COMMON CORE ACHIEVE

Mastering Essential Test Readiness Skills

SOCIAL STUDIES

Mc Graw Hill Education

Bothell, WA • Chicago, IL • Columbus, OH • New York, NY

D0898690

MHEonline.com

Copyright © 2015 McGraw-Hill Education

Send all inquiries to:
McGraw-Hill Education
8787 Orion Place
Columbus, OH 43240

ISBN: 978-0-02-135564-8
MHID: 0-02-135564-9

Printed in the United States of America.

4 5 6 7 8 9 QVS 17 16 15 14

Table of Contents

Table of Contents

Congratulations! If you are using this book, it means that you are taking a key step toward achieving an important new goal for yourself. You are preparing to take your high school equivalency test, an important step in the pathway toward career, educational, and lifelong well-being and success.

Common Core Achieve: Mastering Essential Test Readiness Skills is designed to help you learn or strengthen the skills you will need when you take your high school equivalency test. The program includes four core student modules—*Reading & Writing, Mathematics, Science,* and *Social Studies.* Each of these modules provides subject-level pretests and posttests, in-depth instruction and practice of the core skills and practices required for high school equivalency tests, and a number of additional features to help you master all the skills you need for success on test day and beyond.

How to Use This Book

Before beginning the lessons in each module, take the **Pretest.** This will give you a preview of the types of questions you will be answering on the high school equivalency test. More importantly, it will help you identify which skill areas you need to concentrate on most. Use the evaluation chart at the end of the Pretest to pinpoint the types of questions you have answered incorrectly and to determine which skills you need to work on. The evaluation chart will also help you identify where to go within the module for instruction and practice. You may decide to concentrate on specific areas of study or to work through the entire module. It is highly recommended that you work through the whole module to build a strong foundation in the core areas in which you will be tested.

Common Core Achieve: Mastering Essential Test Readiness Skills includes a number of features designed to familiarize you with high school equivalency tests and to prepare you for test taking. At the start of each chapter, the **Chapter Opener** provides an overview of the chapter content and a goal-setting activity. The lessons that follow include these features to help guide and enhance your learning:

- **Lesson Objectives** state what you will be able to accomplish after completing the lesson.

- **Key Terms and Vocabulary** critical for understanding lesson content are listed at the start of every lesson. All boldfaced words in the text can be found in the Glossary.

- The **Key Concept** summarizes the content that is the focus of the lesson.

- **Core Skills** and **Core Practices** are emphasized with direct instruction and practice in the context of the lesson. Each of the Core Skills and Core Practies aligns to the Common Core State Standards.

- Special features within each lesson include **21st Century Skills, Write About Social Studies, Workplace Skills,** and **Test-Taking Skills** to help you activate high-level thinking skills by using real-word application of these skills.

- **Think about Social Studies** questions check your understanding of the content throughout the lesson.

- **Write to Learn** activities provide you with a purpose for practicing your writing skills.

- The end-of-lesson **Vocabulary Review** checks your understanding of important lesson vocabulary, and the **Skill Review** checks your understanding of the content and skills presented in the lesson.

- **Skill Practice** and **Writing Practice** exercises appear at the end of every lesson to help you apply your learning of content and skill fundamentals.

In addition to the above lesson-level features, this module also includes these features to help you check your understanding as you prepare for the test.

- The end-of-chapter **Review** and **Write about Social Studies** activity test your understanding of the chapter content and provide an opportunity to strengthen your writing skills.

- **Check Your Understanding** charts allow you to check your knowledge of the skills you have practiced, and reference where you can go to review skills that you should revisit.

- The **Answer Key** explains the answers for the questions in the book.

- After you have worked through the book, take the **Posttest** to see how well you have learned the skills presented in this book.

Good luck with your studies, and remember: you are here because you have chosen to achieve important and exciting new goals for yourself. Every time you begin working within the materials, keep in mind that the skills you develop in *Common Core Achieve: Mastering Essential Test Readiness Skills* are not just important for passing the high school equivalency test; they are keys to lifelong success.

This Pretest will help you evaluate whether you are ready to move up to the next level of test preparation. The Pretest consists of 40 multiple choice questions that test your understanding of social studies concepts and your ability to read passages, maps, tables, and charts.

When you have completed the Pretest, check your work with the answers and explanations on pages 11 and 12. Use the Check Your Understanding Chart on page 13 to determine which areas you need to review.

Directions: Read the following questions. Then select the correct answer.

1. A group lobbying for women's rights is an example of which type of interest group?
   A. public
   B. economic
   C. business
   D. special

2. To keep the central government from becoming too strong, the delegates divided its authority; this is known by what term?
   A. separation of powers
   B. checks and balances
   C. popular sovereignty
   D. judicial review

3. Choose the quote that best represents a democracy.
   A. "a government of the people, by the people, and for the people"
   B. "one person or a small group of people seize and exercise absolute power"
   C. Voting is "limited to people with a certain income."
   D. The leader of the government will "inherit their role or use force to get and keep it."

4. A main cause of the rise in totalitarianism in Europe was
   A. the rise of the middle class.
   B. growing religious conflict.
   C. excess public funds for military spending.
   D. an economic depression.

Directions: Use the chart below to answer questions 5 and 6.

Year	Credit Score
2009	560
2010	620
2011	500
2012	540

5. During which year would it have likely been easiest for Ms. Wong to obtain a home loan?
   A. 2009
   B. 2010
   C. 2011
   D. 2012

6. Each credit score is based on financial management during the previous year. During which year did Ms. Wong likely make late payments on bills?
   A. 2009
   B. 2010
   C. 2011
   D. 2012

Directions: Read the following questions. Then select the correct answer.

7. What was the movement that contributed to the United States staying out of World War II until the Japanese attack at Pearl Harbor?

   A. nativism
   B. isolationism
   C. globalism
   D. alliance-building

8. Which of these is a statement that explains a political party's position on issues?

   A. platform
   B. manifesto
   C. goal
   D. mission statement

9. Which term describes people with common concerns who join to influence government policy?

   A. campaign
   B. financial committee
   C. interest group
   D. union

10. The _____ established a church in the American colonies with a strict set of religious beliefs.

   A. Puritans
   B. Cavaliers
   C. Royalists
   D. Minutemen

Directions: Use the map below to answer questions 11–13.

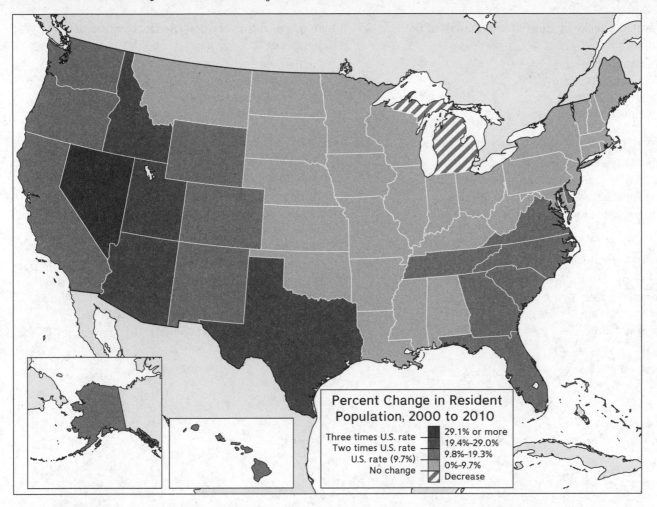

Percent Change in Resident Population, 2000 to 2010

Legend	
Three times U.S. rate	29.1% or more
Two times U.S. rate	19.4%–29.0%
U.S. rate (9.7%)	9.8%–19.3%
	0%–9.7%
No change	
	Decrease

11. Which of the following is an overall trend represented on the map?

   A. The majority of states experienced a decrease in population.

   B. The majority of states experienced a population increase over 29.1%.

   C. The population of most states only increased by 0%-9.7%.

   D. The population of most states increased by twice the U.S. rate.

12. How many states experienced a growth rate greater than the overall US growth rate between 2000 and 2010?

   A. 18

   B. 19

   C. 20

   D. 21

13. Migration was likely highest into which state between 2000 and 2010?

   A. Arizona

   B. Michigan

   C. Nevada

   D. Texas

Directions: Read the following questions. Then select the correct answer.

14. What was the western land located north of the Ohio River called?

    A. Gadsden Purchase
    B. Northwest Territory
    C. Oregon Territory
    D. Frontier Territory

15. The "Trail of Tears" refers to which of these?

    A. the United States invasion of Mexico
    B. the Cherokee lawsuit against Georgia
    C. the fight between Texas and Mexico
    D. the forced relocation of the Cherokee

16. The growth of industry in the United States divided people into

    A. sectional cultures.
    B. social classes.
    C. interest groups.
    D. regional zones.

17. Which organization created the Declaration of Independence?

    A. Parliament
    B. the Federalist Party
    C. the Continental Congress
    D. the House of Representatives

18. Considering that the Constitution has existed for more than two-hundred years, what can you conclude about the twenty-seven amendments?

    A. More amendments are needed.
    B. The twenty-seven amendments came early in US history.
    C. The Constitution is a large, unwieldy document that needs constant revision.
    D. Because of difficulty in enacting, constitutional amendments can only be achieved when national consensus regarding a problem is achieved.

Directions: Read the following questions. Then select the correct answer.

19. Unlike totalitarian systems, the democratic system of the United States allows for citizens to have many

    A. protections.
    B. religions.
    C. civil rights.
    D. beliefs.

20. Which group most recently earned the right to vote?

    A. African American women
    B. women
    C. white men
    D. Japanese Americans

Directions: Use the chart below to answer questions 21 and 22.

Treaty of Versailles (excerpts)

1. Germany accepts responsibility for the war.

2. Germany will pay $33 billion in reparations.

3. Germany may keep only a small army and navy.

4. Nine new nations will be created from territory taken from the Central Powers.

5. The League of Nations will be created.

---

21. What effect did the Treaty of Versailles have on Germany's military?

    A. It guaranteed Germany's right to a strong army and navy.
    B. It kept Germany from maintaining a navy.
    C. It limited the size of Germany's army and navy.
    D. It established international control over the German army.

22. What item in this treaty was created to handle unresolved issues after the war?

    A. the creation of the League of Nations
    B. the collection of reparations payments
    C. the establishment of nine new nations
    D. the assigning of responsibility for the war

Directions: Read the passage below. Then answer the questions that follow.

It is not from the benevolence of the butcher, the brewer, or the baker that we expect our dinner, but from their regard to their own interest. We address ourselves, not to their humanity but to their self-love. . . . Give me what I want, and you shall have this which you want, is the meaning of every such offer; and it is the manner that we obtain from one another the far greater part of those good offices which we stand in need of.

—Adam Smith, *The Wealth of Nations*, 1776

23. The passage seeks to explain which of the following?

A. the formation of social networks
B. the benefits of competition
C. the way that markets work
D. the formation of monopolies

24. According to Smith, how do buyers and sellers behave in a transaction?

A. Buyers and sellers act only in their own self-interest.
B. Buyers act from benevolence, and sellers act from self-interest.
C. Buyers and sellers act from benevolence and self-interest.
D. Buyers act from self-interest, and sellers act from benevolence.

Directions: Use the graph below to answer questions 25 and 26.

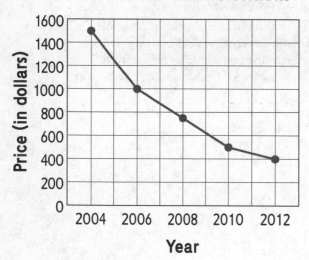

Price of 40" LED Televisions

25. Between which of these years did the price of an LED television decline most quickly?

A. 2004–2006
B. 2006–2008
C. 2008–2010
D. 2010–2012

26. Which of these is the most likely cause of the drop in price over time?

A. decrease in supply
B. increase in demand
C. production delays
D. increase in supply

Directions: Read the following questions. Then select the correct answer.

27. Why were members of the white lower class in the South trapped in poverty?

    A. They worked alongside their enslaved people.
    B. They could not read or write.
    C. They competed with cheap enslaved workers.
    D. They were not interested in working on the plantations.

28. Which of the following was an advantage of the North during the Civil War?

    A. It had more factories with which to supply its armies.
    B. It fought on familiar territory.
    C. It could rely on the labor of enslaved people to free up white men to fight.
    D. It had the support of the British government and navy.

29. Food safety is an example of a _____ policy.

    A. foreign
    B. domestic
    C. economic
    D. state

30. Which branch of government has the power to sign treaties with other nations?

    A. executive
    B. judicial
    C. legislative
    D. only state governments

31. The American government is split into which three branches?

    A. executive, parliamentary, judicial
    B. presidential, prime minster, monarchy
    C. executive, legislative, judicial
    D. judicial, autocracy, legislative

Directions: Use the chart below to answer questions 32 and 33.

GDP per Capita of Selected Countries, 2012

	GDP in 2012 (in trillion $)
Canada	1.8
China	8.4
Mexico	1.2
United Kingdom	2.4
United States	15.7

32. Which of these countries had the lowest GDP (gross domestic product) per capita in 2012?

   A. China
   B. Mexico
   C. United Kingdom
   D. United States

33. Which statement most accurately compares the GDPs per capita of China and the United States?

   A. The GDP of China is about half of the GDP of the United States.
   B. The GDP of the United States and China are very similar in size.
   C. The GDP of China is about twice the GDP of the United States.
   D. The GDP of the United States is about three times the GDP of China.

Directions: Read the following questions. Then select the correct answer.

34. A government in which a single person holds all power is a(n)

   A. dictatorship.
   B. oligarchy.
   C. constitutional monarchy.
   D. democracy.

35. Which group of people wanted to keep immigrants from entering the United States?

   A. industrialists
   B. colonists
   C. settlers
   D. nativists

Directions: Read the passage below. Then answer the questions that follow.

During the period between 1929 and 1933, more than 100,000 businesses failed, causing massive job loss. Without employment, many families lost their homes. With almost 25% of American workers out of work and homeless, shantytowns began to appear in parks and at the edges of cities. These collections of shacks were called Hoovervilles. Although Hoovervilles were made of temporary and makeshift structures, some were organized, with a mayor and governing committees. Even after the Great Depression, Hoovervilles persisted in some areas.

36. The passage describes conditions during which of these times in US history?

A. a period of economic stimulus
B. a period of low unemployment
C. a period of economic boom
D. a period of economic decline

37. The name of these shantytowns implied which of the following?

A. President Hoover enacted effective government programs.
B. President Hoover was the champion of the poor.
C. President Hoover was to blame for economic conditions.
D. President Hoover would not win another election.

Directions: Use the map below to answer questions 38–40.

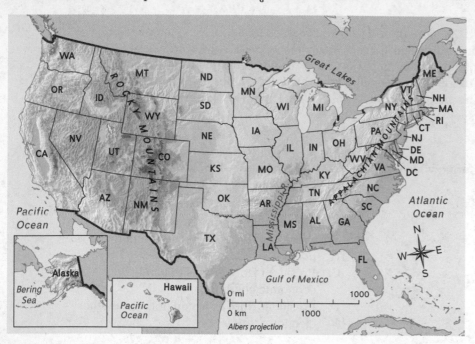

38. Which of these states are separated by a geometric border?

   A. Alaska and Hawaii

   B. Illinois and Missouri

   C. Minnesota and Wisconsin

   D. Wyoming and Montana

39. What physical boundary separates Michigan from Illinois?

   A. river

   B. plains

   C. lake

   D. mountains

40. The Appalachian Mountains help define borders in which section of the United States?

   A. Midwest

   B. Southeast

   C. Northwest

   D. Southwest

1. **D**   Special interest groups are organized around specific issues, such as women's rights.

2. **A**   The central government is split into three parts: judicial, legislative, and executive. This division of power is known as the separation of powers.

3. **A**   In a democracy, the people of a nation rule, either by voting on issues directly or by electing people to represent them.

4. **D**   Leaders in several European countries promised to end the suffering from the depression by setting up totalitarian governments.

5. **B**   Ms. Wong's credit score was highest in 2010, so it would have been easiest for her to get a home loan during that year.

6. **B**   Because Ms. Wong's credit score declined in 2011, it is likely she made late payments on bills in the previous year, 2010.

7. **B**   Isolationism is the policy of avoiding involvement in international affairs.

8. **A**   A platform states the party's position on various issues.

9. **C**   An interest group is a group of people with common concerns who join together to influence government policy.

10. **A**   The Puritans founded many towns in America and set up a church that enforced strict religious beliefs.

11. **C**   The map shows that the majority of the states are shaded light gray, representing a population increase of 0%-9.7%.

12. **C**   There were 20 states that experienced a growth rate greater than 9.7 percent.

13. **C**   Nevada had the highest growth rate, so it is likely that migration of people into the state was highest.

14. **B**   The Northwest Territory was the western land located north of the Ohio River.

15. **D**   In 1832, when the army relocated the Cherokee west of the Mississippi River, thousands of Cherokee died on the forced march.

16. **B**   The growth of industry divided people into three social classes: the wealthy, a growing middle class, and the very poor.

17. **C**   In 1776, the Second Continental Congress created the Declaration of Independence.

18. **D**   Amending the Constitution is a difficult process and not all suggested changes are made.

19. **C**   Civil rights are the rights everyone has to equal protection under the law in the United States.

20. **B**   In 1919, Congress passed the Nineteenth Amendment, which gave women the right to vote.

21. **C**   The treaty stated that Germany could only keep a small army and navy.

22. **A**   The treaty stated that the League of Nations would be created.

23. **C**   The passage seeks to clarify how market forces work.

24. **A**   According to the passage, the buyer and the seller are looking to benefit from a business transaction.

25. **A**   The slope of the graph is steepest between the years 2004 and 2006.

26. **D**   An increase in supply can cause a drop in prices, as sellers try to move inventory.

27. **C**   The white lower class consisted of poor farmers who could not compete with cheap slave labor.

28. **A**   The North had more factories and workshops to produce weapons and clothing for its soldiers.

29. **B**   Food safety is a domestic policy, which is a type of policy related to one's country.

30. **A**   The executive branch has the power to sign treaties.

31. **C**   The national government consists of the executive, legislative, and judicial branches.

32. **B**   The GDP of Mexico was the lowest at $1.2 trillion in 2012.

33. **A**   The GDP of China ($8.4 trillion) is about half that of the United States ($15.7 trillion).

34. **A**   A dictatorship is a type of autocracy in which one person or a small group of people hold all the power.

35. D Nativists wanted to keep immigrants from settling in the United States. They feared immigrants would change American society and traditions.

36. D The passage describes a period of severe economic decline, when businesses failed, jobs were lost, and many families lost their homes.

37. C Using Hoover's name to refer to these towns indicates that some people blamed Hoover, at least in part, for the bad economic conditions.

38. D Wyoming and Montana are separated by a border based on latitude lines.

39. C Lake Michigan separates Michigan from part of Illinois.

40. B The Appalachian Mountains are located in the eastern United States, extending into the southeast.

Check Your Understanding

On the following chart, circle the number of any question you answered incorrectly. In the Reference column, you will see the pages that address the content covered in the question.

Item #	Reference	Item #	Reference	Item #	Reference	Item #	Reference
1	pp. 54–59	11	pp. 278–283	21	pp. 98–105	31	pp. 28–33
2	pp. 28–33	12	pp. 278–283	22	pp. 98–105	32	pp. 176–181, 182–187
3	pp. 16–21	13	pp. 272–277	23	pp. 140–145	33	pp. 176–181, 182–187
4	pp. 98–105, 114–121	14	pp. 72–77	24	pp. 140–145	34	pp. 16–21
5	pp. 218–223, 228–233	15	pp. 72–77	25	pp. 146–151, 158–163	35	pp. 86–91
6	pp. 224–227	16	pp. 206–211	26	pp. 152–157, 182–187	36	pp. 194–199
7	pp. 106–113	17	pp. 16–21, 66–71	27	pp. 78–85	37	pp. 194–199
8	pp. 48–53	18	pp. 22–27	28	pp. 78–85	38	pp. 248–253
9	pp. 48–53	19	pp. 16–21, 114–121	29	pp. 54–59, 128–133, 176–181	39	pp. 248–253
10	pp. 66–71	20	pp. 40–47	30	pp. 28–33	40	pp. 248–253

Chapter 1

Government

The influence of government is all around us. The roads in your neighborhood, the schools in your community, and the practices of many workplaces are all managed by the government. People contribute to their government in many ways. They take part in government by voting, paying taxes, and serving on juries. To be an effective part of government, you must understand how it works.

Bloomberg/Getty Images

In this chapter you will study these topics:

Lesson 1.1
Types of Modern and Historical Governments

How is the US government like the governments of other countries? How was the American government formed? What documents still influence the US government today? Learn about the different types of government.

Lesson 1.2
American Constitutional Democracy

What led the Founders of the United States to create the Constitution? What role does the Constitution play in US government? Learn about the creation of the Constitution and how it can be changed.

Lesson 1.3
Structure of American Government

What are the roles and duties of government leaders? What keeps the central government from becoming too powerful? Learn about the branches of the US government and the powers of the federal and state governments.

Goal Setting

What do you hope to learn in this chapter?

What do you know about your government?

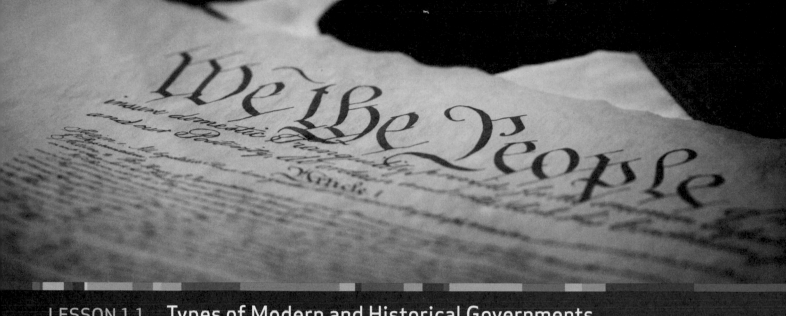

LESSON OBJECTIVES

- Identify and compare types of modern and historical governments
- Explain how types of governments are related
- Identify historical documents that influenced American constitutional democracy and explain the relationships between these documents

CORE SKILLS & PRACTICES

- Compare Ideas
- Analyze Ideas

Key Terms

autocracy
a government in which a single person holds all power

dictatorship
a government in which one person has absolute authority over citizens' lives

oligarchy
a type of government in which only a few people rule

limited government
the principle that a ruler or government is not all-powerful

Vocabulary

analyze
to break information into parts

amendment
a change or addition to a constitution

Key Concept

Governments within a state, country, or region are responsible for establishing order, providing security, and directing public affairs.

Have you ever been in a club or organization? You usually meet regularly, and your group has leaders who run the meetings. The leaders decide, often with input from group members, what the group will do. Local and national governments accomplish many of the same tasks, but they operate on a larger scale.

Types of Government

Throughout history, people have developed different forms of government. The three main types of government are autocracy, oligarchy, and democracy.

Autocracy

In an **autocracy**, a single person holds all power. This is probably the oldest type of government. Autocrats either inherit their role or use force to get and keep it. A monarchy is a government in which a king or queen serves as head of state. Monarchs in Europe from the 1400s to the 1700s and the czars in Russia were autocrats, also known as absolute autocrats. They inherited their positions and sometimes used force to keep them. Modern autocratic monarchies are rare. The king of Saudi Arabia is a modern absolute monarch.

Most monarchies today are constitutional monarchies. Great Britain is one example. The British monarch is mostly the ceremonial head of the British government and has little power. Governmental decision-making is in the hands of the British Parliament, which is a body of government elected by the people. Japan, Sweden, and Spain also have constitutional monarchies.

Dictatorship

A **dictatorship** is a government ruled by one person or a small group of people who seize and exercise absolute power. A dictator controls the government and has absolute authority over citizens' lives. Adolf Hitler in Germany, Joseph Stalin in the Soviet Union, and Benito Mussolini in Italy were all twentieth-century dictators. Kim Jong-Un, the leader of North Korea, is one of the few remaining dictators.

Oligarchy

An **oligarchy** is similar to an autocracy. The difference is that in an oligarchy, a small group of people, not just one person, rules with absolute power. Before and during World War II, Japan was ruled by an oligarchy of army officers and businessmen. Sometimes the group in power will hold elections. However, the only candidates up for election support the oligarchy, and voters must vote for them. This is the form of oligarchy in the People's Republic of China. The only political party is the Communist Party, and few dare to oppose it.

England was an oligarchy in the eighteenth century. The real majority of power was in the hands of a few members of Parliament, and voting was limited to people with a certain income. Some of the ancient Greek city-states and the seafaring Republic of Venice were oligarchies. Greek city-states were ruled by a few leading families, and the Republic of Venice was ruled by elite merchants.

Democracy

Abraham Lincoln said that democracy is "government of the people, by the people, and for the people." In a democracy, the people decide the laws and services they want.

There are two different forms of democracy. One is direct democracy, in which individual citizens vote on issues of government in a meeting of all citizens. This was the form of democracy in ancient Athens, where all male citizens could help govern. Many towns within the New England region of the United States continue to make local decisions through town meetings, which is a form of direct democracy. Few places today are small enough to be governed efficiently by direct democracy. Instead, the people practice representative democracy. They elect representatives who govern in their place. The voters give their representatives the power to make and enforce laws.

The United States is a representative democracy. Senators, representatives, and the president are all elected officials. These leaders are expected to do what the majority of the people want. The United States is also a constitutional democracy. In this kind of democracy, the powers of the government are described in a document called a constitution.

Countries differ in how the chief executive, or head of government, is chosen. Canadians vote for representatives who become members of their parliament, or the legislature. The leader of the political party with the most seats in parliament becomes the prime minister. This means the nation's chief executive answers to representatives rather than directly to the people. This contrasts with a presidential democracy, in which the president, or chief executive, is constitutionally independent of the legislature. The United States has a presidential democracy.

CORE SKILL

Compare Ideas

Read about the three forms of government presented here: autocracy, oligarchy, and democracy. Choose one form of government and write a paragraph explaining its strengths and weaknesses. Describe a situation in which this form of government would be superior to any of the others.

🏴 Think about Social Studies

Directions: Fill in the blank.

1. In a _____ form of government, citizens choose a group of people to govern on their behalf.

2. Most modern _____ are constitutional, not autocratic.

3. Canada has a _____ democracy as its government.

When you **analyze** something, you read it carefully to understand the ideas in the text. Read the passages from the Declaration of Independence and the Virginia Declaration of Rights. Make a list of the similarities in both documents. Think about why the authors decided to include these particular rights and freedoms. What kinds of things were important to the authors during their time? What do you think they were trying to prevent from happening by including these rights in their documents?

Documents That Influenced American Democracy

Several historical documents helped determine the type of government established in the United States. These include the Declaration of Independence, the Virginia Declaration of Rights, and the Magna Carta.

The Declaration of Independence

In the spring of 1776, some colonial legislatures were telling their representatives to the Second Continental Congress to work toward independence. Congress named a committee to prepare a document to declare American independence. The document would explain why the American colonists were rejecting British rule and establishing their own national government. Thomas Jefferson wrote the document, and on June 28, the Declaration of Independence was presented to Congress. They adopted, or approved, it on July 4, 1776.

> We hold these truths to be self-evident, that all men are created equal, that they are endowed by their Creator with certain unalienable rights, that among these are Life, Liberty and the pursuit of Happiness. —That to secure these rights, Governments are instituted among Men, deriving their just powers from the consent of the governed, —That whenever any Form of Government becomes destructive of these ends, it is the Right of the People to alter or abolish it, and to institute new Government, laying its foundation on such principles and organizing its powers in such form, as to them shall seem most likely to effect their Safety and Happiness.

The Virginia Declaration of Rights

The Virginia Declaration of Rights was written by George Mason and adopted in June 1776. This statement of the rights of the people of Virginia set the plan for the government of Virginia.

These are the first two sections of the Virginia Declaration of Rights:

> **Section 1.** That all men are by nature equally free and independent and have certain inherent rights, of which, when they enter into a state of society, they cannot, by any compact, deprive or divest their posterity; namely, the enjoyment of life and liberty, with the means of acquiring and possessing property, and pursuing and obtaining happiness and safety.

> **Section 2.** That all power is vested in, and consequently derived from, the people; that magistrates are their trustees and servants and at all times amenable to them.

Both the Virginia Declaration of Rights and the Declaration of Independence state that all people have certain freedoms and rights, including the right to govern themselves.

The Magna Carta

Limited government is the idea that government is not all-powerful. People have certain rights that government cannot take away. This idea was first set down in the Magna Carta in England in 1215. This document was a first step toward limiting the power of the English monarch and establishing certain rights, many of which are included in the US Constitution.

The following is a paraphrase of part of the Magna Carta:

> **Item 20.** A freeman shall not be punished for a minor crime except to the degree of the crime. For a serious offense, he shall be punished according to the seriousness of that crime.

> **Item 39.** No freeman shall be imprisoned or have his rights taken away except by the lawful judgment of his peers, or equals, and by the law of the land.

The US Constitution

The Declaration of Independence described why colonists were unhappy with British rule and why they were establishing an independent nation. The US Constitution, however, established the structure of the government of this new nation, the United States. The US Constitution was written in 1787. It has three parts: the Preamble, the articles, and the amendments.

The Preamble

The Preamble introduces the Constitution and describes the general purpose for establishing the government. It also declares that the power of the government comes from the people.

> We the People of the United States, in Order to form a more perfect Union, establish Justice, insure domestic Tranquility, provide for the common defence, promote the general Welfare, and secure the Blessings of Liberty to ourselves and our Posterity, do ordain and establish the Constitution for the United States of America.

The Articles

The next section of the Constitution contains seven articles that describe the structure of the government, define the government's powers and responsibilities, and explain the relationship between national government and the states.

The Amendments

Not everyone was happy with the Constitution. Some people did not want a strong central government. Others, like Thomas Jefferson, wanted a bill of rights to ensure that the rights of citizens were protected. In 1789, James Madison presented Congress with a list of suggested **amendments**, or changes. Ten amendments added to the Constitution in 1791 became known as the Bill of Rights. The following is from two of the amendments.

> **Amendment 5:** "No person shall be ... deprived of life, liberty, or property without due process of law."

> **Amendment 6:** "In all criminal prosecutions, the accused shall enjoy the right to a speedy and public trial, by an impartial jury of the State and district wherein the crime shall have been committed."

Both the Magna Carta and the Bill of Rights emphasize the right to justice and due process of law.

Think about Social Studies

Directions: In a notebook, write the Preamble to the Constitution in your own words. Use a dictionary to help you identify synonyms as you work.

WRITE TO LEARN

Find a list of the Bill of Rights online. Choose one of the rights that is important to you and write a paragraph explaining why.

Vocabulary Review

Directions: Complete the sentences using the following key terms and vocabulary words.

amendment	oligarchy	limited government
dictatorship	autocracy	analyze

1. If you _____ the Magna Carta and Virginia Declaration of Rights, you understand their influence on US democracy.

2. A harsh _____ was set up to govern a country after the army generals threw the president out of power.

3. When a change is made to the Constitution, it is called a(n) _____.

4. If a country is controlled by an elite group or a few rich families, it would be considered a(n) _____.

5. In a(n) _____, a single person holds all the power.

6. The idea of _____ was first documented in the Magna Carta.

Skill Review

Directions: Choose the best answer to each question.

1. How is a constitutional monarchy like a democracy?
   A. Individual citizens vote on issues of government.
   B. Representative leaders hold all the power.
   C. A single person holds all the power as head of state.
   D. The people vote for their representative leaders.

2. The United States primarily uses which type of government?
   A. direct democracy
   B. representative democracy
   C. autocracy
   D. oligarchy

3. The Declaration of Independence and the Virginia Declaration of Rights both say that the power of government rests with which group of people?
   A. people being governed
   B. elected representatives
   C. magistrates and trustees
   D. national government

4. How does the Constitution distribute power?
   A. It gives power to officials elected by the people.
   B. It puts power directly in the hands of the people.
   C. It gives the most power to the president.
   D. It gives the most power to a monarch and the nobility.

Skill Practice

Directions: Read the two passages. Then answer the questions that follow.

The English Bill of Rights

The 1600s were a time of conflict between the English king, the English people, and Parliament (the legislature). The conflict ended in 1689 when new monarchs, William III and Mary, accepted the English Bill of Rights. This document helped create a constitutional monarchy. The English Bill of Rights stated that the monarch served at the will of Parliament. The Bill of Rights strengthened the rights of common people. For example, people could no longer be taxed simply because the king wanted money. Laws could not be changed without Parliament's approval. Members of Parliament were to be freely elected. The Bill of Rights guaranteed a just and fair government that answered to the people.

The U.S. Bill of Rights

To protect the rights of Americans, Congress and the states approved the Bill of Rights in 1789. Among the rights protected are the following:

Amendment 1: People have the right to practice any religion they choose.

Amendment 4: People and their homes cannot be searched without probable cause.

Amendment 8: Persons arrested cannot be punished in cruel or unusual ways.

Amendment 9: The rights of the people are not limited to the rights listed in the Constitution.

1. Think about why the English Bill of Rights was written. What do you think the authors of the US Bill of Rights were trying to prevent?

   A. The Bill of Rights was written to prevent the legislature from becoming too powerful.

   B. The Bill of Rights was written to protect American citizens from a strong central government that would take away people's rights.

   C. The Bill of Rights was written to prevent the king of England from claiming more power over the rights of American colonists.

   D. The Bill of Rights was written to prevent the nobility from seizing too much power from average citizens.

2. Look at Amendment 9 of the US Bill of Rights. Why would the authors feel the need to include this amendment?

   A. The authors wanted to make sure that American citizens have the right to assemble peacefully in public places since they didn't have that right under British rule.

   B. The authors wanted to make sure that American citizens had the right to vote whether they were male or female.

   C. The authors wanted to make sure that the rights of American citizens aren't blocked by acts of Congress.

   D. The authors wanted to make sure that the rights of American citizens were not limited only to those listed in the Bill of Rights.

Writing Practice

Directions: If you were to add a new amendment to the Constitution, what would you add and why? Write a paragraph describing your amendment.

LESSON 1.2 American Constitutional Democracy

LESSON OBJECTIVES

- Identify the factors that led to the Constitutional Convention
- Describe some of the compromises in the Constitution
- Summarize the process of amending the Constitution

CORE SKILLS & PRACTICES

- Determine the Relevance of Information
- Read a Bar Graph

Key Terms

federalism
relationship between the states and the national government in which power is shared

executive branch
the branch of government that is headed by the president and carries out the nation's laws

legislative branch
the branch of government that makes the laws

judicial branch
the branch of government made up by the court system

separation of powers
division of central government

Vocabulary

relevant
information that is connected to information you already know

Key Concept

The Constitution was not met with universal approval and had to be changed to get the new American states to approve it.

Organizations rely on sets of rules, or systems, to function effectively. If the system does not work, participants improve it by changing it. These changes often require group members to work together and compromise.

Governments also rely on systems to function. The United States first created a system that was flawed. Leaders recognized the problems and made changes to make the system more effective.

The Need for a Constitution

During the war for independence, Americans set up new governments. They replaced their old colonial charters with new state constitutions. A constitution is a document that outlines a plan of government. A plan was also created for a central, or national, government. Called the Articles of Confederation, this plan created a confederation, or a loose alliance of states. Although the Articles of Confederation provided a national congress, there was no president or national system of courts.

Americans feared a strong central government that could abuse its power. To prevent this, the states retained many important powers of government. They alone had the power to enforce laws, regulate trade, and impose taxes. Each state was a republic, or a government that derives its power from the people. Within the republics, people elected representatives to make and enforce the laws. Most of the state constitutions included a bill of rights, which included "natural rights" that no government should be allowed to violate. These natural rights included the right to hold property, the right to a trial by jury, freedom of the press, and freedom of speech and assembly.

The confederation period after the war was a difficult time for the new nation. During the war, the Continental Congress had borrowed millions of dollars from foreign governments and banks. This debt had to be paid. Lacking the power to tax, Congress could not pay off its debts. Courts began seizing, or taking, farms for nonpayment of debts and taxes. In 1786, more than 1,000 farmers attacked county courts in western Massachusetts and tried to capture muskets from a state arsenal.

Dennis Flaherty/Getty Images

Known as Shays's Rebellion, this attack touched off rebellions against courts and tax collectors in other states, and Congress was powerless to stop them. The attacks frightened many Americans. "We are fast verging on anarchy and confusion," George Washington wrote. Fearing more lawlessness, Congress agreed to revise the Articles of Confederation.

 Think about Social Studies

Directions: Choose the best answer to the following question.

What was the effect of Shays's Rebellion on the nation?

    A. People were concerned that farmers' rights and the rights of landholders were becoming too powerful.

    B. People were concerned with the government's inability to respond to the economic crisis and armed threats to government.

    C. People feared the rebellion highlighted the weaknesses in the Virginia Plan.

    D. People feared the proactive economic policies permitted by the Articles of Confederation.

A Nation Built on Compromise

In May 1787, delegates arrived at the Constitutional Convention in Philadelphia to amend the Articles of Confederation. The loose union of states under the Articles of Confederation had not worked. The members of the Constitutional Convention knew that to survive, the new nation had to have a central government with some power. The delegates who attended the Constitutional Convention based the new government on six principles: popular sovereignty, federalism, separation of powers, checks and balances, judicial review, and limited government.

The power of the United States government comes from the people of the nation. This idea is known as popular sovereignty. Government is able to govern as long as it has the consent, or approval, of the governed. **Federalism** describes the relationship between the states and the national government in which power is shared. In a federal system, power is divided between the states and the national government. Each has its own area of duties and responsibilities.

The delegates were concerned that the central government might become too powerful. To prevent this, the delegates set up three branches of government: the executive branch, the legislative branch, and the judicial branch. Each branch was given its own duties and responsibilities. The **executive branch** is headed by the president and carries out the nation's laws. The **legislative branch** makes the laws, and the **judicial branch** is the court system. This division of central government is known as the **separation of powers**. To keep any one branch of the government from having too much power, the delegates also built in a system of checks and balances. Each branch has duties that check, or restrain, the power of the other two branches. For example, the president nominates federal judges. The Senate then approves or rejects those nominations.

CORE SKILL

Determine the Relevance of Information

When you read, you must judge whether the information is relevant. Something is considered **relevant** if it is connected to what you already know.

Read the following paragraph about Benjamin Franklin.

Carved into the back of the president's chair at the Philadelphia Convention was half of a sun. Benjamin Franklin, a delegate from Pennsylvania, worried about the meaning of that sun. Was the sun setting on the American republic? As the delegates lined up on September 17, 1787, to sign the Constitution, he knew the answer. "Now at length, I have the happiness to know it is a rising and not a setting sun."

Write a paragraph explaining how Franklin's quote is relevant to the new American government.

WRITE TO LEARN

The Bill of Rights contains the first ten amendments to the Constitution. These amendments are important to the freedoms we enjoy today. Write a paragraph about why the Bill of Rights was added to the Constitution.

21ST CENTURY SKILL

Critical Thinking and Problem Solving

The Framers of the Constitution thought about problems the country might encounter in the future when they created the Ninth Amendment of the Bill of Rights. Explain how this amendment protects the freedoms of citizens today.

Another issue the delegates faced was the fair distribution of power between large and small states. To ensure small states had fair representation, the delegates created two separate bodies of the legislative branch. The delegates agreed that each state would receive equal representation in the Senate. The size of a state's population would determine its representation in the House of Representatives. In this way, the House protected the rights of large states and the Senate protected the rights of the small states.

 Think about Social Studies

Directions: Fill-in the blank with the correct term.

1. Citizens of a country retain power through _____.

After considering other issues, such as slavery, delegates wrote a final draft of the Constitution that included a framework of essential principles. The delegates sent the Constitution to the states to be ratified, or formally approved. By 1788, eleven states had ratified the Constitution. By 1790, all 13 states had ratified it.

Amending the Constitution

The United States Constitution is one of the world's oldest written Constitutions. It is also a short document compared to many other constitutions. Its clear, direct language has helped support a stable government for well over two centuries. At the same time, the Constitution has enabled government to adapt to changing times and to deal with challenges that the original framers never dreamed of, such as radio communications to nuclear power to space exploration and more.

The US Constitution is the basic law of the United States. No law—either national or state—is higher than the Constitution. The Framers of the Constitution understood the need to make the Constitution adaptable. They built into the document a way to amend, or change, the Constitution. Today, the Constitution contains 27 amendments. The first 10 are called the Bill of Rights and were promised so the Constitution could win ratification. The other 17 amendments were added over time.

The Bill of Rights

At the time of the writing of the Constitution, many Americans opposed the Constitution despite its separation of powers and system of checks and balances. They worried that Congress or the president would misuse the power and abuse the rights of the people. To win support for ratification, the proponents of the Constitution agreed to add a bill of rights, or list of rights.

The Bill of Rights addresses several of the American people's most important concerns. The first four amendments protect basic rights that Britain violated during the protest over taxes and tea. These include freedom of speech, press, assembly, and religion; the right of citizens and militias to keep and bear arms; the right not to have troops quartered, or live, in a person's house; and freedom from unreasonable searches and seizures of property.

The next four amendments protect Americans against unfair court procedures, trials, and convictions. The Ninth Amendment protects rights not specifically mentioned in the Constitution. The Tenth Amendment is another "catchall" amendment. It reserves to states any powers not delegated to the central government or prohibited by the Constitution.

The Amendment Process

To formally amend, or change, the Constitution is complicated and requires two steps: (1) proposing an amendment and (2) ratifying the proposed amendment. Amendments can be proposed in two ways. First the amendment may be introduced into the House of Representatives and the Senate. Two-thirds of both the House and the Senate must approve the proposed amendment.

Under the second method, two-thirds of the 50 states petition, or request, Congress to call a constitutional convention. The convention proposes, discusses, and approves the amendment. The constitutional convention method of proposing an amendment has never been used.

Once an amendment is approved, there are two ways it can be ratified. In the first way, three-fourths of the state legislatures must ratify it. In the second method, Congress asks the states to call special constitutional conventions to ratify the proposed amendment. If that method is used, then three-fourths of all 50 state constitutional conventions must ratify it. Congress determines which method of ratification to use.

Although it is the basis for the government of a large nation, the Constitution is not a long document. Even with amendments, it is shorter than the rules and guidelines for many organizations. The reason the Constitution is so simple is to keep it timeless. "In framing a system which we wish to last for all ages," James Madison said, "we should not lose sight of the changes which ages will produce." In this way, the Constitution is a living and breathing document that will remain relevant throughout time.

How the Constitution Is Amended

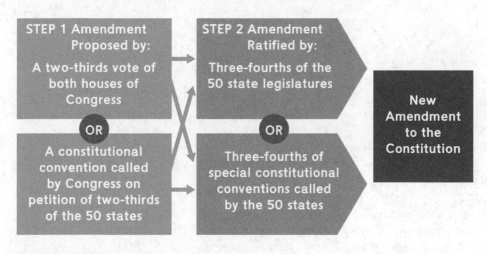

Read a Bar Graph

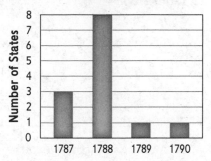

Dates States Ratified the Constitution

Bar graphs are used to compare amounts. The longer the bar, the greater the amount being measured. Bar graphs contain two axes. To understand a bar graph, read the title and the labels on each axis. Look at the graph and answer the following questions:

- In what year did the most states ratify the Constitution?

- Based on the graph, would you conclude that most states were for or against the Constitution? Explain your answer.

 Think about Social Studies

Directions: Choose the best answer to the question below.

1. Why were the system of checks and balances and separation of powers important additions to the Constitution?

  A. Framers wanted a powerful central government.

  B. Framers wanted to prevent one level of government from becoming too powerful.

  C. Framers wanted to limit the power of state governments.

  D. Framers wanted to make the Constitution amendable.

Vocabulary Review

Directions: Complete the sentences using the following key terms and vocabulary words.

executive branch   judicial branch   legislative branch
federalism   relevant   separation of powers

1. The division of central government so that each branch has its own duties is known as

   _____.

2. The courts make up the _____ of the federal government.

3. The _____ of the federal government has the duty to carry out laws.

4. A relationship between the states and the national government in which power is shared is known as

   _____.

5. The _____ of the federal government is the lawmaking body.

6. Information is _____ if it is connected to information you already know.

Skill Review

Directions: Use the graph on page 25 to answer the following questions.

1. Which statement is best supported by the graph?

   A. Most states rejected the Constitution and refused to ratify it.

   B. Most states were satisfied with the Constitution and ratified it quickly.

   C. Many states waited until 1791 to ratify the Constitution.

   D. Only a few states had ratified the Constitution by 1790.

2. In which year did most states ratify the Constitution?

   A. 1787

   B. 1788

   C. 1789

   D. 1790

Directions: Read the passage below. Then answer the questions that follow.

Amendment Six: Rights of the Accused

In all criminal prosecutions, the accused shall enjoy the right to a speedy and public trial, by an impartial jury of the State and district wherein the crime shall have been committed, which district shall have been previously ascertained by law, and to be informed of the nature and cause of the accusation; to be confronted with the witnesses against him; to have compulsory process for obtaining witnesses in his favor, and to have the Assistance of Counsel for his defence.

3. Which members of the American public are protected by the Sixth Amendment?

   A. wealthy lawyers

   B. judges

   C. those suspected of committing a crime

   D. victims of crimes

4. Using context clues, what do you think is the meaning of the term impartial?

   A. not biased

   B. registered to vote

   C. consisting of male and female

   D. witnesses of the alleged crime

Skill Practice

Directions: Read the passage below. Choose the one best answer to each question.

Sherman's Great Compromise

(1) Roger Sherman attended the Constitutional Convention in 1787 as a delegate from Connecticut. (2) He was the most awkward person John Adams had ever seen. (3) A delegate from Georgia called him "unaccountably strange in his manner." (4) Roger Sherman was an odd but honest man. (5) A successful merchant, Sherman was trusted by the people of Connecticut. (6) He knew when to stand firm and when to compromise. (7) At the Constitutional Convention, Sherman put his ability to compromise to good use. (8) He favored the New Jersey Plan, which gave each state an equal vote in Congress. (9) Most delegates wanted representation based on population. (10) Sherman proposed a compromise—give the states equal representation in the Senate, but base representation in the House of Representatives on population. (11) The Connecticut Compromise—known as the Great Compromise—was Sherman's greatest contribution to the new republic. (12) It saved the Philadelphia Convention, which almost broke up over this issue.

1. Which statement best summarizes the relevant information in this passage?

    A. Roger Sherman was the Connecticut delegate at the Constitutional Convention.

    B. Other delegates believed Roger Sherman to be odd and awkward.

    C. Roger Sherman was a good politician and problem solver.

    D. Delegates at the Constitutional Convention could not agree on a compromise for state representation.

2. Which sentence best describes the main idea of this passage?

    A. Sentence 3

    B. Sentence 11

    C. Sentence 9

    D. Sentence 5

3. Which sentence contains the relevant information about Sherman's abilities as a politician?

    A. Sentence 7

    B. Sentence 4

    C. Sentence 3

    D. Sentence 2

4. Which sentence contains the relevant information about the importance of the Great Compromise?

    A. Sentence 5

    B. Sentence 7

    C. Sentence 9

    D. Sentence 12

Writing Practice

Directions: Write a paragraph explaining the factors that led to the Constitutional Convention.

LESSON 1.3 Structure of American Government

LESSON OBJECTIVES

- Identify the role and duties of the president
- Compare and contrast the two houses of Congress
- Explain how the federal and state systems function
- Explain the ways in which federal and state governments are alike and different

CORE SKILLS & PRACTICES

- Read a Chart
- Determine Central Ideas

Key Terms

bicameral
two houses

House of Representatives
federal body that protects the rights of large states

Senate
federal body that protects the rights of small states

referendum
allows citizens to overturn legislation that was passed by legislature or by voters

veto
power of the president to refuse a law

Vocabulary

determine
identify

Key Concept

The federal and state governments provide services to people, but they have unique roles and responsibilities.

Effective teams work well when all members do their share of the work. Like other organizations, the US government relies on its members to fulfill their duties. The Framers of the Constitution structured the government into three branches.

The Three Branches of Government

The men who created the Constitution of the United States did not trust governments with unlimited power. The writers of the Constitution created three branches of government—the executive branch, the legislative branch, and the judicial branch—and took care to divide power among these branches.

The Executive Branch

The Constitution created an executive branch to enforce the laws passed by Congress. It consists of the president, the vice president, and officials in the executive departments. The president's cabinet is also part of the executive branch.

The executive branch is headed by the president. The presidency includes many roles—the president is the chief official of the executive branch, the head of the nation, and the commander in chief of the armed forces. The first job of the president is to run the executive department. In fact, the commitment to run the executive office is part of the oath of office that the president takes at the presidential inauguration. The executive branch is more than the president and vice president. Since 1789, it has evolved into 15 executive departments, more than 50 independent federal commissions, and numerous agencies.

The Executive Office of the President assists the president with day-to-day decisions. Staff in this office advise the president on foreign policy, national security, and other issues. The departments of the executive branch include staff in the areas of agriculture, education, health, energy, commerce and others. The heads of these departments make up the Cabinet. Federal commissions and agencies include the Federal Trade Commission, Bureau of Land Management, Environmental Protection Agency, the United States Postal Service, and the Peace Corp to name a few.

The president has other duties in addition to running the executive office. The president is commander in chief of the armed forces. This role allows the president to use the military to support foreign policy goals. As chief legislator, the president proposes the annual budget and other legislation to Congress.

The executive branch has the power to conduct war; sign treaties; nominate people for federal office; appoint department heads, ambassadors, and federal judges; and issue pardons. However, the president does not have unrestricted power. The checks and balances written into the Constitution limit the president's powers. For example, the presidential power to appoint federal judges and department heads is checked by the Senate. The Senate has the power to approve or reject the president's appointments.

The Constitution also gives the president power to **veto**—or refuse to approve—a law drafted by Congress. However, it limits this power by allowing Congress to override a veto. A vetoed bill can become law if passed in both houses by a two-thirds majority. This allows the two branches to check and balance each other.

The Legislative Branch

Congress is the lawmaking, or legislative, body of the national government. It is a **bicameral** legislature, which means that it has two houses. The upper house is the **Senate**. The lower house is the **House of Representatives**. The Senate is the smaller body, with 100 members, two members from each state. Membership in the House of Representatives was set at 435 in 1913. The number of members for each state is determined by population. States divide their representation into districts. Congress meets for sessions, or periods of time, usually from January until November or December.

The major duties of Congress are to (1) pass laws, (2) represent what members think is best for their constituents, (3) oversee the workings of the federal government, and (4) help their constituents solve problems with the federal government. Constituents are the people back home in the member's state or district.

Congress has the power to tax and appropriate, or authorize the spending of, the income from taxes. The Constitution gives Congress the power to regulate commerce between states and with other nations. Commerce is the buying and selling of goods and services. Congress and the president share military powers. The president is commander in chief of the armed forces. However, the president must ask Congress to declare war and for the funds to fight the war. Congress also has the power to impeach the president or federal judges. Impeachment means to accuse a public official of misconduct in office.

Article I of the Constitution describes the role of Congress in detail. Congress makes the nation's laws. These laws are not just rules for behavior. Congress passes laws that impose taxes, authorize the spending of money, and create government programs. Both houses of Congress must agree on a bill, or proposed law. Once both houses do this, the bill goes to the president. If the president signs the bill, it becomes law.

CORE PRACTICE

Read a Chart

Writers sometimes organize information into charts. Charts are effective tools that convey much information in a small amount of space. Look at the chart on this page. What is the main topic of the chart? What details are provided in the chart?

Executive Branch	Legislative Branch	Judicial Branch
President • Enforces the laws • Acts as commander-in-chief of the armed forces • Appoints ambassadors, judges, and other officials • Makes treaties with other nations	Congress • Writes the laws • Raises troops for armed forces • Decides how much money may be spent on government programs	Supreme Court • Interprets the laws • Reviews court decisions

The Judicial Branch

The judiciary is the third branch of the government. The Constitution gives it the power to decide conflicts between states and between individuals in different states. The judicial branch includes the Supreme Court and any other federal courts that Congress considers necessary.

The US Supreme Court has nine justices, or judges. The Court hears cases for only part of the year and only accepts a few of the many cases it receives for review. However, the decisions of the US Supreme Court greatly affect national policy. That is why a decision by the Court, or an appointment of a justice, creates so much national interest.

Neither the executive nor the legislative branch may throw out a ruling of the Supreme Court. However, there are actions that these branches can take. One is to rewrite the law that the Court found unconstitutional. A second action is to turn the rejected law into an amendment to the Constitution. Congress then passes the amendment and sends it to the states for ratification.

The Supreme Court plays a major role in the system of checks and balances. It can overturn acts of Congress and actions of the president if it finds that they violate the Constitution. The Constitution gives the chief justice power to preside over a trial to impeach the president.

Think about Social Studies

1. What Check does the president have on the power of Congress?

WORKPLACE SKILL

Understand the Purpose of Workplace Documents (flow charts)

Companies often use flow charts like the one shown below to illustrate a process. A company flow chart might show, for example, the steps for developing a new product. Research the process of how a bill becomes a law. Then create a flow chart to illustrate that process.

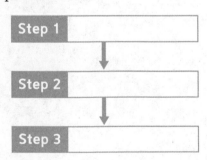

The Power of State Government

The Constitution of the United States created a federal government, but it was not all-powerful. Some powers are shared with the states; others belong only to the states. The Constitution does not necessarily **determine**, or identify, which specific powers belong to the federal government and which belong to state governments. Powers not specifically granted to Congress, or implied under the necessary and proper clause, are reserved to the states. The Tenth Amendment states this clearly.

Only states can set up town, city, or county governments. State legislatures have the power to set up business corporations and regulate trade within the state. Only states can create a police force, establish schools, and pass marriage laws. The Constitution places limits on the powers of the states and places federal law above state law.

The Constitution allows the federal government and the states to make and enforce similar laws. For example, states make laws regulating state elections, while the federal government controls congressional and presidential elections. Both state legislatures and Congress can levy taxes, charter banks, and borrow money. States have court systems to administer justice, including a supreme court. So does the national government. Powers that exist at both levels of government are called concurrent powers.

 Think about Social Studies

Directions: Answer each question, either true or false.

1. Only states can set up county governments.
2. Powers that exist at both the federal and state levels are called concurrent powers.

The Structure of State Government

There are many similarities between the federal and state governments. The states have constitutions and executive, legislative, and judicial branches. Like the branches of the federal government, they act as checks on each other's power.

In addition to the power to make laws, the state legislature has the power to tax, to borrow money, and to spend money. The purpose of the powers of the legislature is to promote the general well-being of the state's citizens. Nebraska is the only state with a unicameral (one house) legislature. The other 49 states have two houses, or bicameral legislatures.

The governor is the chief executive and chief administrator of state government. Governors do not have the same amount of power as the president. Governors share their power with other officers of the executive department. Some of the governor's duties include proposing legislation, vetoing legislation, and calling special, or extra, sessions of the legislature. Governors have limited judicial powers. Governors may pardon, or release, a person from the legal consequences of a crime.

Each state has its own judicial branch and system of laws. The purpose of the state court systems is to interpret and apply state and local laws. State courts include courts of appeals, trial courts, juvenile courts, municipal (city) courts, police courts, and justice courts.

Citizens play important roles in state government. For example, citizens can write laws for the legislature to consider. This action is called a direct initiative. Another power granted to citizens is the **referendum**, which allows citizens to overturn legislation that was passed by legislature or by voters. Some states also allow citizens to vote a state official out of office. This action is known as a recall.

 Think about Social Studies

Directions: Identify the functions below as legislative, executive, or judicial.

1. Chief executive and administrator of state government
2. Organized into houses, either unicameral or bicameral
3. Responsible for interpreting state law

Vocabulary Review

Directions: Complete the sentences using the following key terms and vocabulary words.

referendum	House of Representatives	veto
determines	Senate	bicameral

1. A _____ legislature has two houses.

2. The _____ protects the rights of small states.

3. The Constitution identifies, or _____ many federal and state powers.

4. The power to refuse a law is called _____ power.

5. The _____ protects the rights of large states.

6. The action that allows citizens to overturn legislation that was passed by the state legislature or by

   voters is known as a _____ .

Skill Review

Directions: Examine the chart and answer the following questions.

Other State Executive Officers

Title	Duties
Lieutenant Governor	• Presides over the senate • Succeeds the governor if the governor dies, resigns, or is removed from office
Attorney General	• Represents the state in lawsuits • Offers legal advice to the governor, other state officers, agencies, and the legislature • Provides formal written opinions, or interpretations, of state law, including state constitutional law; these have the force of law within the state
Secretary of State	• Oversees all state records and public documents • Records all official acts of the governor and legislature • Supervises election laws
State Treasurer	• Collects taxes • Pays the state's bills

1. Which state executive officer is a member of the state legislature?

   A. lieutenant governor

   B. attorney general

   C. secretary of state

   D. state treasurer

2. Which executive officer plays a role in the judicial system?

   A. lieutenant governor

   B. attorney general

   C. secretary of state

   D. state treasurer

Skill Practice

Directions: Read the passage below. Then answer the questions that follow.

Of the three branches of government, the Framers had the least to say about the judicial branch. Congress began to spell out the power of the federal judiciary by passing the Judiciary Act of 1789. This act created the first of the lower federal courts. It also gave the Supreme Court the power to review state constitutions and state laws. If they disagreed with the US Constitution, the Court had the power to declare them unconstitutional.

John Marshall added to the power of the federal judiciary. He served as Chief Justice of the Supreme Court from 1801 to 1835. In *Marbury v. Madison*, the Court declared a part of a federal law unconstitutional. In doing this, the Court took for itself the power to review acts of Congress. This is known as the power of judicial review. Since then, neither Congress nor any president has ever argued that the Supreme Court does not have this power.

1. What is the central idea of this passage?

   A. The Framers had little to say about the judicial branch.

   B. The judicial branch was granted the power of judicial review in several ways.

   C. John Marshall created the federal judiciary.

   D. In *Marbury v. Madison*, the Court declared part of a federal law unconstitutional.

2. How did the Supreme Court obtain power of judicial review?

   A. The Supreme Court gained this power through the Judiciary Act of 1789 and through the court case *Marbury v. Madison*.

   B. John Marshall granted the Supreme Court the power of judicial review.

   C. The Supreme Court gained the power of judicial review by a vote of Congress.

   D. It was voted on by the American people.

3. In the passage above, what does the term "declare" mean?

   A. to yell

   B. to argue against

   C. to make an official decision

   D. to create a formal document

4. How does the power of judicial review strengthen the power of the Supreme Court?

   A. It created the federal judiciary.

   B. It grants the Supreme Court the power to review decisions made by the President.

   C. It makes the Supreme Court more powerful than the Constitution.

   D. It grants the Supreme Court the power to review decisions made by Congress.

Writing Practice

Directions: Write a paragraph comparing and contrasting state and federal government structure.

Directions: Choose the best answer to the following questions.

1. What is one disadvantage of a direct democracy?

   A. Citizens must be ruled by a dictator.

   B. Representatives speak for citizens in government.

   C. Large countries cannot be run efficiently with direct democracy.

   D. Citizens must remain loyal to the monarchy.

2. What was one purpose of the Declaration of Independence?

   A. to explain why the colonies were rejecting British rule

   B. to declare the colonists' loyalty to the British monarchy

   C. to persuade colonists to remain loyal to the British king

   D. to set up a new government

Directions: Questions 3 and 4 refer to the following chart.

Competing Plans and the Compromise Solutions

Issue	Virginia Plan	New Jersey Plan	U.S. Constitution
Representation	Based on population or wealth	Equal representation for each state	Upper house (Senate) made up of two delegates from each state; Lower house (House of Representatives) based on population
Executive Branch	Single executive chosen by Congress	Executive committee chosen by Congress	Single executive (president) chosen by the Electoral College; electors selected by individual states
Legislative Branch	Two houses: Upper house elected by the people; Lower house elected by the upper house	One house: appointed by state legislatures	Two houses: Upper house (Senate) selected by state legislatures*; Lower house (House of Representatives) elected by the people
Judicial Branch	National judiciary chosen by Congress	National judiciary appointed by executive committee	National judiciary: Supreme Court and lower courts; Supreme Court justices appointed by the president and confirmed by the Senate

*The Seventeenth Amendment in 1913 changed this. Senators are now elected by the people.

3. The Constitution was built on compromise between different plans for government. How did the constitutional delegates satisfy proponents of the Virginia Plan?

   A. The delegates created a Senate based on state population.

   B. The delegates created a Senate based on wealth of citizens.

   C. The delegates based the lower house on wealth of citizens.

   D. The delegates based the lower house on state population.

4. In what way does the US Constitution best depict a representative democracy?

   A. It includes one house in its legislative branch.

   B. It includes two houses in its legislative branch.

   C. It requires the president to be appointed by Congress.

   D. It requires a national judiciary, including a Supreme Court.

Directions: Use the chart to answer question 5.

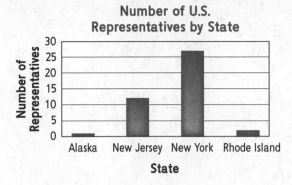

Number of U.S. Representatives by State

Number of Representatives (y-axis: 0, 5, 10, 15, 20, 25, 30)

State (x-axis): Alaska, New Jersey, New York, Rhode Island

5. What can you conclude based on this graph?
   A. The populations of New Jersey and New York are about the same.
   B. The populations of Alaska and Rhode Island are about the same.
   C. Alaska and Rhode Island are geographically the same size.
   D. New Jersey and New York have appointed governors.

Directions: Read the following passage. Then answer questions 6 and 7.

Thomas Jefferson and Constitutional Amendments

Some men look at constitutions with sanctimonious reverence, and deem them like the arc of the covenant, too sacred to be touched. They ascribe to the men of the preceding age a wisdom more than human, and suppose what they did to be beyond amendment. . . . I am certainly not an advocate for frequent and untried changes in laws and constitutions. I think moderate imperfections had better be borne with; because, when once known, we accommodate ourselves to them, and find practical means of correcting their ill effects. But I know also, that laws and institutions must go hand in hand with the progress of the human mind. As that becomes more developed, more enlightened, as new discoveries are made, new truths disclosed, and manners and opinions change with the change of circumstances, institutions must advance also, and keep pace with the times. We might as well require a man to wear still the coat which fitted him when a boy, as civilized society to remain ever under the regimen of their barbarous ancestors. It is this preposterous idea which has lately deluged Europe in blood.

——Thomas Jefferson, in a letter to Samuel Kercheval, June 12, 1816

6. Based on this passage, what can you conclude about Thomas Jefferson?
   A. He does not agree with constitutional amendments.
   B. He believes constitutional amendments are necessary at times.
   C. He believes that change causes great problems.
   D. He thinks people should endure imperfect laws forever.

7. According to Jefferson, what has "deluged Europe with blood"?
   A. constitutional amendments
   B. needless and frequent changes to laws
   C. the lack of progress of institutions and laws
   D. the British monarchy and its ancestors

Check Your Understanding

Lesson	Item Number
Types of Modern and Historical Governments	1, 2, 3
American Constitutional Democracy	5, 7
Structure of American Government	4, 6

WRITE ABOUT President Reagan's Speech at the Brandenburg Gate in West Berlin

Expository writing is writing that explains something. As part of an explanation, you might use examples, definitions, or a combination of both. You might also point out the causes of something or compare one subject to another. Often, you will need to do some research before beginning to write.

Go to page 348 and read the excerpt of a speech President Ronald Reagan gave in West Germany during the Cold War. Using information from the speech, write an expository essay that explains what Reagan believed about the effects of Communism. First, select one or two quotations from the speech. Then, do research to find information that supports Reagan's words. Focus on either the Soviet Union or East Germany following World War II. Be sure that your essay contains an introduction, body, and conclusion.

BEFORE YOU WRITE Create an Outline

Formal outlines follow a pattern of main idea and details. Each main idea is written with a Roman numeral, with the details as letters.

I. Main idea
   A. Detail
   B. Detail
II. Main idea
   A. Detail
   B. Detail

As you read the excerpt from President Reagan's speech, jot down the main idea and any supporting details for each of the four paragraphs. Note any words or lines that particularly interest you. This outline will give you the framework for your expository essay. Pay particular attention to the president's analysis of how Communism affected both the Soviet Union and East Germany, which came under Soviet control following World War II. Notice the tension the president says exists between the free nations of the West and the Communist world.

TIP Use Context Clues

When reading social studies documents, especially primary sources such as speeches, you may find words that are unfamiliar to you. By reading the entire sentence or paragraph, however, you may be able to get a sense of the word's meaning. For example, in the sentence below, the underlined word *comity* may be new to you.

> Freedom replaces the ancient hatreds among the nations with <u>comity</u> and peace.

Before going to the dictionary, look at the surrounding words, or context, for clues. Within the sentence two clues suggest the meaning of *comity*. First, it is something that replaces *ancient hatreds*. Second, it is linked with *peace*. So you can guess that it might mean *accord*. In fact, you would be close to the dictionary definition, which is *social harmony*.

WHILE YOU WRITE Sharpen Your Ideas

An outline is only a starting place. It does not necessarily need to be followed to the letter; rather, it serves as a helpful guide. Sometimes as you reread the passage and begin to write, new ideas will arrive. Let those ideas have their place, if they focus on information that answers the question. Just be sure you are not going off on a tangent, or tossing in your own opinions, unless instructed to do so. Continue to refer to the writing prompt and the task it assigns. Check to make sure that you are following the instructions.

One helpful tool for sharpening writing is to use the acronym WIRMI. Use **W**hat **I** **R**eally **M**ean **I**s to see if you are writing what you intend to say. It will make your writing clearer and the focus of your essay sharper.

> **TIP**   Watch Out for Passive Voice
>
> When the writing is in active voice, the subject is clearly acting. That makes it easy to see who did what.
>
> > Amy <u>ran</u> a marathon.
> > John <u>delivered</u> the message.
>
> Passive voice is wordier and less clear about who is acting. It uses a form of the verb *be*, such as *is* or *was*, plus another verb form, the past participle.
>
> > The marathon <u>was run</u> by Amy.
> > The letter <u>was delivered</u> by John.
>
> Often, such writing is done deliberately to avoid placing responsibility or laying blame.
>
> > The bill <u>was passed</u> by the state legislature.
> > The new law <u>was upheld</u> by the court.
>
> In your writing, avoid passive voice as much as possible. Write in clear, strong prose that lets the reader know what is happening. Use forceful action verbs rather than forms of *be*.

AFTER YOU WRITE Run Spell Check

First make sure you followed the assignment correctly. Did you explain what Reagan believed about Communism? Did you make sure to include a quote or two from the passage? Does your essay have a beginning, a middle, and an end?

When you're satisfied with the content of your essay, check your spelling. Most word processing programs have a spell-check option, usually located under *Tools*. It will catch many errors but not all of them. Spell-check does not notice problems such as *too* instead of *two*, and not all social studies vocabulary terms are in its database. When in doubt, you can always check a reliable dictionary, such as Merriam Webster Online.

Chapter 2

Civics

Have you ever heard people discussing an upcoming election? People often talk about the advantages and disadvantages of the people who are running for office. People also post their opinions about government and its leaders on social media sites. In the United States, citizens are free to express their opinions, and even their disapproval, of their government. That right to expression is guaranteed by the United States Constitution. In this chapter, you will learn about your civil rights and civil liberties.

Jill Braaten/McGraw-Hill Education

In this chapter you will study these topics:

Lesson 2.1
Individual Rights and Responsibilities
How did African Americans and women gain legal rights in the United States? When did women get the right to vote? How are these rights protected?

Lesson 2.2
Political Parties, Campaigns, and Elections
What are political parties? How are candidates elected to public office? Who helps candidates earn votes during an election period? When are elections held and how can people vote?

Lesson 2.3
Contemporary Public Policy
What is public policy? How do people and businesses affect public policy? How can public policy be changed? What are some contemporary public policies of concern today?

Goal Setting
Think about social problems in the United States that you hear about in the news. What is being done to solve those problems by the local or federal government?

What might you do to solve those problems? How can you participate in government to solve problems in your own community?

LESSON 2.1 Individual Rights and Responsibilities

LESSON OBJECTIVES

- Explain how civil rights expanded to include more people
- Understand how African Americans gained the right to vote
- Understand how women gained the right to vote

CORE SKILLS & PRACTICES

- Identify Point of View
- Identify Cause-and-Effect Relationships

Key Terms

civil liberties
freedoms guaranteed by the U.S. Constitution

civil rights
rights everyone has to equal protection under the law

segregation
separation of races

suffrage
the right to vote

Vocabulary

persevere
to continue doing something under difficult circumstances or strong opposition

point of view
how a person feels about, or what a person thinks about, something

Key Concept

Constitutional amendments and new laws have helped extend civil rights to more people in the United States.

Do you want to start a petition to ask the mayor and council to fix up a local park? Do you want to organize a march to city hall to present the petition? In some nations, you would be arrested and sent to jail for these actions. In the United States, though, these actions are legal for all citizens. Although these rights are often taken for granted, they did not come easily for many Americans. Almost 200 years passed before these rights were guaranteed by law to all Americans.

Civil Rights and Civil Liberties

Civil rights are the rights everyone has to equal protection under the law. **Civil liberties** are the freedoms guaranteed by the U.S. Constitution. The Bill of Rights, the first ten amendments to the Constitution, lists many of these civil liberties. Among them are freedom of speech, religion, and assembly.

Civil liberties are the foundation of American government. These freedoms allow us to act and think without interference from the government or fear of unfair treatment. Five basic freedoms are protected by the First Amendment. Following the Civil War, three amendments were passed to help protect African American's rights. Unfortunately, these amendments were not always successful. Southern states passed laws that continued to prevent African Americans from enjoying the same rights and freedoms as white Americans.

In the 1950s, African Americans began to make real progress in winning an equal place. They fought for equal rights in jobs, housing, and education. They also fought against **segregation**, the separation of people of different races. At the time, many African Americans lived with segregation in schools, housing, and many public places.

Library of Congress Prints and Photographs Division [LC-DIG-ppmsca-04297]

First Amendment

Americans' civil liberties begin with the First Amendment. Part of that amendment states, "Congress shall make no law respecting an establishment of religion." This is known as the Establishment Clause. A clause is a separate section in a legal document. Great Britain had established, or made, the Church of England as its official religion. Many citizens of the new United States did not want the government to support any one religion. That is why they wrote the Establishment Clause. Thomas Jefferson once said the Establishment Clause set up "a wall of separation between church and state."

The First Amendment has a second clause about religion. It states that Congress shall not pass any law "prohibiting the free exercise" of religion. This is known as the Free Exercise Clause. Under the Free Exercise Clause, government may not limit what people believe. In other words, people have freedom of religion. That freedom is not absolute, however. The Supreme Court has upheld government limits on what people can do in their religion. For example, federal law bans polygamy—having more than one spouse at a time—although some religions believe in polygamy.

The First Amendment also guarantees freedom of speech and freedom of the press. Speech refers to the spoken word. When the First Amendment was written, "the press" meant the printed word: newspapers, books, and pamphlets. Freedom of the press now extends to movies, radio, television, cable programs, and the Internet. Why are freedom of speech and freedom of the press important? A democracy works best when all ideas—even unpopular ones—are discussed and thought about.

As with religious practice, freedom of speech is not absolute. The government can limit speech that is harmful. Speech is protected when it encourages people to think something. Speech is not protected when it encourages people to take violent actions, provokes a public panic, or contains slander. Slander is knowingly making false statements about someone that damage his or her reputation.

The First Amendment also guarantees people freedom of assembly and the right to petition the government. These freedoms allow people to gather together in private and in public places. The right of people to make their views known to public officials is also guaranteed. However, government can regulate assemblies. For example, city governments issue rules that set when, where, and how protests may be carried out.

> [N]o man shall be compelled to frequent or support any religious worship, place, or ministry whatsoever, nor shall be enforced, restrained, molested, or burdened in his body or goods, nor shall otherwise suffer on account of his religious opinions or belief; but that all men shall be free to profess, and by argument to maintain, their opinions in matters of religion, and that the same shall in nowise diminish, enlarge, or affect their civil capacities.
>
> —Excerpted from *The Virginia Act for Establishing Religious Freedom*, by Thomas Jefferson

CORE SKILL

Identify Point of View

Point of view is how a person feels about, or what a person thinks about, something. Beliefs and values help to shape a person's point of view. To identify someone's point of view:

- identify the author and the author's background
- identify the author's argument or main idea
- look for evidence and reasons the author uses to support the position
- look for emotional words the author uses to sway the reader's opinion

Read the quote on the left from "The Virginia Act for Establishing Religious Freedom," written by Thomas Jefferson in 1786. How do you think Jefferson's point of view about religious freedom might have influenced the First Amendment?

Other Amendments

The remaining amendments in the Bill of Rights cover a variety of topics, such as due process and unreasonable searches and seizures. The Fourth Amendment guarantees due process. It requires the government to act fairly and obey the rule of law. Due process is especially important to people in the criminal justice system. Because of the Fourth Amendment, police cannot just go into a home or business and search it. They must have a search warrant issued by a judge. The Fifth Amendment guarantees that those accused of crimes are not bound to testify against themselves. It also protects a person from double jeopardy—being tried twice for the same crime. The Sixth Amendment guarantees the accused a "speedy public trial" and the right to confront witnesses during a trial.

When the Constitution was written, many Americans were strongly committed to protecting civil rights and civil liberties. Indeed, some states would not ratify the Constitution until political leaders promised that they would pass a bill of rights to provide this protection. Even so, it took almost 200 years for the nation to recognize fully the civil rights of African Americans, women, and other groups.

 Think about Social Studies

Directions: Choose the best answer to the following questions.

1. What is due process?
   A. procedures the government must follow when taking any action against a person
   B. steps the members of the legislative branch must follow when creating laws
   C. requirements a foreign-born person must fulfill to become a citizen of the United States
   D. procedures the federal government must follow when selecting a Supreme Court justice

2. Freedom of assembly implies freedom of
   A. choice.
   B. speech.
   C. the press.
   D. association.

Civil Rights for African Americans

When the Constitution was written, only white, male property owners could vote. Gradually other groups gained the right to vote. After the Civil War, three amendments were written that recognized the civil rights of African Americans. The Thirteenth Amendment ended slavery, and the Fourteenth Amendment said that any person born in the United States is a citizen. It also ensured civil rights for all Americans. However, these amendments did not extend the right to vote to African Americans. In 1870, the Fifteenth Amendment was ratified. This amendment gave all male citizens, even formerly enslaved people, the right to vote.

The Civil Rights movement marked the beginning of protests, court decisions, and public recognition of the need for greater awareness and protection for the rights of African Americans. It took a long time for African Americans to gain the rights of full citizenship and equality under the law.

Individual Rights and Responsibilities

Separate but Equal

Despite these changes, African Americans continued to face discriminatory practices, especially in Southern states. In 1896, in the case *Plessy* v. *Ferguson*, the Supreme Court ruled that segregation, or separation of races, was legal. This decision for "separate but equal" practices caused the rise of Jim Crow laws.

These laws separated African Americans from whites in public places, such as schools, restaurants, and bus stations. Although the Fifteenth Amendment guaranteed African Americans the right to vote, several states passed laws that made voting more difficult. They enacted a poll tax, or a tax on voters. Poor African Americans often did not have enough money to pay this tax, so they could not vote.

Literacy tests were another method states used to prevent African Americans from voting. These laws required potential voters to read and explain a written passage. White people were given easy passages with easy questions. Often, African Americans were given difficult passages to read, with challenging questions to answer, and therefore were more often unable to pass the test.

Warren Court

In 1953, Earl Warren became Chief Justice of the Supreme Court. From that year until 1969, when Warren retired, the Supreme Court gained a reputation for expanding civil rights. One important decision of the Warren Court came in ruling on the discrimination case of *Brown* v. *Board of Education of Topeka, Kansas*. The Court ruled that racial segregation in public schools violated the Fourteenth Amendment. This decision overturned *Plessy* v. Ferguson, at least in education.

Civil Rights Act

In 1963, Martin Luther King, Jr., a civil rights leader, was jailed for his work in the civil rights movement. He wrote a letter from the jail in Birmingham, Alabama, explaining the effects of segregation. He wrote, "Any law that degrades human personality is unjust. All segregation statutes are unjust because segregation distorts the soul and damages the personality. It gives the segregator a false sense of superiority and the segregated a false sense of inferiority."

In 1964, Congress enacted the Civil Rights Act, banning discrimination on the basis of race, religion, gender, or national origin. The law applied to stores, movie theaters, restaurants, stadiums—anywhere people gather or do business. It also banned the use of different registration requirements for African-American and white voters. That same year, the Twenty-Fourth Amendment made poll taxes illegal. The next year, the Voting Rights Act banned literacy tests.

Think about Social Studies

Directions: Choose the best answer to the following question.

1. Segregation is
   A. a civil right.
   B. the social separation of the races.
   C. a form of protest.
   D. nonviolent resistance.

Identify Cause-and-Effect Relationships

When you look for a cause, you are looking for why something happened. When you look for an effect of something that happened, you are looking for a change that results from some influence. Some words that signal a cause are *because, so,* and *since.* Some words that signal an effect are *then, as a result,* and *affect.*

Read the causes below. Then scan the text to identify one effect for each cause listed. On a separate sheet of paper, describe each effect in your own words.

1. In *Plessy* v. *Ferguson* the Supreme Court rules segregation is legal.
2. Southern states enact poll taxes.
3. African Americans are given more difficult literacy tests before voting.

Women's Rights

After the Civil War, the Fifteenth Amendment was passed. This amendment stated that the right to vote could not be denied because of a person's race. Many women were angry when the amendment did not give them the right to vote, or **suffrage**. The right to vote became the goal of women suffragists.

Nineteenth Amendment

In 1869, Susan B. Anthony and Elizabeth Cady Stanton formed the National Woman Suffrage Association (NWSA). The goal of the NWSA was passage of a constitutional amendment giving women the right to vote. This group later became the National American Woman Suffrage Association (NAWSA). In 1915, Carrie Chapman Catt became president of the NAWSA. The final push for the vote was on.

By this time, 11 states had granted women the right to vote in state elections. Women wanted to make sure that suffrage was available to all women across the nation. Women used protest marches and hunger strikes to put pressure on government. In 1919, Congress passed the Nineteenth Amendment, which gave women the right to vote. In the next year, three-fourths of the states ratified the amendment, making it official. Women were able to vote in the 1920 election.

Women Push for More Rights

After this victory, women continued to push for equal rights in other areas. Many women took jobs outside the home during World War II, and many continued to work after the war ended. Women who worked found that they were paid less money than men in similar jobs. Women were also blocked from getting the same jobs as men. Often they had jobs that did not allow them to advance, such as file clerks, sales clerks, or cleaning women.

Married women discovered they could not get credit cards in their own name, only in their husband's name. Single women also found it difficult to get credit.

Women were also inspired by the success of the Civil Rights Movement of the 1950s and early 1960s. That movement saw many advances in the rights of African Americans. Women began to put pressure on Congress to change the laws to guarantee their rights.

In 1963, Congress passed the Equal Pay Act. This law made it illegal to pay men and women differently for the same job. As you read earlier, part of the Civil Rights Act of 1964 banned job discrimination on the basis of gender. That helped working women as well.

The National Organization for Women (NOW) was created in 1966. This organization fought for equal rights for women in jobs, education, and marriage. In the early 1970s, NOW began to campaign for an Equal Rights Amendment (ERA) to the Constitution.

In 1972, Congress passed the Equal Rights Amendment, which states "equality of rights under law shall not be denied or abridged by the United States or by any State on account of sex." Although the Equal Rights Amendment was not ratified, women made other advances. In 1972 Congress also passed Title IX, which requires equal treatment of girls and young women who play sports in school or college. The women's movement had made its mark on civil rights in America.

Women gained more job opportunities and gained a greater voice in government. Women candidates won local and state political offices, seats in Congress, and appointments to the president's Cabinet. In 1981 President Ronald Reagan appointed Sandra Day O'Connor as the first female justice of the US Supreme Court.

⚑ Think about Social Studies

Directions: Choose the best answer to the following question.

1. What did Sandra Day O'Connor mean when she said "The power I exert on the court depends on the power of my arguments, not on my gender"?

   A. Justice O'Connor meant that her gender was just as important as the legal decisions she made on the Court.

   B. Justice O'Connor meant that her gender influenced the legal decisions she made and brought diversity to the Court.

   C. Justice O'Connor meant that while her gender might be important symbolically, as a justice what really mattered was her legal reasoning.

   D. Justice O'Connor meant that her gender was not relevant to her position on the Court.

21ST CENTURY SKILL

Leadership and Responsibility

Great leaders **persevere** to achieve their goals. To persevere means to continue doing something even though it is difficult. Read the following text. Then answer the question.

Ida B. Wells was born into an enslaved family in 1862. As a teacher in Tennessee, Wells was dissatisfied with the education of African-American children. She wrote newspaper articles about the schools. Because of the articles, Wells lost her job. She then began work with a local newspaper. It was the 1890s, and violence against African Americans in the South was common. Wells began to write about the horrors of lynching. In lynching, a group of people seize someone they think is guilty of a crime and hang the person. It was typically carried out by crowds of whites against African Americans. An angry mob attacked the offices of the newspaper. Wells did not stop writing. In 1895, she published the first report on lynching in the United States. Her research showed that between 1878 and 1898, some 10,000 African Americans were lynched. Wells was also a leader for women's rights. She founded the first African-American organization devoted to gaining the vote for women.

What actions showed Wells's ability to persevere?

Vocabulary Review

Directions: Complete the sentences using the following key terms and vocabulary words.

perseverance   suffrage   civil liberties
point of view   segregation   civil rights

1. Freedoms guaranteed by the U.S. Constitution are _____.

2. The right to vote is known as _____.

3. A person's _____ is how he or she feels about, or thinks about, something.

4. Because Martin Luther King, Jr., met with opposition to his civil rights activities, he needed _____ to continue his work.

5. In 1954, the Supreme Court ruled that _____ in education was illegal.

6. Both citizens and aliens are guaranteed _____, or equal protection under the law.

Skill Review

Directions: Choose the best answer to each question.

1. What effect did hunger strikes and protests of women suffragists have on government?
   A. They helped to give women the right to vote.
   B. They eliminated poll taxes for women.
   C. They guaranteed African American males the right to vote.
   D. They ensured women had the right to own property.

2. What was one effect of the Voting Rights Act of 1965?
   A. Poll taxes were banned.
   B. Women were granted to right to vote.
   C. Literacy tests were banned.
   D. Segregation was made illegal.

3. What do you think Martin Luther King, Jr., meant when he said, "All segregation statutes are unjust because segregation distorts the soul and damages the personality?"
   A. Segregation is unjust because of the physical harm it causes.
   B. Separate but equal facilities can not be just because they will never be truly equal.
   C. Laws promoting segregation can never be just because of the psychological damage they cause.
   D. Laws promoting segregation can only be just if they do not harm a person physically or psychologically.

4. What caused women to pressure the government for equal rights?
   A. Women enjoyed working outside the home.
   B. Women wanted equal pay and the right to vote.
   C. Women had a long history of fair treatment.
   D. Women did not want to be treated the same as men.

5. What was the goal of the Equal Rights Amendment?
   A. to guarantee access to voting for disabled Americans
   B. to guarantee equality under the law for women
   C. to strengthen traditional roles of women
   D. to guarantee equality under the law for African Americans

Skill Practice

Directions: Read the passage below. Choose the best answer to each question.

> *Schenck* v. *United States* (1919): "Clear and Present Danger" Rule
>
> (1) During World War I, Congress passed the Espionage Act of 1917. (2) It forbade the speaking, writing, printing, or publishing of anything against the government. (3) Charles Schenck was the general secretary of the Socialist Party. (4) He was convicted of printing and mailing leaflets to 15,000 draftees. (5) The leaflet urged them to refuse to report for military service. (6) Schenck claimed that he was protected by the First Amendment. (7) The Supreme Court ruled against him. (8) The Court agreed that in peacetime, Schenck would be protected. (9) However, in wartime, his "speech" represented a "clear and present danger" to the nation. (10) The Espionage Act was constitutional because Congress had the right to protect the nation.

1. How did World War I affect the Supreme Court's ruling?

   A. The Court ruled that freedom of speech is withheld during wartime.

   B. The Court found Schenck's speech a danger to the nation during wartime.

   C. The Court urged draftees to refuse to report for military service.

   D. The Court protected Schenck's speech as it would during peacetime.

2. Which sentence contains clues about Schenck's point of view regarding freedom of speech?

   A. Sentence 2

   B. Sentence 5

   C. Sentence 6

   D. Sentence 10

3. How would the Supreme Court's decision have been different during peacetime?

   A. The Court would guarantee Schenck's freedom of speech.

   B. The Court would not rule on the case.

   C. The Court's decision would not be different.

   D. The Court would rule against the Socialist Party.

4. The term "espionage" usually refers to spying. Based on the passage above, this term can also refer to

   A. speaking out during peacetime.

   B. actions harmful to the nation.

   C. military service during wartime.

   D. printing and distributing pamphlets.

Writing Practice

Directions: Perseverance was one leadership trait discussed in this chapter. Choose three additional traits you believe are important for effective leaders. Write a brief essay discussing the importance of these traits to good leadership.

Early Voting Center

FRANKLIN COUNTY BOARD OF ELECTIONS

LESSON 2.2 Political Parties, Campaigns, and Elections

LESSON OBJECTIVES

- Explain the role of political parties in U.S. politics
- Discuss the importance of interest groups
- Understand how citizens participate in a democracy

CORE SKILLS & PRACTICES

- Analyze Ideas
- Interpret Political Cartoons

Key Terms

independents
people who belong to no organized political party

interest group
a group of people with common concerns who join together to influence government policy

lobbyists
people who work to sway the opinion of public officials

political party
an organized group of people who share common values and goals

Vocabulary

symbol
a person or object that represents something else

synthesize
to combine things in order to make something new

Key Concept

People can make their views known and influence public policy through political parties and interest groups.

Just as school clubs and community organizations have elected leaders so do local and national governments. Citizens participate by voting for the people they believe will do the best job.

American Political Parties

Political parties exist to help elect people who share their ideals. In the United States, there are several political parties that participate in elections but only two major parties vote for the winning candidates: the Democrats and Republicans.

Two-Party System

A **political party** is an organized group of people who share common values and goals. Members of political parties try to get their candidates elected to office. The United States basically has a two-party system. The Democratic and Republican Parties are the two major parties. Most people who belong to a party belong to one of them. However, the nation has a number of other political parties. These are known as third parties or minor parties. A third party develops when a group of people believes that the major parties are not dealing with some important issue.

Functions of Political Parties

Modern political parties serve several major functions. First, political parties nominate, or choose, people to run for public office. Those chosen are known as candidates. Party officials look for members who will appeal to voters and support the major policies of their political parties.

Second, political parties play a role in governing the nation. Congress is organized along party lines, as are state legislatures. Like legislators, the president and state governors are elected with the support of a political party. The president and governors depend on legislators elected by their party to get laws written and passed.

Political Parties, Campaigns, and Elections

McGraw-Hill Education

Every four years, the national parties carry out one of their most important duties: they hold their national conventions. The conventions have two tasks. They nominate the party's presidential and vice presidential candidates, and they write the party's platform. A platform states the party's position on various issues. It is a promise of what the party will do if elected.

Independents

Between one-quarter and one-third of all registered voters are **independents**. They belong to no organized political party and will often vote for different candidates from different parties. Independents can play a major role in deciding which candidate is elected. Their votes have become increasingly important since the 1990s. The two major parties have about the same number of members. As a result, candidates, especially for president, need to appeal to independents to win.

The two-party system is not the only political system in the world. In fact, most nations have a multiparty system. In this system, there are several major and minor parties. Each party wins some offices, including seats in the national legislature. Often, a major party must partner with a minor party to put together a majority in the legislature. The partnership is known as a coalition. Leaders of the minor party are appointed to the cabinet.

Many European nations and emerging democracies have multiparty systems. A few nations have one-party systems, in which the party and the government are the same. The leaders of the party are the leaders of the government.

 Think about Social Studies

Directions: Choose the best answer to the following question.

1. What is a party platform?
A. a list of a party's candidates
B. a place where party leaders meet
C. a method a party uses to contact followers
D. a statement of a party's beliefs and positions

Political Campaigns and Elections

The right to vote is basic to democracy, and citizens exercise this right on Election Day. Voting comes with a responsibility. That responsibility is to be an informed voter. Candidates and political parties distribute campaign information that is intended to persuade you. Read and listen to campaign information carefully and be aware that it is not objective. Pay attention to the accuracy of the information, so that you can make informed voting decisions.

Analyze Ideas

When you **analyze** ideas, you read carefully to understand the ideas in the text. When you analyze political parties, you try to understand their structure, function, and power. As you read "U.S. Political Parties," make a list of key differences between the two major parties and third parties. Then write a short paragraph explaining why the major parties are more powerful than the third parties in the United States.

A political cartoonist draws a cartoon to illustrate an opinion about a current issue. Examine the political cartoon on this page. Follow these steps to interpret it.

1. Identify the topic of the cartoon.
2. Identify the meaning behind the captions.
3. Identify what is happening in the cartoon.
4. Identify the point of view of the cartoonist.

Presidential Elections

Voters choose electors who meet in December as the Electoral College to choose the president and vice president. The electors in each state meet in their state capitals to vote. The votes are sent to Congress and counted in January. The candidate who has the majority of the electors' votes is declared president.

On election night, newscasters keep a running count of the popular vote and the electoral vote. The popular vote is the number of votes cast by citizens. The electoral vote is the number of electoral votes from each state. Each state's electoral vote is the sum of its two senators plus the number of its members in the House. In all, there are 538 electoral votes. To become president, a candidate must get 270 votes.

The Campaign Trail

Political candidates take part in election campaigns. Campaigns for local and state offices tend to begin during the year the election will be held. In recent years, presidential races have begun as early as two years before the election. Depending on the office, a campaign may laste as long as two years and cost millions of dollars. Long campaigns require a great deal of money to rent offices, pay campaign workers, and run advertisements and Web sites. Campaign money can lead to abuses. Donors of large amounts of money often expect favors in return. As a result, Congress has passed a number of campaign finance laws.

Political cartoons are used to make people think about an issue. They often **synthesize**, or combine, symbols and caricatures to make their point. A **symbol** is a person or object that represents something else. The symbol used for the Democratic Party is a donkey. An elephant stands for the Republican Party.

THE FISHIN' SEASON

■ **Think about Social Studies**

Directions: Choose the correct response.

1. Campaign finance laws are used to prevent _____.
   A. candidates from donating money.
   B. candidates from accepting donations.
   C. candidates from granting favors to donors.
   D. donors from giving large sums of money.

The Influence of Interest Groups

The American Association of Retired Persons (AARP), the National Rifle Association (NRA), and the American Medical Association (AMA) are among thousands of interest groups in the United States.

Working for Issues

An **interest group** is a group of people with common concerns who join together to influence government policy. This may sound like a political party. However, there are important differences between interest groups and political parties. Political parties nominate candidates for public office. Interest groups do not nominate candidates, but they often work for or against candidates during elections. Interest groups generally focus on one or just a few issues. Political parties work for solutions across a range of issues.

Interest groups can be very powerful. For example, political action committees (PACs) raise millions of dollars for candidates. These groups then expect the candidate, if elected, to vote in their favor on laws. Politicians sometimes complain about interest groups. In reality, few candidates today are elected without the support of at least some interest groups.

In addition to contributing to election campaigns, interest groups pressure government officials in other ways. Members testify at government hearings for or against proposed laws. Groups take out media ads to let officials know their views. Group members write letters to their lawmakers and demonstrate in front of the legislature.

Lobbying Lawmakers

The most successful way to influence government is to lobby lawmakers. Lobbying is making direct contact with lawmakers, their staffs, and government officials for the purpose of influencing the passage of laws and regulations. **Lobbyists** are the people who work to sway public officials toward a particular opinion.

Successful lobbyists are paid hundreds of thousands of dollars a year for their work. This means that interest groups with large numbers of members or wealthy members have the most influence. These organizations can afford to hire the best lobbyists.

Some lobbyists set up their own businesses in Washington, D.C., where interest groups hire them. Other lobbyists are employees of large organizations, such as major labor unions. Lobbyists are not limited to trying to influence Congress. Interest groups also use lobbyists to persuade state lawmakers and officials to support their side of issues.

 Think about Social Studies

Directions: In a notebook, answer the following question.

How are political parties and special interest groups different?

Vocabulary Review

Directions: Match the words and their definitions.

1. _____ lobbyists
2. _____ synthesize
3. _____ interest group
4. _____ political party
5. _____ independents
6. _____ symbol

A. people who belong to no organized political party

B. an organized group of people who share common values and goals

C. to combine things in order to make something new

D. something that represents something else

E. people who work to sway public officials toward a particular opinion

F. a group of people with common concerns who join together to influence government policy on a particular issue

Skill Review

Directions: Choose the best answer to each question.

1. Which sentence describes the point of view of the political cartoon in this lesson?

   A. Democrats need to use bait, or incentives, to come up with campaign issues.

   B. Republicans take up more space in the pool, indicating their importance in campaigns.

   C. Democrats and Republicans fish for their issues from different sides of the same pool.

   D. Republicans have more issues in campaigns than Democrats.

2. What is the Electoral College?

   A. a group of electors from each state who choose the president

   B. a college that offers a degree in election campaigning

   C. another name for citizens who vote in state elections

   D. groups of people who work for political candidates

3. Why is it important for candidates of the two major parties to appeal to independents?

   A. Independents belong to a third party, which contributes to the two major parties.

   B. Independents have flexible beliefs and often agree with both major parties.

   C. Candidates of the major parties often need the independent vote to win an election.

   D. The major parties often attack the views of independents to win votes.

4. What would be the best way for a voter to become informed about a political party's position on various issues?

   A. watch television advertisements

   B. read the party's platform

   C. visit the candidates' websites

   D. listen to political talk shows on the radio

Skill Practice

Directions: Read the passage. Then answer the questions that follow.

Shifting Power of Political Parties

After the Civil War, the Republican Party was the dominant party. It was the party that saved the Union and ended slavery. It also supported high tariffs and free homesteads in the West. In the northern states, businessmen, farmers, and many laborers voted Republican. So did most African Americans in states that allowed them to vote. The Democratic Party was strongest in the South and Midwest. Between 1860 and 1932, the Democrats won only four presidential elections.

A shift in power occurred in the 1932 election. The nation was in the depths of the Great Depression. The policies of Republican president Herbert Hoover were not working. Voters elected Democrat Franklin D. Roosevelt. During President Roosevelt's New Deal era, the Democrats supported labor unions, price supports for farmers, and Social Security. Between 1932 and 1968, only one Republican was elected president, Dwight Eisenhower, a World War II general and hero.

1. What is the main idea of the passage?
   A. The Republican Party gained power after the Civil War because it ended slavery.
   B. The most dramatic shift in power happened when African Americans were allowed to vote.
   C. Power shifts between the two major parties have occurred many times in America's history.
   D. Political parties usually shift power after a major war, such as World War II.

2. What caused the power shift in 1932?
   A. Voters wanted to elect a World War II general and hero, so they elected the Republican candidate.
   B. The policies of the Republican president were not working, so voters elected a Democrat for president.
   C. Republicans supported higher taxes, which voters believed would help end the Great Depression.
   D. Voters were discouraged by President Roosevelt's New Deal policies that supported labor unions.

3. In what way does this passage show that voters care about economic issues?
   A. The passage explains the effects of the Great Depression on the nation's economy and a presidential election.
   B. The passage describes how voters feel about economic policies such as support for labor unions and farmers.
   C. The passage analyzes how voters in northern and southern states differ on their positions regarding economic policy.
   D. The passage details the economic problems that resulted in certain party candidates being elected to the presidency.

4. In the passage above, what does the term **dominant** mean?
   A. new
   B. most politically active
   C. won the most elections
   D. supported labor unions

Writing Practice

Directions: In a paragraph, explain how political action groups can contribute to abuses of power by candidates and elected officials.

LESSON 2.3 Contemporary Public Policy

LESSON OBJECTIVES

- Define contemporary public policy
- Identify examples of public policy
- Describe how public policy is made

CORE SKILLS & PRACTICES

- Evaluate Reasoning
- Draw Conclusions

Key Terms

accountable
responsible

domestic
relating to one's own country

issues
concerns

public policy
actions that affect everybody

Vocabulary

bias
belief that certain ideas or people are better than others

conclude
decide

Key Concept

Actions taken by the government to address concerns of the voting public are known as public policies.

Do you think texting and driving should be illegal? Would you like the minimum wage increased? Should the voting age be lowered to allow 16-year-olds to vote? You likely have opinions about these public issues as well as others. Your opinions and the opinions of others help shape the laws that the government creates to manage public problems.

What Is Contemporary Public Policy?

When the US government needs to address a problem affecting citizens, it creates an action plan or a policy. These policies set out to solve problems and prevent future problems from occurring.

Rules and Guidelines

You may have heard the term policy used before, such as school policy, which refers to the rules and guidelines for a school's students, teachers, and administrators. **Public policy** is a broader term and refers to actions that affect the public. The government writes public policy.

Contemporary public policy refers to current public policy, not policies of the past. Because the US government addresses so many issues, thousands of public policies are in effect today, and many impact your life.

Types of Public Policy

Local governments make city and county policies. For example, city governments make policies about health codes at facilities that serve food. State governments make policies that everyone in the state must follow, such as state income taxes. The federal government makes policies that affect everyone in the nation. For example, the minimum voting age is set by federal policy.

Other types of public policy focus on specific topics, such as health, education, and economics. The federal government raising the age that seniors can receive government-funded health care would be an example of a health policy. A state government that implements, or puts into practice,

©iStockphoto.com/EdStock

exams for high school graduation is an example of an education policy. A city government providing tax savings to businesses is an example of an economic policy.

The federal government also has public policy for domestic matters. The term **domestic** means relating to one's own country. Policies that relate to other countries are categorized as foreign policies. These policies guide the activities and relationships with other nations.

How National Policy Is Made

Creating public policy is a complicated process that begins with identifying a problem. After a problem is identified, possible solutions are offered to address the problem. Solutions can come from elected officials, concerned citizens, interest groups, or researchers.

Policy makers compare solutions and choose the one that has the most support. This policy is then passed to Congress for a vote. If a majority of Congress votes for the policy, it is adopted. In some cases, the president can adopt a policy by signing an order. The Supreme Court also has the power to adopt policy by ruling on an important case. After a public policy is adopted, it is then implemented. Government agencies are in charge of implementing new public policies.

As soon as a policy is implemented, the evaluation phase begins. During this phase, policy makers gather information about the effects of the policy and **conclude**, or decide, whether the policy is working. Sometimes the policy needs some changes. Other times, the policy is deemed a failure, and the policy-making process begins again.

Policy-Making Process

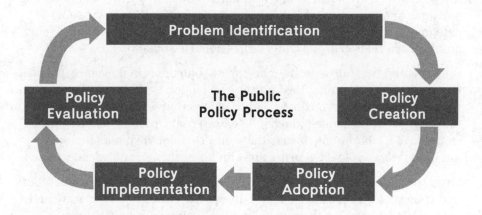

The Public Policy Process

- Problem Identification
- Policy Creation
- Policy Adoption
- Policy Implementation
- Policy Evaluation

🚩 Think about Social Studies

Directions: Answer the following questions.

1. Why is the policy-making process a continuous process?

2. The US government uses _____ to guide its actions with other countries.

CORE PRACTICE

Evaluate Reasoning

Reasoning is the thinking process that leads you to a conclusion. When you evaluate reasoning, you determine whether a conclusion results logically from evidence. Evidence includes facts, opinions, and values. Facts can be proven, but opinions are personal viewpoints. **Bias** is the belief that certain ideas or people are better than others. Values are moral rules or beliefs that often influence people's opinions.

Use the Internet to research your state representative's position on a public policy. Consider whether the representative uses facts, opinions, or values to support his or her position. Is the reasoning logical? Then, write an essay evaluating the representative's reasoning.

Draw Conclusions

Effective readers know how to draw conclusions. Conclusions are judgments or decisions that are formed after careful reading or research of texts. To draw a conclusion, you need to use more than one piece of information. Choose one public policy in the news today. Research reputable online news media sites to learn more about the policy. In particular, note the effects of the policy on you and other US citizens. In a notebook, write a paragraph in which you discuss one conclusion you can draw about the success of the policy. Give evidence to justify your conclusion.

Influences on Public Policy

The US government is **accountable**, or responsible, to the people. Government officials, who are chosen by voters, make public policy. This relationship allows voters to influence public policy by electing officials who support policies that benefit the voters. Voters are not the only influences on public policy, however. Special interest groups and lobbyists also influence contemporary public policy.

Interest Groups

Many types of interest groups affect public policy. Some of these include special interest groups, public-interest groups, and economic interest groups.

Special Interest Groups

Special interest groups are organized around specific issues. For example, the Sierra Club and the National Wildlife Federation are interest groups that address environmental issues. Some issues create groups on both sides. Gun control is one such issue. Handgun Control, Inc., supports background checks on gun purchasers. The National Rifle Association opposes them.

Public-Interest Groups

Public-interest groups work for public policies that will benefit all or most Americans. The groups work for Americans in general, rather than just for their members. Common Cause is an example of this type of organization. It works for openness and fairness in the political system.

Economic Interest Groups

Economic interest groups are concerned with government policies that affect how they do business and how much money they earn. They work for and against government regulations and tax policies. There are four categories of economic interest groups: business and trade groups, labor unions, farm-related groups, and professional associations.

Business and trade groups are made up of companies in the same industry. For example, the National Restaurant Association is made up of people who work in the restaurant business. Labor unions represent people who work in the same job or the same industry. The Fraternal Order of Police is an example of a labor union. Issues that concern union members include minimum wage, Social Security, and similar economic and social policies.

Farm groups include organizations that represent large farmers and others that represent small farmers. These groups are concerned with state and federal laws that affect their products. Professional groups include organizations such as the American Medical Association for doctors. Professional groups deal mostly with regulations related to their profession.

Regulating Interest Groups

State and federal governments have laws about what special interest groups can do. Some laws limit the amount of money they can contribute to a campaign. This is to prevent special interest groups from having more influence than ordinary voters. Supporters of special interest groups, however, believe that these groups help make the wishes of voters known to government officials. Ordinary voters are able to join together to take an active role in government.

Lobbyists

Lobbyists also influence contemporary public policy. Lobbyists are people who work to protect and promote different issues, interests, and reforms. Lobbyists get their name from the days when they would wait in the lobbies of Congress to speak to members of the legislature. Lobbyists work for special interest groups, businesses, and other organizations.

Lobbyists are often former government employees. They may have worked for executive departments or been senators or members of the House of Representatives. These people know how government works. They have friends in agencies and among lawmakers. This closeness between lobbyists and officials can cause concerns about favoritism. As a result, federal law bars members of Congress from becoming lobbyists for at least one year after leaving Congress.

Sometimes lobbyists are lawyers or former reporters. Public relations experts also work as lobbyists. An important job of lobbyists involves public relations. Lobbyists work to make sure that the public images of, or ideas about, the groups they represent are favorable.

Lobbyists use a variety of methods to influence public policy. First, they try to meet with lawmakers or public officials to tell their side of the issues. Lobbyists may make appointments to see lawmakers or officials in their offices.

Another method lobbyists use to influence public policy is to provide government officials with information and reports. At times, lobbyists also help write the bills that come before Congress.

All lobbyists and organizations that work to influence Congress must register with the federal government. They must list their clients and explain all their lobbying activities. Each lobbyist and group must file these reports twice a year.

Think about Social Studies

Directions: Read each statement. Place an S for special interest group, P for public-interest group, or E for economic interest group on the line next to each.

$\boxed{S}$ $\boxed{P}$ $\boxed{E}$

1. _____ includes trade groups and professional associations

2. _____ work for all Americans, not just group members

3. _____ represent large and small farmers

4. _____ organized around special issues

5. _____ focus on environmental issues

21ST CENTURY SKILL

Civic Literacy

Civic literacy includes the knowledge and skills necessary to participate and make changes in your community and society. Participating in society is the first step in making a change. For example, before you can change a policy you first must learn about the policy by attending meetings, talking to officials, and reading related laws. To initiate change in society requires many skills, including communicating, organizing, and planning.

Research a special interest group that interests you. Find out what skills and strategies they used to change a public policy. Then, create a list of skills you believe citizens need to become change-makers in their communities.

WRITE TO LEARN

Imagine you are a lobbyist for a special interest group. Create an outline of the key topics you want to tell lawmakers.

Vocabulary Review

Directions: Complete the sentences using the following key terms and vocabulary words.

issues   domestic   public policy

bias   conclude   accountable

1. Policy makers gather information to _____ whether a policy is working.

2. Public policies address _____ of society.

3. Unlike foreign policies, _____ policies concern only the citizens of the United States.

4. Government officials are _____ for the policies they create.

5. Actions that address the concerns of all citizens are known as _____.

6. Opinions that include _____ are not considered logical reasoning.

Skill Review

Directions: Choose the one best answer to each question.

1. Which is an example of a public policy?
   A. a campaign sign at a local business
   B. hours of operation at a store
   C. state water conservation laws
   D. driving a vehicle without a license

2. Congress passes a law to increase the minimum wage. What type of public policy is this?
   A. foreign policy
   B. education policy
   C. family policy
   D. economic policy

3. What is the name for representatives of interest groups who contact public officials directly?
   A. lobbyists
   B. labor unions
   C. policy makers
   D. public relations experts

4. The state legislature passes a law to ban texting and driving. What type of public policy is this?
   A. economic policy
   B. education policy
   C. health policy
   D. labor policy

5. Reasoning is based on
   A. facts.
   B. opinions.
   C. bias.
   D. judgment.

6. What is an argument in favor of special interest groups?
   A. They only impact local elections.
   B. They encourage corruption among politicians.
   C. They have too much influence on government.
   D. They tell elected officials what the people want.

Skill Practice

Directions: Read the passages below. Then answer the questions that follow.

> People are not naive to the existence of corruption and they know it has worn the face of both Republicans and Democrats over the years. Moreover, the underlying issue of how extensively money influences politics is the original sin of everyone who's ever run for office—myself included. In order to get elected, we need to raise vast sums of money by meeting and dealing with people who are disproportionately wealthy.
>
> —Barack Obama, Senate Floor Debate on Ethics Reform, 2006

> I am in this race to tell the corporate lobbyists that their days of setting the agenda in Washington are over. I have done more than any other candidate in this race to take on lobbyists—and won. They have not funded my campaign, they will not get a job in my White House, and they will not drown out the voices of the American people when I am president.
>
> —Barack Obama, presidential campaign speech, 2007

1. In the second passage, what is the message Obama wanted to give to give to the American voters?

   A. As president, he will not be swayed by lobbyists.

   B. The interests of lobbyists are most important to the presidency.

   C. He will work for lobbyists and special interests if he becomes president.

   D. Lobbyists are an ethical tool for presidents to use.

2. What conclusion can you draw about Obama's point of view on campaign finance?

   A. He will work for lobbyists and special interests if he becomes president.

   B. The interests of wealthy contributors are most important to the presidency.

   C. Campaign contributions are necessary but dangerous.

   D. Lobbyists are an ethical tool for presidents to use.

3. Compare the two passages. How does Obama's presidential campaign speech seem to contradict, or oppose, his Senate floor speech?

   A. In the Senate floor speech, he admits to taking money for his campaign; however, in the presidential speech, he says he has never taken money from lobbyists for his presidential campaign.

   B. In both speeches he is adamant that he has never taken money from lobbyists for any of his campaigns.

   C. He freely admits to taking money from lobbyists to fund all of his campaigns.

   D. In the Senate floor speech, he says he has never taken money for his campaign; however, in his presidential speech he admits to taking money from lobbyists.

Writing Practice

Directions: Consider the role of lobbyists in contemporary public policy. Write a letter to your congressional representative defending or supporting lobbyists. Use evidence from your reading to defend your opinion.

Directions: Choose the best answer to each question.

1. Based on the graph, what can you conclude about the Equal Pay Act of 1963?

    A. The Equal Pay Act successfully met its goals.

    B. The act eliminated salary discrimination in the United States.

    C. Women still face discrimination on the job.

    D. Men do not earn as much as women for the same work.

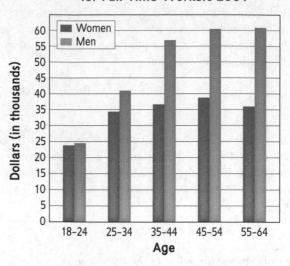

Average Income for Full-Time Workers 2001

2. Why did writers of the Constitution include the Establishment Clause?

    A. They wanted citizens to follow one national religion.

    B. They wanted to model the US government on that of Great Britain.

    C. They believed in the separation of church and state.

    D. They wanted government to support one religion.

3. What was one effect of *Brown v. Board of Education*?

    A. segregation of public schools

    B. voting rights for African Americans

    C. voting rights for women

    D. desegregation of public schools

4. Campaign finance reforms are intended to limit the power of _____.

    A. voters

    B. interest groups

    C. candidates

    D. political parties

5. How do people in the United States influence public policy?

    A. People elect government officials, who are accountable to voters for their actions.

    B. Registered voters can choose public policies at specific times of the year.

    C. People write public policy for consideration by government officials.

    D. People get elected to office and then create public policy.

6. What is the first step in the policy-making process?

    A. policy creation

    B. policy adoption

    C. policy evaluation

    D. problem identification

7. Authorities cannot search a person's home without a warrant because of

    A. double jeopardy.

    B. the Free Exercise Clause.

    C. due process.

    D. the Establishment Clause.

Directions: Read the passage. Then answer the questions that follow.

Campaign Finance

In the past, campaign donors and candidates have found ways around campaign finance laws. The laws regulated hard money. This is money raised and spent by the candidates for Congress and the White House themselves. However, the laws said nothing about soft money. This is money raised and spent for party-building activities, which include registering voters and get-out-the-vote activities on Election Day.

By the 1990s, the two major parties were raising millions of dollars in soft money. There were no laws to govern how much soft money could be raised. Although soft money was supposed to be used only for party building, the parties found ways to use the money to help their candidates.

8. Which of the following statements is an opinion related to the passage?
   A. All campaign finance laws are ineffective.
   B. Soft money is spent on party-building activities.
   C. Campaign finance laws did not regulate soft money.
   D. Millions of dollars in soft money is raised during elections.

9. Based on the passage, why is legislation needed to control the raising of soft money?
   A. Campaign finance reform will end the spending of hard money.
   B. Campaign finance laws only regulate hard money, not soft money.
   C. Without reforms to soft money, the number of people who vote will decrease.
   D. Candidates need to be able to raise more money for their own elections.

Check Your Understanding

Lesson	Item Number
Individual Rights and Responsibilities	1, 2, 3
Political Parties, Campaigns, and Elections	4, 8, 9
Contemporary Public Policy	5, 6, 7

WRITE ABOUT Policy Changes

When you write a sequencing essay, you are putting things in order by time. For example, sportscasters do this when they announce games. Actions in a basketball game are described according to what happens first, then next, and so forth. Listening to a game on the radio, you can follow it in your mind. Perhaps you can even visualize the plays.

Over the course of more than two hundred years, many policies of the government, both nationally and locally, have changed. For example, the XVIII Amendment to the federal constitution made manufacturing, transporting, or selling liquor against the law. Several years later, the XXI Amendment made these activities legal once more. Perhaps you are aware of local laws that have changed over time as well. After reading the essay on voting rights for women, write a sequencing essay addressing a policy change at any level of government.

BEFORE YOU WRITE Make a Time Line

A time line is a visual summary of events in time sequence, or chronological order. You are probably familiar with time lines from reading history books. The date is on one side of a vertical or horizontal line, with the event on the other side. Time lines are a quick visual of events or steps leading to something new, such as a law. Some time lines cover centuries; others include events of only a short time. Notice the time line below.

A History of Voting Rights in the United States

1776 — White men 21 and older can vote; a few states allow African American men to vote

1870 — All men of any race are permitted to vote

1920 — Women gain the right to vote

1970 — Voting age lowered to 18

TIP Vary Sentence Length

When trying to explain policy changes, it is easy to focus on writing short, simple sentences. However, good writing includes a variety of sentence lengths. Just as listening to a person speaking in a monotone quickly becomes boring, so too does reading something that uses sentences that are always the same length. If you have had or babysat children, you get tired of reading the same short sentences to them far sooner than they get tired of hearing them. As we mature, our ears crave variety in sentence structure and length.

One way to check your sentence length is to place a transparent sheet of paper over your finished essay. Note where the periods and capital letters for the ends and beginnings of sentences are located. Are you writing many sentences of the same length? Try combining ideas, always remembering to place either a comma and conjunction or a semicolon between two joined sentences. Note the example below.

> Not all women wanted the right to vote. Some thought it was unladylike.
> Not all women wanted the right to vote; some thought it was unladylike.

WHILE YOU WRITE Use Dates and Time-Clue Words as Transitions

To help the reader follow the action, using time words and dates is helpful. Terms such as *before*, *after*, *when*, and *while* can help the reader track the progress of an event. Using words that relate to the seasons or months of the year is another strategy. *During the first quarter, over the summer*, and *in September* are all examples of subtle cues that can assist the reader.

Beginning each paragraph with a time-signal word or phrase will make it easier for the reader, which is always your goal. Readers who cannot figure out what is happening when will soon stop reading. Help your readers not to be confused by giving them terms that will help move the action forward in time.

TIP   Watch Out for Misused Homonyms

Words that sound alike but have different meanings and different spellings are known as homonyms. Examples include words such as *soar* and *sore*, *here* and *hear*, and *their, they're*, and *there*. Also be aware of near-homonyms, which sound very much alike. Pairs such as *affect/effect*, *complement/compliment*, and *sense/since* can be troublesome. These are the sorts of errors that a computer's spell-check may not catch.

There are memory devices that can help distinguish some pairs of words. For example, the head of a school is a *principal*; the last three letters spell *pal*, which may not have been your experience with the principal but is a good goal. The word *principle* refers to standards of conduct. Another trick is to see the word *here* in the word *there* and to remember that both are place words, thus avoiding using *their* or *they're* when referring to location. If you have trouble with homonyms, devise your own schemes for remembering the difference between words that only sound alike.

AFTER YOU WRITE Proofread Your Essay

Reading and correcting one's own work can be difficult. We have a tendency to read what we intended to write, to see what we thought we had written instead of what is actually on the page.

One way to avoid this tendency is to read the essay or paper from the bottom line up. By forcing the eye to see what is *really* on the page, we can spot errors or omissions more easily. You may also wish to take a ruler or a piece of colored paper to use as a guide as you read, blocking all lines except the one on which you are focusing. Going slowly through the essay line by line may reveal not only errors but also words or ideas that can be made stronger.

Chapter 3

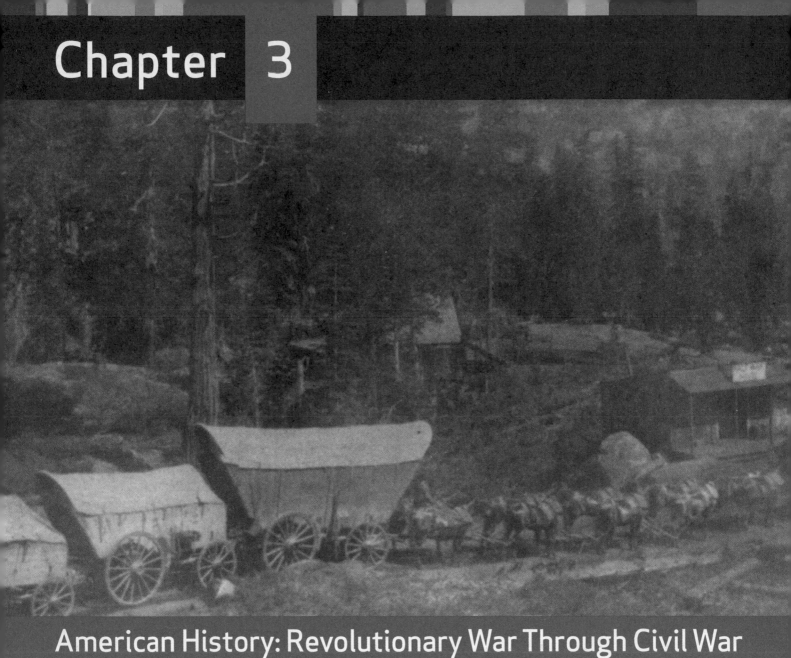

American History: Revolutionary War Through Civil War

The US Constitution is the most powerful law in the United States. It is the law that all other laws must follow. Who wrote the Constitution, and why did they feel they needed to write it? The Constitution was the result of a struggle for independence that culminated in the Revolutionary War. After the war, the new country had to learn to govern itself and face the challenges of a growing population, westward expansion, and conflicts over slavery and states' rights.

In this chapter you will study these topics:

Lesson 3.1
American Revolution

Who fought in the American Revolution and what caused it? Who won the war? Who participated in the first national government? How does the war affect American society today?

Lesson 3.2
A New Nation

How did the nation grow to the size it is today? Who settled different areas of the United States? What effect did the nation's growth have on people other than Americans?

Lesson 3.3
Civil War and Reconstruction

What caused the Civil War? How did the states solve their problem and reunite? How did the Civil War affect people in the South? How did it affect African Americans?

Lesson 3.4
European Settlement and Population of the Americas

Why did people immigrate to the United States? Where did immigrants settle? What issues did immigrants face when they arrived in the United States?

Goal Setting

Think about a time when you argued with your family or close friends. Did you feel divided? How did you come to an agreement?

Americans, too, have disagreed with each other and with other countries. What were the causes of these disagreements? How do they affect you and your society today?

LESSON OBJECTIVES

- Understand the causes of the American Revolution
- Identify the documents that shaped American democratic traditions
- Summarize the provisions of the Articles of Confederation
- Understand how and why the Constitution was developed

CORE SKILLS & PRACTICES

- Summarize Ideas
- Analyze Cause and Effect

Key Terms

boycott
refuse to buy

charter
a written code of rules or laws

colony
a geographic area in a new land that remains loyal to the parent nation

minutemen
soldiers in the colonial militia who were ready to fight at a minute's notice

unicameral
a legislature with one chamber

Vocabulary

declaration
a formal statement

Key Concept

After defeating the British, the new United States established a democratic government built on a foundation of English laws and government.

Disagreements exist in all levels of society. People disagree with each other, states disagree with their governing nation, and countries disagree with other countries. Early American colonists disagreed with the rulers of Great Britain, primarily over rights. These disputes led to the Revolutionary War and to American independence.

English Colonies in America

In 1584, Queen Elizabeth of England asked Sir Walter Raleigh to set up a **colony**, a geographic area in a new land that remains loyal to the parent nation, in North America. The English wanted access to America's gold, fish, timber, furs, and sugar cane. The colonies would also provide a market for English goods.

Raleigh made two attempts to establish a settlement on Roanoke Island, in what is now North Carolina. The first group arrived in 1585 and gained important information on the area. After suffering through a difficult winter, however, the colonists decided to return to England.

Raleigh's second attempt was made in 1587. Shortly after arriving at Roanoke, Virginia Dare became the first English child born in North America. Fighting between Spain and England made it impossible for other settlers to travel to Roanoke with supplies. Three years later, in 1590, colonists arrived to find the Roanoke settlement abandoned. The fate of the Roanoke colonists is still a mystery. By 1606, however, the English were again ready to try settling North America.

Pilgrims

Other colonies were established in what is now Virginia and in present-day New England. In 1620, William Bradford and a group we call the Pilgrims sailed on the *Mayflower* from England. The Pilgrims wanted to be separate from the Church of England. While on the ship, the Pilgrims signed the Mayflower Compact. The Mayflower Compact is a written agreement that set out the rules by which the Pilgrims would govern themselves. These pilgrims founded a colony at Plymouth, Massachusetts.

©Ivy Close Images/Alamy

Puritans

Other settlers soon followed. More than 1,000 English Puritans sailed into Massachusetts Bay on several ships. They founded many towns and set up a church that enforced strict religious beliefs. Puritans who did not follow these rules were expelled, and some set up other colonies. Other colonies were led by people who believed in freedom of religion. Pennsylvania, for example, was a haven for religious minorities.

The people in other colonies set up rules for their settlements. In 1639, leaders in the colony of Connecticut met to sign a charter called the Fundamental Orders of Connecticut. A **charter** is a written code of rules or laws. The charter gave colonists who owned land the right to vote for people to lead the colony. The Fundamental Orders of Connecticut is the first attempt of colonists to establish a government with a constitution. It later helped to shape the US Constitution.

 Think about Social Studies

Directions: Choose the best answer to the following question.

1. What was the significance of the Fundamental Orders of Connecticut?

   A. It established strict religious laws.

   B. It was America's first written constitution.

   C. It established a charter for a new colony.

   D. It separated colonists from the Church of England.

The American Revolution

As time went on, colonists grew separate from England. Policies that seemed reasonable to Britain's king and Parliament outraged the colonists.

Stamp Act

In 1765 Parliament passed a law called the Stamp Act that imposed a new tax on the colonies. Many colonists believed that the Stamp Act threatened a basic right. Until then, the colonists were taxed only by representatives they elected to their colonial legislatures. With the Stamp Act, they were taxed by British Parliament, where they had no representatives. "No taxation without representation," they protested. Many agreed to **boycott**, or refuse to buy, English goods. Under pressure from British merchants, Parliament decided to repeal, or cancel, the Stamp Act in 1766. However, it still insisted it had the right to tax the colonies.

Boston Massacre

In 1767, Charles Townshend, the British finance minister, came up with a new plan that taxed glass, lead, paint, paper, and tea. Knowing what anger this would cause in the colonies, British customs officers insisted upon having soldiers to protect them. In protest, some people in Boston rioted in the streets. On March 5, 1770, a Boston mob attacked some troops with clubs and snowballs. In the confusion, the soldiers fired into the crowd. Five rioters were killed, including Crispus Attucks, an African American. This conflict is known as the Boston Massacre.

Summarize Ideas

A summary tells the most important things that happened and names the most important people. A summary does not include all the ideas or all the details about what happened. A summary is short. It includes just the main ideas and only the most important details to describe or explain the main ideas.

To create a summary, read the information carefully. Include the most important details that describe or explain the main ideas. Do not add your own ideas—a summary does not include your opinion.

Read the section "English Colonies in America." What is the main idea? What details support that idea? Write a paragraph summarizing the information.

Analyze Cause and Effect

When you look for a cause, you are looking for *why* something happened. When you look for an effect of something that happened, you are looking for a result, or a change. Some words that signal a cause are *because, so,* and *since.* Some words that signal an effect are *then, as a result,* and *affect.*

Sometimes authors do not use signal words. You have to think about what you are reading to figure out what is the cause and what is the effect.

In a notebook, identify one conflict that led to the American Revolution. Write a paragraph explaining the causes and the effects of the conflict. Proofread your paragraph for proper spelling and punctuation.

Boston Tea Party

Parliament repealed the Townshend Act, except for the tax on tea. Many colonists remained angry over this tax. On December 16, 1773, a group of colonists boarded a ship docked in Boston that was loaded with tea. They dumped the tea into the harbor, an event they called the Boston Tea Party.

The Continental Congress

Parliament and King George III were tired of conceding to the rebellious colonies. In 1774, Parliament passed a series of restrictive new laws called the Coercive Acts, intended to punish Boston. The Acts, however, had an unintended effect. Colonies rallied behind Massachusetts. Each colony agreed to send delegates, or representatives, to a meeting. In Philadelphia in 1774, the Continental Congress drew up a list of rights that Parliament should respect. But they were not ready to cut their ties to Britain. They declared their loyalty to the king, but they refused to obey Parliament. They also agreed to defend themselves from any attack by the British army.

King George III of England considered the colonists to be in rebellion. "Blows must decide whether they are to be subject to the Country or Independent," he said. In April 1775, British redcoats and colonial **minutemen**, soldiers who were ready to fight at a minute's notice, fought in Massachusetts at Lexington and Concord. The Revolutionary War had begun.

The Second Continental Congress

In May 1775, delegates met again in Philadelphia. This Second Continental Congress sent George III an Olive Branch Petition, offering peace. It again declared the colonists' loyalty to the king and asked for his help in their struggle against Parliament. At the same time, Congress created a Continental army, made George Washington its commander, and printed money to support the troops.

The king rejected the peace petition. The Continental Congress then had to choose between submitting to Britain or declaring independence. In June 1776, the Second Continental Congress created a committee to draft a **declaration**, or formal statement, of independence. Thomas Jefferson wrote the draft. On July 4, Congress approved the Declaration of Independence. It announced to the world that the thirteen former British colonies had become the free and independent United States of America.

The war for independence raged on for years. In 1781, the Americans, with the help of the French, won a major victory at the Battle of Yorktown. In 1783, Benjamin Franklin, John Adams, and other colonial leaders signed the Treaty of Paris with representatives of Britain. This treaty ended the Revolutionary War and recognized the United States as an independent nation.

Think about Social Studies

Directions: Answer the following question on a separate sheet of paper.

What did King George III mean when he said, "Blows must decide whether they are to be subject to the Country or Independent"?

The Confederation Period

During the Revolutionary War, leaders in each colony wrote state constitutions to replace old colonial charters. Most of these constitutions included a bill of rights. Members of Congress wrote the Articles of Confederation, which created an alliance of states and formed a national government.

Articles of Confederation

The Articles of Confederation provided for a congress with a **unicameral** legislature, which means it had one chamber. There was no president or national courts. Congress had the power to declare war, make peace, mint coin and borrow money, and regulate relations with Native Americans. Each state had one vote in Congress, and nine of the thirteen states had to approve a measure for it to become law. The states retained the power to enforce laws, regulate trade, and impose taxes.

The Articles of Confederation proved to be too weak. Congress could not pay off the national debt. This was the money that had been borrowed to carry on the Revolutionary War. Several leaders in Congress wanted a stronger central government. When the states refused, Congress invited delegates to a convention to revise the Articles of Confederation.

Great Compromise

In May 1787, delegates from twelve states met to review the Virginia Plan. It proposed a new government with three branches: a legislature, an executive, and a judiciary. A state's population would determine the number of its representatives in Congress. This plan gave the states with a larger population more votes.

States could not agree on the Virginia Plan. Instead, they agreed to the Great Compromise. This plan made population the basis of representation in the House of Representatives. But it gave each state an equal vote in the Senate. Members of the convention wrote the United States Constitution. The Federalists supported the new constitution. The Anti-Federalists opposed it. By August 1788, the necessary nine states had ratified the Constitution, and the country had a new government.

 Think about Social Studies

Directions: Determine whether each statement is true or false.

1. The office of the presidency was created with the Articles of Confederation. (true/false)

2. The Great Compromise solved a major problem during the Constitutional Convention. (true/false)

Information Literacy

The word *literacy* means knowledge of a particular subject. Information literacy includes the skills you need to find, analyze, and use information.

Practice these skills by researching the Federalists and the Anti-Federalists. Use the Internet to find arguments each group gave for or against the Constitution. Write an essay evaluating the arguments. Which writer used better reasoning to support his or her claim? Be sure to cite the sources you used in your essay.

WRITE TO LEARN

Using a graphic organizer like the one below, map the causes and effects of the Revolutionary War. Add a new row of boxes for each cause that you identify.

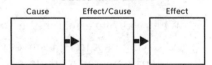

Cause and Effect

| Cause | Effect/Cause | Effect |

Vocabulary Review

Directions: Complete the sentences using the following key terms and vocabulary words.

unicameral   colony   charter
minutemen   declaration   boycott

1. After the Stamp Act, colonists agreed to _____ English goods.

2. The leaders of the Connecticut colony signed a _____ that later served as a model for the U.S. Constitution.

3. The Queen of England set up a _____ in North America to gain access to the resources in the new land.

4. The Second Continental Congress signed a _____ of independence that was drafted by Thomas Jefferson.

5. The soldiers who were prepared to fight with little notice were known as _____.

6. A legislature that has only one chamber is called a _____ legislature.

Skill Review

Directions: Choose the best answer to each question.

1. Rules of laws to govern a settlement were called a
   A. charter.
   B. compact.
   C. article.
   D. policy.

2. What was one effect of the Townshend Act?
   A. Colonists agreed to meet with British Parliament in a congress.
   B. The British sent troops to attack colonists at Lexington and Concord.
   C. A group of colonists attacked British troops in Boston.
   D. The British Parliament repealed the Stamp Act.

3. What was the main cause of the Boston Tea Party?
   A. Parliament passed the Tea Act.
   B. Colonists threw tea into the ocean.
   C. Parliament repealed the Tea Act.
   D. Colonists formed the Continental Congress.

4. What is the significance of the Articles of Confederation?
   A. The British king approved of the Articles.
   B. The Articles was the first plan of government of the united colonies.
   C. The Articles ended the Revolutionary War.
   D. The U.S. Constitution was based on the Articles.

Skill Practice

Directions: Read the passages. Then answer the questions that follow.

Declaring Independence

In January 1776, Thomas Paine published *Common Sense*. Offering "simple facts, plain arguments, and common sense," his pamphlet was an attack on King George III. In it, Paine called the king "a royal brute" who ruled by force. He insisted that the king had lost any claim to the colonists' loyalty and urged the colonists to declare independence. Paine put into words what many colonists were thinking and helped convince others. *Common Sense* became a bestseller. Paine's message also had a political impact. It led many colonists to urge the delegates in Philadelphia to vote for independence.

In the Declaration of Independence, Jefferson took care to explain why the colonists were cutting their ties with Great Britain. People, he wrote, "are endowed by their Creator with certain unalienable Rights." Among them are the right to "Life, Liberty, and the pursuit of Happiness." All people, he said, are justified in getting rid of any government that abuses those rights. He then included a long list of abuses by King George III. He charged with king with trying to establish "an absolute Tyranny over these States." By basing the Declaration on broad principles that apply to all people, Jefferson made the document a declaration of human rights. He defended everyone's right to get rid of an oppressive government. This has made the Declaration a timeless, living document. It continues to inspire people searching for freedom, liberty, and dignity.

1. What was the effect of *Common Sense* on colonists?

    A. The pamphlet spurred colonists to urge delegates to vote for independence.

    B. Colonists decided to side with King George III and Great Britain.

    C. Thomas Jefferson wrote to King George asking for independence.

    D. Thomas Paine charged King George III with being a "royal brute."

2. What is the central idea of the paragraph about the Declaration of Independence?

    A. Thomas Jefferson was an eloquent writer and a great leader.

    B. The Declaration of Independence defends the human rights of all people.

    C. King George III was a tyrant and a brute who could not be trusted.

    D. American colonists were grateful to Thomas Paine for writing *Common Sense*

3. Which definition best matches the use of the word **tyranny** in the second paragraph?

    A. democratic

    B. honored

    C. fair and just rule

    D. cruel and unfair rule

4. Which definition best matches the use of the word **oppressive** in the second paragraph?

    A. democratic

    B. severe

    C. tolerable

    D. agreeable

Writing Practice

Directions: Read the paragraph about *Common Sense* on this page. Write a paragraph describing the effect this print media had on the colonists.

LESSON 3.2 A New Nation

LESSON OBJECTIVES

- Understand how the United States grew geographically
- Identify the causes and effects of the War of 1812
- Explain how westward expansion affected Native American policy

CORE SKILLS

- Sequence Events
- Relate Ideas Within Text

Key Terms

land grant
gift of land

Louisiana Purchase
US purchase of land between the Mississippi River and the Rocky Mountains

Manifest Destiny
belief that the United States should extend boundary to the Pacific Ocean

territory
an area of land that is controlled by a government

Vocabulary

occupy
take possession or control of

sequence
the order in which something happens

Key Concept

After the Revolutionary War, the United States endured conflicts within and struggled with other countries as well.

Creating a new organization is challenging and takes time. New ideas are created and tested. If they do not work, they must be changed. During this time, disagreements among the organization's leaders can occur and must be settled. The United States found itself in this situation after the American Revolution. Growth of the nation brought new challenges and demanded strong leadership.

The Growth of the Nation

The Confederation Congress was not very powerful, but it did accomplish important things. It negotiated the peace treaty that ended the war with Britain. The Treaty of Paris (1783) was favorable to the United States. The boundaries to which Britain agreed created a nation ten times the size of Great Britain and four times larger than France.

The new Congress created by the ratification of the Constitution opened the Northwest Territory to settlement. The Northwest Territory was the western land located north of the Ohio River. The Land Ordinance of 1785 put this land for sale at one dollar per acre. The Northwest Ordinance of 1787 created a way to admit new states into the confederation. It allowed settlers to create their own governments. The ordinance also outlawed slavery in these future territories. A **territory** is an area of land that is controlled by a government. Once a territory had 5,000 adult white males, it could send a nonvoting member to Congress. When the population of a territory reached 60,000, the people could draft a constitution and petition to Congress to become a new state. Five states emerged from the Northwest Territory.

A New President

The growing nation needed a strong leader. In early April 1789, Congress counted the electoral ballots and declared George Washington president. George Washington decided not to wear his military uniform to his inauguration, or swearing in ceremony. He wore a plain, brown suit instead. He wanted people to see the president as an ordinary citizen. Some proposed that the president be called "His Excellency" or "His Highness." Washington asked to be called simply "Mr. President."

With the Senate's approval, President Washington appointed the heads of the departments and the justices of the Supreme Court. Congress passed laws to collect taxes and create a system of federal courts.

European and Native American Troubles

The new president faced troubles with Europe. In 1793, France and Britain went to war. The southern states mainly supported France, the United States's old ally. They accused Britain of taking sailors off American ships. The British also had not withdrawn their soldiers from forts in the frontier, or distant, unsettled areas. Northern merchants favored Britain. They wanted closer relations and expanded trade with the British.

President Washington managed to ease relations with Britain. He sent John Jay to London to negotiate a treaty. In Jay's Treaty (1794), Britain agreed to remove its soldiers from American forts. Some congressmen attacked the treaty, which failed to settle other issues. Spain was concerned about Jay's Treaty and how it would impact Spanish territory in North America. Thomas Pinckney's treaty with Spain (1795) settled the issue by opening the Mississippi River and New Orleans to American trade.

The government also faced a Native American crisis. Tecumseh, a Shawnee leader, tried to unite the Native American groups in the Ohio Valley against the settlers there. The United States army put down this uprising at the Battle of Fallen Timbers (1794). Defeated, the Native Americans signed the Treaty of Greenville (1795), in which they agreed to leave the Ohio Valley.

The Louisiana Purchase

George Washington's presidency ended in 1796, and John Adams became the new president. He served four years before Thomas Jefferson was elected the third US president. Under Jefferson's leadership, the United States grew.

In early 1803, France offered to sell the Louisiana Territory to the United States. Buying this land would more than double the nation's size. It would give western farmers the right to ship their produce down the Mississippi River. But President Jefferson believed in a strict interpretation of the Constitution, which said nothing about the United States buying new territory.

Despite his doubts, Jefferson agreed to purchase more land. He signed a treaty with France to buy Louisiana for $15 million. The **Louisiana Purchase** gave the United States the land between the Mississippi River and the Rocky Mountains. In the spring of 1804, Meriwether Lewis and William Clark led an expedition to explore Louisiana. They followed the Missouri River to its source, crossed the Rocky Mountains, and finally reached the Pacific Ocean. The Lewis and Clark Expedition returned in 1806 with a wealth of information about the Far West.

 Think about Social Studies

Directions: Choose the best answer to the following question.

1. The Northwest Ordinance
   - A. denied a bill of rights for settlers.
   - B. allowed for the spread of slavery.
   - C. encouraged the sale of land to speculators.
   - D. provided a method for petitioning for statehood.

Sequence Events

Sequence is the order in which something happens. Knowing the sequence of events in history can help you understand and remember them better. There are two ways to identify the sequence of events. One is to look in the text for the dates of events. There are also words that can help you figure out sequence. Some words that signal sequence include *first, second, third, next, then, now, sooner, later, finally.*

Read the section "The Growth of the Nation." As you read, look for dates. Create a timeline of the dates and their corresponding events.

When you read, it is important to relate, or connect, ideas in the text. To connect ideas, determine the relationship among them. Relationships can be cause and effect, sequence of events, main idea and details, or compare and contrast.

Read the section titled "Declaration of War." Consider how the information relates to a declaration of war. Then write three events that led to the declaration of war in 1812.

War of 1812

In 1810, Congress repealed trade restrictions and opened trade with Britain and France. Congress promised to cut off trade with either nation if American rights were not protected. However, many Americans were angry that France and England kept impressing, or forcing, American sailors to serve on their ships. They were demanding war.

Declaration of War

Western settlers accused Britain of arming Native Americans in the Ohio Valley. They also had their eye on good farmland in British Canada. Americans also blamed the British for increasing tensions with Native Americans. In the Northwest, the Shawnee posed a serious threat to settlers. Shawnee leader, Tecumseh, had tried years before to unite the Ohio Valley Native American groups against the settlers. In 1811, one thousand militiamen defeated the Native Americans at the Battle of Tippecanoe. Tecumseh and hundreds of survivors escaped to Canada to seek British help.

In 1810, Western and Southern voters elected congressmen who shared their pro-war views, including Henry Clay of Kentucky and John C. Calhoun of South Carolina. These War Hawks helped persuade Congress to declare war against Britain on June 18, 1812.

Outcome of War

To save money, Congress slashed the size of the army. The nation had to rely on poorly trained state militia troops. In 1814, Britain attacked the United States. British ships sailed up the Chesapeake Bay, landing troops near Washington, D.C. The militia defending the city fled. The British marched into the city, setting fire to the White House and the Capitol. They tried unsuccessfully to capture Baltimore.

In December, General Sir Edward Packenham landed 7,500 troops south of New Orleans. He wanted to capture the city and use it as a base to **occupy**, or take control of, the Mississippi Valley. American General Andrew Jackson blocked his advance with 4,500 militiamen. When the British attacked on January 8, 1815, Jackson's frontier hunters stopped them. The British suffered 2,000 casualties, including General Packenham. The survivors withdrew. Unknown to either general, the Treaty of Ghent (Belgium), which ended the war, had been signed two weeks earlier. By signing the treaty, Britain agreed to restore, or give back, any territories they had taken during the war.

⚑ Think about Social Studies

Directions: Match the following people with their role in the War of 1812.

1. _____ Tecumseh
2. _____ Andrew Jackson

3. _____ Henry Clay
4. _____ Edward Packenham

A. general in the American militia

B. Native American leader who opposed settlers

C. British general injured in battle

D. US congressman known as a "War Hawk"

Manifest Destiny

After the War of 1812, Americans entered a period called the Era of Good Feelings. The American people were united and felt strongly about their nation. Americans believed their destiny was to occupy the land from the Atlantic Ocean to the Pacific Ocean. This idea came to be known as **Manifest Destiny** and led to thousands of settlers moving to the western frontier. Settlers moved into the Ohio Valley and west to Mississippi and Louisiana. The area beyond the frontier was still known as Indian Country.

Westward Expansion

In the 1820s, Americans first settled in Texas, which was then part of Mexico. The Mexican government offered Americans a large **land grant**, or gift of land, to settle in Texas. Mexico needed American settlers to help defend its Texas frontier. Each family received thousands of acres of ranch land at little cost. However, they came to dislike Mexican laws and customs, and wanted to govern themselves.

In 1836, American settlers in Texas declared their independence, and war broke out between Texans and Mexico. Texas defeated Mexico and was independent until 1845. In that year, the United States chose to annex, or add, Texas as a state. Mexicans and US troops clashed over land claimed by Mexico in the Mexican American War. In 1848, the United States won the war and gained more western lands, including what are now Arizona, Nevada, California, and Utah.

Removing Native Americans

American settlers continued to pressure the federal government to take over Native American lands. Settlers had gained lands in conflicts with Native Americans in the west. Now they wanted land in the south. After Andrew Jackson was elected president in 1828, he began using his presidential power to claim more land for American settlers.

The state of Georgia was trying to force the Cherokee off their land. The Cherokee, who could read and write, knew how to protect their rights. The group filed suit against the state in the Supreme Court. When the Court ruled in the Cherokee's favor in 1832, Jackson refused to enforce its decision. He ordered the army to remove the Cherokee. The army relocated them to "Indian Territory" west of the Mississippi River. Thousands of Cherokee died on the forced march known as the Trail of Tears. By 1837, Jackson and his successor Martin Van Buren had forced more than 45,000 Native Americans to leave their land and move west.

 Think about Social Studies

Directions: Choose the best answer to the question.

Why is the period of time following the War of 1812 called the Era of Good Feelings?

    A. Americans were happy with the land they held and did not want more.

    B. Relations between Mexico and American settlers were better than ever.

    C. Andrew Jackson inspired good feelings in Native Americans.

    D. Americans were united and had strong national feelings.

WRITE TO LEARN

Write a paragraph explaining how the Treaty of Greenville affected the settlement of the Northwest Territory.

21ST CENTURY SKILL

Apply Technology to a Task

The Internet, presentation software, and spreadsheets are just a few tools that you can use when researching and presenting information. Technology also allows people from various parts of the world to work together to complete tasks. In a group, gather more information about President Jackson's Native American policies. Use e-mail and shared online documents to communicate about and create an essay evaluating the policies. Be sure to include evidence to support your reasoning.

Vocabulary Review

Directions: Evaluate the meaning of the italicized word in each sentence. Then label each sentence as true or false.

_____ 1. When you *sequence* information, you look for date and words such as *first, last,* and *finally.*

_____ 2. General Sir Edward Packenham wanted to *occupy* the Mississippi Valley.

_____ 3. The *Louisiana Purchase* gave the United States land west of the Mississippi.

_____ 4. *Manifest Destiny* was one of the factors that lead to the War of 1812.

_____ 5. The US government could not control any *territory* that was not a state.

_____ 6. Mexico gave US settlers *land grants* so that settlers could defend Mexican borders.

Skill Review

Directions: Choose the best answer to each question.

1. Which event occurred after the British burned Washington, D.C.?
   A. British troops landed near Washington, D.C.
   B. The United States declared war on England.
   C. US troops stopped the British at New Orleans.
   D. George Washington became president.

2. How did the Louisiana Purchase benefit Americans?
   A. It allowed settlers to ship products down the Mississippi River.
   B. It amended the Constitution to allow land purchases.
   C. Americans could settle land east of the Mississippi River.
   D. Native Americans and settlers could live peacefully in the frontier.

3. How did President Washington show that he was an "ordinary citizen"?
   A. He demanded people call him "His Highness."
   B. He wore a regal outfit to his inauguration.
   C. He dressed in his military outfit in public.
   D. He asked to be called "Mr. President."

4. How did western expansion affect many Native American groups?
   A. They were forced off their land by settlers.
   B. They were able to fight alongside settlers against the British.
   C. They were given voting rights and recognition as states.
   D. They were able to win a Supreme Court case to protect their land.

Skill Practice

Directions: Read the passage. Then answer the questions that follow.

> The Trail of Tears
>
> Groups of Cherokee set out on the "trail of tears" to Indian Territory late in September 1838. In the following account, a traveler from Maine described the condition of the Cherokee when they passed through Kentucky.
>
> *"We met several detachments [of Cherokee] in the southern part of Kentucky on the 4th, 5th, and 6th of December. . . . The sick and feeble were carried in wagons . . . a great many ride on horseback and multitudes go on foot—even aged females, apparently nearly ready to drop into the grave, were traveling with heavy burdens attached to the back—on the sometimes frozen ground, and sometimes muddy streets, with no covering for the feet except what nature had given them. . . . We learned from the inhabitants on the road where the Indians passed, that they buried fourteen or fifteen at every stopping place."*
>
> —Quoted in John Ehle, *Trail of Tears: The Rise and Fall of the Cherokee Nation*
> (New York: Doubleday, 1988)

1. Based on this passage, which outcome of the Trail of Tears is most likely?

   A. The Cherokee were allowed to move back to Georgia.

   B. The Cherokee arrived healthy and safe to their new home.

   C. Few Cherokee died on the journey to Indian Territory.

   D. Many Cherokee lives were lost on the journey.

2. Based on this passage, what is the author's point of view of the Cherokee removal?

   A. The author believes Native American removal policies are cruel.

   B. The author would like to see more Cherokee removed from the frontier.

   C. The author supports the relocation of Native Americans.

   D. The author is neutral about the Cherokee's journey.

3. What does the name "trail of tears" symbolize?

   A. It symbolizes the national feeling of Americans after the War of 1812.

   B. It symbolizes how the settlers mourned the removal of Native Americans.

   C. It symbolizes the sadness the Cherokee felt upon being removed from their land.

   D. It symbolizes the happiness settlers felt after the Cherokee were moved west.

4. Which definition best matches the use of the word **multitudes** in the quote above?

   A. they young

   B. the healthy

   C. only a few

   D. many people

Writing Practice

Directions: Some congressmen were known as *War Hawks*. Explain the meaning of this term and why it was used to identify congressmen with certain beliefs.

LESSON 3.3 Civil War and Reconstruction

■ LESSON OBJECTIVES

- Identify the events and issues that led to the Civil War
- Understand the advantages and disadvantages of the North and the South during the Civil War
- Recognize how Reconstruction affected the South and newly freed African Americans

■ CORE SKILLS & PRACTICES

- Recognize Persuasive Language
- Analyze Point of View

Key Terms

abolitionists
people who wanted to end slavery

sectional
local

slave codes
laws that enslaved African Americans and their children

surrender
stop fighting

triangular trade
triangle shaped trade route

Vocabulary

persuasive language
language used to influence a reader's opinion

Key Concept

The Civil War began as an attempt to preserve the Union, but it ended with the abolition of slavery in the United States.

People feel discriminated against, or treated unfairly, at times in their life. Unfair treatment because of race, religion, or country of origin is illegal in the United States. In the history of the United States, many people have protested to end this type of discrimination. In the 1860s, there was a civil war to end the enslavement of African Americans.

Slavery in the United States

The South had long survived by growing cash crops that provided a steady income. Wealthy farmers owned large farms, or plantations, where they grew the main cash crops: tobacco and cotton. Plantation owners needed many workers to plant and harvest these crops. They tried using white workers called indentured servants, but many ran away and could not be found.

In 1619, a Dutch slave trader sold the first enslaved Africans in Virginia. The number of enslaved people grew slowly. It was cheaper for a planter to import a servant than to buy an enslaved person. However, servants who ran away were difficult to recover. They blended into the white population. Every five years or so, planters had to train new workers. In time, they decided that enslaved workers cost less in the long run. By 1700, enslaved Africans were common throughout the southern colonies.

The trade routes brought many enslaved Africans to the colonies. Many of the slave traders followed a route that became known as the **triangular trade**. This is because the routes formed the shape of a triangle. On one leg, traders brought sugar and molasses from the West Indies to the colonies. These products were used to make rum, which was shipped to Africa and traded for enslaved workers. The enslaved people were then shipped to the West Indies and the colonies.

As the number of enslaved people increased, the colonies enacted **slave codes**. These laws further limited the rights of enslaved people and their children and ensured they could not obtain freedom.

Political Changes

The slavery issue promoted **sectional**, or local, interests. In 1819, Missouri asked to be admitted to the Union as a slave state. This would upset the balance that existed in Congress of eleven slave states and eleven free states. The Missouri Compromise (1821) admitted Missouri as a slave state. To restore the balance, it admitted Maine as a free state. To settle the question for the future, Congress drew a line on a map from Missouri to the Rocky Mountains. Any new state south of that line would be admitted as a slave state; any north of it would be a free state.

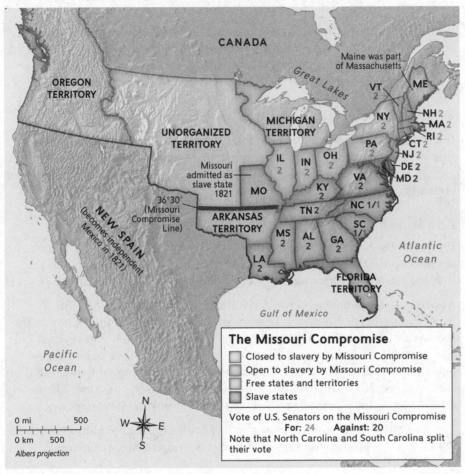

CANADA

Maine was part of Massachusetts

Great Lakes

OREGON TERRITORY

UNORGANIZED TERRITORY

MICHIGAN TERRITORY

Missouri admitted as slave state 1821

36°30' (Missouri Compromise Line)

NEW SPAIN (becomes independent Mexico in 1821)

ARKANSAS TERRITORY

VT 2

ME

NY 2

NH 2

MA 2

RI 2

PA 2

CT 2

NJ 2

DE 2

MD 2

IL 2

IN 2

OH 2

KY 2

VA 2

MO

TN 2

NC 1/1

MS 2

AL 2

GA 2

SC 1/1

LA 2

FLORIDA TERRITORY

Atlantic Ocean

Gulf of Mexico

Pacific Ocean

The Missouri Compromise

- Closed to slavery by Missouri Compromise
- Open to slavery by Missouri Compromise
- Free states and territories
- Slave states

Vote of U.S. Senators on the Missouri Compromise
For: 24   **Against:** 20
Note that North Carolina and South Carolina split their vote

0 mi 500
0 km 500
Albers projection

N W E S

Labor in the South

The most powerful families in the South were the big plantation owners. They were the upper class, along with the merchants who bought and sold their cotton. Wealthy planters owned thousands of acres and had hundreds of enslaved people who worked under an overseer.

The majority of the whites in the South were middle-class farmers. They owned small farms and a few enslaved people. These farmers often worked in the fields and owned modest farmhouses.

The white lower class consisted of poor farmers who owned neither enslaved workers nor land. Most worked as hired farm laborers. Competing with cheap slave labor kept them in poverty.

Most enslaved people in the South worked in cotton fields. White men called overseers forced them to work hard. Some enslaved people often worked from before sunup until after dark in the fields.

CORE PRACTICE

Recognize Persuasive Language

People use **persuasive language**, or language used to influence a reader's opinion, to win other people over to their point of view. Persuasion tends to appeal to the reader's emotions. To identify persuasive language, look for strong words that show the author's emotion.

Read the following excerpt from a speech given by Frederick Douglass on July 5, 1852. List the emotional words Douglass used.

What, to the American slave, is your 4th of July? I answer; a day that reveals to him, more than all other days in the year, the gross injustice and cruelty to which he is the constant victim. To him, your celebration is a sham; . . . your sound of rejoicing are empty and heartless; . . . your prayers and hymns, your sermons and thanks-givings, . . . are to him, mere bombast, fraud, deception, impiety, and hypocrisy—a thin veil to cover up crimes which would disgrace a nation of savages.

A few enslaved people worked in the plantation owner's house. They did housework and helped raise the plantation owner's children. Some enslaved people ran away, but if they were caught, they were severely punished. This often made many enslaved people too fearful to try and escape.

Economic Changes

In 1793, Eli Whitney invented the cotton gin. This simple machine removed seeds from raw cotton. The cotton gin could work fifty times faster than a person could. A gin was also cheap and easy to make. The cotton gin increased the wealth of plantation owners.

While the South put its money into crops, the North supported factories and shops. New machines and factories changed where and how people worked, and new factories attracted workers to the Northeast. In 1813, a mill was built where workers could spin, weave, and dye cloth in the same factory. This mill helped make New England the textile center of the United States. The growth of mills and factories increased the demand for cotton.

During this time, known as the Industrial Revolution, new methods of transportation arose. Railroads connected most cities in the Northeast. New canals and steamships increased the amount of goods that could be shipped by water.

Abolition Movement

By the 1830s, Americans placed greater value on social equality. More people opposed slavery. They saw that it violated the Declaration of Independence. These reformers wanted slavery to end immediately.

Abolitionists, people who wanted to end slavery, included African Americans such as Frederick Douglass and Sojourner Truth. Both of them former enslaved workers, they gave speeches and wrote books against slavery. William Lloyd Garrison, a white newspaper editor in Boston, published the first issue of *The Liberator*. The newspaper demanded that all enslaved people be freed. Many women also supported abolition. They attended meetings, helped raise money, and signed antislavery petitions.

The abolition movement in the North, however, only made relations with the South worse. Many southerners felt that their way of life was being attacked.

 Think about Social Studies

Directions: Review the map on page 79. Then choose the best answer to the following questions.

1. What was the name of the territory closed to slavery by the Missouri Compromise?
   - **A.** Oregon Territory
   - **B.** Michigan Territory
   - **C.** Arkansas Territory
   - **D.** Unorganized Territory

2. Which territory was opened to slavery by the Missouri Compromise?
   - **A.** New Spain
   - **B.** Florida Territory
   - **C.** Oregon Territory
   - **D.** Arkansas Territory

Civil War and Reconstruction

Civil War

Fearful that the new Republican president, Abraham Lincoln, would demand the abolition of slavery across the South, Alabama, Florida, Georgia, Louisiana, Mississippi, South Carolina, and Texas seceded from the Union in the winter of 1861. Together they formed the Confederate States of America with Jefferson Davis as their president. Eight slave states in the Upper South remained in the Union, waiting to see how President Lincoln would respond.

In his Inaugural Address on March 4, 1861, President Lincoln said that he would not abolish slavery, but he would defend the Union. "In your hands, my dissatisfied fellow-countrymen, and not in mine, is the momentous issue of civil war." Lincoln was afraid the states of the Upper South would secede if the North attacked first.

The Battles Begin

On the morning of April 12, 1861, Jefferson Davis's army fired on Fort Sumter, a federal fort in the harbor of Charleston, South Carolina. The fort surrendered the next afternoon. With the outbreak of war, Virginia, North Carolina, Tennessee, and Arkansas decided to join the Confederacy. Four border states—Missouri, Kentucky, Maryland, and Delaware—remained in the Union. The western counties of Virginia also remained loyal. In 1863, they joined the Union as the state of West Virginia.

President Lincoln asked the states for 75,000 state troops and hoped to quickly end the war by capturing the Confederate capital of Richmond, Virginia. However, Union troops were defeated by a Confederate army at the Battle of Bull Run near Washington, D.C., on July 21, 1861. This battle proved the North would need a large and well-trained army to defeat the South.

In 1862, Union troops again tried to take Richmond with General George B. McClellan and a well-trained army. Confederate General Robert E. Lee stopped their advance. After a seven-day battle, the Union army withdrew. The North had again failed to defeat the Confederates.

In September, General Lee tried to invade the North. He attacked Union troops in Maryland. This battle was the bloodiest one-day battle of the Civil War. Though the Battle of Antietam was deemed an inconclusive outcome, the Union did stop Lee's objective of winning a major victory in the North. The cost of the battle was high. Estimated casualties of those killed or wounded totaled over 22,000.

The Union success at Antietam gave Lincoln enough political clout to change the course of the war. On January 1, 1863, Lincoln issued the Emancipation Proclamation, which freed all enslaved people in the Confederacy. Many enslaved people in border states would not be freed until the Thirteenth Amendment was ratified in 1865. Some enslaved people who were freed as the troops advanced into the South joined the Union army. More than 130,000 black soldiers and sailors fought on the Union side.

There was more fighting to come after Antietam. The Battle of Gettysburg lasted four days, claimed a total of about 48,000 casualties, and prevented the Confederates from getting help from Britain. By the end of that summer, Union gunboats controlled most of the Mississippi River. Along the Atlantic and Gulf coasts, the Union navy blocked Confederate ports. The Union wanted to keep the Confederates from getting supplies from Europe.

You can find many primary sources from the Civil War period by searching the Internet. Primary sources include letters, diaries, and newspaper articles written by people from that time period. Many were written by eyewitnesses.

Type "abolitionist documents" into a search engine. Evaluate the search results for reliable sources for the documents. Reliable sources include government and educational institutions. These have .gov or .edu in their URL. Choose three sites and read the documents there. Make a list of these websites.

The End of War

General Grant spent 1864 battling Robert E. Lee's army. He lost more men than Lee, but was determined to wear Lee down. In early April 1865, Grant's army finally surrounded Lee's troops in western Virginia. On April 9, 1865, General Lee agreed to **surrender**, or stop fighting. The Civil War had finally ended, and the United States of America had been preserved.

The Civil War was the bloodiest and most costly war in American history. It took the lives of 360,000 Union and 260,000 Confederate soldiers at a cost of $20 billion. The South lost two-thirds of its wealth in property, half of its farm equipment, and two-fifths of its livestock. It paid dearly for its attempt to secede from the Union.

The Two Sides Compared

The North had several advantages in the war. It had more factories and workshops to produce weapons and clothing for its soldiers. It also had more railroads, banks, and men of military age—those between eighteen and forty-five years old. The Confederate army never had enough tents, blankets, and uniforms. Its soldiers often fought barefoot.

The South also had advantages. Most of the battles took place in the South, so Confederates fought on familiar ground. They also knew they did not have to defeat the North to win. The Confederate states could gain their independence by wearing down the North. A draw was as good as a victory.

 Think about Social Studies

Directions: Complete the statement below with the correct term that follows the statement.

1. The North was able to produce more weapons and clothing during the war because it had more _____. (farm equipment, factories)

Reconstruction

After the Civil War, the nation had to begin the task of Reconstruction. Leaders had to decide how the Southern states would retake their place in the Union. Before Congress and President Lincoln could compromise on a plan, the president was assassinated on April 14, 1865.

With the death of Lincoln, Vice President Andrew Johnson became president. Like Lincoln, Johnson did not wish to punish the South. Johnson believed that Reconstruction was the job of the president, not Congress. Johnson's plan included the following main points:

- Most ex-Confederates could be pardoned if they swore loyalty to the Union.
- States had to write new constitutions that repealed secession.
- The states had to ratify the Thirteenth Amendment, which abolished slavery.
- Once a state constitution was written, a state could hold elections. Those who were elected could then take their seats in Congress. The states would then be considered Reconstructed.

African American rights were not part of this plan. As Southern states recovered after the war, they established laws known as black codes. Under black codes, African Americans could not own guns or gather in groups after dark. They could do only certain jobs, like farm work. If they could not prove they had a job, they could be arrested.

Black codes angered Northerners. The Radical Republicans in Congress sponsored constitutional amendments to protect the rights of African Americans. The Fourteenth Amendment made African Americans citizens. The Fifteenth Amendment gave African American men the right to vote.

Formerly enslaved people were facing hard times across the South. Many African Americans became poor sharecroppers. Many white Southerners were angry because they did not like that formerly enslaved people were gaining more rights. They showed their anger by forming secret societies like the Ku Klux Klan, which terrorized African Americans and those who supported them.

By the 1870s, many Northerners were tired of Reconstruction. The nation's economy was not doing well. People were worried about having jobs and earning enough money to live. They turned away from the problems of African Americans.

🚩 Think about Social Studies

Directions: Choose the best answer to the following question.

1. How was President Johnson's plan favorable to Southern states?
   A. Slavery remained legal in the South.
   B. Southern states were not harshly punished for leaving the Union.
   C. Southern states were not required to write new constitutions.
   D. The South was only required to pay for some the damage done during the Civil War.

Analyze Point of View

A person's point of view is shaped by his or her family, religion, education and reading, friends, personal experiences, and time period. Follow these steps to analyze point of view:

1. Identify the author or the speaker. What is the person's background?

2. Identify the argument or issue. Find the main idea and supporting details of the piece of writing or speech.

3. Identify the facts used to support the argument. Distinguish facts from opinions.

4. Examine the kinds of words and phrases that the speaker uses. Do some words and phrases seem more favorable to one side of the issue or the other?

Write a short essay describing Reconstruction from the South's point of view. Be sure to write clearly and use correct punctuation and spelling.

WRITE TO LEARN

Describe the effects of Reconstruction on formerly enslaved people.

Vocabulary Review

Directions: Complete the sentences using the following key terms and vocabulary words.

abolitionist   triangular trade   slave codes
surrender   sectional   persuasive language

1. The Civil War ended in 1865, after General Lee agreed to _____.

2. Authors who try to influence a reader's opinion often use _____.

3. Southern states enacted _____, which enslaved African Americans and their children forever.

4. The Missouri Compromise was agreed on because the North and the South had _____ interests.

5. African American and white _____ worked in many ways to free enslaved African Americans.

6. Enslaved people were brought into the United States on a shipping route known as the _____.

Skill Review

Directions: Choose the one best answer to each question.

1. What was the North's greatest advantage over the South in the Civil War?

   A. more military-age men

   B. more farmland

   C. fewer enslaved people to defend

   D. shipping routes

2. What effect did the cotton gin have on the economy of cities in the North?

   A. It created more low-paying field jobs for poor whites.

   B. It decreased the demand for cotton and for textiles.

   C. It provided more cotton to factories, which grew to produce more textiles.

   D. It decreased demand for slave labor because it worked faster than enslaved people.

3. Which statement best describes why President Lincoln wrote the Emancipation Proclamation?

   A. Freed enslaved people could work in Northern factories and mills.

   B. The president did not believe enslaving people was morally right.

   C. The Confederate army could not win without enslaved people.

   D. Freed enslaved people would join the Union army.

4. Which statement would abolitionists most likely say?

   A. "All men, including African Americans, should be free to own enslaved people."

   B. "All men and women are free to pursue life, liberty, and happiness."

   C. "White men, above all others, should determine the rights of American citizens."

   D. "Women and African Americans should be allowed to own land."

Skill Practice

Directions: Read the passage below. Then answer the questions that follow.

The Gettysburg Address

The Battle of Gettysburg took place on July 1–3, 1863. Thousands of soldiers from both the North and the South died and were laid to rest in the same cemetery. President Lincoln delivered a short speech that has become known as the Gettysburg Address in a ceremony at the cemetery on November 19, 1863.

Fourscore and seven years ago our fathers brought forth on this continent a new nation, conceived in liberty and dedicated to the proposition that all men are created equal. Now we are engaged in a great civil war, testing whether that nation or any nation so conceived and so dedicated can long endure. We are met on a great battlefield of that war. We have come to dedicate a portion of that field as a final resting-place for those who here gave their lives that that nation might live. It is altogether fitting and proper that we should do this. But in a larger sense, we cannot dedicate, we cannot consecrate, we cannot hallow this ground. The brave men, living and dead who struggled here have consecrated it far above our poor power to add or detract. The world will little note nor long remember what we say here, but it can never forget what they did here. It is for us the living rather to be dedicated here to the unfinished work which they who fought here have thus far so nobly advanced. It is rather for us to be here dedicated to the great task remaining before us—that from these honored dead we take increased devotion to that cause for which they gave the last full measure of devotion—that we here highly resolve that these dead shall not have died in vain, that this nation under God shall have a new birth of freedom, and that government of the people, by the people, for the people shall not perish from the earth.

1. Which sentence best represents the purpose of President Lincoln's speech?
   A. Lincoln wants to persuade the nation to remain united and follow the principle of freedom.
   B. Lincoln wants to persuade more men to sign up to fight for the Union.
   C. Lincoln wants to inform citizens about the purpose of the cemetery.
   D. Lincoln wants to inform those who died in battle that they are not forgotten.

2. Which answer best describes what Lincoln means when he states "The world will little note nor long remember what we say here, but it can never forget what they did here."
   A. No one should forget that many Confederate soldiers died at Gettysburg.
   B. People will not forget a speech given by the president during a war.
   C. People should not forget the death of the soldiers and should work to find a solution.
   D. Both sides are at fault, and one side will need to compromise to avoid more battles.

Writing Practice

Directions: Imagine you are an abolitionist, speaking to a group of plantation owners. Write a brief speech convincing them to free their enslaved workers. Be sure to include emotional words and evidence that supports your point of view.

LESSON 3.4   European Settlement and Population of the Americas

LESSON OBJECTIVES

- Understand why new immigrants came to America
- Identify where the new immigrants settled
- Understand how immigrants were received

CORE SKILLS & PRACTICES

- Summarize Ideas
- Find Details

Key Terms

pull factors
reasons that bring people to the United States

push factors
reasons that force people to leave their native countries

nativists
native-born people who wish to limit immigration

settlement houses
privately run neighborhood centers that provide services for the poor

tenements
large buildings of apartments where the poorest people live

Vocabulary

social class
levels of society that are based on economic success

Key Concept

As immigrants came to America, they settled in cities and spread throughout the growing West.

Many people in the United States are new to the country. Some came as children, others as adults. Those who were born here often have parents or grandparents who came from other countries. What motivated them to make such a big move? In this lesson, you will learn about the people who moved to the United States during the 19th and 20th centuries and the factors that pushed and pulled them to leave their countries.

The Growth of Immigration

Between 1820 and 1920, more than 33 million people moved to the United States from other countries. These immigrants hoped to make a better life for themselves and their families. Immigrants are people who leave one country to settle in another.

The reasons that force people to leave their native countries are called **push factors**. Among the push factors were poverty, lack of religious freedom, and political oppression. In many countries, small farms could no longer support large families. With little income, people had no reason to stay in their native countries. Religious persecution also forced people to leave their homelands. In Russia and Poland, Jews were harassed for practicing their religion.

Democracy, religious freedom, and economic opportunity brought people to the United States. These are called **pull factors** because they attract immigrants. Some Europeans were attracted by the belief that American streets were "paved with gold."

Immigrants contributed to the growth of cities. Immigrants from Europe arrived in port cities on the East Coast. Many of the newcomers, including women and children, went to work in the northeastern states. The men took work as bricklayers, carpenters, or street vendors, or did whatever other work they could find. Those who could afford the train fare continued west. Some went as far as Detroit and Chicago. There, they found work in new factories. In the late 1800s, immigrants provided the labor that helped the nation's industries grow.

Chinese and Japanese immigrants arrived on the West Coast in port cities like San Francisco and Seattle. They settled mainly in the West. Many became farmers or worked in construction. Mexican immigrants settled in the Southwest, and many became farm workers.

 Think about Social Studies

Directions: Choose the best answer to the following question.

1. What did the idea that American streets were "paved with gold" mean to immigrants?

   A. Americans were rich.

   B. America was full of opportunities.

   C. America provided many jobs to bricklayers.

   D. Streets in America were literally paved with gold.

Life in America

Throughout the 1800s, newly invented farm machines were being used to plant and harvest crops. This reduced the need for farm workers. At the same time, falling farm prices caused some families to lose their farms.

Factories, mills, and other city businesses needed workers. People from the countryside were pushed from their farms by changing conditions there. They were pulled to cities in search of work. In 1840, there were 131 cities in the nation. By 1900, the number had increased to 1,700. By 1920, more than half of all Americans lived in cities.

The Social Classes

The growth of industry in the United States divided people into social classes. **Social class** describes levels of society that are based on economic success. Cities were divided into three social classes: the wealthy, a growing middle class, and the very poor. The very wealthy lived in the city centers. They built large homes taken care of by servants, wore elegant clothes, and went to the opera and the theater. They owned horses and carriages.

The middle class was growing. New industries like railroads and new businesses like department stores created new kinds of jobs. Teachers, doctors, lawyers, sales clerks, bank tellers, and people who worked for the government were all part of the middle class. A growing number of middle-class families moved to new neighborhoods on the edges of cities. New streetcar lines connected these suburbs, or residential areas, to places of work downtown.

The working class were the poorest people. Some worked building the new skyscrapers, digging subway tunnels, or making steel or building train cars in factories. The working class lived farthest from the city center. Their neighborhoods were close to the factories, railroad yards, and slaughterhouses.

Immigrants tended to settle with others from the same ethnic group. The Chinese lived in one section of a city, the Italians in another. This is why neighborhoods were given names like "Chinatown" and "Little Italy." Many working class families lived in tenements. **Tenements** were large buildings of apartments where the poorest people lived. Tenements had no elevators, and some lacked running water. Families of six or more crowded into one or two rooms.

CORE PRACTICE

Summarize Ideas

A summary includes the main ideas of a piece of writing and only the most important details that describe or explain those main ideas. It does not include all of the details in the original piece. Summarize the information in the section "The Growth of Immigration." Follow these steps:

- Read the text carefully.
- Take notes in your own words that include the main ideas.
- Include the most important details that describe or explain the main ideas.
- Do not add your own ideas—a summary does not include your opinion.
- Be short. Be complete. Be accurate. Write clearly.
- Use correct punctuation, spelling, and grammar.

Find Details

Readers often need to find details in a text to answer questions. To find details related to a specific topic, first read the headings. Find the heading that matches your topic or comes closest to it. Then skim the text under that heading for the details. When you skim text, you look for key words. For example, to find details about the wealthy class in the United States, you would look under the heading "The Social Classes" and skim the text to find the key word *wealthy* or words related to wealth. Under what heading would you look to find information about where immigrants settled in America? Skim the text under that heading and list three details describing the effects of this settlement pattern.

The Challenges of Cities

The rapidly growing cities had serious problems. Sewage flooded basements and garbage piled up in the streets. Over-crowding and poor sanitation, or hygiene, caused outbreaks of disease. Smoke and grime from burning coal polluted the air. Sometimes disasters struck. Fires gutted entire business sections in Chicago, Boston, and other cities.

A number of reformers tried to clean up cities and help the poor. Jane Addams established Hull House, in Chicago, in 1889 to aid the poor and immigrants. It was a **settlement house**. Settlement houses are privately run neighborhood centers that provide services for the poor. Hull House offered medical care, day care, and classes learning the English language and other skills. Single working women could live in Hull House's boardinghouse. Addams's work became the model for settlement houses in other cities.

⚑ Think about Social Studies

Directions: Choose the best answer to the following question.

1. In the 1900s, middle-class Americans were most likely to live in

   A. mansions   C. tenements

   B. suburbs   D. settlement houses

2. What effect did industrialization have on cities?

   A. Farms were hiring more people and the farming industry grew.

   B. Immigrants tended to settle in areas where there were other people of the same ethnic group.

   C. Cities were becoming over-crowded and sanitation and pollution became problematic.

   D. The many factories and mills discriminated against women and children in the workplace.

Discrimination Against Immigrants

Not all native-born Americans welcomed immigrants. The newcomers often spoke their own languages and had their own customs and traditions. They were Roman Catholic, Jewish, and Buddhist at a time when most native-born Americans were Protestant. They also feared that immigrants would take jobs away from Americans.

Many native-born Americans feared that immigrants would change American society and traditions. These **nativists**, as they were known, wanted to prevent immigrants from coming to the United States. Nativists were generally Protestants, and they wanted to block the entry of Catholics and Jews. They also disliked immigrants from Asia. As a result of pressure from nativists, Congress passed the first immigration law in 1882. The Chinese Exclusion Act halted immigration from China for 10 years. Chinese Americans protested the policy, but it did no good.

About 1890, a new social movement arose in the United States. It was composed of people who believed in reform and the improvement of society. They called themselves progressives. Some progressives wanted to see changes in the way government worked. Others wanted controls on big business. Still others wanted social reforms. Many ideas of the progressives became enacted into law.

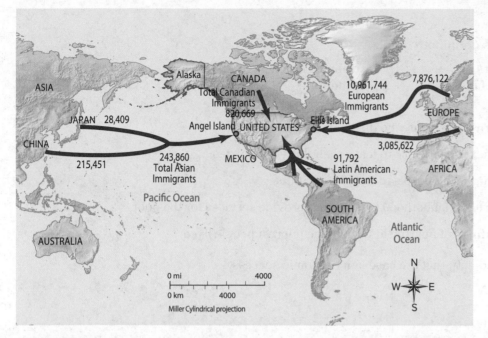

Prior knowledge—what you already know—is important in learning. You can often connect new things you learn to prior knowledge. Some tests require you to read a passage. To understand what you read, your brain connects it to what you already know. One connection technique is to turn headings into questions and then answer them. For example, you might turn the heading "Discrimination Against Immigrants" into the following questions: "What do I know about immigration?" "What is discrimination?" "What types of discrimination have I seen or read about in the past?" Then answer your questions. As you read, relate the ideas in the text to what you already know. Practice this technique with other headings in this chapter. Share your questions with a partner.

The reforms of the Progressive Era did not include everyone, however. By 1902, Chinese were prevented from entering the United States permanently. In 1924, Congress passed a law ending most immigration from Asia. That same year, it also put limits on the number of immigrants from certain areas of Europe. Jews and Catholics were not barred from immigrating. But once in the United States, they faced prejudice. As more Jews arrived from Eastern Europe, anti-Semitism, or discrimination against Jews, increased.

In the late 1800s and early 1900s, Mexican immigrants added to the number of Latinos in the United States. The first Mexican immigrants left lives in poverty to search for work. Later immigrants were pushed by violence from the Mexican Revolution. Like other immigrant groups, they found themselves living in poor sections of cities. Called barrios, these areas often had no running water, no paved streets, and no electricity. Mexicans learned to depend on one another for support.

WRITE TO LEARN

List some of the reasons immigrants came to the United States.

 Think about Social Studies

Directions: Refer to the map above to answer the following questions.

1. Which answer characterizes immigration to the United States in the late 1800s?

   A. Many enslaved Africans arrived.

   B. People came mainly from northern and southern Asia.

   C. People came mainly from northern and southern Europe.

   D. The majority of immigrants came from Latin America and Canada.

2. What is the total number of immigrants arriving from Asia?

   A. 28,409

   B. 91,792

   C. 243,860

   D. 3,085,622

Vocabulary Review

Directions: Write each word next to its definition.

push factors   nativists   settlement houses
pull factors   social class   tenements

_____ **1.** native-born Americans who disliked immigrants

_____ **2.** reasons that force people to leave their native countries

_____ **3.** reasons that bring people to the United States

_____ **4.** privately run neighborhood centers that provide services for the poor

_____ **5.** large buildings of apartments where the poorest people lived

_____ **6.** levels of society that are based on economic success

Skill Review

Directions: Choose the best answer to each question.

1. Which of the following immigrants settled mainly on the western coast of the United States?

A. immigrants from Europe

B. immigrants from Africa

C. immigrants from Mexico

D. immigrants from Japan and China

2. Which of the following events helped lead to the growth of cities?

A. Cities provided healthy, safe living spaces.

B. Settlement houses were built to help the poor.

C. Progressive reforms made cities safer.

D. Farm machines replaced farm workers.

3. Which group of people did Jane Addams have the most in common with?

A. nativists

B. wealthy city dwellers

C. immigrants

D. progressives

4. What is an example of a pull factor for Jewish immigrants?

A. freedom of religion

B. settlement houses

C. religious persecution

D. anti-Semitism

Skill Practice

Directions: Read the following passage. Then answer the questions that follow.

The Muckrackers

(1) During the Progressive Era, some journalists wrote about wrongdoing in business and government in order to bring about change. (2) These journalists were called muckrakers because they uncovered ugly aspects of American life. (3) Muckrakers attacked a wide range of problems. (4) For example, Lincoln Steffens wrote about corruption in city politics. (5) Upton Sinclair wrote about unsafe and unhealthy conditions for workers in the meatpacking industry. (6) Ida Tarbell wrote about the unethical business practices of the Standard Oil Company. (7) John Spargo used his writing to campaign for an end to child labor. (8) While each muckraker addressed a different issue, they found similar abuses and injustices.

1. Which sentence best summarizes the passage?
   A. Sentence 4
   B. Sentence 3
   C. Sentence 2
   D. Sentence 1

2. Which sentence provides the best evidence about the lack of workplace safety?
   A. Sentence 3
   B. Sentence 4
   C. Sentence 5
   D. Sentence 8

3. Based on the passage, what conclusion can you draw about muckrackers?
   A. They were nativists who did not believe in immigration.
   B. They believed in fairness for all people living in the United States.
   C. The working class did not trust muckrackers because they stirred up trouble.
   D. City politicians and large businesses appreciated the work of muckrackers.

4. Which group of people might be most interested in the work of John Spargo?
   A. children in poor families
   B. mothers in wealthy families
   C. children in wealthy families
   D. fathers in middle-class families

Writing Practice

Directions: Imagine you work at Hull House, the settlement house run by Jane Addams. Write a letter to a family member describing your work and explaining how it differs from the ideas of nativists. Be sure to use correct spelling, punctuation, and grammar in your letter.

Directions: Choose the best answer to each question.

1. What was one effect of the colonists' protests of the Stamp Act?

   A. British Parliament imposed a tax on English goods.

   B. Colonists agreed to pay taxes on English goods.

   C. Parliament repealed the Stamp Act.

   D. The Boston Massacre occurred.

2. Which of the following events occurred first?

   A. Crispus Attucks was killed in the Boston Massacre.

   B. The pilgrims founded the town of Plymouth, Massachusetts.

   C. Colonists dumped British tea into the Boston harbor.

   D. The British Parliament repealed the Townshend Acts.

Directions: Questions 3 and 4 refer to the following map.

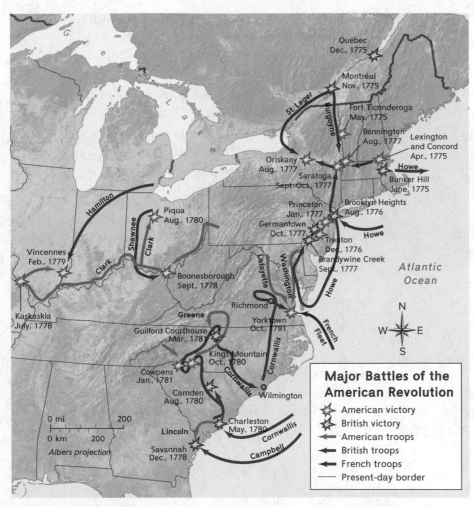

3. Which battle was won by American colonists?

   A. Savannah, Georgia

   B. Germantown, Pennsylvania

   C. Brooklyn Heights, New York

   D. Saratoga, New York

4. According to the map, where did most battles take place?

   A. the New England region

   B. the southeastern coastline

   C. west of the Great Lakes

   D. along the Mississippi River

Directions: Choose the best answer to each question.

5. How did the Treaty of Greenville affect Native Americans in the Ohio Valley?

   A. Tecumseh and other Native Americans agreed to remain in the Ohio Valley.

   B. Tribes were paid for their land in the Ohio Valley.

   C. Tribes agreed to leave the Ohio Valley.

   D. A truce was agreed on by the Americans and the Native American tribes.

6. Anti-Semitism is discrimination against _____.

   A. Mexican immigrants

   B. Jewish people

   C. Chinese immigrants

   D. Japanese people

Directions: Questions 7 and 8 refer to the passage below.

Kate Cumming was born in Scotland in 1835. Her family moved to Mobile, Alabama, when she was a child. When the Civil War began, she was twenty-six and a true daughter of the Confederacy. At first she kept busy helping to put on concerts and plays to raise money for the troops.

In April 1862, Union and Confederate troops clashed near the village of Shiloh, Tennessee. The Confederate army needed volunteers to care for the wounded. Cumming set forth for the hospital. Cumming was totally unprepared for what she found at Corinth. "Nothing that I had ever heard or read had given me the faintest idea of the horrors witnessed here," she wrote in her diary. "Gray-haired men—men in the pride of manhood—beardless boys . . . mutilated in every imaginable way, lying on the floor . . . so close together it was almost impossible to walk without stepping on them."

For the next three years, Cumming journeyed from one Confederate hospital to another. After leaving the hospital at Corinth, she wrote in her diary, "I shall ever look back on these two months with sincere gratification, and feel that I have lived for something."

7. Which statement provides the best summary of the passage?

   A. Old men and boys were wounded in the war.

   B. A woman of the Civil War took on an important role by caring for the wounded.

   C. Women of the South helped the war effort by putting on concerts and plays.

   D. Kate Cumming moved to the South and kept a diary.

8. What phrase from the passage is the best example of persuasive language?

   A. "she was twenty-six and a true daughter of the Confederacy"

   B. "I . . . feel that I have lived for something"

   C. "beardless boys . . . mutilated in every imaginable way"

   D. "troops clashed near the village of Shiloh"

Check Your Understanding

Lesson	Item Number
American Revolution	1, 2, 3, 4
A New Nation	5
Civil War and Reconstruction	7, 8
European Settlement and Population of America	6

WRITE ABOUT Causes and Effects of War

When you write a cause-and-effect essay, you are showing direct relationships between events. You are familiar with cause and effect in everyday life. A blizzard overnight (cause) results in schools closing (effect). Sometimes sentences are written so that the effect is presented first. The police officer gave the young driver a ticket (effect) because he ran a stop sign (cause). Sometimes a chain reaction of causes and effects occurs. In that case, the effect can become the cause of the next event. Read the cause-and-effect essay on page 350. Then write your own cause-and-effect essay on an aspect of the Civil War.

BEFORE YOU WRITE Create a Chart

Charts provide a simple visual that can help organize your thoughts. The most basic format is a two-column chart like the one below. Notice that an effect can become a cause in a chain of events.

CAUSE	EFFECT
Led by Pontiac, Native Americans attack British forts and colonists on their land.	King George III issues the Proclamation of 1763, restricting settlers to east of the Appalachians.
Colonists disregard the ruling, moving into Ohio.	Further unrest between settlers and Native Americans occurs.
Further unrest between settlers and Native Americans occurs.	Britain sends more soldiers and builds more forts.

If you wish, you can make different forms of the chart, including arrows to show the progression of events.

Cause: Colonies cancel orders for British goods.

Effect: British workers lose their jobs.

TIP Use Compound Sentences Correctly

One way to achieve sentence variety is to write compound sentences. Doing so joins two short complete sentences into one longer sentence and avoids a choppy feel. Notice the compound sentences below.

British soldiers were stationed in private homes, <u>but</u> the colonists disapproved of their presence.
Colonists often threw snowballs at the soldiers<u>;</u> they also called them names, such as lobsterbacks.

The two sentences show the two correct ways of forming compound sentences. To join two complete sentences, you may use a comma **followed** by a conjunction. The comma does not go after the conjunction. Common conjunctions include *and, or, for, not,* and *but.*

You may also place a semicolon between the two sentences without the conjunction.

A comma splice occurs when neither method is followed, and the sentences simply run together.

WHILE YOU WRITE Use Cause-and-Effect Clue Words

Some words clearly show cause-and-effect relationships. A list of the most frequently used terms is below. By placing these words as transitions between sentences or paragraphs, you help the reader see the relationships between events and ideas. Remember that your goal is always to make the writing smooth for your reader. Sloppy writing leads to confusion, which will generally discourage your readers.

as a result	for that reason	so
because	led to	so that
consequently	in order to	therefore
due to	produced	thus

TIP   **Watch Out for Possessive Nouns**

Possessive nouns show ownership. Most often, possession is shown by use of an apostrophe and an s.

Lisa's car   Maria's notebook   James's book

To form the possessive for plural nouns, simply place an apostrophe after the s.

bedrooms'   families'   companies'

Some nouns have irregular possessive forms. If the noun does not end in s, add an apostrophe and an s.

children's toys   mice's tails   women's work

When in doubt, check a print or reliable online dictionary.

AFTER YOU WRITE Revise

One quick way to improve your writing is to replace *be* verbs with action words. Go through your essay looking for every use of the words *am, are, was, were, be, been* and *being*. Substitute an action verb wherever possible. Doing so will make your writing more vivid.

Another quick trick is to look for prepositional phrases. Make sure you haven't written a string of them, which is easy to do. For example, this sentence has three prepositional phrases at the end of it. *We walked to the store on the corner for a treat.* The sentence can be improved with little work: *For a treat, we walked to the corner store.*

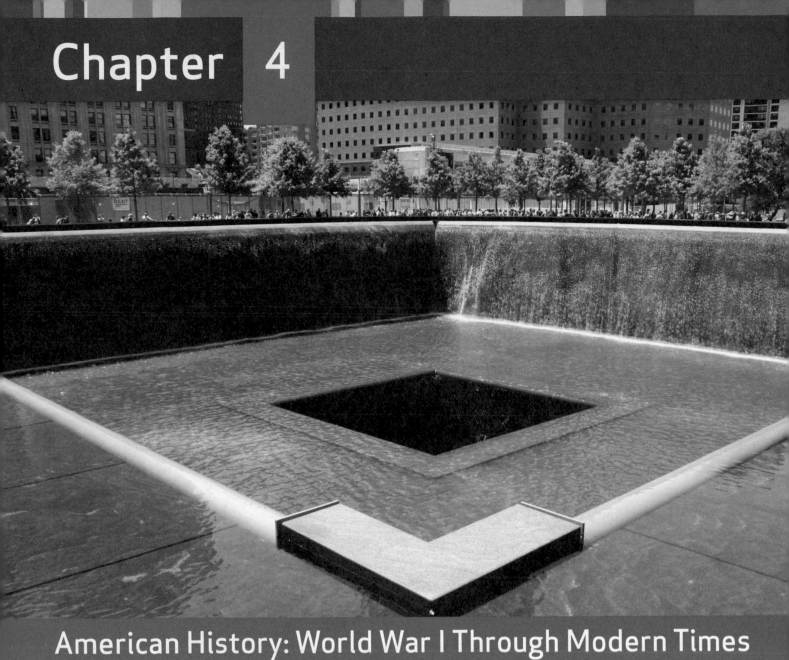

Chapter 4

American History: World War I Through Modern Times

Think about various groups or organizations you have participated in at school, at work, or in your community. Who made up the groups? Were the participants similar to or different from you? How did you get along with others who did not agree with you? The United States is a participant in a diverse global community. Relationships with other countries became increasingly important in the 20th century.

©iStockphoto.com/vivalapenler

In this chapter you will study these topics:

Lesson 4.1
World War I

What caused World War I? How did the war affect Europe and the United States? How did the United States plan for global peace after the war?

Lesson 4.2
World War II

What events led to World War II? Why did the United States enter the war? How did the war affect life in the United States?

Lesson 4.3
The Cold War

How did communism spread throughout the world? What did the United States do to stop communism? What was the Cold War? What countries were affected by the Cold War?

Lesson 4.4
Societal Changes

What was the Great Society? How effective were its programs? Who was Richard Nixon and how did he affect politics? How did the collapse of communism affect Eastern Europe?

Lesson 4.5
Foreign Policy in the 21st Century

What is terrorism? What happened on September 11, 2001, in the United States? How did the events of that day affect US foreign policy?

Goal Setting

The United States is a major world power that has participated in wars outside its borders. Have you seen news reports about wars in other parts of the world? Who was involved in these wars? How do the wars affect citizens of the United States?

LESSON 4.1   World War I

■ LESSON OBJECTIVES

- Identify the causes of WWI
- Explain the effects of WWI on Europe and the U.S.
- Understand how and why the League of Nations was formed

■ CORE SKILLS & PRACTICES

- Make Predictions
- Sequence Events

Key Terms

imperialism
governing of weaker nations or colonies by more powerful nations

League of Nations
an organization designed to help nations settle disputes peacefully

militarism
a policy of aggressive military preparedness

nationalism
a feeling of pride in and loyalty to one's nation

Vocabulary

alliance
a group of countries joined together in a common cause

revolution
the overthrow of a government or ruler and replacement with another government.

Key Concept

World War I resulted from alliances being formed throughout the world.

Think about disagreements you have seen between family members or friends. Did other people get involved in the disagreement? Did they take sides? Disagreements between countries can cause other countries to take sides. Sometimes problems are solved through peaceful compromises. Other times, fighting breaks out. World wars occur when the most powerful countries go to war.

The United States Becomes a World Power

By the 1890s, overseas expansion and **imperialism** slowly began to appeal to more Americans. Imperialism is the governing of weaker nations or colonies by more powerful nations, such as Great Britain and France. As the world's leading producer of steel and oil, the United States had more miles of railroad than any other country. It extended from the Atlantic Ocean to the Pacific. Some Americans thought it was time for the United States to become a world power.

At the same time, European nations were competing for territory and economic gain in Asia and Africa. The Industrial Revolution speeded up the economic development of Europe and the United States. It also established the way industrial nations viewed their colonies. They began to see the colonies as markets for goods as well as sources of raw materials.

The factories and mills of the Industrial Revolution required vast amounts of raw materials. Regions in Africa, Asia, and Latin America had raw materials in abundance. Once goods were produced, business owners needed markets. Africa, Asia, and Latin America represented huge new markets. Setting up colonies ensured that the flow of raw materials continued. It also ensured that the home country controlled the sale of goods in the colonies.

Everywhere US businessmen looked, they saw new customers. Everywhere government leaders looked, they saw new power for the nation. A spirit of nationalism also motivated imperialists. **Nationalism** is a feeling of pride in and loyalty to one's nation. Setting up colonies was one way to show how one nation was more powerful and wealthy than another. Europe had been an imperial power for over a hundred years. The United States began to build an overseas empire.

If the United States was going to build an empire, it had to be ready to defend it. This was the argument of both business leaders and naval officers. Congress listened to the argument and budgeted money to build a modern navy.

 Think about Social Studies

Directions: Choose the best answer to the following question.

1. Which factor contributed to the rise of imperialism?
   A. desire to expand the navy
   B. desire to empower other nations
   C. desire to expand the railroad system
   D. desire to expand U.S. trade and power

World War I

The Great War, later known as World War I, began in Europe in 1914. The United States proclaimed its neutrality and did not enter the war until 1917. Many Americans thought it was a problem for Europeans to solve.

Tensions in Europe

There were several long-term causes that eventually led to World War I. Beginning in the mid-1800s, several European countries began to unite, transforming politics across the continent. In the early 1900s, an arms race in Europe set the stage for war. In a show of **militarism**, which is a policy of aggressive military preparedness, European nations competed with each other to build the largest army or navy. The arms race was driven by nationalism and fear.

Nationalism also affected ethnic groups who did not have their own nation. One such group was the Slavs who lived in Austria-Hungary. They began to demand an independent country. For protection, European countries formed defensive alliances. An **alliance** is a group of countries joined together in a common cause. They agreed to come to one another's aid if attacked. The alliance system formed by Austria-Hungary, Germany, and the Ottoman Empire became known as the Central Powers. Great Britain, France, and Russia formed an alliance called the Allied Powers. Tensions in Europe were so high, an advisor reported to President Wilson in 1914, that "it only requires a spark to set the whole thing off."

There were also short-term causes of the war. The assassination of Austria-Hungary's Archduke Franz Ferdinand, in 1914, provided the spark. The archduke was killed by Gavrilo Princip, a Serbian nationalist. The Serbs supported independence for the Slavs. Very quickly, Austria-Hungary declared war on Serbia.

This brought Austria-Hungary's allies—the Ottoman Empire and Germany—into the conflict. They would be joined later by Italy. Serbia's allies—Great Britain, Russia, and France—then declared war against the Central Powers.

United States Response to War

Under President Woodrow Wilson, the United States adopted a policy of neutrality. The United States would not favor one side or the other. This was consistent with the nation's policy of avoiding "permanent alliances with

Make Predictions

Often, social studies and history texts are like stories. They tell about events that happened and the people, or characters, who took part in those events. One helpful reading strategy when reading stories is to make predictions. As you read, you guess what will happen next. Then you read to find out if your prediction is correct. Read the section titled "The United States Becomes a World Power." Predict what might happen as a result of the nationalism and imperialism in Europe and the United States combined with the United States wanting a larger, more powerful navy. Then read the section "World War I" to find out if your prediction is correct.

European Alliances, 1914

- Allied Powers
- Central Powers
- Neutral Nations
- ← Initial troop movements of Central Powers

any portion of the foreign world" as George Washington said in 1796. The United States was determined to stay out of European affairs. It was difficult, however, for Americans to remain neutral in their thinking. They shared many traditions and values with the British and still respected France as a friend to America during the Revolutionary War. On the other hand, many Americans of German descent favored Germany. Many Irish Americans also sided with the Central Powers. They hoped that a British defeat would free Ireland from British rule.

However, the warring nations did not always respect neutrality. Great Britain blocked merchant ships from entering German ports. As a result, American ships could not carry goods to Germany and the other Central Powers. German submarines, known as U-boats, attacked American merchant ships sailing to Great Britain.

Even President Wilson found it difficult to be perfectly neutral. He issued several strong warnings to Germany about attacking merchant and passenger ships. Wilson protested Britain's actions but not vigorously. Wilson's two-sided approach did little to keep the United States neutral.

Steps to War

On May 7, 1915, Germans torpedoed the passenger liner *Lusitania* as it crossed the Atlantic. The loss of 123 American lives and approximately 1,200 European lives shocked Americans and brought angry protests from President Wilson. Germany was afraid the United States would enter the war. To prevent the United States from joining the conflict, Germany announced that its submarines would stop attacking nonmilitary ships. Germany's pledge lasted less than a year. The turning point for America came in 1917.

In January 1917, British agents deciphered a German telegram that became known as the Zimmermann Telegram. In the telegram, a German foreign minister named Arthur Zimmermann asked the German ambassador to

Mexico to declare war against the United States if the United States joined the war in Europe. In return, Mexico would receive New Mexico, Texas, and Arizona. Americans were furious.

On February 1, Germany began unrestricted submarine warfare. Germany believed that they could conquer Britain before the United States entered the war. Several American ships were torpedoed, killing passengers and crew. The Zimmermann Telegram and the continued attacks on American ships changed the public's mind. President Wilson went before Congress on April 2, 1917, and asked for a declaration of war against Germany.

The Home Front

One of the first things that needed to be done was to mobilize, or prepare, the army and navy. In May 1917, Congress passed the Selective Service Act. All men aged 21 to 30 had to register for the draft. Almost three million men were drafted, or called, for active duty.

Factories had to switch from making consumer goods, like cars, to making war goods, like tanks and uniforms. In factories, women often took the place of the men who went to war. During the war, more than one million women took jobs outside the home. African Americans were also hired to fill empty factory jobs in the North.

The Battlefield

When American soldiers arrived in France in June 1917, Europe had been at war for three years. The Allies were fighting the Central Powers on two fronts. The Western Front lay across France and Italy. The Eastern Front lay between the Central Powers and Russia. It was to the Allies advantage that Germany fought a two-front war. But that changed in 1917.

Europe During World War I, 1914–1918

- Allied Powers
- Central Powers
- Neutral Nations
- Allied victories
- Central victories
- Indecisive

0 mi 500
0 km 500
Azimuthal Equidistant projection

Major Battles

1. Tannenberg, Aug. 1914
2. 1st Marne, Sept. 1914
3. Gallipoli, Apr. 1915–Jan. 1916
4. Verdun, Feb.–Dec. 1916
5. Somme, July–Nov. 1916
6. Château-Thierry and Belleau Wood, June 1918
7. 2nd Marne, July 1918
8. St.-Mihiel, Sept. 1918
9. Argonne, Sept.–Nov. 1918

Sequence Events

Sequence is the order in which events happen. A timeline is one way to arrange the sequence of events. You can see that one thing happened before or after another from the location of events on the timeline. Sometimes you have to figure out sequence without a timeline or signal words in text, such as *first, next,* and *finally.* A flowchart can help you. Start with the first event and fill in each event in the order in which it happened. The flowchart presents the main ideas. Details are left out. Create a flowchart of events for the section titled "World War I."

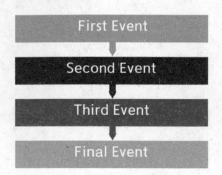

First Event

Second Event

Third Event

Final Event

Russia had suffered during the war, and soon the government collapsed during a revolution to overthrow the czar, led by Vladimir Lenin. A **revolution** is the overthrow of a government or ruler. Lenin's government pulled Russia out of the war in December 1917. In March 1918, the new Russian government signed a treaty with Germany. Germany no longer had to fight on two fronts. It could send all its troops to fight on the Western Front.

Germany used its new force to break out of the French lines. By June 1918, the Germans had pushed to within 40 miles of Paris. From June through mid-July, the Allies, including American troops, fought to keep the Germans from advancing any farther.

Then the Allies went on the offensive. From mid-July to the end of September, the Allies slowly advanced. Finally, they broke through the German lines during the seven-week Battle of the Argonne Forest. The German government asked for peace and an armistice, or agreement, was signed at the 11th hour of the 11th day of the 11th month—November 11, 1918. The Treaty of Versailles officially ended the war on June 28, 1919.

⚑ Think about Social Studies

Directions: Choose the best answer to the following question.

1. In 1917 Germany offered Mexico an alliance against the United States in the
   - **A.** Treaty of Versailles.
   - **B.** Allied Alliance.
   - **C.** Battle of Argonne Forest.
   - **D.** Zimmermann Telegraph.

After the War

The war ended with an armistice. The German kaiser, or emperor, had been overthrown and the new German government asked for peace. In 1919, the Allies negotiated a peace treaty.

Wilson's Peace Plan

President Wilson had his own idea of what peace in Europe should look like. He believed that there should be no winners or losers in the war. The future of the world depended on treating Germany and the other Central Powers fairly.

Wilson's peace plan was called the "Fourteen Points." It outlined a new world order based on freedom of the seas, free trade, and arms reduction. The Fourteen Points also ended secret treaties between countries and called for open diplomacy, or negotiations between nations. Wilson also called for national self-determination. This would allow ethnic groups in Central Europe and Turkey to set up their own nations.

Finally, he proposed a **League of Nations**, a new organization designed to help nations settle disputes peacefully.

The Paris Peace Conference

The Paris Peace Conference was the first time an American president traveled to Europe while in office. Wilson went to promote his Fourteen Points, but the leaders of France and Britain wanted to punish Germany for all of Europe's suffering during the war. The other Allied countries were more interested in their own security than in securing a more stable world order.

Great Britain, France, and Italy wanted to punish Germany. France had suffered two invasions by Germany in 44 years. The French prime minister wanted to make sure this did not happen again. Both France and Great Britain wanted reparations, or money, for their nations' losses in the war. Along with the United States, these "Big Four" dictated peace terms to Germany and the other Central Powers.

One of the biggest changes was the change to the land occupied by the Central Powers. The negotiators at the peace conference redrew the map of Eastern Europe. They took land from Germany, Austria-Hungary, and Russia. The redrawn map included the new, independent nations of Finland, Latvia, Estonia, Lithuania, Poland, Czechoslovakia, Austria, Hungary, and Yugoslavia.

The points in the Treaty of Versailles indicated:

- Germany accepted responsibility for the war.
- Germany would pay $33 billion in reparations.
- Germany could keep only a small army and navy.
- Nine new nations were to be created from territory taken from the Central Powers.
- The League of Nations was created.

Wilson returned to the United States to urge the Senate to ratify the treaty. He realized that the treaty had weaknesses, but he believed that the League of Nations could settle unresolved issues. Republicans, led by Senator Henry Cabot Lodge of Massachusetts, objected to the League. They were afraid that joining the League would mean that the United States would lose its sovereignty, or the ability to act on its own. They thought they would be committing the United States to go to war any time another nation was attacked. Wilson refused to compromise with proposed changes. The Senate voted twice and each time rejected the treaty. As a result, the United States never joined the League. Instead, it signed a separate treaty with Germany in 1921.

Think about Social Studies

Directions: Match each word to its definition.

national self-determination   reparations
sovereignty   kaiser

_____ 1. ability to act on one's own

_____ 2. idea that ethnic groups can set up their own nations

_____ 3. money for a nation's losses during war

_____ 4. German emperor

TECHNOLOGY SKILLS

Apply Technology to a Task

In school and in the workplace, you may need to educate or train others. Visual aids can help learners understand topics. Using appropriate software, create a multimedia presentation that includes a slide show of the major events of World War I. Use Internet resources to find photos, maps, and other graphics to include in your presentation. Be sure to cite the sources of your visuals. Write a script to use during your presentation, or create an audio file to accompany your slide show.

WRITE TO LEARN

Nationalism was increasing before World War I. Imagine you are a nationalist. Write about how you feel about your country and why.

Vocabulary Review

Directions: Complete the sentences using the following key terms and vocabulary words.

revolution   militarism   imperialism

alliance   League of Nations   nationalism

1. Governing of weaker nations or colonies by more powerful nations is known as _____.

2. Germany, the Ottoman Empire, and Austria-Hungary formed a(n) _____ so that they could aid one another militarily.

3. A policy of aggressive military action is known as _____.

4. While fighting in World War I, Russia's government changed due to a(n) _____.

5. President Wilson proposed the _____ to help countries settle disputes peacefully.

6. A feeling of pride in and loyalty to one's nation is called _____.

Skill Review

Directions: Choose the best answer to each question.

1. Which of the following events occurred after the United States entered World War I?

   A. Germans sank the passenger liner *Lusitania*.

   B. The Zimmermann Telegram became public.

   C. European countries formed alliances.

   D. The Russian czar was overthrown.

2. How did the Treaty of Versailles reduce the militarism of Germany?

   A. It stated Germany had to reduce its military forces.

   B. It protected Germans from military actions.

   C. It provided only a few troops for German armies.

   D. It banned Germany from having an army.

3. Which of the following was a short-term cause of the war?

   A. increased militarism and nationalism

   B. the colonization of less-powerful countries

   C. the assassination of Austria-Hungary's archduke

   D. increased markets due to the Industrial Revolution

4. How did the draft affect industry in the United States?

   A. Businesses replaced white, male workers with women and African Americans.

   B. Men went to war and were unable to purchase goods from businesses.

   C. Businesses had to close because they did not have enough workers.

   D. Businesses hired children to replace male workers who were drafted.

Skill Practice

Directions: Read the passage. Then answer the questions that follow.

Wilson's Fourteen Points Speech

(1) In regard to these essential rectifications of wrong and assertions of right we feel ourselves to be intimate partners of all the governments and peoples associated together against the Imperialists. (2) We cannot be separated in interest or divided in purpose. (3) We stand together until the end. (4) For such arrangements and covenants we are willing to fight and to continue to fight until they are achieved; but only because we wish the right to prevail and desire a just and stable peace such as can be secured only by removing the chief provocations to war, which this program does remove. (5) We have no jealousy of German greatness, and there is nothing in this program that impairs it. (6) We grudge her no achievement or distinction of learning or of pacific enterprise such as have made her record very bright and very enviable. (7) We do not wish to injure her or to block in any way her legitimate influence or power. (8) We do not wish to fight her either with arms or with hostile arrangements of trade if she is willing to associate herself with us and the other peace-loving nations of the world in covenants of justice and law and fair dealing. (9) We wish her only to accept a place of equality among the peoples of the world, —the new world in which we now live, —instead of a place of mastery.

—*Woodrow Wilson, in an address to Congress, January 8, 1918*

1. Which sentence best describes Wilson's position on punishment of Germany?

   A. Sentence 1

   B. Sentence 3

   C. Sentence 5

   D. Sentence 7

2. In which sentence does Wilson acknowledge that the United States is a world power among other countries?

   A. Sentence 1

   B. Sentence 3

   C. Sentence 5

   D. Sentence 9

3. Read the final two sentences. What does the Fourteen Points plan require from Germany?

   A. Germany must obey the governments of peace-loving nations.

   B. Germany must not seek to master, or take over, other countries.

   C. Germany will not be treated equally until they pay reparations.

   D. Germany will have to provide free trade to Allied countries.

4. In sentence 4, what does the term **provocations** mean?

   A. causes

   B. hardships

   C. opponents

   D. supporters

Writing Practice

Directions: President Wilson wanted a "just peace," a "peace without victory," that would not punish Germany and Austria. He did not want nations to have a reason for another war. The leaders of France and Britain wanted revenge. In your opinion, who won out in the final peace treaty? Write a paragraph explaining your answer. Cite evidence for your conclusion.

LESSON 4.2 World War II

LESSON OBJECTIVES

- Understand the events that led up to World War II
- Explain why the U.S. entered the war
- Understand how the war affected life in the U.S.

CORE SKILLS & PRACTICES

- Identify Author's Bias
- Understand the Main Idea

Key Terms

fascism
a dictatorship in which the state is more important than individuals

internment
the confining or segregating of people during war

isolationism
a policy of avoiding involvement in international affairs

totalitarian government
a government that controls all aspects of a nation

Vocabulary

depression
a period of low economic activity and high unemployment

propaganda
false or exaggerated statements

Key Concept

After World War I, three totalitarian governments formed in Europe and began World War II.

The term power hungry *is often used to describe people who have a strong desire for power. Often these people will abuse others, disobey rules, and rewrite the rules to give themselves more power. As you will read in this chapter, unlimited government power can have severe consequences for a nation and the world.*

The Rise of Dictators

After World War I, people in Europe and the United States were tired of war. The League of Nations was created to ensure that a global war would never happen again. However, its 40-member nations could not agree on policies, and the United States never joined the League.

Europe's economic problems, stemming from World War I, continued to increase. In the 1920s the world was hit with a massive **depression**. A depression is a period of rising unemployment and low economic activity. It began in Europe and spread around the world.

By the early 1930s, the economy of the United States had also collapsed. The depression caused great hardship everywhere. Leaders in several countries promised to end the suffering by setting up totalitarian governments. A **totalitarian government** is one that attempts to control the politics, economy, society, and culture of a nation.

Fascism in Italy

The first person to set up a totalitarian government was Benito Mussolini in Italy. Mussolini used the economic fears of the middle class to form the Fascist Party in 1919. By 1925, he had set up a dictatorship that was called **fascism**. According to fascism, the state is more important than individuals. In a fascist state, individuals and companies may own businesses and land, but the government controls how they are run.

National Archives and Records Administration

Hitler's Germany

The conditions that helped Adolf Hitler take over Germany were similar to those that helped Mussolini take over Italy. Germany was deep in debt and had been politically unstable since the end of World War I. Germans were angered at their treatment by the Allies at the Paris Peace Conference. Germany was also suffering from the worldwide depression. However, the Allies insisted that Germany continue to pay the huge reparations, or compensation, called for by the Treaty of Versailles.

After the war, many nationalist political parties were developing in Germany. Adolf Hitler joined the National Socialist German Workers' Party, better known as the Nazi Party and became its leader. Hitler appealed to nationalists and the desperate German people. He promised to stop the payment of reparations, rebuild the German military, and create a new empire.

At the beginning of 1933, the president of the German Republic was forced to make Hitler chancellor. The Nazis formed a coalition with a majority of seats in the German Parliament. Hitler had Parliament suspend the constitution. The law was whatever Hitler decided.

By 1934 no one could challenge Hitler. The only political party allowed in Germany was the Nazi Party. Nazism took over Germany. Nazism is a form of totalitarianism which states that Germans are racially superior and the Nazi *führer*, or leader, is the supreme ruler. Hitler used terror and **propaganda**, or false statements, to maintain control and achieve his policies. The Gestapo, his secret police, spied on possible enemies. Anyone who opposed Hitler could be sent to a concentration camp—a type of prison camp.

Hitler set up massive public works projects to employ people. Funding was provided to private industry to create jobs. Hitler also stopped World War I reparation payments and set about re-arming Germany. Thousands of jobs were created to help build and equip the military.

War in Europe

In 1935, Mussolini seized Ethiopia in Africa. The following year, Hitler sent soldiers into the Rhineland, between Germany and France, in direct violation of the Treaty of Paris. In March 1938, Hitler took Austria. In March 1939, all of Czechoslovakia was given to the Germans to avoid potential war. Later that year in August, Hitler and Joseph Stalin, the dictator of the Soviet Union, agreed not to attack each other. This meant that Hitler did not have to worry about defending his eastern border. On September 1, 1939, Germany invaded Poland. Within two days, Great Britain and France declared war on Germany.

 Think about Social Studies

Directions: Choose the best answer to the following question.

1. One of the factors that contributed to the rise of Hitler and other European dictators was
   A. American aggression.
   B. joblessness and resentment.
   C. the economic boom of the 1920s.
   D. the failure of any nation to adopt the League of Nations.

CORE PRACTICE

Understand Author's Bias

Bias presents only one point of view or one side of an issue. Bias may be stated or unstated. A person may say that he or she supports a particular point of view. Or you can determine whether bias is present using other information. To identify bias, ask yourself the following questions:

- Is more than one point of view presented?
- Who is speaking? To what groups does he or she belong?
- Are there facts to support the point of view?
- Is any emotional language used like *all*, *never*, *no one*, *greedy*, *corrupt*, or similar words?

Use Internet resources to find propaganda from World War II. Identify the bias in the text.

World War II

By September 1940, German soldiers had overrun and seized every nation in Western Europe except Great Britain, Sweden, and Switzerland. Many Americans remembered the troubles of World War I and wanted the United States to remain neutral. These people believed in **isolationism**, that the United States should not get involved in another war in Europe.

From 1935 to 1937, Congress passed a series of Neutrality Acts. American companies could not sell weapons to nations at war. As Hitler's goals became clearer, President Franklin D. Roosevelt became alarmed. He worked with Congress to pass laws that allowed the United States to sell, lend, or lease war materials to Great Britain.

The United States Enters the War

By 1941, Hitler had added the nations of the Balkans to his German empire. In June, he then turned against Stalin and invaded the Soviet Union.

As war raged in Europe, Japan sought to destroy American naval power in the Pacific and seize the European colonies in Southeast Asia. On December 7, 1941, Japanese planes bombed the American naval base at Pearl Harbor, Hawaii. They destroyed a large part of the Pacific fleet, and, more than 3,500 military personnel were killed or wounded. The next day, President Roosevelt asked Congress for a declaration of war against Japan.

After the United States declared war on Japan, Germany then declared war on the United States. Italy, the third Axis power, also declared war. The nations fighting the Axis powers called themselves the Allies. The main Allies included the United States, France, Great Britain, and the Soviet Union.

Fighting the Axis Powers

WRITE TO LEARN

Write a journal entry from the point of view of a soldier landing on the beach at Normandy during Operation Overlord.

The Allies first decided to stop the Axis in Europe and North Africa before turning the full force of their armies and navies against Japan. In October 1942, the British defeated the Germans at the battle of El Alamein, Egypt. In November, the Allies invaded Algeria and Morocco and fought their way east.

In February 1943, the Nazi army suffered its first major defeat at the Battle of Stalingrad. In September, Italians removed Mussolini from power, but Hitler refused to accept this defeat. He ordered his soldiers to return Mussolini to power and to hold Italy. During the winter of 1943–1944, the Allies fought their way north on the Italian Peninsula. In June 1944, they took Rome. However, fighting continued in Italy until the end of the war in 1945.

The final push against Germany began with the invasion of France on D-Day, June 6, 1944. American General Dwight D. Eisenhower, the commander of Allied forces in Europe, ordered the invasion of France, known as Operation Overlord. More than 2 million Allied troops landed on the beaches of Normandy.

Over the rest of 1944 and into 1945, the Allies slowly made progress. In the spring of 1945, Germany was surrounded by Allied troops. Hitler committed suicide the last week in April, and Germany surrendered on May 7, 1945. The Allies declared May 8, 1945, V-E Day for "Victory in Europe."

The Holocaust

Adolf Hitler's hatred toward Jews began many years before World War II. By 1942, Hitler had decided on a "final solution" for ridding Germany and Europe of Jewish people. The result was the Holocaust, the genocide committed against the Jewish people by the Nazis. The Holocaust also included Poles, other Slavic peoples, Roma (also known as Gypsies), and those with mental illness or mental disabilities—anyone Hitler considered undesirable.

Governments in nations conquered by Germany helped carry out the Holocaust. Like the Germans, they arrested Jews and jammed them into railroad freight cars. The cars took these people to concentration camps in Eastern Europe, such as Auschwitz in Poland. Many died during the trip from lack of air and food.

When the prisoners arrived at the camps, the ill and weak were marched directly to the gas chambers to be put to death. The healthy were taken to barracks. German guards required them to work in war factories or on farms. Most died from starvation and exhaustion. Between 9 million and 12 million people died in the Holocaust. About 6 million were Jews.

As the Allies pushed into Germany and Poland, they found the concentration camps. Half-dead, human skeletons greeted them through barbed wire fences. Their German guards had fled. After the war, the Allies tried German and Austrian leaders for these war crimes. The message was clear. Government officials and military officers were responsible for their actions. They were not above international law.

Understand the Main Idea

The main idea is the theme or idea that a piece of writing is mostly about. The chapter title tells you the main idea of the chapter. The lesson title tells you the main idea of the lesson. Each paragraph also has a main idea. Often it will be stated in the first sentence of the paragraph. Sometimes the main idea of a paragraph is unstated. Then you have to figure out the main idea from the details in the paragraph.

Read the paragraphs in the section titled "War in the Pacific." Identify the main idea of each paragraph. Determine whether the main idea is stated or unstated.

War in the Pacific

By early 1942, the Japanese had captured European colonies in Southeast Asia and the islands in the western Pacific. Although the Allies decided to defeat Hitler first, they did not give up fighting in the Pacific. They planned a two-pronged strategy to fight the Japanese. One prong, or branch, was made up of land forces. The second prong consisted of naval forces to fight at sea.

The Allies began pushing the Japanese back. By April 1945, they were only 800 miles from Tokyo, Japan's capital. Japan's civilian leaders and Emperor Hirohito were willing to end the war. However, Japan's military leaders refused to surrender.

President Franklin Roosevelt died suddenly on April 12, 1945. Vice President Harry Truman was immediately sworn in as president. It was then that Truman learned about the atomic bomb. President Roosevelt had established a top-secret project in 1941 to develop an atomic bomb. The damage from such a bomb would be horrendous. Truman sought advice from military advisors. They thought an invasion of the Japanese islands would be costly. It would take months, and thousands of American soldiers and Japanese civilians and soldiers would be killed.

During the summer of 1945, the Allies again offered Japan a chance to surrender. Its military leaders again refused. On August 6, an American plane dropped an atomic bomb on the city of Hiroshima. Between 80,000 and 120,000 people were killed. Thousands more died from burns and radiation poisoning. The Japanese military leaders still did not surrender. A second bomb was dropped on the city of Nagasaki on August 9. Another 35,000 to 75,000 Japanese died. Japan finally surrendered on August 14, 1945. World War II was over.

Peace Agreements

Planning for peace had gone on at the same time as planning for war. The peace agreements reached at the Yalta Conference in 1945 were particularly important. The leaders agreed to

- divide Germany into four military zones and to govern them after the war;
- accept a communist government in Poland until elections could be held;
- and accept communist-backed governments in countries the Soviet Union had freed from the Nazis

Think about Social Studies

Directions: Write the numbers 1 through 4 to put these events in sequence.

_____ **1.** Japan attacks the naval base at Pearl Harbor.

_____ **2.** Germany invades the Soviet Union.

_____ **3.** The United States drops the atomic bomb on Japan.

_____ **4.** Hitler commits suicide.

Americans During the War

As the country had done in World War I, the United States prepared to fight. This meant increasing the size of the armed forces. Americans from all walks of life joined the military. Young men were drafted into service, and others volunteered. Women also signed up to serve in noncombat roles.

African Americans enlisted in the military. Initially, they were placed in segregated units and kept out of combat. African American leaders protested this segregation. President Roosevelt ordered that African Americans be trained for combat. By the end of the war, most African Americans were still serving in segregated units. However, they were often commanded by African American officers.

Latinos and Native Americans also served the country. A group of 400 Navajo, known as the Navajo Code Talkers, helped the marines use the Navajo language to send secret messages. The Japanese were never able to break the code.

Roosevelt wanted to ensure that veterans did not return to hard economic conditions after the war. In 1944, just days after D-Day, the president signed the GI Bill. The law provided veterans with money for education, loans for home purchases, and job counseling. It also provided for hospital facilities for veterans.

Japanese Internment

Japanese Americans also fought in the war. Even so, Japanese people in America and Japanese Americans suffered a grave violation of their civil rights during the war. In early 1942, the US War Department classified the West Coast as a military zone. This allowed the War Department to remove anyone considered a threat to national security.

Many officials and other Americans feared that Japanese Americans would help Japan in the war. As a result, about 120,000 Japanese and Japanese Americans were taken from the West Coast. Some were immigrants, but about two-thirds were born in the United States. Forced to leave their homes and jobs, they were sent to **internment**, or relocation, camps.

With barbed wire and guard towers, the camps were like prisons. Some families were separated once they arrived at the camps. Some Japanese Americans were killed by guards. Others became ill and died without medical care. The interned families spent most of the war in the camps.

One Japanese American named Fred Korematsu refused to leave California. He took his case all the way to the Supreme Court. In 1944, the Court ruled that the government had acted within its rights. According to the president's order, the War Department had the power to remove people from any area termed a military zone. Shortly after, however, the Court ruled that loyal citizens could not be held against their will and by 1945, Japanese Americans were released back to their homes.

 Think about Social Studies

Directions: Choose the best answer to the following question.

1. Why would the US War Department classify the West Coast as a military zone?
   A. The War Department hoped more men would enlist in the army.
   B. The War Department was concerned with the safety of citizens on the West Coast following the attack on Pearl Harbor.
   C. This allowed the War Department to forcibly remove Japanese Americans to internment camps.
   D. Because the GI Bill would offer money for education and loans for homes to people living in this area.

Employers want to hire people who can use reasoning to solve problems. Two types of reasoning are commonly used in the workplace: inductive and deductive reasoning. Inductive reasoning involves drawing a conclusion from specific information. For example, a patient at a doctor's office may have a runny nose, a fever, and a cough. The doctor might conclude from these details that the patient has a cold. Another type of reasoning is deductive reasoning. This involves working from more general ideas to specific ones. Scientists employ deductive reasoning when they use the scientific method.

Use Internet resources to read about various jobs. Cite examples of deductive and inductive reasoning you find in the job descriptions.

Vocabulary Review

Directions: Complete the sentences using the following key terms and vocabulary words.

fascism   totalitarian government   internment
isolationism   depression   propaganda

1. To influence people to believe in their ideas, governments sometimes lie or exaggerate by using

   _____.

2. US citizens who believed the United States should not be involved in the war in Europe were practicing

   _____.

3. A dictatorship in which the state is more important than individuals is _____.

4. Germany created a _____, in which Hitler controlled the politics, society, culture, and

   economy of the nation.

5. Japanese Americans from the West Coast were placed in _____ camps during the war.

6. A high period of unemployment may be an indication of a(n) _____.

Skill Review

Directions: Choose the best answer to each question.

1. Which factor contributed to the rise of the Nazi Party?

   A. the poor economy in Germany

   B. lack of American military strength

   C. Japan's attack on Pearl Harbor

   D. Mussolini's dictatorship in Italy

2. What caused the United States to enter the war?

   A. Germany's attack on the Soviet Union

   B. Great Britain's request for assistance

   C. the attack on Pearl Harbor

   D. the need for increased manufacturing of weapons

3. What was the main reason Hitler created concentration camps?

   A. Hitler had intense feelings of anti-Semitism.

   B. Hitler needed people to work on farms for no pay.

   C. Hitler did not need Jewish people to serve in his army.

   D. Hitler thought Jews would fight for the Allies.

4. Which statement best explains the reason why the United States used the atomic bomb against Japan?

   A. President Truman wanted to show Japan that the United States had a stronger military.

   B. An invasion of Japan would cost the United States thousands of lives and take months to finish.

   C. American military leaders were afraid Japan would drop an atomic bomb on the United States if the war did not end.

   D. The United States wanted to punish the Japanese for the attack on Pearl Harbor.

Skill Practice

Directions: Read the passage. Then answer the questions that follow.

Nazis created propaganda not only for Germans but also for Allied soldiers. The following is an example of a Nazi leaflet.

Five questions for the American soldier:

1. Are you certain of finding a job if you have the good luck to get back to the States safe and sound from the war?

2. Won't the best jobs be held by those who were wiser than you and avoided taking part in the war?

3. What security have you for your existence if you come back from the war sick and wounded, minus a limb or even blinded?

4. Is your family sufficiently provided for if you are one of the many who will never see America again?

5. Are your savings secure against inflation which is threatening the USA as a result of the absurdly high war loans, or will you and your family be reduced to beggars after the war?

Now, Jim, don't think and wait—life is short. You have only one chance! Escape from this bloody business.

This will conduct you safely through our lines.

1. Which phrase from the leaflet provides the best evidence of the author's bias?

   A. "Are your savings secure against inflation?"

   B. "Are you certain of finding a job?"

   C. "Don't think and wait—life is short."

   D. "This will conduct you safely through our lines."

2. What is the purpose of the pamphlet?

   A. to inform the soldiers about the poor American economy

   B. to describe to soldiers the types of injuries they may encounter

   C. to convince American soldiers to surrender and go home

   D. to encourage American soldiers to go to school after the war

Writing Practice

Directions: Imagine you have been sent to an internment camp. Write a letter to President Roosevelt describing the conditions at the camp. Explain to the president how you feel as an American citizen sent to the camp.

LESSON 4.3   The Cold War

■ LESSON OBJECTIVES

- Explain the spread of communism throughout the world
- Understand how the United States matured as a world power
- Understand how the world reacted to the Cold War

■ CORE SKILLS & PRACTICES

- Identify Implications
- Use Maps, Charts, and Graphs

Key Terms

containment
US policy to block further Communist expansion

Marshall Plan
US plan to provide aid to help Europe rebuild after WW II

NATO
organization designed to stop Soviet expansion in Europe

Truman Doctrine
US policy of aiding countries threatened by communism

Vocabulary

negotiate
to discuss something formally in order to make an agreement

refugee
a person who flees a country because of war or danger

Key Concept

After World War II, the United States and the Soviet Union began a Cold War that kept tensions high between the countries.

You may have heard of the phrase "cold shoulder." When you give someone the cold shoulder, you purposefully ignore that person because of some conflict between the two of you. Typically, tensions are high in such a situation, and one wrong move by either one of you could escalate the conflict. The United States experienced a situation similar to this called the Cold War. For several years, tensions were high between the United States and a former World War II ally.

A Broken Alliance

During World War II, President Franklin D. Roosevelt met several times with Winston Churchill, prime minister of Great Britain, and Joseph Stalin, dictator of the Soviet Union. The purpose was to plan wartime strategy and the postwar peace. However, Stalin did not share the same goals for peace as Roosevelt and Churchill. It quickly became clear that Stalin wanted to create a zone of Communist nations between the Soviet Union and the rest of Europe. Communism is a totalitarian system of government in which the state plans and controls the economy, and all goods are shared by the people.

Different Goals

During their wartime conferences, the leaders made a number of agreements about what would happen after the war. Some of the most important were made at the Yalta Conference in 1945. The three leaders agreed that Germany would be divided into four military zones once the war had ended. The United States, Great Britain, the Soviet Union, and France would each govern a zone.

The leaders also discussed what would happen in Eastern Europe. Roosevelt and Churchill insisted that Stalin hold free elections in the Soviet-occupied nations of Eastern Europe. Stalin agreed, but in the end he broke his promise. Instead, he imposed Communist governments on East Germany, Poland, Czechoslovakia, Hungary, Romania, and Bulgaria. He also helped the Communist side in a civil war in Greece and tried to take territory from Turkey.

The alliance that won World War II quickly split apart after the war. The Western Allies—including the United States and Great Britain—were on one side. These countries had democratic governments and capitalist economic systems that allowed for private property and let businesses earn profits. On the other side were the Soviet Union and the nations of Eastern Europe that it controlled. The Soviet army cut off these nations from any contact with the West. This separated Europe into two blocks of nations divided by what Winston Churchill called an "iron curtain." He also warned that Stalin would not be satisfied with controlling only Eastern Europe, but that he aimed to spread communism throughout the world.

The Soviet Union became the enemy of the United States. In 1949, it exploded its first atomic bomb. Now both the United States and the Soviet Union had nuclear weapons. The threat of nuclear war had a strong effect on each country's foreign policy.

The United Nations

One development of the postwar world that the leaders agreed to during their wartime meetings was the creation of the United Nations (UN). The UN would replace the League of Nations. Its purpose would be to negotiate disputes between nations. To **negotiate** is to discuss something formally in order to make an agreement. If an agreement could not be reached, the UN could also use force, if necessary, to stop aggressor nations. In 1945, an international conference drew up a charter, and the United Nations was founded.

A Security Council of 15 nations would be responsible for maintaining world peace. Ten seats on the council would rotate among various members of the UN, but the United Kingdom, China, France, the Soviet Union, and the United States would each have a permanent seat. To settle any disputes, these five powers had to agree. If any one of them voted against a proposed action, that action was defeated. This power proved to be an obstacle to world peace as the United States and Soviet Union clashed on many issues.

⚑ Think about Social Studies

Directions: Identify each statement as applying to the Soviet Union, Great Britain, or United States by writing the name of the country in the space provided.

_____ 1. Winston Churchill was prime minister.

_____ 2. This country had a totalitarian government.

_____ 3. Joseph Stalin was the leader of this Communist country.

_____ 4. Great Britain was an ally of this country.

The West Responds to Communism

In the years immediately after World War II, countries in Western Europe looked to the United States for leadership. The British people were exhausted after the war. Many of their cities, factories, and shipyards had been badly damaged by German bombs. Much of France also lay in ruins, and the same was true of other countries as well. The only nation with the energy and resources to oppose Soviet expansion was the United States.

Identify Implications

An implication is a suggestion. Writers often imply something will happen rather than directly stating it. As a reader, you must figure out what the writer is suggesting. To do this, use your own knowledge as well as information from the text.

As you read the section "A Broken Alliance," think about the implications the writer is making. What caused the alliance between the United States and the Soviet Union to break down? When the writer states, "the Soviet Union became the enemy of the United States." What might this mean for the people of the United States?

Use Maps, Charts, and Graphs

During the Cold War, the Soviet Union expanded the areas under Communist control. The United States provided aid to countries to prevent the further spread of communism. A map of Cold War countries can help you visualize the conflict. Follow these steps to answer the questions below:

- Read the title of the map. What is it about?
- Read the map key. What does each color stand for?
- Look at the placement of color on the map.
- Reread the explanation for each color to be sure you understand what it shows.

Examine the map on this page. Identify the countries under Communist control and those that were members of NATO. Explain the importance of West Germany to the Soviet Union and to the rest of Europe. Why might the Soviet Union and NATO both want control of West Germany?

In 1947, President Harry S. Truman promised to aid nations struggling to remain democratic. In a message to Congress, he asked for $400 million. The aid helped Turkey refuse Soviet demands. It also kept Greek Communists from coming to power. This new policy of providing aid to countries threatened by communism was called the **Truman Doctrine**.

President Truman also supported the **Marshall Plan**, which provided economic aid to help Europe rebuild. The plan provided $13 billion to Western Europe. They used the money to rebuild their cities and get their capitalist economies growing again. Aid was offered to Stalin for the Soviet Union, but he rejected it.

Truman's Containment Policy

The goal of the Truman Doctrine and the Marshall Plan was **containment**. President Truman adopted this policy as a way to block further Communist expansion. The United States would provide money, equipment, weapons, and military support to nations threatened by communism.

In 1948, a crisis arose in Berlin, the former capital of Germany. Like Germany itself, Berlin—deep in Communist East Germany—had been divided into western-controlled zones and a Soviet-controlled zone. When Great Britain, France, and the United States united their three zones of West Germany, Stalin responded with a blockade of Berlin. No car, train, or boat was allowed to enter the West Berlin zones. President Truman then launched the Berlin Airlift. For ten months, American and British planes airlifted millions of tons of supplies to West Berliners. In May 1949, Stalin finally ended the blockade.

Europe in 1952

- ☐ Communist control
- ☐ Divided nation
- ☐ NATO member
- ☐ Neutral nation

In 1949, the United States and 11 European nations formed a new military alliance. Known as the North Atlantic Treaty Organization (**NATO**), it was designed to stop Soviet expansion in Europe. In response, the Soviet Union and seven communist nations formed the Warsaw Pact in 1955. They pledged that an attack against one was an attack against all.

The United States's policy of containment stopped the expansion of communism in Europe. It also kept the United States and the Soviet Union from fighting each other. Though the two countries were bitter rivals for power and influence, they never fought. For that reason, their conflict is called the Cold War. However, these great powers continued to support their democratic or Communist allies. Containment led to an uneasy peace.

Part of the Cold War was an arms race. Both the United States and the Soviet Union competed to build more nuclear bombs and missiles to carry them.

The Berlin Wall

In June 1961, Nikita Khrushchev tried another tactic to oppose the United States. He had become premier, or leader, of the Soviet Union in 1958. He insisted that the United States, France, and Great Britain sign a peace treaty with East Germany. The treaty would end the division of Berlin, with all four zones joined together—under the control of Communist East Germany. Khrushchev wanted to stop East Germans from escaping through West Berlin. Each week, about 4,000 people fled East Germany through West Berlin.

John Kennedy, the newly elected US president, refused Khrushchev's demands. Instead the president asked Congress for three billion dollars more in defense spending. He sent more troops to West Berlin. He called to active duty some reserve units of the army. He also asked for money to build bomb shelters across the United States. These were in case of a nuclear attack by the Soviets.

The crisis ended in August 1961. Khrushchev had a wall built between East and West Berlin. The wall was made of concrete, steel, and barbed wire. East German soldiers patrolled it 24 hours a day. The Berlin Wall stopped the large-scale flow of East Germans to the western zones. Still, some people continued to climb over the wall to democratic West Berlin.

 Think about Social Studies

Directions: Choose the best answer to the following questions.

1. What method did President Truman use to "fight" communism?
   A. arms race
   B. containment
   C. Warsaw Pact
   D. negotiation

2. How did the Soviets respond to the creation of NATO?
   A. It led the Soviets and other communist nations to form the Warsaw Pact.
   B. It led to the creation of the Berlin Wall.
   C. They responded by blockading Berlin.
   D. They responded by invading East Germany.

Communism Outside of Europe

In the 1950s, the island nation of Cuba faced huge problems. Its economy was based on sugar plantations, owned mostly by companies in the United States. American support helped keep Fulgencio Batista, a harsh dictator, in power. The Cuban people were generally poor, many lived in shacks, and most lacked health care.

The Cuban Revolution

A young lawyer named Fidel Castro led a revolt that succeeded in overthrowing Batista on January 1, 1959. His revolution was successful, and Castro set up a Communist government. He also began taking over American-owned businesses and property. Thousands of Cubans fled rather than live under communism. Most of the refugees came to the United States. A **refugee** is a person who flees his or her own country because of war or other danger.

The US Central Intelligence Agency (CIA) came up with a plan to remove Castro from power. First it would use Cuban exiles who had fled the island when Castro came to power to invade Cuba. Then, the CIA thought, Cubans who did not support the Revolution would join the exiles and together they would overthrow Castro. President Kennedy was unsure of the plan. Military advisers and the CIA, however, were sure it would work.

President Kennedy agreed to the plan but with one important change. The United States would give the exiles weapons and ships but not supply air support. There would be no shelling of Castro's soldiers by bombers. About 1,500 exiles landed in Cuba on April 17, 1961. The Bay of Pigs invasion, however, was a disaster. Castro's forces killed or captured the invaders. No rebellion against Castro occurred.

The Cuban Missile Crisis

The crisis with Cuba continued. The United States regularly sent spy planes over Cuba. During the summer of 1962, the spy cameras began showing pictures of military construction. By October, it was clear that the Soviets had built secret nuclear missile bases in Cuba that were capable of reaching many major American cities.

On October 22, 1962, President Kennedy announced that the Soviets had placed long-range missiles in Cuba. More missiles were on their way to Cuba on Soviet ships.

Kennedy ordered a military blockade around Cuba. US warships were to keep the Soviet ships from reaching Cuba. If any missiles were fired from Cuba, the United States would launch a nuclear attack against the Soviet Union.

Americans feared an attack would happen at any time. Secret letters went back and forth between Kennedy and Khrushchev to resolve the crisis. Finally, Kennedy agreed not to invade Cuba. He also agreed to remove US missiles from Turkey, which was on the Soviet border. Khrushchev, in turn, agreed to remove the missiles from Cuba.

The Cuban missile crisis scared Americans. Never had the threat of a nuclear attack been so close, or so real. A special phone line, called the hot line, was set up between the president and the Soviet premier. In case of a future crisis, they could reach each other directly and quickly.

The Cuban Missile Crisis: October 14–28, 1962

MIG Jet bomber range=800 mi.
Medium ballistic missile range=1,500 mi.
Intermediate ballistic missile range=2,500 mi.

0 mi   1000
0 km   1000
Miller projection

The Vietnam War was and remains a controversial conflict. Many Americans did not agree with President Johnson and did not believe the United States should have entered the war. Use reputable Internet resources to gather more details about why the United States entered the war. Then find information about antiwar demonstrations during the Vietnam War. After completing your research, choose a position: either for or against Johnson's decision to fight in Vietnam. Then create a slide show that depicts your findings and supports your position.

WRITE TO LEARN

Read the text about the spread of communism in the world. Write a paragraph about how this spread led to fear of communism in the United States.

The Vietnam War

The period after World War II was marked by decolonization, the process by which colonies become independent nations. People in Africa and many parts of Asia no longer accepted living in colonies ruled by a European government. India and Pakistan were among the first to win independence. One of the longest struggles took place in Vietnam, which had been under French control.

In 1945, Ho Chi Minh led communist forces in a guerilla war against the French. Defeated militarily, the French granted independence to Vietnam. But Vietnam was partitioned in two, with a Communist controlled north and a non-Communist controlled south.

Both Presidents Eisenhower and Kennedy supported South Vietnam. In 1965, President Lyndon B. Johnson increased the number of American troops in Vietnam. After years of bitter fighting, the United States finally withdrew its combat troops from Vietnam in 1973. More than 58,000 American soldiers were killed and 300,000 were wounded during the war. In 1975, North Vietnam took over South Vietnam, creating one Communist nation.

 Think about Social Studies

Directions: Study the map above. Choose the best answer to the following question.

1. Which cities are located within the medium ballistic missile range?

   A. Chicago and New York   **C.** New York and Los Angeles

   B. Los Angeles and Chicago   **D.** Miami and Los Angeles

Vocabulary Review

Directions: Complete the sentences using the following key terms and vocabulary words.

NATO   Truman Doctrine   negotiate
containment   Marshall Plan   refugees

1. After Fidel Castro took control of Cuba, many Cuban _____ fled to the United States.

2. The policy of providing aid to countries threatened by communism was the _____.

3. The United States and its allies formed _____ to stop Soviet expansion in Europe.

4. President Truman supported the _____, which provided economic aid to help Europe rebuild after World War II.

5. The United States adopted a policy of _____ in an effort to block the spread of communism.

6. Kennedy and Khrushchev worked together to _____ an agreement to settle the Cuban Missile Crisis.

Skill Review

Directions: Choose the best answer to each question.

1. Examine the map on page 119. Which US city would provide the most logical entry point for Cubans fleeing Castro's government?

   A. Chicago

   B. Los Angeles

   C. Miami

   D. New York

2. Why did the Soviet Union construct the Berlin Wall?

   A. to prevent citizens in East Germany from fleeing the Communist country

   B. to prevent citizens of West Germany from entering East Germany

   C. to keep US military troops from attacking East Germany

   D. to block the spread of communism in Europe

3. Why might people in Europe have worried about a missile strike on US soil during the Cuban missile crisis?

   A. A missile strike would create massive destruction in the United States.

   B. The United States would attack Europe if it was bombed by the Soviets.

   C. A missile strike against the United States would likely cause another world war.

   D. Fidel Castro would gain power in the United States after a missile strike.

4. Why did the United Nations have difficulty settling disputes?

   A. China did not play a major role in world affairs.

   B. The Soviet Union and the United States could not agree on solutions to conflicts.

   C. The Soviet Union did not participate in the UN.

   D. The UN and NATO could not agree on issues related to communism.

Skill Practice

Directions: Read the passage. Then answer the questions that follow.

Cuban Missile Crisis Address to the Nation

On the night of October 22, 1962, President Kennedy made this statement to the American people regarding the Soviet missiles in Cuba:

Good evening, my fellow citizens:

This Government, as promised, has maintained the closest surveillance of the Soviet military buildup on the island of Cuba. Within the past week, unmistakable evidence has established the fact that a series of offensive missile sites is now in preparation on that imprisoned island. The purpose of these bases can be none other than to provide a nuclear strike capability against the Western Hemisphere. . . .

The 1930's taught us a clear lesson: aggressive conduct, if allowed to go unchecked and unchallenged, ultimately leads to war. This nation is opposed to war. We are also true to our word. Our unswerving objective, therefore, must be to prevent the use of these missiles against this or any other country, and to secure their withdrawal or elimination from the Western Hemisphere.

Our policy has been one of patience and restraint, as befits a peaceful and powerful nation which leads a worldwide alliance. We have been determined not to be diverted from our central concerns by mere irritants and fanatics. But now further action is required, and it is under way; and these actions may only be the beginning. We will not prematurely or unnecessarily risk the costs of worldwide nuclear war in which even the fruits of victory would be ashes in our mouth; but neither will we shrink from that risk at any time it must be faced.

1. What is President Kennedy implying in his last sentence?
    A. The United States will not participate in another world war.
    B. The United States cannot afford another world war.
    C. The United States will continue on a course of patience and restraint.
    D. The United States will go to war if the Soviets do not withdraw.

2. President Kennedy states that the 1930s taught the United States a clear lesson: "aggressive conduct, if allowed to go unchecked and unchallenged, ultimately leads to war." What is he comparing the Soviet spread of communism to?
    A. the spread of communism in Vietnam
    B. the rise of Hitler and World War II
    C. the Confederates and the Civil War
    D. Great Britain and the American Revolution

Writing Practice

Directions: Imagine you were an American living in October 1962 who heard President Kennedy's speech to the people of the United States. Write a letter to the president about the Cuban missile crisis. Do you agree with his tough stand? Or does it frighten you? Include evidence and reasons to support your position.

LESSON 4.4   Societal Changes

LESSON OBJECTIVES

- Understand domestic issues in the second half of the twentieth century
- Explain US politics and the scandals that took place
- Understand how communism affected US foreign policy

CORE SKILLS & PRACTICES

- Integrate Concepts
- Paraphrase Information

Key Terms

détente
a relaxing of tensions

Great Society
a set of domestic policies which helped those in need

impeach
to charge a public official with misconduct with the intent to potentially remove from office

poverty line
the minimum income that a family of four needs to live

Vocabulary

media
methods of communication used to reach the public

scandal
an event that is legally or morally wrong

Key Concept

During the second half of the twentieth century, the United States struggled with scandals at home and communism abroad.

What makes a "Great Society"? Good jobs for everyone? The opportunity to go to college? Owning a home? People define a great society differently. Even the president has ideas about what makes a great society. Sometimes presidents implement policies that affect people's daily lives in an effort to achieve a society that is good for all people of the nation.

The Great Society

By 1963, the Kennedy administration had brought new hope and ideals to the American people. The economy was strong. The president's ideas and visions were exciting. However, history was about to be changed forever. On November 22, 1963, President Kennedy was shot while riding through Dallas, Texas, in an open car. After the assassination, Lyndon B. Johnson, the vice president, was sworn in as president.

Building on the public sympathy after the assassination, President Johnson was able to show the public his ideas for the future. President Johnson believed the government had a responsibility to help those in need. He presented his ideas to the American people in a set of policies known as the **Great Society**. The programs fell generally into four areas—health and welfare, housing, education, and consumer and environmental protection.

The War on Poverty

President Johnson's first opportunity came with his State of the Union speech in January 1964. He declared an "unconditional war on poverty" and asked for funding to help those living at or below the **poverty line**. This is the minimum income that the government believes a family of four needs to live adequately.

Within months, Congress passed the Economic Opportunity Act. The act set up the Office of Economic Opportunity (OEO). This agency managed ten new programs to aid the poor. The goal of all of them was to fight the causes of poverty. One of these programs, VISTA, helped poor people improve their lives in cities, rural areas, and Native American reservations. The Job Corps helped high-school dropouts with job training and counseling. The Community Action Program gave poor people a greater voice in government decisions affecting their neighborhoods.

Civil Rights

In addition to his other programs, President Johnson also promoted legislation to end racial segregation. The Civil Rights Act of 1964 was the strongest civil rights law the nation had ever had. Discrimination was now against the law in any public location and during voting registration. The Civil Rights Act also set up the Equal Employment Opportunity Commission (EEOC). Its job was to investigate charges of discrimination in the workplace.

In March of 1965, President Johnson proposed a sweeping Voting Rights Act. The law gave federal officials the power to register African Americans in districts where local officials were keeping them from voting. All laws that discriminated against African Americans, such as literacy tests, were banned. Congress acted swiftly and passed the bill.

The Vietnam War

The conflict in Vietnam was building when President Johnson took office. The president ordered bombing raids on North Vietnam and sent US troops to South Vietnam to help them fight the communists.

The antiwar movement in the United States had been growing slowly. The ability of the Viet Cong to continue fighting wherever and whenever they wanted stunned Americans. US troops were not trained to fight a guerrilla war. The nightly TV news showed high-level US officials describing how well the war was going. The reports from troops and officials on the ground in South Vietnam were vastly different. The same news programs showed more and more body bags coming home. Many in the nation stopped believing what the government said.

In time, the public became bitterly divided. Many antiwar activists were young people, especially white, middle-class college students. They took to the streets in large, loud antiwar demonstrations. Antiwar protestors were shown on television, being beaten by police.

 Think about Social Studies

Directions: Identify the following statement as fact or opinion.

1. At the end of the Vietnam War, South Korea surrendered to the North and came under Communist control.

The Nixon Administration

In March 1968, President Johnson said he would not run for reelection. Richard Nixon, the Republican nominee, won the election. President Nixon set out to end President Johnson's social programs. He said they were too costly and gave the federal government too much power over people's lives. The president called his policies New Federalism. Under New Federalism, President Nixon planned to return more power and more tax money to the states.

Media Literacy

Media is a term used to describe methods of communication used to reach large masses of the public. Mass media includes newspapers, television, and the Internet. Mass media has an effect on people's opinions. During the Vietnam War, mass media influenced the American public's opinion about the war. Use the Internet to research the media's role in the anti-war movement. Study the images of the war in newspapers, in magazines, and on television. Select three images that you feel most powerfully influenced people's opinions of the war. Create a multimedia presentation explaining the effect these images had on the American public.

Integrate Concepts Presented in Different Ways

You can present information in several ways. Tables are good tools to use to sort and organize information. To make a table, follow these steps:

1. Decide on the categories you need to use to sort the information.

2. Create the form for your table. You will need a column for each category and a row for each topic you want to include under each category.

3. Find the information to complete your table and fill in the table. Sometimes, you might not find information for every box in every row.

Create a table about the costs of the Vietnam War. Use the Internet to find information about the number of soldiers killed or wounded and the financial costs of the war. Be sure to label your columns and rows and add a title for your table.

Nixon also promised to end the war. In 1973, the Vietnam War ended with the Paris Peace Accord. Many Americans considered the war a major defeat for the United States. Many also thought it was a war that the nation should not have entered.

The Watergate Scandal

President Nixon had several triumphs while he was president. However, many people remember him for his downfall, which came to be known as the Watergate Scandal. A **scandal** is an event that is upsetting because it is legally or morally wrong. The year 1972 was a presidential election year. The president and his advisors wanted to find out as much as they could about the Democratic Party's election plans. The Democratic National Committee headquarters was in the Watergate, a building in downtown Washington, D.C. On June 17, 1972, five men broke into the offices to find the Democrats' election plans. The men were caught and arrested.

The Senate began an investigation. Rather than perjure themselves by lying under oath, some officials talked. One official testified that the president secretly taped all conversations in his office. Congress demanded the tapes. The president eventually handed over the written transcripts of the tapes. The president's role in the break-in was apparent.

The House Judiciary Committee voted to **impeach** the president, or charge a public official with misconduct with the intent to potentially remove from office. Before the articles could be passed in the House of Representatives, and to avoid further disgrace, Richard Nixon resigned the presidency on August 9, 1974. He was the first president in US history to resign. His vice president, Gerald Ford, was sworn in as president.

 Think about Social Studies

Directions: Choose the best answer to the following question.

1. Based on context clues, what is the meaning of *resign*?
   A. to claim, or confiscate
   B. to step down or vacate
   C. to safeguard or protect
   D. to accept that something is unavoidable

Communism in China and the Soviet Union

Though the Watergate scandal damaged Nixon's reputation, his contributions to international policy helped the United States through the Cold War. Throughout his career, President Nixon had been a strong anticommunist. However, in 1971 he changed his views and the nation's policy. President Nixon adopted what became known as **détente**. This means a relaxing of tensions. He realized that it was more important to avoid nuclear war than to take a hard line against Communists. As part of détente, the United States in 1971 agreed to allow the People's Republic of China to take the seat reserved for China at the United Nations. The next year, the president visited China, ending twenty-five years of Cold War silence. The goal was to begin communication between the two nations. The United States also lifted limits on trade and travel with the People's Republic of China.

In writing reports, you often need to paraphrase what you have read. When you paraphrase, be careful not to write word for word what you have read. Use your own words and keep the important details as well as the main idea. A paraphrase may be about the same length as the original. To paraphrase, remember to:

• state the main idea

• include all important details

• make it as long as needed

Read the information in the text about Nixon's relations with China. Follow the steps to paraphrase the content in your own words.

While President Nixon hoped to improve relations with China, his policy also had another goal. By becoming friendly with China, he hoped to force the Soviet Union to be less threatening. After World War II, China and the Soviet Union were allies. However, they soon became rivals for world power. Their shared border also was a trouble spot. President Nixon hoped to play the two nations against each other.

Détente was working with the Soviet Union, too. In 1972, President Nixon and Leonid Brezhnev, head of the Soviet Union, signed the Strategic Arms Limitation Treaty (SALT). The treaty froze the production of long-range missiles that could be used for attack. They also agreed to ease trade barriers.

During Nixon's presidency, the Soviet Union maintained the Berlin Wall. Almost 20 years later, Mikhail Gorbachev, the Soviet leader who came to power in 1985, began to allow greater freedom. He changed the Soviet policy by refusing to intervene militarily in the affairs of satellite nations. This led to a greater freedom of movement for people living in Communist-controlled nations. Soon, a new government had been established in East Germany. The Berlin Wall came down in 1989, and a united Germany was formed in 1989.

Democracy in other Eastern European nations followed. Poland became the first satellite nation to hold democratic elections. Bulgaria and Hungary followed. Gorbachev's reforms helped to dissolve the Soviet Union and create a new Russia.

WRITE TO LEARN

Pick one of the programs from the Great Society and explain how it was intended to change a condition in society.

🚩 **Think about Social Studies**

Directions: Write the numbers 1–4 to order these events in sequence.

_____ **1.** A united Germany is formed.

_____ **2.** President Nixon travels to China.

_____ **3.** The Strategic Arms Limitation Treaty is signed.

_____ **4.** The Berlin Wall comes down.

Vocabulary Review

Directions: Complete the sentences using the following key terms and vocabulary words.

media   scandal   Great Society
détente   impeach   poverty line

1. President Johnson implemented a set of policies called the _____ that helped those in need.

2. The House Judiciary Committee voted to _____ President Nixon.

3. President Nixon established a policy of _____, which relaxed tensions with communist China.

4. An event that is legally and morally wrong and upsets people is known as a(n) _____ .

5. Newspapers, television, and the Internet are types of _____ that can influence large masses of the public.

6. The minimum income that the government believes a family of four needs to live adequately is known as the _____.

Skill Review

Directions: Choose the best answer to each question.

1. How did Americans' opinions of the Vietnam War differ from the opinions of US government officials?

   A. Americans approved of the war but President Nixon did not.

   B. Americans thought the United States was winning the war.

   C. Americans disapproved of the war, even though officials said it was going well.

   D. Americans believed the president should be impeached for his policies in Vietnam.

2. How did the Voting Rights Act affect African Americans?

   A. More African Americans became registered to vote.

   B. African Americans were given the constitutional right to vote.

   C. African Americans had to pass literacy tests to vote.

   D. Fewer African Americans were allowed to take literacy tests.

3. What was the purpose of Nixon's détente policy?

   A. Nixon wanted to increase trade with China and the Soviet Union.

   B. The president wanted to ease tensions with communist nations to avoid war.

   C. The president wanted to become an ally to China to fight the Soviet Union.

   D. The United States wanted to settle the border of China and the Soviet Union.

4. What can you conclude about Mikhail Gorbachev's policy to stay out of the affairs of satellite nations?

   A. All satellite nations will remain communist countries.

   B. Gorbachev will enforce communism in satellite nations.

   C. Fewer satellite nations will have communist governments.

   D. The Soviet Union will go to war with the satellite nations.

Skill Practice

Directions: Read the passage. Then answer the questions that follow.

The Effects of Policy on the US Economy

The Great Society and the Vietnam War hurt the US economy. Businesses laid off workers and some even closed. To help the economy, President Nixon cut taxes and increased government spending. The economy began to improve. By the time Gerald Ford was sworn in as president in 1974, the economy had slowed again. Inflation, the sharp rise in prices, had become a huge problem. He asked businesses to limit increases in wages and prices. He also asked the public to conserve energy. The high price of fuel was feeding inflation. The president then cut government spending. Nothing worked. In 1976, Jimmy Carter was elected president. In many ways, the election of 1976 was a vote against Ford's failed economic policies.

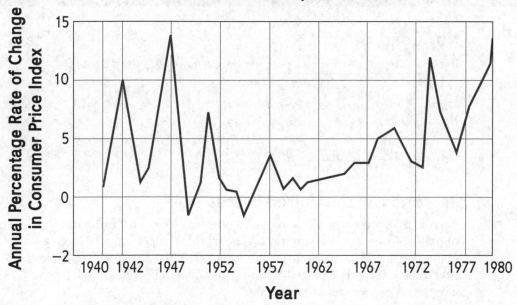

Rate of Inflation, 1940–1980

Source: U.S. Bureau of the Census

1. Based on this graph, what can you conclude about President Carter's economic policies?

   A. President Carter's policies reduced inflation and improved the economy.

   B. President Carter's policies decreased inflation, workers' wages, and the price of goods.

   C. President Carter's policies failed, which resulted in rising inflation.

   D. President Carter's policies succeeded in improving the US economy.

2. Which statement best paraphrases the information in the passage?

   A. Despite the efforts of three presidents, the US economy did not grow in the 1970s.

   B. President Ford was unable to succeed in building the US economy.

   C. The American people were frustrated with the economy in the 1970s.

   D. The rising costs of fuel and wages caused a rise in US inflation.

Writing Practice

Directions: President Nixon was a controversial president. Do you believe he was a good president? Write an essay answering that question. Support your answer with evidence from the text.

LESSON 4.5   Foreign Policy in the 21st Century

LESSON OBJECTIVES

- Understand the events of the 9/11 terrorist attack
- Understand how the 9/11 terrorist attack affected US foreign policy
- Explain how the world reacted to the war on terror

CORE SKILLS & PRACTICES

- Conduct Research Projects
- Evaluate Evidence

Key Terms

terrorism
political strategy that uses violence against people or property to achieve a goal

militants
people who use violence to achieve their goals

foreign policy
the principles used to guide interaction with other nations

insurgents
rebels

Vocabulary

embassy
a building that houses an ambassador and other representatives

conduct
perform

Key Concept

In the first decade of the twenty-first century, the United States experienced a terrorist attack that reshaped government and policies.

Think of a time when you suffered a great loss. Do you remember that time well? How does that loss affect you today? Many Americans can tell you where they were on the morning of September 11, 2001. On that day, the United States suffered a great loss that continues to affect its people and its foreign policy.

Terrorism in the United States

Terrorists, people who use force or the threat of force to frighten their opponents, operate in all regions of the world. They attempt to force a change in government by threats or violence. This strategy is known as **terrorism**. Terrorists have different goals. The following are the four main categories of terrorist organizations:

1. nationalist groups who want to create their own nations
2. urban guerrillas (independent soldiers) who want to overthrow the government in power
3. Radical Islamic **militants**, people who use violence to achieve their goals, who want to create a nation of Palestine
4. Radical Islamic militants who are fighting Western, especially US, influences in the Middle East

The US State Department lists 37 major terrorist organizations around the world. There are other smaller groups as well. These terrorist groups use suicide bombing, airplane hijacking, kidnapping, car bombing, and assassination as weapons of terror.

Countries all around the world have suffered terrorist attacks. The United States has been targeted by terrorists several times. In 1993, six people died when terrorists set off a truck bomb in the garage of the World Trade Center in New York City. In 1998, terrorists bombed US embassies in Kenya and Tanzania. An **embassy** is a building that houses an ambassador and other representatives of a country. More than 200 people died. Two years later, the USS *Cole* was bombed in the port of Yemen. Seventeen US sailors were killed and 39 were injured.

Bri Rodriguez/FEMA News Photo

The Middle-Eastern terrorist group known as al-Qaeda was linked to both the attack on the USS *Cole* and the US embassy. Al-Qaeda is a network of radical Islamic fundamentalists who use terrorism to advance their cause. The vast majority of the world's 1 billion Muslims, or followers of Islam, do not support terrorism. Muslim fundamentalists call for a return to a society strictly based on Islamic teachings. To many such people, Western culture undermines traditional Muslim values. Another factor that creates strong anti-American feeling is US support for Israel. The few Muslims who favor bin Laden's methods believe the need to create a pure Muslim society calls for drastic acts.

The leader of al-Qaeda, Osama bin Laden, was from a wealthy family in Saudi Arabia. In the 1980s, he fought in Afghanistan against the Soviets. After the Soviets left Afghanistan, bin Laden organized al-Qaeda. His goal was to force Westerners out of the Middle East. He was particularly angered by US troops stationed in Saudi Arabia. The United States had stationed troops there during the Persian Gulf War from 1990 to 1991. After the war, US forces remained in Saudi Arabia.

The Attacks of 9/11

The attack of September 11, 2001, was the result of several years of planning. Nineteen members of al-Qaeda hijacked four airplanes filled with passengers. Two planes were flown into the World Trade Center towers in New York City, and one into the Pentagon, the US military headquarters in Washington, D.C. Passengers on the fourth plane learned from cell phone calls about the other attacks. They put up strong resistance, and the hijackers crashed the plane into the ground in Pennsylvania. Government officials believe it had been headed for either the Capitol or the White House in Washington, D.C. More than 3,000 people died in these attacks.

President George W. Bush reacted strongly and quickly. Osama bin Laden operated out of Afghanistan. He had found a safe place under the

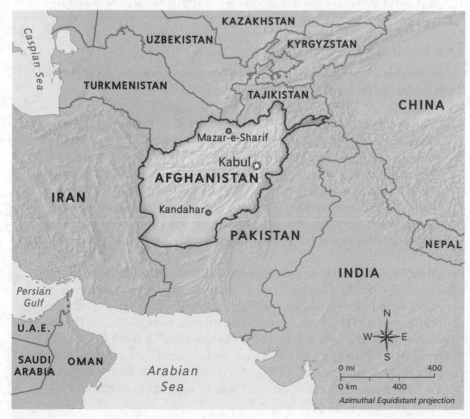

The Middle East has been an area of conflict for hundreds, if not thousands of years. In 1948, Israel was founded, and militant groups have been attacking Israel since the 1980s. Their aim is to establish an independent nation of Palestine. Use Internet and library resources to **conduct**, or perform, research into the Israel-Palestine conflict. In particular, find out the role the United States has played in the region. Create a video documentary of your findings and present it to your class.

fundamentalist government of the Taliban. The Taliban had come to power after the Soviet Union withdrew from Afghanistan. Within a month, the United States launched a war against Afghanistan. Three months later, the Taliban government was overthrown. A new pro-Western government was set up. The United States and several other nations sent troops to Afghanistan as peacekeepers.

At home, the president proposed a new Department of Homeland Security. It combined a number of existing agencies and duties. The goal was to better coordinate the nation's security to prevent another terrorist attack.

The president also signed the USA Patriot Act into law. The law allows the United States government to:

- detain foreigners who are suspected of terrorism for seven days without charging them with a crime.
- monitor e-mail and Internet use and tap telephones of suspects.
- make search warrants valid across state lines.
- order United States banks to investigate sources of large foreign bank accounts.
- prosecute terrorist crimes without any limitations or time restrictions.

 Think about Social Studies

Directions: Use the map on page 129 to answer the following question.

1. Which countries border Afghanistan?
   A. Iran, Turkmenistan, Uzbekistan, and Oman
   B. Iran, India, Kazakhstan, Kyrgyzstan, and Tajikistan
   C. Iran, Turkmenistan, Uzbekistan, Tajikistan, and Pakistan
   D. Iran, Turkmenistan, Uzbekistan, Tajikistan, and Saudi Arabia

The Global War on Terror

On September 20, 2001, in an address to the nation and the world, President Bush declared the war on terror.

"The enemy of America is not our many Muslim friends. It is not our many Arab friends. Our enemy is a radical network of terrorists and every government that supports them. . . . This is not just America's fight. And what is at stake is not just America's freedom. This is the world's fight, this is civilization's fight, this is the fight of all who believe in progress and pluralism, tolerance and freedom. We ask every nation to join us. We will ask and we will need the help of police forces, intelligence service, and banking systems around the world."

President Bush's speech was an appeal to allies in the fight against terrorism. The North Atlantic Treaty Organization (NATO) responded by invoking, or using, Article 5 of the Washington Treaty. Article 5 states that an attack on a NATO ally is an attack on all members of NATO. This was the first time in history Article 5 had been invoked. On October 9, 2001, NATO declared that forces from its member nations would take military action in support of the United States. Led by NATO allies, these forces included troops from many nations. Their goal was to remove al-Qaeda and the Taliban from Afghanistan.

The United Nations (UN) also responded. It passed Resolution 1373. This resolution requires UN member nations to act to end terrorism. UN members must deny all forms of support to terrorist groups. They cannot harbor, or safely keep, them in their territory. They also must share information about terrorists with other governments.

The Iraq War

By 2002, President Bush had shifted the foreign policy focus to Iraq. **Foreign policy** is the principles a nation uses to guide its interactions with other nations. Years earlier Saddam Hussein had agreed to destroy Iraq's weapons of mass destruction, or WMD. WMD include nuclear, chemical, and biological weapons. The UN sent weapons inspectors to Iraq to look for weapons, but Hussein refused to let UN inspectors into Iraq. He declared that he had no WMD.

The United States and Great Britain believed that Iraq had WMD. The UN refused to go to war with Iraq. In October 2002, Congress voted to allow the president to use force to end the Iraqi weapons program and remove Hussein from power. President Bush ordered the attack. Within weeks, US and British forces captured Baghdad, the capital of Iraq. Inspectors were sent to look for the weapons. No weapons were found.

Although major combat operations ended quickly, the fighting did not stop right away. **Insurgents**, or rebels, began to appear. Some were rival groups who fought one another as well as US forces. Others were loyal to the former dictator. Foreign fighters also entered Iraq to join in the insurgency. More US troops died during the insurgency than during the brief war which lasted less than a month. Saddam fled into hiding, but was captured later that year and put on trial for crimes against humanity. As violence began to decline in Iraq, the United States was able to establish a new embassy in Baghdad in January 2009.

The Election of 2008

President Bush's second term was over at the end of 2008. Frustrated with the ongoing war in Iraq, Americans elected Barack Obama as president in 2008. President Obama promised to remove all US troops from Iraq. This was finally accomplished in late 2011. However, troops remained in Afghanistan. There they searched for Osama bin Laden and fought the Taliban. On May 2, 2011, US forces attacked a compound in Pakistan, where bin Laden was believed to be hiding. The al-Qaeda leader was killed.

 Think about Social Studies

Directions: Choose the answer that completes each statement.

1. In his speech, President Bush declared (Saudi Arabia, terrorists) as an enemy.
2. Members of (the UN, NATO) sent troops to Afghanistan to find and capture bin Laden.
3. President Bush ordered an attack on (Iraq, Afghanistan) to remove Saddam Hussein from power.

Evaluate Evidence

Authors often try to influence readers. To do so, authors make claims, or declare things to be true. Unsupported claims are those that cannot be proved as fact. Often these claims are emotionally charged. That is, they bring out feelings in the reader. Like authors, speakers often try to influence others through speeches. Use the Internet to research speeches given by government leaders after the September 11 attacks. Identify the unsupported claims in the speeches. Then identify the emotional words the speaker uses.

WRITE TO LEARN

The United States supported groups who fought the Soviets in Afghanistan in the 1980s. Research the roles of both Osama bin Laden and the United States in that conflict. Write a summary of your findings.

Vocabulary Review

Directions: Complete the sentences using the following key terms and vocabulary words.

foreign policy   **terrorism**   **embassy**
conduct   **militants**   **insurgents**

1. Some Islamic fundamentalists are _____ who use violence to achieve their goals.

2. Terrorists often _____ research on the targets of their violence.

3. A(n) _____ is a building in another country that houses an ambassador.

4. After major combat operations ended in Iraq, US troops had to fight _____ .

5. The principles a nation uses to guide its interactions with other nations is called _____ .

6. The goal of _____ is to force a change in society by using violence.

Skill Review

Directions: Choose the best answer to each question.

1. What was the purpose of President Bush's speech on September 20, 2011?

   A. to declare war on Afghanistan

   B. to inform the nation of the September 11 attacks

   C. to convince other countries to fight against terrorism

   D. to explain the effects of terrorism

2. How did the UN respond to claims of WMD in Iraq?

   A. They sent weapons inspectors to Iraq but did not declare war on the nation.

   B. They refused to declare war or send weapons inspectors to Iraq.

   C. They believed President Bush and assisted the United States in war.

   D. They adopted a resolution stating that Iraq was an enemy of the UN.

3. How did the September 11 attacks affect US foreign policy?

   A. The United States stated it would take over countries that harbored terrorists.

   B. The United States decided to capture all dictators who harbor terrorists.

   C. The United States declared it would take action against any country that supports terrorists.

   D. The United States took the position of international peacekeeper in countries that suffer terrorist attacks.

4. According to the text, what was the major challenge to US troops in Iraq?

   A. capturing bin Laden

   B. fighting the insurgency

   C. killing Saddam Hussein

   D. decreasing terrorism

Skill Practice

Directions: Read the passage. Then answer the questions that follow.

Excerpt from President Obama's Speech on Terrorism

May 23, 2013

(1) With the collapse of the Berlin Wall, a new dawn of democracy took hold abroad, and a decade of peace and prosperity arrived here at home. (2) And for a moment, it seemed the 21st century would be a tranquil time. (3) And then, on September 11, 2001, we were shaken out of complacency. (4) Thousands were taken from us, as clouds of fire and metal and ash descended upon a sun-filled morning. This was a different kind of war. (5) No armies came to our shores, and our military was not the principal target. Instead, a group of terrorists came to kill as many civilians as they could. (6) And so our nation went to war. We have now been at war for well over a decade. . . . (7) Today, Osama bin Laden is dead, and so are most of his top lieutenants. (8) There have been no large-scale attacks on the United States, and our homeland is more secure. (9) Fewer of our troops are in harm's way, and over the next 19 months they will continue to come home. (10) Our alliances are strong, and so is our standing in the world. (11) In sum, we are safer because of our efforts.

1. Which of the following sentences includes an unsupported claim?
   A. Sentence 4
   B. Sentence 5
   C. Sentence 7
   D. Sentence 10

2. Which sentence would most likely invoke emotions in the listener?
   A. Sentence 2
   B. Sentence 4
   C. Sentence 8
   D. Sentence 9

3. Which sentence provides evidence that the attacks were a different kind of war?
   A. Sentence 5
   B. Sentence 6
   C. Sentence 7
   D. Sentence 8

4. Which sentence indicates that the United States is safer?
   A. Sentence 2
   B. Sentence 4
   C. Sentence 6
   D. Sentence 8

Writing Practice

Directions: Some critics claim the USA Patriot Act violates the freedoms guaranteed by the Constitution. Take a position either for or against the Patriot Act. Write an essay explaining your position. Include evidence to support your argument.

Directions: Choose the best answer to each question.

1. Which of the following events occurred first?
   A. The archduke of Austria-Hungary was assassinated.
   B. The Germans bombed the *Lusitania*.
   C. Congress passed the Selective Service Act.
   D. The Russian czar was overthrown.

2. Which of the following terms was outlined in the Treaty of Versailles?
   A. Germany gained the countries of Austria, Hungary, and Latvia.
   B. Germany was required to pay reparations to France and Great Britain.
   C. The United States would join the League of Nations.
   D. France and Great Britain could keep only a small army.

3. In an effort to prevent the spread of communism, President Johnson sent troops to _____.
   A. Vietnam
   B. Poland
   C. Great Britain
   D. Cuba

4. What was the purpose of the GI Bill?
   A. to convince men to fight in the war
   B. to provide the war dead with a funeral
   C. to make sure returning soldiers did not face hard economic times
   D. to provide land and housing to families of deceased soldiers

Directions: Questions 5 and 6 refer to the following text.

Roosevelt's Declaration of War

After the attack on Pearl Harbor, President Roosevelt made the following address to Congress:

Yesterday, December 7, 1941—a date which will live in infamy—the United States of America was suddenly and deliberately attacked by naval and air forces of the Empire of Japan. . . . The attack yesterday on the Hawaiian Islands has caused severe damage to American naval and military forces. I regret to tell you that very many American lives have been lost. In addition American ships have been reported torpedoed on the high seas between San Francisco and Honolulu. . . . Hostilities exist. There is no blinking at the fact that our people, our territory, and our interests are in grave danger.

With confidence in our armed forces—with the unbounding determination of our people—we will gain the inevitable triumph—so help us God.

5. What is the purpose of the president's speech?
   A. to keep the United States out of World War II
   B. to convince Congress to declare war on Japan
   C. to persuade Americans to join the US Navy
   D. to increase the number of US troops in Hawaii

6. Who is the president appealing to in this speech?
   A. Congress
   B. America's allies around the world
   C. the American people
   D. the US military forces

Directions: Question 7 refers to the following map.

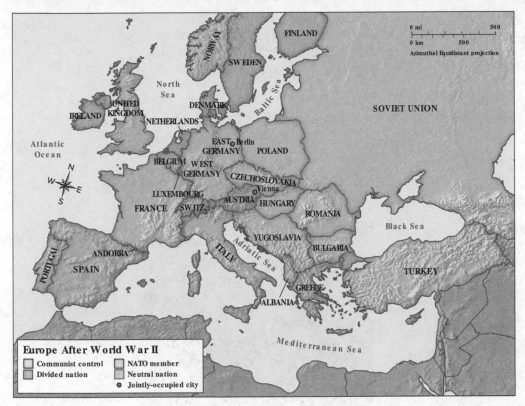

7. Which country did not join NATO after World War II?

   A. Poland

   B. Norway

   C. Greece

   D. Spain

8. President Johnson's efforts to help poor people was known as the _____.

   A. Economic Opportunity Program

   B. Job Corps Program

   C. War on Poverty

   D. War for Wealth

9. What event resulted in a united Germany?

   A. World War II

   B. fall of the Berlin Wall

   C. war in Vietnam

   D. Nixon's policy of détente

10. What is the common trait of all terrorist groups?

    A. They want to fight Western influences.

    B. They use fear to accomplish their goals.

    C. They want a nation of Palestine.

    D. They use urban guerillas to fight their enemies.

Check Your Understanding

Lesson	Item Number
World War I	1, 2
World War II	4, 5, 6
The Cold War	3, 7
Societal Changes	8, 9
Foreign Policy in the 21st Century	10

WRITE ABOUT Propaganda

Propaganda is material that is written or created to convince the reader or viewer to think in a particular way about a product, an issue, an event, or a person. Propaganda may include opinions and some half-truths, rather than facts. The following questions are helpful in analyzing material that may be propaganda:

• What is the topic of the writing, cartoon, advertisement, or poster?

• Who is responsible for the piece? Did it come from a company, political party, or government?

• What is the message of the piece? Does it exaggerate or present only one side?

Read the essay on page 351. Then read the following information and identify the propaganda techniques used in the images below.

During World War I, the United States had a Committee on Public Information. One part of it was the Division of Pictorial Publicity. The director urged painters and illustrators to contribute work to be used for propaganda. He wanted both to create support for the war and to encourage people to buy bonds, which would help pay for troops and equipment. In response, people sent in about 700 posters, and in 1918, during the Fourth Liberty Loan Drive, the illustrator Joseph Pennell created an image of New York City. He put in red flames and debris to make it look like the city had been bombed, which could not happen because enemy aircraft could not fly across the Atlantic. Even still, the image was used extensively during the war.

BEFORE YOU WRITE Look for Propaganda Techniques

When you examine written or created material, you may encounter one of the four common propaganda forms explained below. As you read or view an item, look for these techniques:

• **Bandwagon:** Everyone else is doing it. Political parties use this method all the time. "If party members support Candidate A, then you should too, as a loyal party member."

• **Name Calling:** using terms that stir up dislike, fear, or anger to turn people against others. During the Vietnam War, for example, opponents called Senator Barry Goldwater "trigger-happy," making him seem too ready to fight.

• **Plain Folks:** using words or images to convince people that someone is "just like us." This is another popular technique used by politicians from the past to the present. President William Henry Harrison was born into wealth and privilege, but his campaign in 1840 often featured a log cabin and portrayed him as a simple frontiersman.

• **Testimonial:** using a famous person to promote a product or support a political candidate. For example, singer Bruce Springsteen campaigned for Senator John Kerry in the 2004 presidential election.

Identifying Propaganda

TIP Writing Effective Paragraphs

By definition, an effective paragraph is one that gets your point across. Three parts make up an effective paragraph. The first is a topic sentence, usually at the beginning of the paragraph. The topic sentence states the main idea. The next few sentences give supporting details. These might be examples, explanations, or descriptions. The final sentence is the conclusion, which summarizes the details and restates the main idea. Notice the example below.

Main idea: African Americans became opposed to the Vietnam War.

Supporting details: Dr. Martin Luther King, Jr., and other civil rights leaders saw that the war was draining money from Great Society programs. They also saw the number of soldiers in Vietnam who were African American. African Americans made up 10 percent of the population in the mid-1960s. However, they made up 20 percent of those drafted.

Conclusion, restating main idea: By 1968, 70 percent of African Americans opposed the war.

To create your own effective paragraph, you may wish to make a simple outline or list. Doing so can help you keep the paragraph focused.

WHILE YOU WRITE Connect with Your Audience

A skilled writer tries to connect with those who will read his or her words. Although this is especially true for those creating propaganda, it is equally the case for more common writing. A good writer sometimes creates an "ideal reader," the one who will understand his or her point of view. Word choice and tone are two ways to connect. In persuasive writing it is important to get readers on your side. The most direct form of persuasion—propaganda—does this well. President Franklin D. Roosevelt, for example, gave "Fireside Chats" on the radio during his presidency. He always began these speeches with the words "My friends . . . ." By doing so, he connected with his listeners.

TIP Watch Out for Sentence Fragments

A sentence contains a subject, a verb, and a complete thought. All three elements must be present. Simple complete sentences are also known as independent clauses because they can stand on their own. Some clauses may have a subject and verb, but not a complete thought. Those clauses are termed *dependent*, because they rely on the rest of the sentence to complete their thought. Look at the example below:

> *Because college costs have risen. Some students have to delay starting college.*

The first part of the example is a sentence fragment. It begins with a capital letter and ends with a period, but it does not contain a complete thought; it is dependent on the next clause to make it meaningful. Generally, it is possible to eliminate a fragment by joining it to a nearby sentence. Notice the revisions, which create a complex sentence, with one independent and one dependent clause.

> *Some students have to delay starting college because college costs have risen.* OR
> *Because college costs have risen, some students have to delay starting college.*

AFTER YOU WRITE Revise

In an ideal situation, you will be able to set aside your first draft for a period of time. When you return to it with fresh eyes, you will perhaps see ways to improve the writing. These improvements may include fixing errors in spelling or grammar. They might also include better ways to organize the writing. Whenever possible, write the paper ahead of time so that you can leave it alone for a while. Then try to read it as though you had never seen it before. Does each sentence say exactly what you intend for it to say? Can it be improved at all?

Chapter 5

Fundamentals of Economics

In economics, the word *market* describes buyers and sellers exchanging money for goods and services. A market economy is when ordinary people decide what to sell and what to buy. Buyers have to make a choice of what they can buy based on limited resources available to them. Sellers also have to make choices between limited resources. They do this by using four factors of production: natural resources, human resources, capital resources, and entrepreneurship. By using comparative advantage and specialization, they work hard to make their businesses productive and profitable.

©Ariel Skelley/Blend Images/Corbis

In this chapter you will study these topics:

Lesson 5.1
Markets, Monopolies, and Competition

How does a market economy take advantage of self-interest? How does competition affect the marketplace? Is a monopoly good or bad for the economy?

Lesson 5.2
The Factors of Production

What is scarcity and how is it related to choice? What are the four factors of production and how do businesses use them?

Lesson 5.3
Profits and Profitability

Why are workers and businesses willing to take risks? How does productivity increase profit? Is incentive related to risk taking?

Lesson 5.4
Specialization and Comparative Advantage

What is the advantage of specialization to businesses? What is comparative advantage? Why is interdependence important to the international marketplace?

Goal Setting

What do you hope to learn about the fundamentals of economics in this chapter?

What do you know about how businesses increase productivity and compete in the marketplace?

LESSON 5.1 Markets, Monopolies, and Competition

LESSON OBJECTIVES

- Explain the difference between goods and services
- Give examples of goods and services
- Contrast competition and monopoly

CORE SKILLS & PRACTICES

- Predict Outcomes
- Synthesize Ideas from Multiple Sources

Key Terms

goods
products made to be sold

service
useful work that does not create an actual product but meets someone's need and is sold in the market

market
a relationship that makes buying and selling easier

competition
a process of offering price, quality or other advantages to two or more suppliers to try to gain the business of a buyer

monopoly
the control or domination of an industry by a single supplier

Vocabulary

outcome
result or consequence

Key Concept

Buyers and sellers exchange goods and services in a market. Monopoly occurs when a business in a market has no competition, but with many businesses, competition can thrive.

Your local grocery store may be convenient, but its prices are high, and its vegetables aren't very fresh. After another store opens nearby, the first store makes some improvements. It has weekly sales and offers fresher vegetables. Why did the first store change? To attract the same customers as the newer store, it must show why it is the better choice. Customers benefit from the improved service.

Markets

Every country has an economic system. An economic system consists of all of the ways that people have developed to decide what goods and services to produce, how to produce those goods and services, and for whom to do so.

Exchanges Between Buyers and Sellers

Goods are products made to be sold, such as cell phones, hair brushes, and meat. **Services** are useful work that does not create an actual product but meets someone's need and is sold in the market. Examples are cell phone calling plans, hair styling, and meal preparation.

Goods and services are exchanged in markets. In economics, a **market** is more than a place where people buy and sell goods. It is any arrangement that makes buying and selling easier. In many large markets, buyers and sellers never meet. These exchanges can take place in different ways. Long ago, people traded goods directly. For example, a person might trade a grinding stone for a woven basket.

In complex civilizations where people perform specialized tasks, barter does not work for most exchanges. The invention of money thousands of years ago made trading easier. At some point, people started to accept stones, beads, shells, or gold disks in exchange for goods or services. The amount offered, or the price, depended on how much the buyer wanted an item and how much money the seller was willing to accept in trade.

Market Economy

In a market economy, ordinary people decide what, how, and for whom to produce goods and services with little or no government involvement.

A market economy takes advantage of self-interest. Workers exchange their labor for wages and salaries. They use this income to buy goods and services. Owners of resources provide these resources for payment. Owners of businesses use their income to buy resources to produce goods and services and to purchase new equipment to modernize or expand their business.

Economists consider a market economy an efficient approach to production and distribution. It allocates scarce resources according to the supply of those resources and the demand for various goods and services. However, it puts those without the money to pay for the resources at a disadvantage.

⚑ Think about Social Studies

Directions: Complete each statement below.

1. A market is an exchange between _____ and sellers of _____ and _____.

2. A market is any arrangement that makes _____ and _____ easier.

Competition

Markets differ in terms of the number of suppliers. **Competition** is a market in which two or more suppliers try to sell similar goods or services to consumers. Competition gives buyers freedom of choice. If buyers are offered several alternatives, sellers cannot raise prices on a whim. Competition forces sellers to use resources efficiently and respond to consumer needs.

Competitive Markets

Economists have identified six conditions that determine how competitive a market is:

1. The number of buyers and sellers in the industry
2. Whether products are identical or unique
3. The degree to which individual firms control price
4. The amount of information available to producers and consumers
5. The ease of entry and exit from the industry
6. The role of government

The Number of Buyers and Sellers in the Industry Let's say a farm in Iowa produces an average of 625,000 bushels of corn annually. That sounds like a lot, but it is only a small percentage of the over 9 *trillion* bushels American farmers harvest each year. The presence of thousands of farmers makes the corn market competitive.

Predict Outcomes

An **outcome** is a result or a consequence. When you think about outcomes, you are thinking about what will happen in a situation as a result of some action. Predicting outcomes is one way to understand a concept more fully. Reread the section on market economies. Imagine a country where the government tells people what they can produce and how much of it they can produce. How do you think this approach might affect the economy?

Synthesize Ideas from Multiple Sources

Why is access to information about a product and its price important for both buyers and sellers? Think of an example from your own experience, such as information on computers, cars, or children's clothing. Write a paragraph describing the product, where you found the information, and how it influenced your choice of purchase.

Whether Products Are Identical or Unique Corn is an example of an identical product. The Iowa farmer's crop is essentially the same as corn raised on thousands of other farms. Buyers have no reason to prefer his or her crop, so they will expect to pay the same price for it as they would for corn grown elsewhere. If the farmer grew purple corn containing a rare health-giving substance, he would be able to ask more for it, and the market for his crop would be less competitive.

The Degree to Which Individual Firms Control the Price In a perfectly competitive market, individual buyers and sellers cannot influence the price of a product. If the Iowa farmer stopped planting tomorrow, neither the nation's supply of corn nor its price would change.

The Amount of Information Available to Producers and Consumers Both buyers and sellers have access to the information they need in a perfectly competitive marketplace. Our Iowa farmer gathers news about prices and advances in agricultural technology from trade journals, equipment manufacturers, government bulletins, and the Internet. Potential buyers of his corn can consult the same sources.

The Ease of Entry and Exit from the Industry In a perfectly competitive industry, sellers and buyers are free to enter or leave the market at will. If the price of corn rises, our farmer's neighbors may plant more of it. If the price falls, some may switch to other crops.

The Role of Government Governments try to keep producers from getting together to set prices or limit supplies of a product. They try to ensure that markets are competitive, with many independent suppliers. That way there is little chance of one supplier taking over.

 Think about Social Studies

Directions: Fill in the blank.

In a _____ market, there are many buyers and sellers.

Markets, Monopolies, and Competition

Blend Images/SuperStockx

Monopolies

The opposite of perfect competition is monopoly. A **monopoly** is a market structure in which one firm dominates, or controls, the sale of a good or service. Like perfect competition, pure monopoly is an extreme that exists only in theory.

Characteristics of a Monopoly

The following six characteristics define a monopoly:

1. A single company produces all or nearly all of an industry's output.
2. A monopoly produces a unique product, one for which there is no easy substitute. Electricity from your local power company may be a good example.
3. Because it does not have to worry about what rivals are charging, a monopoly has a great deal of control over price.
4. Monopolies have all of the information about their market and they seldom share it with buyers.
5. When a monopoly exists, competitors find it very difficult to enter the industry. Monopolies may control raw materials necessary to produce a good or service. In the early 1900s, U.S. Steel Corporation controlled the steel industry because it owned its own coal and iron mines. Coal and iron are needed to make steel.
6. When prices are controlled by the actions of a single company, the market works less efficiently, so the government often steps in to keep competition alive.

Antitrust Acts

The Standard Oil Company was one of the nation's first monopolies. By 1878, it controlled about 90 percent of the nation's oil refineries. Its business practices led to the passage of the Sherman Antitrust Act, which forbids contracts, schemes, deals, or conspiracies to limit trade.

Antitrust laws like the Sherman Antitrust Act of 1890 and the Clayton Antitrust Act of 1914 are examples of government action to keep markets competitive. A trust is another name for a monopoly, and antitrust laws try to prevent new monopolies from forming and break up those that already exist.

 Think about Social Studies

Directions: Choose the best answer to the following question.

1. Which of the following are characteristics of a monopoly? Choose all that apply.
   A. Several companies produce all of an industries output.
   B. Competitors find it difficult to enter an industry.
   C. The market works efficiently.
   D. Companies have all the information about their market and seldom share it.
   E. Companies produce a unique product.

WRITE TO LEARN

Research more about Standard Oil's monopoly on the Internet. Write a paragraph describing the process the company took to form a monopoly and the practices it used to stay a monopoly as long as it did.

21ST CENTURY SKILLS

Information, Communication, and Technology Literacy

The passage about Standard Oil presents information about Standard Oil's monopoly. The same information could have been included in an audio presentation. Write a sentence or two stating the advantages of each type of communication. Name two other possible ways to communicate information about the subject.

Vocabulary Review

Directions: Complete the sentences using the following key terms and vocabulary words.

monopoly   markets   outcome

competition   goods   service

1. Insurance is an example of a(n) _____.

2. In the late 1800s and early 1900s Standard Oil was a powerful _____.

3. The consequence of an action is a(n) _____.

4. _____ encourages firms to improve their products and keep their prices fair.

5. Many _____ are manufactured with the aid of complex machines.

6. _____ are controlled by the laws of supply and demand.

Skill Review

Directions: Choose the best answer to each question.

1. Why does the government step in when there is a monopoly?

   A. Lawmakers want monopolies to supply different goods or services.

   B. Lawmakers want monopolies to treat their employees more fairly.

   C. Lawmakers want to restore freedom of choice to the market.

   D. Lawmakers want a greater share of the monopoly's profits.

2. How does a market take advantage of self-interest?

   A. It sets the cost of goods and services.

   B. It allocates scarce resources to those with more money.

   C. It allows buyers and sellers to make their own decisions.

   D. It allows workers to buy items for their wages.

3. What's the best way to make a product more competitive?

   A. making it less unique

   B. making it more unique

   C. providing more information about a product

   D. providing less information about a product

4. How might the creation of a monopoly affect an industry and its customers?

   A. Because they do not have competitors, monopolies can prevent customers from receiving goods and services.

   B. Because they do have competitors, monopolies can flood the market with products, creating higher prices for goods and services.

   C. Because they do not have competitors, monopolies can charge higher prices and deliver lower quality goods and services.

   D. Because they do have competitors, monopolies can charge lower prices and deliver higher quality goods and services.

Skill Practice

Directions: Read the passage below. Then answer the questions that follow.

A technological monopoly results when a firm develops a new technology that is used to produce a new product. To protect that product, the firm applies for patents. In the drug industry, for example, companies spend huge sums of money on research. They then obtain a patent on those drugs, giving them the exclusive right to sell that medication for 20 years.

Similarly, copyright law protects works of art, literature, songs, and other creative material. The author or artist keeps the rights to the work for his or her lifetime plus 50 years.

1. Many people complain about the high price of medication. What would happen if drug companies did not have patent protection for their new products?

   A. The drugs would be of a lower quality.

   B. People would complain.

   C. Their costs would be higher.

   D. Drug companies would not develop new drugs.

2. What would happen if people were legally allowed to download and use all software, books, music, photographs, drawings, and other creative works from the Internet for free?

   A. The fans of professional authors, songwriters, artists, and photographers would send them money.

   B. Professional authors, songwriters, artists, and photographers would eventually stop creating new works for publication.

   C. Professional authors, songwriters, artists, and photographers would make bad art in retaliation.

   D. All of the above

3. If you write a book, a story, or a song that becomes a classic, what will happen to the rights after you die?

   A. The rights will pass to your spouse, your children, or other designated heirs.

   B. The rights expire once you die.

   C. Whoever publishes your work will own the rights.

   D. The rights become public domain, or free for anyone.

4. In the passage above, what does the term "exclusive" mean?

   A. partial

   B. available for everyone

   C. limited or reserved

   D. long-term

Writing Practice

Think about competition between businesses in your neighborhood. What have local businesses done to draw customers? Do they use social networking on the Internet or do they place ads in local papers? What businesses do you think will fade away and why?

LESSON 5.2 The Factors of Production

LESSON OBJECTIVES

- List the factors of production
- Understand the relationship between labor and capital
- Discuss the importance of entrepreneurship

CORE SKILLS & PRACTICES

- Make Inferences
- Analyze Ideas

Key Terms

natural resources
anything found in nature that can be used to produce goods and services

labor
efforts of people who process natural resources or produce services

capital
equipment used to process natural resources into goods or to deliver services

entrepreneurship
human creativity that produces new products or services

Vocabulary

inference
to reach a conclusion or opinion based on facts or evidence presented

scarce
rare or short supply

Key Concept

The factors of production, which include natural resources, labor, capital, and entrepreneurship, are used to produce goods and services.

Suppose you develop a new kind of vegetable and sell it at a local farmer's market. You use natural resources like sunlight, water, and soil. You use labor of planting, weeding, and harvesting. You invest money in seeds and tools as capital. You become an entrepreneur. Natural resources, labor, capital, and entrepreneurship are the four factors of production that make all markets work.

Scarcity and Choice

We have many wants and needs, such as buying a new car, paying for food and housing, or going on a family vacation. Yet our resources are limited. We only have so much money to spend on these items. This means we have to make a choice. Choosing between limited resources demonstrates the concept of scarcity.

Value and Scarcity

Usually people describe something that is rare or in short supply as **scarce**. In economics, scarcity has a slightly different meaning. Scarcity has two important characteristics. To be scarce, an item must have value. It must be useful to someone. Second, an item must be in short supply in comparison to the number of people who would like to own the product.

Gasoline is a good example. In the 1850s, when workers refined oil to make kerosene, they threw out the gasoline they accidentally produced. It was not valued because no one had a use for it at that time. Forty years later, in 1893, two Americans invented a gasoline-powered car. By 1920, nine million of those cars were on the road in the United States, and gasoline had become a scarce resource.

The supply of gasoline did not change much between 1850 and 1920. The only thing that changed was the value attached to gasoline. Economists refer to this kind of scarcity as relative scarcity. The world has a large supply of gasoline, but it is scarce in comparison to the number of people who want it. People today need gasoline to keep their cars running.

moodboard/Getty Images

Making Choices

In choosing one thing over another, we make a trade-off. We give up one thing in order to have another. You and a friend decide to go to a ball game. That decision has a cost that goes beyond the price of your tickets. In going to the game, you are also giving up the next best alternative. It is what you would have done if you had not gone to the game. For example, you might have spent the afternoon catching up on yard work. The **opportunity cost** of watching the game was falling behind on yard work. Opportunity cost is the cost of the next-best use of time and money when choosing to do one thing over another. It refers to the next-most attractive alternative. Whenever you choose one thing over another, you give up that alternative. This is the opportunity cost of choosing to do one thing rather than another.

The Four Factors of Production

The problem of scarcity affects individuals, families, businesses, and nations, because no one has an unlimited supply of resources. The four types of resources needed to produce goods and services are the factors of production: natural resources, human resources, capital resources, and entrepreneurship. Each of these four factors of production is vital to the health of an economy. If one factor is weak, the entire system suffers.

 Think about Social Studies

Directions: Answer the following questions.

1. What are the characteristics of scarcity?
2. Explain how trade-offs help people maximize their resources.
3. Give an example of a resource in which scarcity depends on where people live.

Natural and Human Resources

Two of the four factors of production involve natural resources and human resources.

Natural Resources

Natural resources are anything found in nature that can be used to produce goods and services. Economists sometimes refer to this factor of production as *land* with the understanding that it includes much more than soil. Land is a natural resource, as are oil and water. Air, plants, animals, iron ore, and other minerals are all natural resources. Environments like forests, mountains, oceans, and deserts are natural resources as well.

Natural resources are either renewable or nonrenewable. Today, coal, oil, and natural gas are the major sources of energy powering homes, businesses, and transportation. They are called nonrenewable natural resources because there is a limited supply of them and they cannot be easily replenished. Other natural resources, such as trees, are renewable because they can be planted and grown. Some trees, however, take a long time to grow so they are scarce and have a higher monetary value. Because renewable natural resources can be replenished, their supply is not limited.

CORE PRACTICE

Make Inferences

Ideas are not always directly stated in a text. Sometimes you need to make an inference, or educated guess, by connecting your own knowledge and experience with the information presented. Read these two sentences: "In the 1850s, when workers refined oil to make kerosene, they threw out the gasoline they accidentally produced. Forty years later, in 1893, two Americans invented a gasoline-powered car." What inference can you make about what happened to the value of gasoline?

Analyze Ideas

One way of analyzing ideas is to read a passage and identify the main idea and the details that support the main idea. Read the passage on natural resources again. Identify the main idea and three supporting details.

Human Resources

Human effort is needed to change natural resources into finished goods and services. That effort is sometimes called labor. **Labor** is defined as the efforts of people who process natural resources or produce services. Labor means more than physical work. It also includes jobs that involve planning, organizing, managing, and distributing.

For example, a gas station uses natural resources of the land it is built on and the gas and oil that it sells. It also uses human resources to pump the gas, add oil to cars, and make repairs. Other examples of human resources include factory workers, teachers, doctors, and farmers.

Technological advances have made it possible for companies to hire people around the country, even worldwide. While many people still work in a traditional office setting, more and more companies and employees are taking advantage of telecommuting, or working outside of the office. Many companies are also expanding to other countries to take advantage of lower taxes and cheaper labor. Thanks to technology, the physical distance between countries does not always matter.

⚑ Think about Social Studies

Directions: Fill in the blanks.

1. Human effort changes _____ resources into goods and services.
2. The human effort needed to create goods and services is called
   _____ .
3. Oil and gasoline are examples of _____ resources.
4. Trees are a(n) _____ resource because they can be replenished.

Capital and Entrepreneurship

Capital and entrepreneurship are also factors of production.

Capital

Capital refers to the technology, tools, and other equipment used to process natural resources into goods or to deliver services. These components have a financial value. Machines such as drill presses, boilers, and pumps are examples of capital. So are office buildings, storage sheds, and warehouses. Technology might include computers, microscopes, MRIs, and supermarket checkout scanners. Tools can range from a simple wrench or screwdriver to a more complicated jackhammer or concrete saw. When capital combines with natural resources and labor, more goods and services are produced.

In 1901, a young machinist named Henry Ford started a car company. At first, he struggled to stay in business. Automobiles were very expensive. A 1912 Ford cost $600—more than a year's wage for most people. There was good reason for the high price. Early cars were difficult to construct. It took a team of workers 12 hours and 28 minutes to build just one.

Ford knew he could lower the cost of his cars if he could make production more efficient. The following year, with new tools and methods, he produced a car every 90 minutes. By 1916, the cost of a Ford had dropped to $360. The number of workers did not change, but the new technology increased their productivity. By 1916, Ford had sold well over one million cars.

Entrepreneurship

Every business firm begins with an entrepreneur. Some entrepreneurs are inventors who develop new products or more efficient ways of producing an existing product. Others simply see a need in the community or the nation—for a laundromat, a movie theater, or a more energy-efficient computer—and set out to fill that need. In doing so, entrepreneurs take risks. **Entrepreneurship** refers to the human creativity and organization that produces new products or services.

In a market economy, producers are the people who transform natural resources, labor, and capital (three of the four factors of production) into goods and services. Entrepreneurs start new businesses and introduce new products and services.

 Think about Social Studies

Directions: Select the best answer to the following question.

1. Which of the following are examples of capital?
A. land, cash register, building, construction worker
B. gas pump, baker, ATM, petroleum
C. cell phone, mannequin, sales associate, leather
D. office building, checkout scanner, screw driver

21ST CENTURY SKILL

Use Internet Resources

Go online and research a famous entrepreneur. Find information about the person on an educational site (with a .edu extension), a personal Web site created by an individual, and a reputable news site. Compare and contrast the information you find. Is one site more reliable than another? Is there an indication of bias? Which site would you trust for the most accurate information? Why?

WRITE TO LEARN

Imagine you are starting your own business. Write a paragraph describing the factors of production you would need in your business and the steps you would take to establish them.

Vocabulary Review

Directions: Complete the sentences using the following key terms and vocabulary words.

opportunity cost   natural resources   entrepreneurship
labor   capital   scarce

1. The founding of a new computer company is an example of _____.

2. Your _____ is when you choose one activity over another.

3. The people who work in an office or factory are the _____ of a business.

4. Water, minerals, and forests are examples of _____.

5. The dishes, silverware, stoves, and freezers are part of a restaurant's _____.

6. When a valuable item is in short supply, it is _____.

Skill Review

Directions: Choose the best answer to each question.

1. Why are entrepreneurs important to the economy?

   A. Entrepreneurs donate a great deal of money to charity.

   B. Entrepreneurs provide jobs for those who make luxury items.

   C. Entrepreneurs use innovation to create new products or services.

   D. Entrepreneurs pay high property taxes that fund city services.

2. How does capital contribute to the production of goods and services?

   A. It causes some natural resources to become more scarce and expensive.

   B. It gives entrepreneurs the natural resources they need to start a business.

   C. It provides land and human resources that allow the goods and services to be made.

   D. It provides the tools, machinery, and buildings that help produce goods and services.

3. Scarcity is based on the idea that

   A. people have to make a choice between limited resources.

   B. many natural resources are nonrenewable.

   C. more capital produces more goods and services.

   D. individuals, families, businesses, and nations all have resources.

4. Ford increased the sales of his automobiles by

   A. building new highways.

   B. establishing labor unions in his factories.

   C. shutting down the assembly line.

   D. by increasing production and lowering the price.

Skill Practice

Directions: Read the passage below. Then answer the questions that follow.

Suppliers use three of the factors of production—natural resources, labor, and capital—to produce a product or service. A change in the amount of any one of these production resources can affect supply in the long run. In the short run, only a change in labor is likely to impact production. To understand why only labor can be increased in the short run, think about a company that produces the most popular running shoe on the market. To keep up with the demand, the company has to produce more shoes. The fastest way to increase production is by hiring extra workers. Building a new factory, developing a new manufacturing process, or adding machines requires more time and expense.

1. What is the most cost-efficient option to keep up with increasing demand?

   A. Hiring and training new workers

   B. Building a new factory

   C. Hiring a new manager

   D. Lowering wages

2. In the long run, what will happen to supply if demand continues to increase and the firm does not upgrade its facilities?

   A. The company will have to stop making its product.

   B. Prices on the product will go up.

   C. The equipment will start to wear out and workers will not have room to do their jobs effectively.

   D. The company will have to hire new workers to learn new jobs more efficiently.

3. Which of the three factors of production mentioned here is the hardest for a firm to control? Why?

   A. Weather

   B. Wars

   C. Holiday rushes on a particular product

   D. Natural resources

4. How could entrepreneurship work with labor and capital in this shoe company to increase supply?

   A. An entrepreneur could develop a new shoe assembly strategy or invent a new machine to perform tasks more efficiently.

   B. An entrepreneur could hire more workers to increase productivity.

   C. An entrepreneur could find investors to pour money into the company.

   D. All of the above.

Writing Practice

Businesses in the United States often look for labor in other nations. Sometimes, they build factories in other nations, too. Do you think this is a good idea? How would this affect the factors of production? Write a paragraph stating your opinion. Support your ideas with specific examples. Include an introductory sentence and a conclusion.

LESSON 5.3 Profits and Productivity

LESSON OBJECTIVES

- Explain why profit is important in a market economy
- Describe the relationship between productivity and profit
- Discuss the role of incentive in making a profit

CORE SKILLS & PRACTICES

- Interpret Graphics
- Use Context Clues

Key Terms

market economy
an economy where people are free to decide what, how, and for whom to produce goods and services

net income
amount left after total expenses are subtracted from income

productivity
the amount of goods and services a worker can produce in a certain amount of time

depreciation
a decrease in value

incentive
encouragement to try new ideas or invent new products

Vocabulary

strategy
carefully devised plan

Key Concept

The possibility of increased profits is an incentive for business owners to take risks, expand, and try various strategies that will increase productivity.

Suppose a neighbor pays you to mow his lawn using his mower. To expand your business, you take a risk and buy a used mower and spend your weekend passing out flyers. If other neighbors hire you to mow their lawns, you will cover the cost of your equipment and start making money—a profit. If nobody uses your service, you will lose your investment. In a market economy, risk-taking increases the quantity and quality of available goods and services.

Risks and Profits

In a market economy businesses and workers are willing to take risks in order to make a profit. However, they try to minimize risks by keeping expenses as low as possible.

Taking Risks

In a **market economy**, workers exchange their labor for wages or salaries, and people are free to decide what, how, and for whom to produce goods and services. These people are willing to risk some time or wealth in the hope of making a profit.

A profit is money earned after all expenses are paid, or the extent to which an individual or group is better off after buying or selling a good or service. A person may gain money or satisfaction from the exchange. The hope of making a profit motivates both consumers and producers to participate in various markets.

How risky is a new business? More than 50 percent of all small businesses fail within the first four years. Entrepreneurs are willing to take risks in the hope that their business will make a profit. One way to understand how profits differ from sales is by examining an income statement—a report showing a business's sales, expenses, and profit for a certain period of time.

In the figure on this page, the total sales for the first three months of the year (the first quarter) equals $1,000. To figure out the firm's **net income**— the amount of money it has left over after expenses and taxes are subtracted from income—subtract expenses ($800) and taxes ($80) from total sales. The remainder ($120) is the firm's net income, or profit.

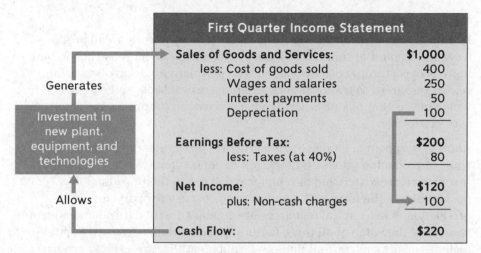

First Quarter Income Statement	
Sales of Goods and Services:	**$1,000**
less: Cost of goods sold	400
Wages and salaries	250
Interest payments	50
Depreciation	100
Earnings Before Tax:	**$200**
less: Taxes (at 40%)	80
Net Income:	**$120**
plus: Non-cash charges	100
Cash Flow:	**$220**

Generates — Investment in new plant, equipment, and technologies — Allows

CORE SKILL

Interpret Graphics

Study the chart titled First Quarter Income Statement. The arrows show a cycle, which is a repeating series of events or actions. Describe in a few sentences how the cycle of reinvesting creates profits.

Controlling Expenses

One way companies try to minimize the risk of failure is by controlling their expenses. Every business has expenses. Wages are an ongoing expense. So are interest payments, the fees paid to a bank or another lender for borrowing money. Other expenses include tools, office supplies, packaging, electricity, heat and air conditioning, telephone service, postage, and transportation costs.

One expense listed under costs on the chart does not involve a cash payment. That charge is called **depreciation.** Depreciation is an expense a firm takes into account for wear and tear on its machines and other capital goods. It is later added to the net income to determine the firm's cash flow. Cash flow is determined by adding net income plus non-cash charges like depreciation.

Every firm decides how its cash flow will be used. Some of it may be paid back to the owners of the business as their reward for risk-taking. Some of the funds may be reinvested in tools and equipment or marketing in order to produce more products and hopefully generate more sales and profits. As long as a firm is profitable and its reinvested cash flow is larger than depreciation, the firm is likely to grow.

Think about Social Studies

Directions: Fill-in-the-blank with the correct term.

profit   expenses   risk

1. You must deduct _____ and taxes from total sales to determine profit.
2. A net income represents a company's _____.
3. _____ can result in increased profits.

People depend on each other to produce needed goods and services. For example, if the bakery did not do its baking overnight, the restaurant would not have fresh bread for customers in the morning. Write a sentence or two explaining one thing you make or do that someone else depends upon. What would happen if you did not do your part?

Productivity and Profits

Individuals and businesses invest in capital in the hope of increasing productivity in the future. Increasing productivity should lead to increased profits.

Productivity

Productivity is the amount of goods and services a worker can produce in a certain amount of time. Increasing productivity can increase profit, but there is opportunity cost associated with productivity. It involves using scarce resources to train workers or purchase new tools and equipment, which means that businesses will have less money for producing goods and services today.

Another way people increase productivity is by developing new and better ways of producing goods and services. Many companies spend time and resources on research and development to expand their production possibilities in the future. The opportunity cost is a drop in current production. When capital resources are combined with natural and human resources, the value of all three factors of production increases. Capital includes goods such as buildings and equipment that are used to produce other goods or services. Capital boosts productivity.

The assembly line is an example of how new techniques can boost productivity. First used in the meat packing industry in the 1800s, assembly lines consisted of powered chains taking meat carcasses from worker to worker. The workers remained in place while the meat came to them. The chain moved at a steady pace, which forced workers to keep up with it. In 1913, Henry Ford became famous for using assembly lines to build his automobiles. By 1914, his assembly lines were so successful that cars became affordable to the middle class. Assembly lines transformed manufacturing and made mass production possible.

Production Costs

Productivity also affects production costs. Productivity increases if the same quantity of input (work, for example) produces more output (quantity supplied). When Henry Ford and his engineers reorganized the way cars were made, workers were able to turn out more cars (output) in the same amount of time (input). Productivity decreases if the same quantity of input produces less output.

⚑ Think about Social Studies

Directions: Read the sentence below. Then choose the words that correctly complete the sentence.

capital	production	opportunity cost

A temporary decrease in _____ can be a(n) _____ of investing in _____.

Incentives and Risk Taking

Individuals and businesses are more willing to take risks and invest in new products if they are encouraged to do so with incentives.

Incentive in a Market Economy

In a market economy, individuals and businesses have the right to own property. They are also able to freely buy and sell land, a business, a car, their skills, or other goods. The right to own property gives people an incentive or motive to produce goods and services. **Incentive** is encouragement to try new ideas or invent new products.

Incentive in a Traditional Economy

Traditional economies are different from market economies. They change very little from one generation to the next. People have no incentive to try new ideas or invent new products. Entrepreneurship has little value in a traditional economy. The other three factors of production—natural resources, human resources, and capital resources—also have limited value, because they cannot be bought or sold. Even though people may own mines, land, or other property, they are not free to buy or sell those resources. Workers are not free to improve their lives by finding a new job or acquiring a new skill. No modern country has a traditional economy because it is difficult to avoid the technological and social changes that are part of the modern world.

Incentive in Business

Making a profit is an important incentive for starting a business. But business owners are not the only ones who need incentives to make profits. Employees who work for businesses are motivated by wages, bonuses, and tips they make from working at their jobs. Successful business owners develop **strategies**, or plans to achieve certain goals, to ensure they and their employees have the incentive needed to make their business profitable. Customers also need incentives to buy products and services. When marketers produce effective advertisements that persuade customers to buy their products and services, sales increase, and companies make profits.

In some economies that are not market economies, companies may not have incentive to do their best or show ingenuity. For example, the government of India used to own many businesses. For 12 years, the employees at one company showed up for work and were paid regularly. However, they never produced a product that could be sold. Because the government determined how much the company produced, there was no incentive for the company to compete in the marketplace. Because workers would get paid no matter how many items were sold, they had no incentive to work harder or use ingenuity to improve sales.

 Think about Social Studies

Directions: Choose the best answer to the following question.

1. In a market economy, people and businesses

A. are free to buy land and sell land.

B. are traditional.

C. have no incentive.

D. do not make much money.

CORE PRACTICE

Use Context Clues to Understand Meaning

Read the following passage and answer the question.

In a pure command economy, the government makes most of the decisions about production and distribution. It identifies the economy's needs and decides which goods and services to produce and how to create them.

Is the United States a command economy? Why or why not?

WRITE TO LEARN

Write a paragraph outlining what must happen before a business can be profitable. Think about the repeatable steps a business must take.

Vocabulary Review

Directions: Complete the sentences using the following key terms and vocabulary words.

incentive   market economy   productivity
net income   depreciation   strategy

1. Using context clues is a good _____ for building a powerful vocabulary.

2. People in a/an _____ are free to decide what goods and services to sell.

3. A decrease in the value of a company's machinery or equipment due to wear and tear is known as

    _____.

4. The amount of money a company has left after it subtracts expenses and taxes is its _____.

5. When Ford increased his _____ he produced more cars in the same amount of time.

6. Possible profits are a/an _____ to take risks in business.

Skill Review

Directions: Choose the best answer to each question.

1. Why are business owners willing to take risks to expand?

   A. They have never lost money before.

   B. They believe the risk is minimal.

   C. They don't think they can lose their money.

   D. They expect to make greater profits.

2. Combining capital resources with natural and human resources

   A. creates a market economy.

   B. lessens production.

   C. increases the value of all three factors of production.

   D. decreases the value of all three factors of production.

3. How do businesses minimize risks?

   A. by becoming entrepreneurs

   B. by creating an income statement

   C. by keeping expenses as low as possible

   D. by reducing cash flow

4. Modern countries do not have a traditional economy because they

   A. have no incentive to do so.

   B. believe it is difficult to ignore technological innovations.

   C. do not have enough capital resources.

   D. think traditional economies are too remote.

Skill Practice

Directions: Read the passage below. Then answer the questions that follow.

In the manorial system in Europe (starting in the fifth century), most people were peasant farmers. They were bound to the land and forced to work the soil for food and to make money for the owner of the estate. Some workers were also craft workers, like blacksmiths or shoemakers, while others had food production jobs, like bakers. During the Middle Ages (from the eleventh to the fourteenth centuries), these specialized jobs developed further. Eventually they organized into craft guilds, where master craft workers supervised young apprentices and taught them their trade. Parents could then pick a trade for their children to be apprenticed into, rather than having the children grow up to do the same work the parents had done. This was the beginning of modern professions.

1. This passage describes the gradual phasing out of an outdated economy. Which economy was the society moving toward?

   A. traditional

   B. capitalism

   C. traditional mixed with market

   D. capitalism mixed with market

2. How is the form of job training described in this passage the same as training we have today?

   A. Some modern professions still have apprenticeships to learn the trade.

   B. Farmers often take apprentices to teach them what they know.

   C. Craft guilds today take on more apprentices than in the Middle Ages.

   D. Shoemakers usually pick their craft because it is a family trade.

3. Blacksmithing is a job that still exists today. Which statement explains how it has changed since the Middle Ages?

   A. Blacksmiths have not changed since the Middle Ages.

   B. Blacksmiths are no longer central to the economy.

   C. Blacksmiths now make more shoes for horses.

   D. Blacksmiths now make more metal decorations.

4. What can you infer is meant by "they were bound to the land"?

   A. Peasant farmers were tied down.

   B. Peasant farmers lived in large farm houses.

   C. Peasant farmers had no other options but to farm and work the land to survive.

   D. Peasant farmers led difficult, unpleasant lives.

Writing Practice

Some people say that market economies are based on greed. Do you agree? State your opinion. Include facts and examples to support your opinion and finish with a strong concluding statement.

LESSON 5.4   Specialization and Comparative Advantage

■ LESSON OBJECTIVES

- Explain how specialization can increase profit and result in interdependence
- Define "comparative advantage" and explain the importance of opportunity cost

■ CORE SKILLS & PRACTICES

- Identify Facts and Details
- Gather Information

Key Terms

absolute advantage
the ability to produce a product or service using fewer resources than other producers require

comparative advantage
the ability to produce goods or services at a low opportunity cost compared to other producers

opportunity cost
the alternative that one gives up when making choices

specialization
to concentrate on the production of a few goods and services

Vocabulary

efficient
capable of producing desired results with little waste

interdependence
two or more producers' reliance on one another

Key Concept

Specialization increases productivity and provides businesses with a comparative advantage but also leads to interdependence.

Have you ever tried to throw a party and do everything yourself? You send out the invitations, bake the cake, clean the house, put up the decorations, cook a meal, and prepare some kind of entertainment. Think about how much faster and easier it would be if several of your friends help out. You can each specialize on one task and depend on each other to throw a fantastic party. In a similar way, businesses use specialization and interdependence to increase their own productivity.

Specialization

Some people are better at some things than others. They may have skills, knowledge, or resources that others lack. The same is true of businesses and nations. By concentrating on a few tasks rather than trying to do everything, they can accomplish more with fewer resources.

Focusing on a Few Goods and Services

Concentrating on the production of a few goods and services is called **specialization**. You specialize when you focus on making a few goods or performing a few services rather than trying to produce everything you need.

In the early 1700s, most Americans grew their own food, wove wool into cloth, tanned leather, and built furniture. These people tried to be self-sufficient. That is, they tried to produce all of the goods and services their families needed. People today specialize. They farm, or build houses, or fix automobiles, or teach children, or create music. Few people try to produce everything they need.

Absolute Advantage

The same is true of states and nations. About one-third of all of the potatoes grown in the United States come from Idaho. Potatoes can be grown in other parts of the country as well, but they are especially well suited to Idaho's climate and soil. Idaho has an absolute advantage in growing potatoes. Absolute means total, or complete. An **absolute advantage** is the ability to produce a product or service using fewer resources than other producers require. Farmers in Idaho can grow potatoes using fewer resources than farmers in other states have to use.

Idaho is not well suited to growing oranges. The climate is too cold. To grow oranges, Idaho farmers would have to plant orange trees in large greenhouses that they could heat during the cold winter months. Idaho does not have an absolute advantage in growing oranges. Farmers in places like Florida and Southern California can produce oranges more efficiently than can those in other states. To be **efficient** is to be capable of producing desired results without wasting materials, time, or energy. Florida and California have an absolute advantage in producing oranges. They can produce oranges using fewer resources than other producers require.

 Think about Social Studies

Directions: Choose the best answer to the question below.

1. How does a nation benefit from specialization?

   A. A nation can be more profitable if it produces a limited assortment of goods for which it is well-suited.

   B. A nation can reduce the number of items it imports if it produces many different products.

   C. A nation can increase the amount of items it exports if it specializes in a product.

   D. A nation can benefit from specialization by producing more oranges and potatoes.

Comparative Advantage

Specialization allows individuals and businesses to focus on what they do best rather than trying to produce everything they need. What determines which goods or services an individual or business produces? You may think they should produce only those for which they have an absolute advantage. In fact, they should produce only those for which they have a *comparative* advantage.

Low Opportunity Cost

Comparative advantage is the ability to produce goods or services at a relatively low opportunity cost than others. What is opportunity cost? **Opportunity cost** is the next most attractive alternative that one gives up when making economic choices. Idaho farmers could choose to grow apples instead of potatoes. When they choose to grow potatoes, apples are their opportunity cost.

When companies have a comparative advantage, they do not have to have an absolute advantage. That is, they do not have to produce goods or services more efficiently than everyone else. According to the law of comparative advantage, those with the lower opportunity cost should specialize in that product or service even if they do not have an absolute advantage.

CORE PRACTICE

Identify Facts and Details

When you read, it is important to distinguish among facts, opinions, and reasoned judgments (opinions backed by facts) in order to fully understand the information Read the following excerpt and identify any facts, opinions, and reasoned judgments you find.

In comments to reporters afterwards, [World Bank President] Kim said the bank's comparative advantage lies in large-scale, "transformational" projects that can impact many people and address big problems, rather than focusing on small pilot projects.

He pointed to the example of $340 million the bank approved in August to finance a hydropower plant in central Africa's Great Lakes region to bring electricity to the power grids of three countries.

But the bank's increased support for such projects could put it in conflict with some aid groups, who contend big projects are more likely to disrupt the environment and displace people.

— "World Bank pledges more funds for poor in troubled states" by Anna Yukhananov, *Reuters*, October 1, 2013

Production Possibilities of A and B

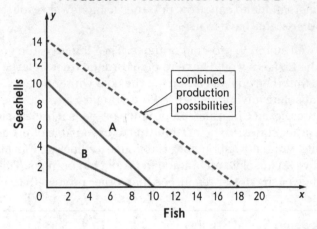

How Comparative Advantage Works

To understand how the law of comparative advantage works, imagine two people, Tim (A) and Juanita (B). They live on an island, and they both collect seashells and catch fish. The graph shows that Tim (A) can produce more fish and shells more efficiently than Juanita (B) in one day's time. That means that Tim (A) has an absolute advantage over Juanita (B) in both collecting shells and catching fish.

Notice that if Tim (A) decides to gather 10 seashells a day, he will not be able to catch any fish. Similarly, if Juanita (B) decides to catch 8 fish, she will not be able to collect seashells. Since both Tim and Juanita make trade-offs, they also have opportunity costs.

Tim has to give up 1 fish for every shell he collects. Juanita gives up 2 fish for each seashell she gathers and one-half of a seashell for each fish she catches. If each of them spends half of his or her day collecting shells and the other half fishing, Tim's output would be 5 shells and 5 fish, and Juanita's output would be 2 shells and 4 fish. Their combined total would be 7 shells and 9 fish.

Advantage of Specializing

Suppose they decide to specialize. Because the opportunity cost of catching fish is lower for Juanita (B) than it is for Tim (A), Juanita has a comparative advantage in producing fish, even though Tim has the absolute advantage. If Tim only collects shells and Juanita only catches fish, their combined output will be 10 shells and 8 fish.

By working together, they have gained 3 seashells and given up only 1 fish. However, if Tim catches 1 fish and collects 9 seashells, they have a combined output of 9 fish and 9 seashells. Compared to their production if they each split their time between the two activities, they have gained 2 seashells with no loss of fish.

By specializing, they have expanded their combined production possibilities. Even though Tim has an absolute advantage over Juanita for both fish and seashells, both benefit if they specialize.

Specialization and Comparative Advantage

Think about Social Studies

Directions: Fill-in-the-blank to complete each sentence by selecting the correct word or words at the end of each sentence.

1. A company that concentrates on producing only a few types of goods or services is practicing _____. (comparative advantage/specialization)

2. Opportunity costs are like _____. (trade-offs, models)

3. A company with a comparative advantage _____ produce goods or services more efficiently than anyone else. (needs to, does not need to)

Interdependence

Tim and Juanita choose to trade because each is better off as a result of their exchange. Trade is the activity or process of buying, selling, or exchanging goods or services. Individuals and businesses in a market economy tend to make choices that improve their lives. In this case, Tim and Juanita chose to specialize, which boosted the production possibilities for both of them.

Businesses and nations make similar choices. The US economy is linked to dozens of other nations around the world. **Interdependence** happens when producers rely on one another for information, resources, goods, and services.

Businesses are also interdependent. A company that makes automobiles is a good example. The design, natural resources, parts, and much of the labor that goes into producing automobiles involve not just the auto company but also other businesses in the same country and around the world. That interdependence has made cars more affordable than ever before.

Interdependence can seem like a bad idea when an event in another country has a negative effect on businesses close to home. In 2011 when an earthquake and tsunami hit Japan, the combined disasters halted production of cars in Japan. As a result, the supply of those cars in the United States fell.

Overall, however, interdependence benefits people in all countries. The gains made in productivity as a result of increases in specialization usually offset the negative effects.

 Think about Social Studies

Directions: Choose the best answer to the following question.

1. Why do nations engage in trade?

A. to protect home industries

B. to dump unwanted currency

C. to solve the problem of scarcity

D. to get rid of what they do not want

CORE SKILL

Gather Information

Look around your home or workplace and find a common everyday object. Think about how the object was made and the interdependence involved in its manufacture. Where did the raw material come from? How was the raw material transported to the manufacturer? How many parts make up this object and where did they come from? How was the object assembled and then distributed?

Go online and research your object to find the answers to these questions. Make a list of the jobs, companies, and countries involved in making your object and getting it to stores.

WRITE TO LEARN

Imagine you own your own small business. Describe the decision-making process you go through when deciding which products to produce with your limited resources. Include the concepts of specialization and interdependence in your process.

Vocabulary Review

Directions: Complete the sentences using the following key terms and vocabulary words.

absolute advantage	**comparative advantage**	**efficient**
interdependence	**opportunity cost**	**specialization**

1. A business that specializes in producing only the goods and services that can be made at a relatively low opportunity cost has a/an _____.

2. A company that produces something without wasting materials, time, or energy is _____.

3. If a bakery makes and sells only pies and not cakes, cookies, or donuts, it is practicing _____.

4. A company that produces a product or service by using fewer resources than other companies require has a(n) _____ in producing that product or service.

5. Two producers that need each other for information and resources are an example of _____.

6. A Florida citrus grower can grow oranges for a slightly lower cost than he can grow grapefruits, so he chooses to grow oranges. Not growing grapefruits is his _____.

Skill Review

Directions: Use the graph to answer the questions that follow.

Production Possibilities for Yard Work (based on a 20-hour workweek)

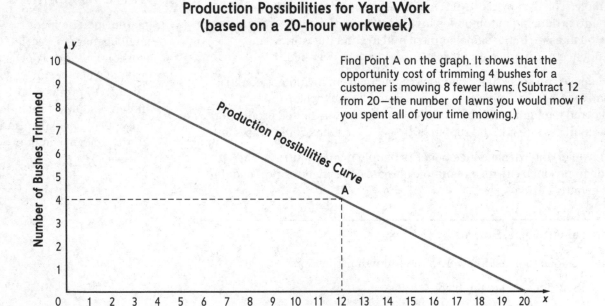

Find Point A on the graph. It shows that the opportunity cost of trimming 4 bushes for a customer is mowing 8 fewer lawns. (Subtract 12 from 20—the number of lawns you would mow if you spent all of your time mowing.)

1. What is the opportunity cost of trimming 6 bushes for a customer?

   A. 8 lawns mowed

   B. 12 lawns mowed

   C. 6 bushes trimmed

   D. 8 bushes trimmed

2. If only 3 bushes are trimmed, how many lawns can be mowed?

   A. 6 lawns

   B. 10 lawns

   C. 12 lawns

   D. 14 lawns

Skill Practice

Directions: Read the passage below. Then answer the questions that follow.

India's economy has grown about 7 percent every year since 1997. Contributing significantly to this growth is its high-tech businesses. Because so many Indian people speak English, India exports information technology to other countries. Its companies are leaders in designing software and selling the services to support it.

Indian companies also sell a range of services related to business processing. For example, a company in the United States or France will outsource operations such as accounting to companies in India. Other services that are outsourced to India include processing insurance claims and loan applications and reading medical X-rays. Computers and the Internet make this kind of long-distance rapid transfer of information possible—and cheap.

Many of these high-tech companies are Indian-owned and operated. However, U.S. businesses such as IBM, Hewlett-Packard, and Electronic Data Systems have their own branches in India. They employ thousands of Indians to work on information technology service projects.

1. According to the passage, which specialization played a major role in India's high growth rate?
   A. insurance claims
   B. loan applications
   C. medical x-rays
   D. information technology

2. When U.S. businesses employ Indians workers, they are participating in
   A. comparative advantage.
   B. interdependence.
   C. specialization.
   D. trade.

3. Other companies besides India have large populations of English speakers. What other reason can you infer for U.S. companies to export their services to India?
   A. Indian companies have a high growth rate.
   B. Indian companies are less expensive.
   C. Indian companies specialize in accounting.
   D. Indian companies are owned by many U.S. companies.

Writing Practice

Imagine you are starting your own business and you want to describe one aspect of it to someone who doesn't know the business. List the steps required to perform a vital task, such as preparing the night's special entrée, or fixing a leaky radiator, or building a Web page. Make sure to include every step, even the ones that seem obvious to you, and be sure to define any technical terms or jargon. They probably won't be obvious to someone not familiar with your business. Put the steps in chronological order.

Directions: Read the passage, and then answer the questions that follow.

> Think of all the materials and parts in a modern automobile. Car manufacturers have assembly plants to put all these parts together into a finished vehicle. But they usually rely on other companies to provide the raw materials or finished parts for each car. Some suppliers provide steel and aluminum for vehicle bodies. Others provide finished parts, such as seat belts, dashboards, seats, tires, door handles, windows, windshield wipers, filters, and lights.

1. Why might auto manufacturers buy a finished part, such as a door handle, instead of making it themselves?

   A. The part is cheaper when produced by a company specializing in its production.

   B. Auto manufacturers do not have a workforce that could produce such parts.

   C. It would take more raw materials for the auto manufacturer to produce the part.

   D. There is a low opportunity cost for the auto manufacturer to produce the part.

2. The auto manufacturer and its seat belt supplier could best be characterized as which of these?

   A. interdependent

   B. competitive

   C. inefficient

   D. entrepreneurial

3. Why would it be in the best interest of the auto manufacturer to have multiple companies producing windshield wipers instead of just one?

   A. Only the wiper makers producing the best product would survive in the market.

   B. Windshield wipers must be different for each car, so many companies are needed.

   C. Competition between windshield wiper makers would lower the cost of wipers.

   D. Specialization ensures that windshield wipers will cost less to the auto maker.

Directions: Answer the following questions.

4. Which of these is true about a market economy?

   A. Entrepreneurship is seldom rewarded.

   B. Natural resources cannot be bought or sold.

   C. Individuals are able to buy and sell property.

   D. Most goods remain the same for generations.

5. Which of these is most disadvantaged in a market economy?

   A. a farmer producing many crops

   B. a business purchasing new equipment

   C. a worker exchanging money for goods

   D. a craftsperson bartering for food

Directions: Use the following diagram to answer questions 6–8.

Circular Flow of Economic Activity

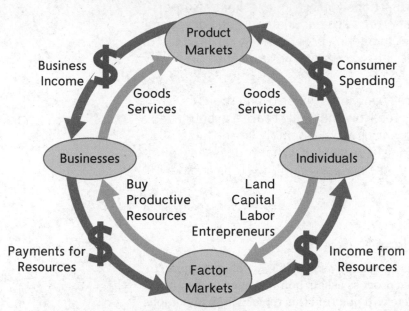

6. The circular flow model shows how a market economy organizes the production and consumption of goods and services. According to this diagram, how are the factors of production bought and sold in a market economy?

   A. through the use of factor markets

   B. through increases to business income

   C. through the use of product markets

   D. through spending by consumers

7. According to the diagram, which of these is likely to increase when businesses invest money in labor and capital?

   A. capital and labor availability

   B. production of goods and services

   C. consumer spending for goods

   D. overall unemployment

8. What is one way entrepreneurs are likely to obtain income in the market economy?

   A. by buying goods and services from product markets

   B. by inventing and selling new management methods

   C. by becoming employees at established companies

   D. by receiving payments for natural resources

Check Your Understanding

Lesson	Item Number
Markets, Competition, and Monopolies	3, 5
Factors of Production	6, 7
Profits and Productivity	4, 8
Specialization and Comparative Advantage	1, 2

WRITE ABOUT Business Production

A process essay describes in order the steps needed to accomplish a goal. Think of processes with which you are already familiar. Perhaps you are an excellent baker or can change a flat tire quickly. You follow certain steps in a particular order. Forgetting one of the steps, such as adding baking powder to banana bread batter, can lead to disaster. The steps must be in order; it's impossible to remove a tire without first loosening the lug nuts.

The same principles apply in economics generally and in business productions specifically. Factories are set up in a step-by-step flow that will create a product at the end of the line. Read the sample essay on Henry Ford's assembly line on page 352. Then imagine a business you might enjoy working in or owning. What processes would you need to follow or to set up? Write a process essay describing the steps and how you would implement them.

BEFORE YOU WRITE Brainstorm Ideas

When you brainstorm, you jot down as many ideas as quickly as possible, without stopping to edit or to judge the ideas. To write a well-developed process essay, you will need to discover a topic and several steps that must be followed. Where will you find this topic? Think about jobs that you have had. If you worked the line at a fast food restaurant, there was definitely a process to building a burger or a burrito. If you worked in an office, there was a process to opening and distributing the mail or to answering the telephone. If you were a library aide, you put books and other materials in order before you went out on the floor to shelve them. Use your own work experiences or those of a friend or family member to develop ideas for your process essay.

TIP   Use Graphic Organizers

Some people can organize their ideas just by making a list of them on a sheet of paper. For many of us, however, a visual diagram is helpful, especially to aid in uncovering the steps in a process. You may wish to use a graphic organizer similar to the one below. Feel free to design a graphic organizer that will best help you see the steps in the process about which you are going to write.

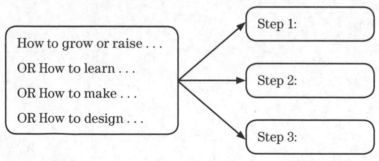

WHILE YOU WRITE Use Time-Order Transitions

Any process can be broken down into steps. When writing about a process, using words that help the reader follow each step is key. Each step needs to be written in the order in which it is done. If you have ever tried to follow a friend who stops to say while telling a story, "Oh, I forgot to mention that earlier . . . " you know how frustrating that can be. Each new step deserves a transition word to help readers know what to do and when to do it. The following words are often used for keeping steps in correct time-order.

after	meanwhile	
before	next	third
finally	now	when
first	second	while
later	then	

TIP   Watch Out for Subject-Verb Agreement

When writing in standard English, it is important to be sure that subjects and verbs agree in number. That is, a singular subject demands a singular verb, while a plural subject requires a plural verb. This is the case whether the subject is a noun or a pronoun. *He, she,* and *it* are all singular pronouns that need singular nouns. If the verb is a regular verb, the verb must end in s to match a singular subject.

   He talks.   She walks.   It runs.

On the other hand, a plural subject needs a verb that does not end in s.

   We serve.   They catch.

AFTER YOU WRITE Ask a Friend to Check Your Work

After you have written your process essay, ask a friend to read it over and see whether he or she can follow the steps. Is the writing clear? Have time-order words been inserted to help the reader? Ask your friend to give an honest evaluation. Were there times when it was hard to follow what you were saying? Revise your essay based on the suggestions your reader offers.

Chapter 6

Microeconomics and Macroeconomics

As you go through each day, you make many economic decisions. What should you buy for lunch? Do you need to pay any bills? Should you add more money to savings? These are all decisions that affect your personal economy. Economics is the study of how goods and services are produced, distributed, and consumed. Your personal economic decisions fall within the field of microeconomics. Microeconomics is concerned with the economic behavior of individuals, businesses, and markets within an economy. Macroeconomics focuses on a bigger picture—the policies that govern the larger economy, as well as indicators of economic health.

In this chapter you will study these topics:

Lesson 6.1
Microeconomics

How does the market economy affect your life? What happens to prices when there is high demand for a product? What about when demand is low but supply is high? How do buyers and sellers benefit when the markets are in equilibrium?

Lesson 6.2
Macroeconomics and Government Policy

How does the federal government participate in the economy? What is the relationship between revenues and expenditures? What are federal fiscal and monetary policies?

Lesson 6.3
Macroeconomics, the GDP, and Price Fluctuation

How do economists measure the health of an economy? What is the gross domestic product and how is it calculated? How do inflation and deflation affect economic activity?

Goal Setting

Think about what you already know about the economy. As a consumer, how do you participate? How might changes in supply and demand affect your economic life?

Now think about what else might be important to know about the economy. How do government regulations affect your economic life? What happens to your personal economy when inflation or deflation occurs?

LESSON OBJECTIVES

- Identify the relationship between supply and demand
- Interpret graphs of supply and demand curves
- Explain market equilibrium

CORE SKILLS & PRACTICES

- Interpreting Charts and Graphs
- Analyze Information

Key Terms

demand curve
a graph that illustrates the quantity of a good demanded at different prices

law of demand
as the price of a good rises, the demand falls; as the price falls, the demand rises

market equilibrium
the point at which demand is equal to supply

supply curve
a graph that illustrates the quantity of a good supplied at different prices

supply and demand
forces that influence the exchange of goods and services in a market economy

Vocabulary

median
middle number when numbers are sorted least to greatest

Key Concept

The forces of supply and demand determine the market prices of most products and resources in the US and global economies.

Popular new technology products often sell out quickly. Those who did not get to the store in time have to wait for more products to be shipped to stores. Sometimes the price of the product increases because so many people want it. This scenario illustrates the market forces of supply and demand.

Market Influences

Markets are important to the US and global economies. In economics, the word *market* describes the exchange of goods and services. These exchanges take place between buyers and sellers. The study of these exchanges, and the behaviors of the individuals participating in the exchanges, is known as microeconomics. Microeconomics includes the economic behavior of individual buyers and sellers, or businesses, in an economy.

Nations with a market economy allow the forces of **supply and demand** to influence the markets. The supply side of the market includes producers of products and services (sellers). The demand side includes those who purchase goods and services (buyers). Buyers and sellers influence the market by choosing what to buy and sell. The price of the goods and services is set by sellers, however, buyers influence the price by purchasing more or less of the product.

Prices send signals to both producers (sellers) and consumers (buyers). A rise in prices is a signal to producers that it is time to increase production. To consumers, it is a signal to buy fewer goods. Falling prices let sellers know it is time to cut back on production or make something else. Low prices let buyers know it is time to stock up on an item.

In a market economy, government plays a limited role in a country's economic activity. The United States has a mixed economy. A mixed economy is one in which government does not control the economy but regulates it by passing laws to help control it. Some regulations include environmental protection and workplace safety laws. Some countries do not allow market forces to work. In these countries, the government controls most economic activity. The governmentsets the price of products and

Jose Luis Pelaez Inc/Blend Images LLC

controls the number of products made and sold. This type of economy is known as a centrally planned economy.

In market exchanges, buyers and sellers must answer different questions. The questions faced by sellers are related to supply, the amount of a product businesses are willing and able to produce at a specific price in a certain time. The questions faced by buyers are related to demand—how much to purchase and at what price. Demand is the amount of goods and services consumers are willing to buy at various prices.

Think about Social Studies

Directions: Select the correct definition for the following term.

1. microeconomics

A. producers of goods and services

B. those who purchase goods and services

C. exchange of goods and services

D. the economic behavior of individual buyers and sellers, or businesses, in an economy

Laws of Supply and Demand

According to the **law of demand**, as the price of a good rises, the demand for it falls, and as the price falls, the demand rises. In economics, laws like this one are descriptions of what is likely to happen—if all other things are equal. For example, a new smart phone comes on the market and is extremely popular. Even though the price is high, many people will still buy it because it is desirable to them.

Demand Schedule

Economists illustrate the relationship between price and demand in two ways. One way to show this relationship is in a demand schedule. This is a list that shows how price affects the demand for a product. The demand schedule on this page shows the demand for CDs at several different prices. At $30, no one is willing to buy a CD. At $20, just one will be sold. At $5, the number jumps to eight.

Another way to look at the information is to use a graph. Look at the graph on this page. The line on the graph is formed by plotting the points from a demand schedule. The resulting **demand curve** illustrates the quantity of a good or service that is demanded at different prices. Notice that the curve slopes downward. A downward slope shows a negative relationship—as one variable increases, the other decreases.

Interpreting Charts and Graphs

Charts and graphs make understanding large amounts of information easier. To interpret, or read, a chart, first read the main title and the title of the columns. Then read the information under the headings. Relate the data, or information, in one column to that in other columns on the same row.

Line graphs include a vertical axis, also called the y-axis. The horizontal axis is called the x-axis. To interpret a line graph, read the main title. Then read the title for each axis. These titles represent a variable, because their value can change. Study the points plotted on the graph. Trace the line and look for a trend, or the general direction of change.

Study the chart and graph on this page. Then answer the following questions in your notebook.

1. What pattern do you see in the first column of the demand schedule? What pattern do you see in the second column?

2. How does this trend relate to the demand curve in the graph?

Demand Schedule

Price of CDs	Quantity Demanded
$30	0
25	0
20	1
15	3
10	5
5	8

Demand Curve

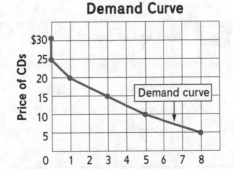

Analyze Information

Information is presented in various forms, including text, illustrations, charts, and graphs. When you analyze economic information, you may need to perform mathematics calculations. Those calculations can include mean, median, and mode. These calculations help you to understand information more completely.

The mean is sometimes referred to as the "average." To find the mean, add all of the numbers in the data set. Then divide the sum by the number of points in the data set. The **median** is the middle number when the numbers are sorted least to greatest. If there is an even amount of numbers, the mean of the two middle numbers is the median. The mode is the number that occurs most frequently.

Follow the steps listed above to find the mean, median, and mode of the price data in the supply schedule.

In a market economy, sellers must consider how much to sell and at what price. According to the law of supply, if all other things are equal, the higher the price of a product or service, the more of it suppliers will offer for sale. As the price falls, so will the quantity supplied.

Profit Motive

The law of supply is based on the profit motive—the desire of individuals and businesses to make money. Therefore, the relationship between the price of a good or service and the quantity supplied is a positive one. That is, if the price rises, the quantity supplied also rises. If the price drops, the quantity supplied goes down as well.

Supply Schedule

The relationship between price and the quantity supplied can be shown with a supply schedule. A supply schedule is a list that shows the quantities supplied of a product at various prices during a particular time period. The supply schedule on this page shows the supply for CDs at several prices. At $30, suppliers will provide eight CDs; at $20, six will be offered; and at $5, they do not provide any CDs.

Like demand schedules, supply schedules can also be graphed. Connecting the points plotted from a supply schedule forms the **supply curve**, which illustrates the quantity of a good or service that is supplied at different prices. Unlike a demand curve, it slopes upward. An upward slope shows a positive relationship—as one variable increases, the other also increases.

Supply Schedule

Price of CDs	Quantity Supplied
$30	8
25	7
20	6
15	4
10	2
5	0

Supply Curve

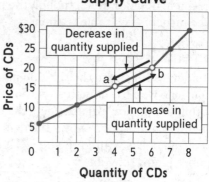

A supply curve begins with the preferences of individual sellers. The points along the curve show the sellers' willingness to provide a good or service at a particular price. Sellers can be individuals or companies. Economists can find out the total number of products in a market by adding the individual supply curves of all suppliers in the market. This total number is known as the market supply.

Think about Social Studies

Directions: Identify each statement as either *buyer* or *seller*.

1. The demand curve relates to the _____.
2. The supply curve relates to the _____.
3. A consumer is also known as the _____.
4. A producer is also known as the _____.

Market Equilibrium

According to the law of demand, the higher the price, the smaller the quantity demanded. If the quantity demanded is greater than the quantity supplied, a product shortage occurs. For example, a popular, new electronics product, such as a cell phone or video game, that sells out quickly in stores. When demand for a product is greater than its supply, rising prices act as a way of rationing, or limiting, the demand for that product. The higher the price of the new product, the shorter the lines will be to purchase it.

The higher the price of a good or service, the larger the quantity supplied. If the quantity supplied is greater than the demand, prices are likely to fall. Clearance sales are a sign of a surplus—a situation in which the quantity supplied of a good or service is greater than the demand.

The aim of the market is to compromise between the interests of the buyers and the interests of the sellers. **Market equilibrium** is reached when demand is equal to the supply. At that point, buyers have no incentive to offer more money for a product, and sellers have no incentive to reduce the price.

To illustrate market equilibrium, the supply curve and demand curve are included in the same graph. The place where the two curves cross each another is the equilibrium price. The graph shows the CD example. At $15 per CD, suppliers will produce 600 million CDs, and buyers will purchase the entire supply.

Graphing the Equilibrium Market

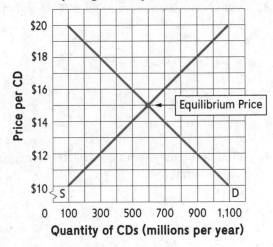

Financial, Economic, Business, and Entrepreneurial Literacy

The effects of supply and demand are evident in all areas of the economy, including the cost of gas, rent, and groceries. Even tickets to a sporting event are affected by supply and demand. Many people do not want to see a team with a losing record, so demand for tickets is low. Low demand causes low ticket prices. However, people want to attend games of winning teams. The demand for tickets to these games is great, and the games often sell out. High demand leads to high prices. High demand can have some harmful consequences. For example, demand for tickets causes some people to resell tickets illegally for many times their original cost.

Research how demand creates a black market, or illegal marketplace, for products. Write a brief paragraph describing the effects of the black market on the economy.

WRITE TO LEARN

In your notebook, describe how the forces of supply and demand determine prices of goods and services.

 Think about Social Studies

Directions: Choose the best answer to the following question.

1. Why do you think the equilibrium price is also known as the price that "clears the market"?

A. Because no one will want to buy the good or service at this price.

B. Because the price of the good or service will be so low there will not be any competition.

C. Because the price of the good or service will cause the demand to match the supply.

D. Because the demand for the good or service will greatly exceed the supply.

Vocabulary Review

Directions: Complete the sentences using the following key terms and vocabulary words.

law of demand   supply curve   median

supply and demand   demand curve   market equilibrium

1. The point when demand for a product is equal to the supply of the product is known as

_____.

2. The _____ of a set of data is found by arranging the numbers from smallest to largest

and then choosing the middle number in the arrangement.

3. When the price of a product falls, the demand for that product usually increases. This is known as the

_____.

4. The _____ shows a negative, or downward slope, on a graph.

5. The _____ shows a positive relationship, or upward slope, on a graph.

6. In a market economy, the forces of _____ influence the markets.

Skill Review

Directions: Refer to the demand chart and demand curve on page 169 to answer the questions. Choose the best answer to each question.

1. If the pattern in the demand curve were continued, how many CDs would be sold if the price were $2.50?

  A. 1

  B. 5

  C. 8

  D. 9

2. How many CDs are sold when the price is $12.50?

  A. 3

  B. 4

  C. 5

  D. 6

3. What is the median number of CDs shown in the demand chart?

  A. 8

  B. 4

  C. 2

  D. 0

4. What is the mean number of CDs shown in the demand chart?

  A. 2.83

  B. 3.5

  C. 4.25

  D. 5

Skill Practice

Directions: Read the passage. Then answer the questions that follow.

A report on the effect the U.S. Civil War (1861–1865) had on the shoe industry:

"The shoe business is in a most thriving condition. The war reduced a part of the country to bare feet, and as the existing shoe factories had during the war only been able to supply the loyal states, the extension of their market makes them very busy. Wonderful progress has been made in the shoe business within a few years. A machine is had for everything, and girls to tend machines, and men to finish when the machines stop. There is a machine to roll the leather, which was formerly hammered; a machine to split the leather, which was done slowly by hand in other times; . . . machines to stitch the upper leathers or cloths, and bind the edges; and finally, a more important machine that sews the upper to the sole; and then there are machines for putting on the heels and forming them. By these means, from five to ten times the work can be done by a given number of hands than could have been accomplished twenty years ago under the old system."

— *The Merchants' Magazine and Commercial Review*, 1865

1. What does the report suggest about the way shoemakers in the 1860s increased the quantity supplied?
   A. Machinery helped increase the supply of shoes to meet the demand after the Civil War.
   B. In general, people were not happy that machines replaced workers.
   C. Workers were able to produce as many shoes as machinery could produce.
   D. Machinery lowered demand for shoes and increased their price after the Civil War.

2. Why was the supply of shoes insufficient in Southern states during the war?
   A. Factories in Southern states did not use machinery to make shoes.
   B. Shoe factories in the South had to ship all of their shoes to the Northern states.
   C. Shoe factories in the north could not sell shoes to people in Southern states.
   D. Laws prevented Southern states from opening shoe factories during the war.

3. How might increased supply of shoes affect their price in the South?
   A. The price would not change.
   B. The price would decrease.
   C. The price would increase.
   D. The price would level off.

4. Based on the context clues, what do you think the word **bind** means?
   A. to decorate or embellish
   B. to shine or polish
   C. to fasten or secure
   D. to dye or add coloring

Writing Practice

Directions: Write a response to the following question: How does the law of supply contrast with the law of demand?

LESSON 6.2 Macroeconomics and Government Policy

LESSON OBJECTIVES

- Explain the relationship between revenue and expenditures
- Describe the fiscal and monetary policies used by the federal government
- Discuss the purpose of tariffs

CORE SKILLS & PRACTICES

- Identify Comparisons and Contrasts
- Interpret Meaning

Key Terms

expenditures
money that is paid out by a government

fiscal policy
taxing and spending policies of a government

monetary policies
strategies for controlling the size of the money supply and the price of credit

subsidy
government payment to an individual or business to encourage or protect a particular economic activity

tariff
tax on an import

Vocabulary

contrast
to show differences

Key Concept

The federal government uses fiscal policies and monetary policies to manage the economy.

When you manage your household budget, you are managing a small economy. You may track how much money you make and how you will spend that money. Your budget might include a savings plan to meet short-term goals, such as a new stove, as well as long-term goals, such as money for retirement. The federal government also manages an economy, but on a much larger scale. Because of its size and complexity, the federal government has implemented many laws and policies to manage the economy.

Federal Revenue and Expenditures

The federal government collects income so it is able to perform its business. Taxes provide most government income, or revenue. The government also borrows money to help pay for its expenses.

Revenue

Each year, the federal government collects around $2.5 trillion in income. Almost half of this revenue comes from income taxes that are paid by individuals or businesses. Most of the remainder comes from Social Security and Medicare payroll deductions. Other taxes make up a small percentage of total revenue, as does the budget deficit. The deficit is the amount of revenue that the country must borrow to meet its financial obligations.

The government borrows money by selling bonds and other securities to individuals and businesses. When you buy a savings bond, you are loaning the government money. After a certain amount of time, the government pays off its bonds, notes, and other bills, with interest. Because savings bonds are backed by the US government, they are considered a safe investment for consumers.

Expenditures

The government uses revenue to cover **expenditures**, or money that is paid out by the government to conduct business. The largest percentage of expenditures for human resources, which includes government employment

Macroeconomics and Government Policy

and benefits, Medicare, Social Security, and veterans' benefits and services. Defense spending is also a major expenditure. Other expenditures include interest on the national debt, and spending on energy, transportation infrastructure, education, the environment, and international affairs. Percentages of expenditures can change over time, as shown in the two charts.

These expenditures are also investments because the government receives something in return. Some of the biggest projects the American government invested in after 1900 include the Panama Canal, Hoover Dam, and the Interstate Highway System. What the United States received for its investment was a shorter route from the Atlantic to Pacific Ocean, a hydroelectric power plant, and a network of high-speed roads.

CORE PRACTICE

Identify Comparisons and Contrasts

The circle graphs on this page were produced using data from the US Federal Office of Management and Budget. What do these circle graphs compare? Why might it be useful to compare the information in the charts? Write a statement that **contrasts** or shows the differences in the information that is shown.

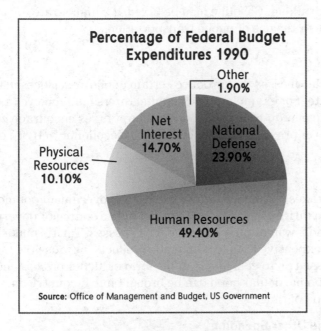

Percentage of Federal Budget Expenditures 1990

- Other 1.90%
- Net Interest 14.70%
- National Defense 23.90%
- Physical Resources 10.10%
- Human Resources 49.40%

Source: Office of Management and Budget, US Government

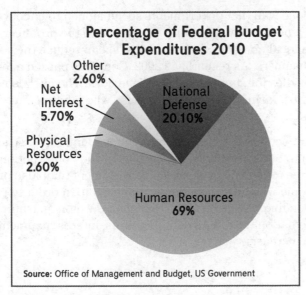

Percentage of Federal Budget Expenditures 2010

- Other 2.60%
- Net Interest 5.70%
- National Defense 20.10%
- Physical Resources 2.60%
- Human Resources 69%

Source: Office of Management and Budget, US Government

Think about Social Studies

Directions: In a notebook, list three types of government expenditures and describe how each type directly or indirectly affects your family.

Macroeconomics and Government Policy

List the pros and cons of keeping taxes low to stimulate the economy.

Federal Fiscal and Monetary Policies

The government must have specific plans in place to legally obtain and spend revenue. To manage its economy effectively, it must also have specific plans related to money supply, credit, and interest rates. The federal **fiscal policy** includes all policies that relate to taxing and spending. Federal **monetary policies** establish strategies for controlling the size of the money supply and the price of credit.

The fiscal policies that direct taxation and federal spending are determined by both Congress and the president. Federal tax policies are designed to raise money. They may also be designed to influence the behavior of individuals or businesses. For example, some goods that can harm health, such as cigarettes or alcohol, are often taxed at a high rate to discourage smoking or drinking. Gasoline may be taxed at a higher rate to encourage conservation or the use of public transportation.

Fiscal Policies

Alternately, businesses that produce certain goods or services may be taxed at a lower rate. For example, some manufacturers may receive tax breaks for producing energy-efficient products. Lower taxes encourage companies to charge lower prices, thereby increasing the economic activity of consumers.

Tariffs

Tariffs are taxes on imports. In the 1800s, the government got most of its revenue from tariffs. Those taxes were not only a source of government funds but also a way of protecting local businesses. Tariffs make imported goods more expensive than locally made products, because the tax on the import is passed on to consumers in the form of higher prices. Quotas limit how much of a particular good can be brought into a country during a specific period of time.

Subsidies and Other Spending

Subsidies are one way that governments spend money to encourage local production of a product. A **subsidy** is a payment to the producer or consumer of a local good or service. A subsidy can reduce the cost of that product to consumers. As recently as 2002, Congress passed a law that increased subsidies for soybeans, wheat, and corn. The law also contained subsidies to dairy farmers, as well as to those who plant peanuts, lentils, and chickpeas.

During difficult economic times, the government may increase spending on projects to try to boost the economy, such as hiring construction workers to repair or replace roads and bridges. The government may also provide more benefits to people who are struggling economically. In order to pay for this increase in spending, the government may borrow money, leading to an increase in the national debt. As debt increases, interest payments on that debt may also increase.

Regulations

A regulation is a rule that controls or directs a business or industry in order to protect consumers or the nation as a whole. Regulations are not taxes, but they can have a similar effect on businesses and the overall economy. In 1906, for example, Congress passed the Pure Food and Drug Act. It created an agency that tested all foods and medicines to ensure that they were safe for human consumption. The law had a variety of effects, one of which was to make many foods and drugs safer. However, many foods and drugs became more expensive, as new regulations required companies to add steps to their production process, thus increasing costs. In general, increased or tighter government regulations tend to raise costs, with some exceptions. For example, regulations that promote efficiency in manufacturing, or encourage competition, can lower costs and stimulate the economy.

Market Failures

In a market economy, the market does not always work. Market failures occur as a result of imperfect competition and gaps between the private cost and the social cost of behaviors or actions. In the past, some businesses formed monopolies to limit competition. Others engaged in price discrimination. In 1914, Congress passed the Clayton Antitrust Act, which outlawed price discrimination. That same year, Congress also created the Federal Trade Commission (FTC). The FTC can issue rulings that force a company to stop unfair practices.

Monetary Policies

The federal government uses monetary policies to control the size of the money supply and the price of credit. The Federal Reserve Act of 1913 created a Federal Reserve Board to manage the monetary policies of the United States.

The Federal Reserve System, or "The Fed," is the central bank system of the United States. As the nation's official bank, it receives government deposits, makes government loans, manages the money supply, and sets interest rates. The Fed also monitors private banks, to prevent bank failures.

The Fed manages the money supply to make sure an appropriate amount of money stays in circulation. Increased economic activity requires more money, and The Fed can release more money as the economy grows. However, too much money circulating in the economy can cause a rise in prices, called inflation. Too little money in circulation can slow economic activity, so The Fed must determine the right balance.

The Fed can also manage the economy by adjusting interest rates. During a weak economy, The Fed may lower interest rates, to encourage individuals or businesses to take out loans or consume more goods. During a strong economy, The Fed may raise interest rates to prevent inflation.

 Think about Social Studies

Directions: Choose the best answer to the question below.

1. When the Fed writes lending rules for banks, it is acting as a

A. government banker.

B. money supplier.

C. regulator.

D. a subsidy.

Interpret Meaning

During a difficult economic period, The Fed lowers interest rates and reduces the money supply. A nonprofit organization argues that both of these actions could negatively impact consumers and the economy. What does the organization mean by this statement? Use the information about monetary policy to write a paragraph supporting the viewpoint of the organization. Then write a paragraph from your own viewpoint. This paragraph could support, or corroborate, the conclusions of the organization, or challenge those viewpoints.

Vocabulary Review

Directions: Complete the sentences using the following key terms and vocabulary words.

expenditures	fiscal policy	monetary policies
contrast	tariff	subsidy

1. A(n) _____ is a tax on an import.

2. A nation's _____ determines how it taxes individuals or businesses and spends revenue.

3. Government _____ might include money spent to repair bridges and roads.

4. A(n) _____ is a government payment that encourages local production of a product or service.

5. Charts are a good way to compare and _____ information.

6. The Federal Reserve is responsible for carrying out the nation's _____.

Skill Review

Directions: Choose the best answer to each question.

1. Which of these is a government expenditure?
   A. cigarette tax
   B. corn subsidy
   C. Pure Food and Drug Act
   D. tariff on foreign cotton

2. Which of these actions would The Fed likely take if economic activity were increasing rapidly and the money supply were high?
   A. Add money to the economy and lower interest rates.
   B. Remove money from the economy and lower interest rates.
   C. Add money to the economy and raise interest rates.
   D. Remove money from the economy and raise interest rates.

3. Which of these activities would be most influenced by actions taken by The Fed?
   A. A disabled veteran seeks medical care.
   B. Greek olives cost more than California olives.
   C. A couple applies for a homeowner's loan.
   D. Georgia farmers receive money to grow peanuts.

4. What is the single largest source of revenue for local governments?
   A. income tax
   B. intergovernmental revenue
   C. property tax
   D. sales tax

Skill Practice

Directions: Read the passage below. Then choose the best answer to the questions that follow.

A Century of US Central Banking

In his 2013 speech at a conference sponsored by the National Bureau of Economic Research, Federal Reserve Chairman Ben S. Bernanke discussed the evolution of Federal Reserve policymaking over the last 100 years.

"In the words of one of the authors of the Federal Reserve Act, Robert Latham Owen, the Federal Reserve was established to 'provide a means by which periodic panics which shake the American Republic and do it enormous injury shall be stopped.' In short, the original goal of the Great Experiment that was the founding of the Fed was the preservation of financial stability… How should a central bank enhance financial stability? One means is by assuming the lender-of-last-resort function…under which the central bank uses its power to provide liquidity to ease market conditions during periods of panic or incipient panic… However, putting out the fire is not enough; it is also important to foster a financial system that is sufficiently resilient to withstand large financial shocks. Toward that end, the Federal Reserve, together with other regulatory agencies… is actively engaged in monitoring financial developments and working to strengthen financial institutions and markets…What about the monetary policy framework? In general, the Federal Reserve's policy framework… include[s an] emphasis on preserving the Fed's inflation credibility, which is critical for anchoring inflation expectations…We have also continued to increase the transparency of monetary policy."

—Chairman Ben S. Bernanke at "The First 100 Years of the Federal Reserve: The Policy Record, Lessons Learned, and Prospects for the Future," a conference sponsored by the National Bureau of Economic Research, Cambridge, Massachusetts, July 10, 2013

1. According to Chairman Bernanke, one way The Fed helps to preserve financial stability is by
   A. providing liquidity to the system during periods of panic.
   B. creating periodic panics.
   C. emphasizing inflation credibility.
   D. increasing transparency of monetary policy.

2. Liquidity is when assets can be easily converted to cash. Why would liquidity help ease market conditions during periods of panic?
   A. It helps The Fed regulate inflations rates.
   B. It allows The Fed to work with other regulatory agencies.
   C. It anchors financial expectations of inflation.
   D. It allows The Fed to quickly loan money to companies.

3. What is the most likely definition of "inflation credibility"?
   A. assuming lender-of-last-resort function
   B. providing financial stability through regulating inflation
   C. engaging in financial monitoring of regulatory agencies
   D. preventing periodic panic and providing liquidity

4. In the passage above, what does the term **resilient** mean?
   A. fire resistant
   B. financially secure
   C. monitored
   D. able to recover

Writing Practice

Directions: If you were able to influence US fiscal policy, what would be your priorities and why? Write a paragraph describing this.

LESSON 6.3 Macroeconomics, the GDP, and Price Fluctuation

LESSON OBJECTIVES

- Explain why the GDP is an important economic measure
- Contrast inflation and deflation
- Explain the significance of the unemployment rate

CORE SKILLS & PRACTICES

- Read Charts
- Integrate Visual Information

Key Terms

gross domestic product (GDP)
the dollar value of all final goods and services produced in a nation during a single year

inflation
a rise in the general level of prices over time

deflation
a drop in the general level of prices over time

unemployment rate
the percentage of people in the labor force who actively looked for a job during a particular month but could not find one

Vocabulary

integrate
combine to make a whole

cyclical
reoccurring in the same order

Key Concept

Measures such as an economy's GDP, inflation or deflation rate, and unemployment rate provide economists with ways to measure an economy's health.

Skilled workers build cars and trucks in the various automobile manufacturing plants around the United States. The value of vehicles they produce as well as the number of workers on the job and the number of people looking for work are both indicators of the nation's general economic health.

Gross Domestic Product

Cars, trucks, and all other goods and services produced in the United States are part of the nation's **gross domestic product (GDP)**. GDP is the dollar value of all final goods and services produced in a country during a single year. It includes the value of all the cars, the advertising to sell all those cars, the loans that help people buy those cars, and the gasoline sold to fuel those cars. GDP is an important gauge of the strength of the economy, as it measures total output or production of a country's economy.

Calculating GDP

GDP is determined by multiplying the quantity of all final goods and services by their prices. It is first calculated for each of three broad categories: consumer spending, government spending, and investments. The results are added together to form GDP.

Only final goods and services are included in GDP. For example, a new car that is manufactured in the United States is a final good that would be included in GDP. The seat belts, mirrors, tires, and other parts that became part of the car are considered intermediate goods. As a result, they are not included in GDP. However, if someone who already owns a car buys new tires—and if those tires were made in the United States—they are considered final goods. They would then be counted in the GDP the year they are sold.

Goods made in other countries are not part of GDP. Neither is the sale of used goods or transactions that take place outside of organized markets, such as jobs done at home, are not counted.

©iStockphoto.com/RicAguiar

GDP Fluctuations

Economists calculate GDP quarterly, or every three months. They use the percentage change in GDP from one quarter to the next to see economic trends. The chart shows quarterly percentage changes of GDP from 2007 to the second quarter of 2013.

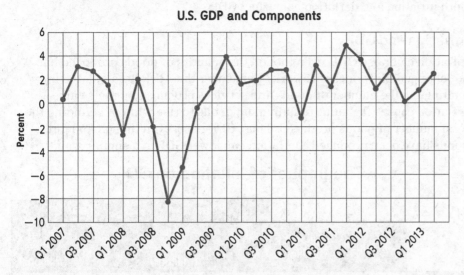

U.S. GDP and Components

Source: https://www.thrivent.com/wallstreettoyourstreet/images/marketcommentary/2013/2013_0219_US_GDP_and_Components_200.jpg

Limits of GDP

GDP is a useful indicator of economic output and the health of an economy, but it has limitations. Because it includes only transactions in organized markets, work outside those markets is uncounted. In a country where bartering is common, GDP can underestimate economic output. GDP can also count negative events as beneficial. Wars and natural disasters can raise GDP, however these events can have an overall negative effect on a nation.

 Think about Social Studies

Directions: Answer the following questions.

1. According to the chart above, in which quarter did the GDP have the largest drop?

   A. Q1 2008

   B. Q4 2008

   C. Q1 2011

   D. Q4 2011

2. Using the chart above, how many quarters had positive growth in GDP?

   A. 6

   B. 10

   C. 13

   D. 20

Read Charts

The graph on this page shows changes in US GDP (based on 2009 dollars) from 2007 to the second quarter of 2013. However, it does not show the actual GDP itself. Instead, it shows the percentage of change in the GDP from one quarter to the next. For example, in 2011, GDP increased by 4.5 percent between Q3 (the third quarter) and Q4 (the fourth quarter). According to the graph, how did GDP change between Q3 and Q4 of 2008?

Inflation and Deflation

Inflation is a rise in the general level of prices over time. As prices go up due to inflation, the purchasing power of a dollar declines. **Deflation** is the opposite of inflation; it is a drop in the general level of prices over time. As prices go down due to deflation, the purchasing power of a dollar increases. Both inflation and deflation can affect GDP.

Inflation and GDP

Inflation can raise GDP, even though the quantity of goods produced has not changed. How does this work? Remember that GDP is calculated by multiplying the number of goods and services produced by their value. Inflation causes the value of individual goods to rise without changing the total number of goods produced. Thus, GDP rises, even though no more goods have been produced. Deflation can lower GDP in a similar way.

The Impact of Inflation on GDP

	Product	Quantity (millions)	Year 1 Price (per 1 unit)	Year 1 Dollar Values (millions)	Year 2 Price (per 1 unit)	Year 2 Dollar Values (millions)
Goods	Automobiles	6	$20,000	$120,000	$22,000	$132,000
	Tires	10	$60	$600	$70	$700
	Shoes	55	$50	$2,750	$55	$3,025
	...*	...*	...*	...*	...*	...*
Services	Haircuts	150	$8	$1,200	$10	$1,500
	Tax Filing	30	$150	$4,500	$160	$4,800
	Legal Advice	45	200	$9,000	$220	$9,900
	...*	...*	...*	...*	...*	...*
Structures	Single Family	3	$75,000	$225,000	$80,000	$240,000
	Multifamily	5	$300,000	$1,000,000	$330,000	$1,650,000
	Commercial	1	$1,000,000	$1,000,000	$1,100,000	$1,100,000
	...*	...*	...*	...*	...*	...*

NOTE: ...*other goods, services, and structures

Total Gross Domestic Product = $9 trillion

Total Gross Domestic Product = $9.9 trillion

Rising inflation can cause a slowdown of economic activity. Inflation decreases consumer spending because the amount of goods and services people can buy for their money falls as prices rise. Families and businesses may put off large purchases or investments during periods of inflation. Since they are buying less, producers will make less. As a result, economic activity slows.

Think about Social Studies

Directions: Fill in the blanks.

1. _____ is the increase in prices over time.

2. When prices fall, the GDP can _____ even if the same number of goods is produced.

3. A decrease in prices over time is called _____.

4. Families are _____ likely to buy a house during a period of inflation.

Unemployment

The **unemployment rate** is the percentage of individuals in the civilian labor force who actively looked for a job during a particular month and could not find one. High unemployment is a signal that the economy is not working efficiently and that resources are being wasted. Low unemployment signals an efficient economy.

Causes and Effects of Unemployment

Unemployment happens when people leave their old jobs for any number of reasons and have not yet found new jobs. These people have the skills for the jobs available in the economy, so their unemployment is usually brief. Unemployment can occur seasonally, based on holidays or weather patterns. It can also be **cyclical**, happening again and again in the same order, in response to changing business cycles. During a recession, for example, many people are laid off because there is no longer a demand for the goods and services they provide. Or sometimes a company tries to save money during a recession by laying off workers. Once the economy recovers and demand increases, these workers are sometimes rehired.

Sometimes unemployment can occur when a significant change in the economy reduces the demand for a particular group of workers and their skills. Technological innovations, changes in consumer demand, or decisions by businesses or governments can result in this structural unemployment. For example, when the printing industry became digital, jobs for manual typesetters disappeared. Retraining unemployed workers is often necessary with structural unemployment.

A high unemployment rate affects almost every part of the economy, and it places economic hardship on those who can least afford it. Government programs such as unemployment insurance and federal welfare help people to meet basic needs and participate in the economy while unemployed.

In a time of high unemployment, the government may also take steps to try to boost the economy. It may increase spending, for instance. By buying more goods and services, the government hopes to spur businesses to produce more. That will lead them to hire more workers, which reduces the unemployment rate.

Think about Social Studies

Directions: Choose the best answer to each question.

1. What could it mean when the unemployment rate increases?

A. The overall number of jobless people has decreased.

B. Companies have become less efficient over time.

C. The economy is not working as efficiently as before.

D. Inflation has decreased, thereby decreasing GDP.

2. Which of these workers is most likely to undergo seasonal unemployment?

A. a newspaper reporter

B. a dentist

C. an automotive worker

D. a farmworker

Vocabulary Review

Directions: Complete the sentences using the following key terms and vocabulary words.

gross domestic product	**inflation**	**integrate**
deflation	**cyclical**	**unemployment rate**

1. When the _____ is low, a very high percentage of people can find jobs.

2. _____ causes prices to decrease.

3. A rise in the GDP without a rise in the number of goods produced is an indicator of _____.

4. By looking at a bar graph and reading related text, you can _____ the information in both to better understand the ideas presented.

5. The _____ of a nation is a measure of the value of its goods and services produced.

6. Unemployment that is _____ happens again and again in response to business cycles.

Skill Review

Directions: Choose the best answer to each question.

1. Which of these would count toward the US gross domestic product?

   A. a washing machine made in Sweden and sold in the United States

   B. a homeowner paying a neighborhood teen for mowing the lawn

   C. a car made in the United States and sold in the United Arab Emirates

   D. clothing once made in the United States that is sold at a secondhand shop

2. People who stay home to take care of their children are not counted in the unemployment rate. Why not?

   A. They have a job that allows them to participate in the economy.

   B. They are not considered to be "working" by economists.

   C. They are not collecting government unemployment benefits.

   D. They are not actively searching for a job outside the home.

3. Which of these would be the most likely reaction to inflation?

   A. reduction in household spending

   B. decrease in the gross domestic product

   C. rapid increase in unemployment

   D. increased purchase of luxury items

4. An increase in the purchasing power of a dollar is a sign of

   A. deflation.

   B. inflation.

   C. rising prices.

   D. unemployment.

Skill Practice

Directions: Read the passage and examine the chart below. Then answer the questions that follow.

In a September 2012 article in *Business Insider*, Joe Weisenthal criticizes a speech made by former President Bill Clinton. In that speech, Clinton stated: "We do need more new jobs, lots of them, but there are already more than three million jobs open and unfilled in America today, mostly because the applicants don't have the required skills. We have to prepare more Americans for the new jobs that are being created in a world fueled by new technology."

Weisenthal takes issue with Clinton's statement that unemployment is more structural rather than cyclical. Weisenthal states: "All of the evidence shows that *lack of demand* is the problem, not the structure of the economy." He includes data from the US Department of Labor, presented in the chart below, as well as other data.

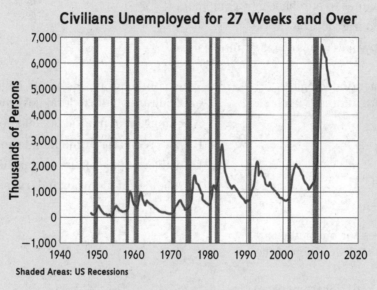

Civilians Unemployed for 27 Weeks and Over

Shaded Areas: US Recessions

Source: U.S. Department of Labor: Bureau of Labor Statistics

1. How does the chart indicate that unemployment can be caused by lack of demand?

   A. Unemployment occurs in highly predictable cycles.

   B. Levels of unemployment have been increasing over time.

   C. Unemployment spikes during each period of recession.

   D. Unemployment decreases gradually but increases sharply.

2. What aspect of the data in the chart indicates that there was also structural unemployment occurring around 2012?

   A. Unemployment appeared to be decreasing around 2012 after a spike.

   B. Unemployment around 2012 was not part of a predictable cycle.

   C. Unemployment in 2012 was not correlated to a previous recession.

   D. Unemployment in 2012 was at a higher level than in previous periods.

Writing Practice

Write an essay that compares and contrasts economic conditions during a period of high unemployment versus a period of low unemployment.

Directions: Read the passage and then answer the questions that follow.

In a 2011 speech about his proposed economic stimulus plan, President Obama proposed the following measures for improving the American economy:

- An extension of payroll tax cuts for employees
- A cut in the payroll tax for all businesses
- A waiver of the payroll tax for businesses that hire new workers or give raises to current workers
- Tax credits for companies that hire the long-term unemployed
- Subsidies for job training programs
- An extension of unemployment benefits
- Tax incentives for companies to purchase new equipment
- Funding for highway and transit projects
- Programs to help homeowners refinance their mortgages

1. The job training programs mentioned by the president are best designed to address which of these issues?

   A. cyclical unemployment

   B. low unemployment

   C. structural unemployment

   D. low consumer confidence

2. The tax credits and incentives for businesses are fiscal policies meant to accomplish which of the following?

   A. raising money for the federal government

   B. promoting hiring and spending by companies

   C. reducing the size of the federal deficit

   D. improving infrastructure with more funding

3. Which of the proposals would result in a direct expenditure by the federal government?

   A. extension of payroll tax cuts for workers

   B. tax credits for hiring long-term unemployed

   C. waiver of payroll tax for businesses

   D. funding for highway and transit projects

Directions: Answer the following questions.

4. Which of these would count toward GDP in the United States?

   A. work within the household done by the homeowner

   B. work done by a neighbor as part of a bartering agreement

   C. services performed by a nurse in a medical center

   D. tools manufactured in China for sale in the American market

5. How can deflation negatively affect the economy?

   A. It can lower gross domestic product.

   B. It can increase unemployment.

   C. It can reduce demand for products.

   D. It can cause prices to increase.

Directions: Use the following supply and demand curve to answer questions 6–8.

Supply and Demand for Computer Tablets

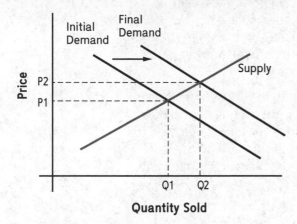

6. What trend is shown in initial demand as prices of computer tablets increase?

   A. As tablet price increases, demand increases.

   B. As tablet supply increases, demand increases.

   C. As tablet price increases, demand decreases.

   D. As tablet supply increases, demand decreases.

7. What does the point (Q2, P2) represent on this chart?

   A. the point of median supply and demand

   B. a point where supply exceeds demand

   C. a point where demand exceeds supply

   D. market equilibrium at final demand

8. What effect on the market for computer tablets is shown by the change from initial to final demand?

   A. a decrease in demand related to a decrease in supply

   B. an increase in prices related to an increase in demand

   C. a decrease in supply related to an increase in prices

   D. an increase in supply related to a decrease in demand

Check Your Understanding

Lesson	Item Number
Microeconomics	6, 7, 8
Macroeconomics and Government Policy	2, 3
Macroeconomics, the GDP, and Price Fluctuations	1, 4, 5

WRITE ABOUT Microeconomics and Macroeconomics

When economists write about aspects of the economy that affect individual consumers, such as supply and demand, they are discussing microeconomics. On the other hand, macroeconomics deals with global questions and issues such as employment and inflation. Macroeconomics generally deals with a country as a whole and may examine its government. Microeconomics tends to focus on one market, such as computers, and look at supply and demand.

When you write a compare-and-contrast essay, you show how two or more things are alike and different. Comparing is showing how things are alike. Contrasting shows how they are different. They are sometimes used to persuade a reader that one choice is better than another. This technique is used often in political campaigns. Read the essays on page 353. Then write a compare-and-contrast essay on microeconomics and macroeconomics.

BEFORE YOU WRITE Make a Graphic Organizer

Having a visual plan before you begin to write helps focus your essay. One way to accomplish this is by using a graphic organizer. A Venn diagram can help organize your main points to show how two things are alike and different. By placing what is unique to each idea in separate ovals then showing ideas that overlap, you can create a structure for your essay.

TIP   Develop a Structure

Two major ways exist to organize a compare-and-contrast essay. In the block method, all the information on one idea or thing is presented first. The next paragraph or section discusses all the points of the second idea or thing.

A second method, alternative comparison, involves selecting main points and first discussing one then the other item being compared. In this method, each paragraph offers a detail and covers both comparing and contrasting of that detail.

Select whichever method works best for your topic, then stick to it. An example of each method is shown below in outline form.

Block Method
- I. Chevrolet Volt
  - A. gas mileage
  - B. size
  - C. interior design

- II. Honda Prius
  - A. gas mileage
  - B. size
  - C. interior design

Alternative Comparison
- I. Gas mileage
  - A. Chevrolet Volt
  - B. Honda Prius

- II. Size
  - A. Chevrolet Volt
  - B. Honda Prius

- III. Interior design
  - A. Chevrolet Volt
  - B. Honda Prius

WHILE YOU WRITE Use Comparison and Contrast Words

Transitions offer your reader a chance to follow your thinking. Often, they are used at the beginning of a new paragraph. They act as signals to a point about to be made, just as traffic signs can give an automobile driver clues about the road ahead. The following words and phrases are common transitions for comparison and contrast.

also	conversely
again	despite
likewise	even though
in comparison	instead
in contrast *or* by contrast	on the one hand . . . on the other hand
in the same way	regardless
similar to	still
however	yet

TIP Watch Out for Dangling and Misplaced Modifiers

When words, phrases, or clauses are not in the right place, they are called dangling modifiers. When the writing calls for a modifier (from the word *modify*, or *change*), be sure to place it as near as possible to the word it modifies. Failing to do so can create some amusing mistakes. Notice the sentence below.

> When only a little girl, my mother took me to Philadelphia.

As it is written, the sentence states that when the mother was a little girl, she took her child to Philadelphia, which is clearly not possible. One way to revise that sentence would be to add a subject to the introductory clause.

> When **I** was only a little girl, my mother took me to Philadelphia.

Adjectives and adverbs are single-word modifiers. They should be used sparingly, not sprinkled all over an essay. When they are used, place them before or after the word they modify. The meaning of a sentence can change, based on where the modifier is placed, as shown below. Be sure you are writing what you intend to say.

> Diego went out with **just** his jacket on.
> Diego **just** went out with his jacket on.
> **Just** Diego went out with his jacket on.

AFTER YOU WRITE Double-Check Your Conclusion

Just as the introduction sets out the main idea, the conclusion restates that idea in different words. It is meant to be a summary of the essay. The same thing is true of speeches. You may have heard a speaker finish by saying, "To sum up" or "In conclusion" before restating his or her theme. Your conclusion should be more than a repeat of the introduction. Incorporate ideas that have supported the main idea as you conclude your essay.

Chapter 7

Economics and History

The actions of people and their governments affect the economy. Government policies, wars, and alliances are a few actions of government that affect the American and the global economies. Saving money and purchasing goods are actions of people that affect the economy. Together, people and governments create economic events. Some of these events have had major effects on the worldwide population. This chapter describes some of these events.

In this chapter you will study these topics:

Lesson 7.1
Major Economic Events
What were some major economic events in US history? How have economic events shaped US government? What government policies resulted from major economic events?

Lesson 7.2
The Relationship Between Politics and Economics
What is the relationship between political and economic freedoms? What is the impact of war on an economy? What is colonization and how did the economy influence it?

Lesson 7.3
The Scientific and Industrial Revolutions
What was the Scientific Revolution? How did scientific discoveries change the American economy? How did technological advances in the 19th century change the lives of workers?

Goal Setting
Think about technology you use every day, such as a cell phone, a car, or even a light bulb. How does that technology affect your life? How does it affect business? How might it affect the nation's economy?

LESSON 7.1 Major Economic Events

LESSON OBJECTIVES

- Explain how major economic events shaped the US government
- Discuss how government policies developed as a result of economic events

CORE SKILLS & PRACTICES

- Analyze Information
- Identify Point of View

Key Terms

business cycle
the repeated pattern of growth and decline of an economy

expansion
period when a country's GDP grows

Great Depression
a severe decline in the US economy during the 1930s

recession
a decline in a country's GDP for at least two quarters

stimulus
government policies to provide relief for workers and create business reforms

Vocabulary

standard of living
the necessities or comforts essential to life or aspired to by an individual

Key Concept

The federal government has responded to economic events in a variety of ways, for example, by developing stimulus programs and regulating businesses.

Think of a time when you had extra money to spend. Did you buy items you wanted, such as clothes or a restaurant meal? Or did you spend it on items you needed, such as gas for a car or clothes for children? The United States as a whole functions like individuals. It has periods of financial ups and downs. When the economy is doing well, many of its citizens do well. When it hits a tough time, many citizens suffer.

Booms and Busts

Throughout its history, the United States has experienced economic booms (when the economy does well) and busts (when the economy does poorly). During booms, businesses do well, they hire workers, and individuals prosper. During busts, businesses lose money or close, they stop hiring, and individuals struggle. The cycle from boom to bust and back to boom is called the **business cycle**.

Changes in the gross domestic product (GDP) signals whether the economy is in a boom or in a bust. GDP is the total value of goods and services produced in a country in one year. It is one way economists measure the health of an economy. During a boom, GDP grows because the economy grows. This is called economic **expansion**. When the growth peaks, inflation sets in. Inflation is an overall increase in prices of goods and services. Inflation reduces demand because consumers do not want to purchase items that cost too much. GDP shrinks, and the economic bust sets in.

The low point in the business cycle is a called a trough. When the economy is in a trough, it is in a recession, which is a decline in a country's GDP for at least two quarters. During a **recession**, businesses suffer or fail. They stop hiring people and cut wages. Consumers stop purchasing many goods and services because they have lost their jobs or are working for reduced wages. A severe, long-lasting recession is known as a depression.

The Roaring Twenties

One of the biggest busts in history was preceded by a time known as the Roaring Twenties, which refers to the 1920s. During this time, consumers began to demand more items to make their lives easier and more enjoyable. Mass production, the making of large amounts of goods by machines, answered the demand.

Machines were used to make an assembly line, where workers produced goods. For example, in an automobile assembly line, one person attaches the left door and another person puts on the right door. Henry Ford used the assembly line to mass-produce automobiles at a greatly reduced cost. In 1910, the Ford Model T cost $950. By 1924, as a result of mass production, a Model T cost $300. This made automobiles affordable for millions of middle-class families.

 Think about Social Studies

Directions: Match these terms with their definitions.

1. boom   **A.** low point in the business cycle
2. bust   **B.** increase in prices of goods and services
3. inflation   **C.** period when the economy does well
4. trough   **D.** period when the economy does poorly

The Great Depression

Much of the wealth of the 1920s was on paper. It was not in the form of real money that people had in the bank but was based on the value of their investments. Many people invested their savings in stocks, or shares, in corporations. Shares were bought and sold on the stock market.

By the end of the 1920s, more investors were buying stocks on margin. They did not pay the full price of the stocks. Instead, they paid 10 percent of the price and borrowed the rest. The idea was that when the value of the stock went up, they would sell the stock and have enough money to repay the loan and make a profit. This worked as long as the value of stocks kept going up.

During the summer of 1929, however, stock prices started to fall. By September, there were serious problems. A massive sell-off of stocks began on October 21, 1929. As investors saw the value of stocks fall, more and more of them sold their stocks. The stock market dropped sharply and kept dropping. October 29, 1929, came to be known as "Black Tuesday." Sixteen million shares of stock were sold on that day. This was two to four times as many as usual.

Life During the Depression

This stock market crash led to the **Great Depression**, a severe decline in the US economy during the 1930s. The economy continued to worsen throughout 1930. Some investors saw their savings wiped out in the crash. Others lost their savings when banks failed. Banks failed because investors, business owners, and farmers could not repay their loans.

CORE PRACTICE

Analyze Information

One of the benefits of economic growth is a higher **standard of living**. The term *standard of living* refers to the overall quality of life, the minimum needs and the luxuries that are necessary for people to survive and to improve their living conditions. The nation's wealth is evident in the items found throughout the homes of you and your neighbors— televisions, computers, indoor plumbing, and electric lights. The nation's standard of living is also evident in the number of cars on the road and in the quantity and quality of goods in stores and supermarkets. The United Nations developed the Human Development Index (HDI) to measure a country's economic and social development and standard of living. Find the HDI of the United States on the Internet. How does it compare with the HDI of other nations? Discuss your findings with your classmates.

Understand the Question

When taking a test, if you do not understand what the question is asking, you probably will not be able to choose the right answer or write an appropriate response. To understand test questions, follow these steps:

1. Read the question carefully. Look for key words in the question, such as *then*, *least*, and *not*.

2. Think about what the question is asking. For example, if the question states, "What caused the Great Depression?" you might think "They are asking me to list the factors that caused the severe economic depression of the 1920s. I have to think about circumstances that existed before the Depression that led to it, not the effects of the Depression."

3. For multiple choice questions, make sure you understand the question before reading the answer choices.

Use these steps when answering the questions at the end of this lesson.

Companies stopped buying equipment and began laying off workers in an effort to save money. As more businesses closed, more workers lost their jobs. Farmers lost their farms as well, and more banks failed. By the end of 1932, 12 million workers—25 percent of the workforce—were unemployed. Some 30,000 businesses failed in 1932 alone. Some families piled into a car and drove off in search of jobs. Banks foreclosed on homes when owners fell behind in their loan payments.

The Great Depression affected countries worldwide. In Europe, leaders of several countries promised to end the suffering by setting up totalitarian governments. The poor economy created the conditions that led to World War II.

⚑ Think about Social Studies

Directions: Choose the best answer to the following question.

1. What contributed to the stock market crash in 1929?

A. Brokers repaid their bank loans.

B. People bought everything factories produced.

C. Investors panicked when stock prices fell.

D. Stock prices went up in value after a steep drop.

The Government Responds

President Herbert Hoover did not believe that the federal government should step in, believing that the American economy could eventually recover on its own. Many European countries had implemented socialism after World War I and were not recovering economically. Hoover blamed socialism for the poor conditions in Europe and didn't want the same thing to happen to the United States. He asked companies to remain open and not to reduce wages. Little came of Hoover's requests, however.

By 1931, Hoover realized that the federal government had to do something. He supported federal government spending on public works projects. These projects created jobs and provided relief, or aid, for the unemployed. They are called public works projects because they fund the building of buildings or other structures such as libraries, dams, or highways.

In 1932, Hoover asked Congress to pass a law creating the Reconstruction Finance Corporation. It lent money to banks, railroads, and insurance companies. Hoover then agreed to the Emergency Relief and Construction Act, which provided money to state governments for relief and for public works. While Hoover did take these steps, they came too late to stop the Depression. Farmers, in an effort to raise prices, destroyed their crops. At the same time, however, some Americans were starving. Hoover's time was running out.

Roosevelt's New Deal

In the 1932 presidential election, Franklin Delano Roosevelt defeated Hoover to become president. The next year, in his Inaugural Address, Roosevelt pledged to help the American people. His program to do so was called the New Deal. The New Deal provided **stimulus**—government policies to provide relief for workers and create business reforms. He believed that banks and corporations had to change the way they operated. Not all his ideas worked, but Americans were relieved that the government was acting.

Roosevelt immediately declared a bank holiday on taking office. This meant closing banks temporarily so that people would not withdraw all their deposits. The president sent Congress the Emergency Banking Relief Act, and Congress passed it. Under this law, the accounts of all banks were reviewed. Banks that had financial resources could reopen at the end of the holiday. Congress set up the Federal Deposit Insurance Corporation (FDIC), which still operates today. This agency insures the money people deposit in banks. The insurance guarantees that people will still have the money in their bank account if a bank fails. These actions restored people's confidence in banks.

In May 1933, Congress set up the Civilian Conservation Corps (CCC), the Federal Emergency Relief Agency (FERA), and the Public Works Administration (PWA). These agencies put people to work so they would have money for food and shelter. They replanted forests, built schools, and fixed roads.

Roosevelt then asked Congress to set up the Agricultural Adjustment Administration (AAA) to pay farmers to produce fewer crops. Sending fewer crops to market would raise crop prices. That would provide farmers with more income.

Congress also approved the Tennessee Valley Authority (TVA). It built dams and power plants to provide the South with cheap electricity. The National Recovery Administration (NRA) was created to help establish fair trade practices. The NRA also helped establish minimum wages, cap working hours, and reduce unemployment.

In January 1935, Roosevelt proposed the Works Progress Administration (WPA) to complete construction projects. The National Labor Relations Act (NLRA) helped workers and labor unions. Between 1933 and 1943, union membership rose from just over 2 million workers to almost 14 million.

The Fair Labor Standards Act (FLSA) replaced some of the NRA codes. This law set a maximum work week at 40 hours. That same year, Congress passed a law creating Social Security (SS). For the first time, American workers would have old-age pensions so they could retire. The NLRA, FLSA, and SS are still in operation today.

By the late 1930s, economic recovery was still uncertain. However, people felt more confident about the future. Roosevelt's New Deal turned the tide from a hands-off government to one that intervened in times of economic difficulty. Today, the government continues to take an active role in the US economy.

Think about Social Studies

Directions: Choose the correct organization to complete the sentence.

FDIC   **WPA**   **AAA**

1. The _____ helps to prevent people from losing money if a bank fails.

2. The _____ provided economic stimulus for farmers.

3. The _____ was part of a stimulus program that created construction jobs.

CORE SKILL

Identify Point of View

Point of view is how a person feels about, or thinks about, something. Beliefs and values help to shape a person's point of view. Age, sex, ethnic background, and religion influence beliefs and values. Follow these steps to identify someone's point of view:

- Identify the author and the author's background. How might these affect what the person thinks?

- Identify the author's argument or main idea. Did the author leave anything out? Is the author emphasizing just one side of the issue?

- Look for emotional words or phrases such as *right-wing*, *leftist*, *lovely*, or *delightful*.

- Look for opinions as well as facts in what the author says.

Some politicians were critical of Roosevelt's New Deal. Use the Internet to research their stance. Write an essay about government reforms from the point of view of Roosevelt's conservative critics.

WRITE TO LEARN

Imagine you are an unemployed worker during the Great Depression. Write a letter to President Hoover or Roosevelt persuading him to help you and others like you.

Vocabulary Review

Directions: Complete the sentences using the following key terms and vocabulary words.

recession   expansion   Great Depression
standard of living   stimulus   business cycle

1. The United States has endured several boom-to-bust movements known as the _____.

2. Not as severe as a depression, a(n) _____ occurs during an economic trough.

3. During the 1920s, people had a higher _____ and were able to purchase goods that they could not afford before.

4. The Roaring Twenties was a period of economic _____, when the economy and GDP grew.

5. The _____ occurred during the 1930s and caused the government's role in the economy to change.

6. President Roosevelt's New Deal provided _____ for the nation's struggling economy.

Skill Review

Directions: Choose the best answer to each question.

1. What caused the bank failures during the Great Depression?
   A. People could not repay loans.
   B. People moved to find work.
   C. Consumer goods were sold at lower prices.
   D. Farmers were unable to purchase equipment.

2. Which event occurred first?
   A. President Hoover passed the Emergency Relief and Construction Act.
   B. President Roosevelt was elected to office.
   C. The assembly line made consumer goods more affordable.
   D. Many banks and businesses closed after Black Tuesday.

3. What view of government involvement in the economy was held by Franklin Roosevelt but not Herbert Hoover?
   A. Local governments should solve their own economic problems.
   B. The federal government should help regulate the national economy.
   C. Involvement in the economy by the federal government might lead to socialism.
   D. Charitable organizations, not the federal government, should take responsibility for helping the unemployed.

4. What program was created to generate electricity for a region?
   A. Civilian Conservation Corps
   B. the Tennessee Valley Authority
   C. the Works Projects Administration
   D. the National Recovery Act

Skill Practice

Directions: The excerpt below is from a speech given by President Barack Obama. Read the excerpt then answer the questions that follow.

The President's Speech on the Economy—January 2009

We start 2009 in the midst of a crisis unlike any we have seen in our lifetime, a crisis that has only deepened over the last few weeks. Nearly two million jobs have been now lost, and on Friday we're likely to learn that we lost more jobs last year than at any time since World War II. Just in the past year, another 2.8 million Americans who want and need full-time work have had to settle for part-time jobs. Manufacturing has hit a twenty-eight year low. Many businesses cannot borrow or make payroll. Many families cannot pay their bills or their mortgage. Many workers are watching their life savings disappear. And many, many Americans are both anxious and uncertain of what the future will hold. . . .

It is true that we cannot depend on government alone to create jobs or long-term growth, but at this particular moment, only government can provide the short-term boost necessary to lift us from a recession this deep and severe.

Only government can break the cycles that are crippling our economy—where a lack of spending leads to lost jobs which leads to even less spending; where an inability to lend and borrow stops growth and leads to even less credit.

That's why we need to act boldly and act now to reverse these cycles. That's why we need to put money in the pockets of the American people, create new jobs, and invest in our future. That's why we need to restart the flow of credit and restore the rules of the road that will ensure a crisis like this never happens again.

1. What is President Obama's opinion regarding the federal government's role in the economy?

   A. The federal government should not interfere in economic activities.

   B. The federal government caused much of the economic troubles in 2008.

   C. The federal government plays a role in US economic success.

   D. The federal government should provide credit cards to US citizens.

2. What economic situation is President Obama describing in his speech?

   A. boom

   B. expansion

   C. depression

   D. trough

3. Based on this passage, what would you expect President Obama to do?

   A. to agree with President Hoover on economic issues

   B. to look to Roosevelt's New Deal for solutions

   C. to support laws that increase costs of goods

   D. to declare war to improve the economy

Writing Practice

Directions: President Franklin Roosevelt's three goals for the New Deal were relief, reform, and recovery. Write a critique of Roosevelt's New Deal. In your opinion, was the New Deal effective? What programs were most crucial to economic recovery?

LESSON 7.2 The Relationship Between Politics and Economics

LESSON OBJECTIVES

- Explain the relationship between political and economic freedoms
- Identify the economic causes and impacts of wars
- Discuss how economic factors led to colonization

CORE SKILLS & PRACTICES

- Compare and Contrast
- Make Inferences

Key Terms

annexation
taking control of another country or territory

foreign aid
money, goods, and services given to another nation

industrialized nations
countries with developed economies and advanced infrastructures

laissez-faire
"let it be" approach to governing business

Open Door Policy
a policy that gave all nations equal trading rights in China

Vocabulary

humanitarian
helping others

Key Concept

Politics and economics interact with each other in complex ways that affect the entire society.

Professionals such as hair stylists, dentists, architects, plumbers, and many others are all required by law to have licenses to practice their trade. The licenses ensure that the professional understands his or her trade and is safely qualified to practice it. What if government did not make such requirements? Although your relationship with your hair stylist or dentist may seem like a small part of the economy, government legislation and politics create large effects at the local and national levels.

Political and Economic Freedom

In the United States, the balance between personal freedom, as outlined in the Constitution, and economic freedom is frequently addressed. The Bill of Rights and other amendments guarantee freedoms for people of the United States.

Government Influence

These personal freedoms apply to personal economics as well as the American economy. For example, Americans are free to choose any occupation, which pays them a salary. They are free to change occupations and thus alter their income. Americans are free to spend their earnings as they choose, in any businesses that they choose.

Businesses also enjoy freedoms in the United States. Citizens can open businesses to sell products and services. Business owners choose what products they would like to sell and the price at which they would like to sell those products. Whether the business is successful depends on the market, not on direct control of the government.

Although the government does not dictate what businesses can sell or what type of job a person must have, government officials, lobbyists, and voters influence business. For example, before the Great Depression, government took a **laissez-faire** or "let it be" approach to business. The idea of laissez-faire is to keep government from interfering in economic affairs. Economists thought this approach was the best for growing an economy.

Economic Stimulus

During the Great Depression, an economist named John Maynard Keynes argued that government should manage the economy. Keynes believed that governments could create demand for products by spending money and that this economic stimulus would end the depression.

President Roosevelt used Keynes' ideas in the New Deal plan. Roosevelt created government programs to put people to work, regulate business, and protect workers. At the time, Americans were pleased with government involvement in the economy. Many Americans were poor, hungry, out of work, and, in some cases, homeless.

At other times in history, the political climate has influenced laws and policies that affect the economy. In 2009, President Barack Obama urged Congress to pass the American Recovery and Reinvestment Act. This law allowed government to spend money on programs that would help revitalize the economy and ease the recession.

 Think about Social Studies

Directions: Choose the best answer to the following question.

1. Based on your understanding of the term laissez-faire, from which French phrase do you think the term originated?

   A. "to monitor closely"

   B. "to treat fairly"

   C. "to intervene"

   D. "to leave alone"

The Politics of Imperialism

Politics also plays a part in interactions among countries. The policy of imperialism—the governing of weaker nations or colonies by more powerful nations—is an example of the influence of politics on the economy. In the late 1800s, the United States was a powerful country. It was the world's leading producer of steel and oil. Farmers and ranchers had largely settled the frontier. The United States extended from the Atlantic Ocean to the Pacific.

New Markets

The United States needed new markets for the goods it produced. As the nation grew, more crops and more goods were produced than Americans could use. This problem resulted in the hard economic times of the 1870s and 1890s.

Overseas markets would allow the economy to continue to grow. Racist ideas about Anglo-Saxon superiority also helped support overseas expansion. Many Americans believed that Christian, English-speaking nations were better than others. Like Europeans in the sixteenth and seventeenth centuries, they thought it was the duty of Americans to bring their civilization to the people of Asia and the Pacific. Overseas expansion and imperialism appealed to many Americans.

Compare and Contrast

When you make a comparison, you study two or more individuals, groups, ideas, events, or objects. Then you look for the ways they are alike (compare) and the ways they differ (contrast) from each other.

Use the Internet to research two types of economies: centrally planned and pure market (or laissez-faire). Create a Venn diagram showing the similarities and differences between the two economic styles. Then write a brief statement that describes the benefits and drawbacks of each type of economy.

Make Inferences

An inference is a statement that interprets and explains the meaning of facts. It is not a fact, but it is based on facts. To make inferences, follow these steps:

- Identify the stated facts. Ask yourself: What are the facts in this piece of reading?

- Review what you already know about the topic, person, or event.

- Use the new information (the stated facts), what you already know, logic, and common sense to form a conclusion.

Based on the information in the text, what can you infer about the feelings of Hawaiians regarding imperialism?

Foreign Markets

By the 1870s, settlers from the US mainland were growing sugarcane on large plantations in Hawaii. In 1875, the planters signed a trade treaty with the United States. The treaty allowed them to sell their sugar in the United States without paying a tariff. A tariff is a tax on goods brought into a country for sale. All other foreign sugar was taxed. As a result, the non-native Hawaiian planters became very wealthy and powerful. They forced the Hawaiian king to grant them control of the legislature. When he died in 1891, his sister Liliuokalani became queen. She tried to regain control of the government.

In 1893, the planters forced the queen from office and applied for annexation by the United States. **Annexation** means taking control of another country or territory. President Grover Cleveland refused. Later, President McKinley, who supported imperialism, annexed Hawaii in 1898.

During this time, the United States also took military action in Latin America. The United States helped the Central American country of Panama gain independence. In exchange, Panama gave the United States the right to build a canal across Panama. This man-made, narrow waterway would allow ships to pass between the Atlantic and Pacific Oceans. Americans believed these actions were necessary to protect their economic interests.

In the 1890s, the United States became interested in China's natural resources. The United States proposed the **Open Door Policy** in 1899. Under this policy all nations would have equal rights to trade in China. This made it easier for US companies to do business in China.

Think about Social Studies

Directions: Write the numbers 1–4 to sequence the events.

_____ Non-native planters gain control of the legislature in Hawaii.

_____ The United States proposes the Open Door Policy.

_____ The United States annexes Hawaii.

_____ The Hawaiian queen is forced from office.

The Relationship Between Politics and Economics

The Economics of War

Countries fight each other for natural resources. For centuries, economics has been a major cause of war. Wars take place all over the world and involve developing nations as well as **industrialized nations**. Industrialized nations are countries that have strong economies, well-developed infrastructures, and high standards of living. Some countries experience many wars. For example, over the last 40 years, nearly 20 African countries have experienced at least one civil war. The region is also home to many smaller conflicts.

Destruction

The destruction caused by many years of war is tremendous. War always increases poverty. Many people are injured or killed. Homes and business are destroyed. Jobs are hard to find. Almost everything that allows a city or a nation to function efficiently—electricity, running water, sewage systems, roads, and buildings—is ruined and needs repair. Food is scarce because farm fields are used as battlegrounds.

It takes money and effort to rebuild a nation after fighting stops. Once a conflict has ended, nearly everything has to be rebuilt. Roads, bridges and other parts of a nation's infrastructure often require extensive repair. Adding to the challenge is that all these things must be done at the same time because everything is interconnected.

Unstable Governments

War also indirectly affects a country's economy. Wars create unstable governments. Political instability scares away investment. Without investment, however, countries are unable to develop their economies and improve welfare, causing more dissatisfaction and increasing political instability. How, then, can the cycle be broken? One way is through foreign aid. **Foreign aid** consists of the money, goods, and services that the government of one nation gives to help the government of another nation.

Why do developed nations offer foreign aid? Many do so for **humanitarian** reasons because they are concerned with improving people's lives and reducing suffering. Nations also provide aid for economic reasons. Foreign aid can expand a nation's markets for exports and provide new opportunities for foreign investment.

Politics are also a reason for providing aid. Nations use foreign aid to protect their own security. Economic aid is often a part of a military alliance with a developing nation. Through such alliances, the United States has gained overseas military bases. The United States has also used foreign aid to win allies in the United Nations and other international groups.

🚩 Think about Social Studies

Directions: Choose the best answer to the following question.

1. The "Open Door" referred to efforts to

A. trade with China.

B. trade with Hawaii.

C. prevent Japan from trading with Korea.

D. annex Hawaii.

Vocabulary Review

Directions: Complete the sentences using the following key terms and vocabulary words.

annexation   laissez-faire   industrialized nations
humanitarian   foreign aid   Open Door Policy

1. A policy that allowed countries equal trading rights in China is known as the _____.

2. Some countries provide _____ aid to other nations in need to improve people's lives and help end suffering.

3. The United States gives _____ to other nations in need, which includes money, goods, and services.

4. Hawaiians did not agree with the _____ of Hawaii by the United States.

5. Countries are considered _____ if they have well-developed economies, advanced infrastructures, and a high standard of living.

6. Before the Great Depression, the United States practiced a(n) _____, or "hands off," approach to governing business.

Skill Review

Directions: Choose the best answer to each question.

1. Why did the United States adopt the Open Door Policy?
   A. to prevent trade between the United States and China
   B. to keep other countries from doing business in China
   C. to help the Chinese transition to a laissez-faire business approach
   D. to protect US economic interests in China

2. What was one cause of US imperialism?
   A. a period of economic prosperity in the late 1800s
   B. the need to expand the US economy
   C. the request of Hawaii to be annexed
   D. the need for US troops in Latin America

3. Which answer includes reasons why nations provide foreign aid to war-torn countries?
   A. to declare war and annex countries
   B. to help other people out of kindness and gain allies
   C. to take over other countries and promote imperialism
   D. to destabilize foreign governments and create a recession

4. Why did President Roosevelt use the economic ideas of John Maynard Keynes in his New Deal plan?
   A. to limit the involvement of government in the economy
   B. to deregulate business and promote investment in the economy
   C. to stimulate the economy and end the depression
   D. to create unions that would protect workers' rights

Skill Practice

Directions: Read the passage. Then answer the questions that follow.

The Panama Canal

By 1900, the United States had political and economic interests in the Pacific. For example, it had recently annexed Hawaii and taken control of the Philippine Islands in the Pacific. The United States needed to be able to move its warships and merchant ships quickly from one coast to the other. The only way to do this was to build a canal through Central America. The best place seemed to be Panama, which was then part of Colombia. A French company had already started a canal there in 1881.

When there seemed no other way to gain control of the area, the United States aided a rebellion in Panama in 1903. President Theodore Roosevelt sent warships to threaten Colombia. Colombia had little choice and allowed the rebels to declare independence. The Panamanians gave the United States control of what became the Panama Canal Zone. The canal opened in 1914.

1. According to the passage, why did Panama give the United States control of the area?

    A. Panama wanted to repay the United States for helping with the rebellion against Colombia.

    B. Panama wanted to prevent the United States from attacking Colombia.

    C. President Roosevelt threatened Panamanian rebels with warships.

    D. The United States bombed Panama until the country gave over control of the canal.

2. Based on this passage, what can you infer about France?

    A. France wanted to colonize Panama.

    B. France had military or economic interests in Latin America.

    C. France wanted to wage war with Panama.

    D. France suffered a recession and was unable to finish the canal.

3. Based on this passage, what was President Roosevelt's view of imperialism?

    A. He did not agree with expansion or imperialism.

    B. He did not want to gain control of the canal.

    C. He believed imperialism was good for the United States.

    D. He thought imperialism was a poor military strategy.

4. Which statement supports the assumption that the United States had a more powerful army than Colombia?

    A. Colombia had little choice and allowed the rebels to declare independence.

    B. The Panamanians gave the United States control of what became the Panama Canal Zone.

    C. The United States needed to be able to move its warships and merchant ships quickly from one coast to the other.

    D. When there seemed no other way to gain control of the area, the United States aided a rebellion in Panama in 1903.

Writing Practice

Directions: Anti-imperialists quoted the Declaration of Independence in their argument against imperialism. Write an essay arguing for or against imperialism. In your essay, refer to the statement from the Declaration that all people are created equal and have the right to life, liberty, and the pursuit of happiness.

LESSON 7.3 The Scientific and Industrial Revolutions

■ LESSON OBJECTIVES

- Discuss how the Scientific Revolution changed the American economy
- Identify how the Industrial Revolution changed the American economy and workers' lives

■ CORE SKILLS & PRACTICES

- Interpret Meaning
- Identify Cause and Effect

Key Terms

cottage industry
system in which workers manufacture products at home

Industrial Revolution
the time period when machines replaced hand tools in the manufacturing of goods

scientific method
the process used by scientists for testing theories using careful observation

Scientific Revolution
the time period when numerous scientific theories were developed

urbanization
significant increase in the number and size of cities

Vocabulary

innovation
process of introducing something that is new

Key Concept

Today's world has been shaped by the technological advances that came about as a result of the Scientific and Industrial Revolutions.

What technological device do you feel is most important? Is it television, which broadcasts news, information, and entertainment worldwide? Or is it a smart phone, which allows people a method of wireless access to information and to other people? Or perhaps a GPS, which provides a method to navigate, or move about in, the world. All of these devices are the products of scientific discovery that began hundreds of years ago.

The Scientific Revolution

Cars, televisions, computers, cell phones, and video cameras—all of these devices, and many others, are the result of science. Science is a method of learning about the natural world. The **scientific method** is the process used by scientists for testing ideas and theories through experiments and careful observation. A theory is a general statement that attempts to explain facts observed by scientists.

The **Scientific Revolution** is the name given to a time period when numerous scientific theories were developed. A revolution is a time of sudden and dramatic change. The Scientific Revolution lasted from the late 1500s to the early 1600s. During this time, people began to question old ideas about the world around them. They used reason, or rational thinking, to look for new answers.

Scientists were making so many discoveries and overturning so many ideas that it seemed like a revolution. Ptolemy, a Greek astronomer in the A.D. 200s, developed the idea that the planets revolved around Earth. From then on, most people assumed that was how the galaxy worked. But in 1543, Nicholas Copernicus published a book disagreeing with this theory. He stated that all the planets, including Earth, revolve around the sun. In the early 1600s, Galileo Galilei used the telescope to observe the sky. What he saw confirmed that Earth moved around the sun.

The Scientific and Industrial Revolutions

Other scientists followed and built on the ideas of Ptolemy, Copernicus, and Galileo. Isaac Newton explained why the planets orbit the sun. Andreas Vesalius described the structures of the human body. Joseph Priestley discovered oxygen, and Antonie van Leeuwenhoek discovered cells in living matter. In fact, van Leeuwenhoek made and used a simple microscope to observe the cells. These scientists used technological devices, such as microscopes and telescopes, to make their discoveries.

Scientific inventions continued and influenced other areas of life. The technology that allowed long sea voyages was developed. These included the compass and the astrolabe. These technological devices made European exploration possible.

Fast-forward to today, and the effects of the Scientific Revolution can still be seen. Over the centuries, scientists have used the scientific method to advance human knowledge and create new technologies, such as computers, smart phones, and television, that have changed the way people live.

 Think about Social Studies

Directions: Choose the best answer to the following question.

1. Which of the following best summarizes the ideas of Copernicus?

A. The sun orbits the Earth.

B. The Earth orbits the sun.

C. the stars orbit the Earth.

D. The moon orbits the sun.

The Industrial Revolution

Technological advances that exist today are also the result of the Industrial Revolution. In the early 1800s, the economies of Western Europe and the United States were based on farming, the making of goods by hand, and trading. During the time period known as the **Industrial Revolution**, machines replaced hand tools in the manufacturing of goods. More people left their farms to work in factories. Within 100 years, many nations had become industrial giants.

The Industrial Revolution began in the 1780s in Great Britain. Britain at that time had all the factors of production that were needed to succeed in changing from an agricultural to an industrial society. The country had the people needed to work in manufacturing. Manufacturing depended on natural resources. Britain had the iron and coal needed to make machines and run steam engines.

In addition, Britain had money to invest in railroads and factories, as well as the markets where it could sell the manufactured goods. It also had a colonial empire to supply other needed materials. India, for example, sent tons of raw cotton to England's new textile, or cloth-making, mills.

Britain was the center of a revolution in technology. Inventors created new machines that made goods faster and cheaper than goods made by hand. The invention of the steam engine created a new source of energy and a revolution in transportation.

Creativity and Innovation

Innovation is the process of introducing something that is new. Technological inventions are examples of innovation. Inventors use their knowledge and creativity, or imagination, to create products of value that improve people's lives. People see the value of the products and purchase them.

Inventions can change the course of history. Think about the compass and its effect on exploration. This seemingly simple tool made overseas travel a possibility for the colonists. Without it, they would never have crossed the Atlantic Ocean safely and founded the United States.

Use the Internet to read about important inventions in history. Then choose one that you believe has the most impact on your life today. Present your idea to the class and explain why it is most important.

CORE SKILL

Interpret Meaning

The term *interpret* means "to understand." When you interpret meaning, you understand a text in such a way that you can explain it. Often this involves using your own knowledge as well as facts from the text. Context clues and knowledge of figurative language will also help you interpret meaning. Figurative language is a way of describing something indirectly. For example, the text describes nations that used technology in the 1800s as "industrial giants." The term *giant* does not refer to the actual size of the nation but their economic success.

Use the Internet to read about steam engines. In a notebook, explain in your own words how a steam engine works. Then describe how the steam engine affected not only the textile industry but other industries in the United States, including transportation.

The Factory System

Before people worked in factories, they worked in their own homes or in workshops. Cloth, for example, was made in steps by different workers in their homes, or cottages. This system in which workers manufactured products at home was known as the **cottage industry**.

A series of inventions in the late 1700s changed the textile industry. These inventions included the flying shuttle, the spinning machine, and the cotton gin. Machines powered by water and steam led to the factory system of production. Investors built factories to house these machines, and factory owners hired workers to run them. By the mid-1800s, Great Britain was the leading industrial nation in the world.

Technology and industry spread to the United States in the early 1800s. Entrepreneurs in New England invested in the first textile factories. Entrepreneurs are people who organize, operate, and assume the risk for a new business. Improvements in technology similar to what happened in the textile industry caused changes in other industries.

 Think about Social Studies

Directions: Choose the best answer to the following question.

1. How were cottage industry workers affected by inventions in the textile industry?

   A. Workers had more work to bring into their homes.

   B. Workers began to take jobs in factories rather than working in their homes.

   C. More people began to work.

   D. Farming jobs became more numerous.

The Rise of Cities

Between 1800 and 1850, the population in Europe and the United States grew rapidly. Workers needed to live close to factories and mills. At the same time, changes in farming meant that fewer farm workers were needed. People were being pushed out of rural areas.

This increase in the number and size of cities in Europe and the United States is called **urbanization**. Living conditions in cities were terrible for workers. They gathered in neighborhoods near where they worked. These very poor, crowded neighborhoods became known as slums. People lived in five- and six-story apartment buildings called tenements. Whole families crowded into tiny, two-room apartments. People got their water from hand-operated pumps. Cities also had no garbage collection or sewer systems. Waste piled up in streets and alleys. Diseases spread quickly through these urban areas.

Cities may have offered work, but the work paid poorly. The work day was long and hard. Working conditions in the new factories and mills were dangerous. Factories could be boiling hot in summer and freezing cold in winter. They lacked large windows to let in fresh air and furnaces to heat the rooms in winter. Dust in the air in textile factories sickened workers.

Men and women worked 12- to 16-hour days. However, women were typically paid 50 percent of what men were paid. Children, too, worked because their families needed the money. Most countries did not require all children to attend school in the early 1800s. Tired workers were sometimes careless. Accidents could cost workers a finger, a hand, an eye, or even their life. There was no medical insurance to pay for medical care for injured workers. Until the late 1800s, there were no labor unions to demand shorter working hours and safe and healthful working conditions.

The horrible working conditions in factories in the 1800s led to the development of labor unions. Groups of workers formed organizations to protest the conditions. They also wanted reforms like shorter working hours, age limits for working children, and safety measures.

The New Middle Class

For hundreds of years, there had been a middle class of craftworkers, merchants, shop owners, and professionals such as lawyers and doctors. The Industrial Revolution created new members of the middle class. These new members were the men who provided the money to build the new factories and the men who managed the new businesses.

Middle-class families lived around the central city of working-class neighborhoods in areas known as suburbs. They had large, well-built, single-family homes with yards. Often, they had a servant or two. The wives did not work outside the home. Their job was to manage the servants, raise the children, and make a pleasant home for their husbands when they came home from work.

 Think about Social Studies

Directions: Select the term that best completes the sentence.

1. In the 1800s, there was a large increase in the number and size of (farms, cities).

2. Industrialization created a new middle class, who lived in (tenements, suburbs).

3. Groups of workers who wanted workplace-safety reforms were known as (entrepreneurs, labor unions).

The cause is what makes something happen. The effect is what happens—or the outcome of the cause. Looking for cause and effect helps us understand history. We can better understand why something happened in the past (effect) if we know what other people, conditions, or events helped make it happen (cause).

In your notebook, make a cause-and-effect chart like the one below. List three causes and three effects of urbanization.

WRITE TO LEARN

Describe the effects of urbanization on populations in cities and rural areas.

Vocabulary Review

Directions: Complete the sentences using the following key terms and vocabulary words.

cottage industry   innovation   Industrial Revolution
urbanization   scientific method   Scientific Revolution

1. In the 1800s, the rise of factories shut down home textile workers, or the _____.

2. Scientists use the _____ to test ideas and theories through experiments and careful observation.

3. Factories led to _____, which is a significant increase in the number and size of cities.

4. A time period when numerous scientific theories were developed is known as the _____.

5. Technological devices of today are a result of _____ in the past.

6. The _____ began with textile factories in Great Britain and eventually spread to the United States.

Skill Review

Directions: Choose the best answer to each question.

1. What was one effect of urbanization in American cities?
   A. a wealthy lower class
   B. a reduction in factory work
   C. increased wages for workers
   D. spread of diseases

2. Why do historians call the period of industrialization the "Industrial Revolution"?
   A. because there were violent revolts
   B. because it dramatically changed life in many places
   C. because it led to the overthrow of leaders
   D. because it stopped scientific advances

3. What was one factor that led to the Industrial Revolution in Great Britain?
   A. natural resources, such as coal
   B. a large rural population
   C. safe working conditions
   D. lack of transportation

4. Which invention directly affected the population of American cities in the 1800s?
   A. the compass
   B. the steam engine
   C. the plow
   D. the telescope

5. What was one factor that led to the organization of labor unions?
   A. overcrowding in tenements
   B. workplace accidents
   C. working conditions for entrepreneurs
   D. living conditions in suburbs

6. The majority of industrial workers in the early 1800s
   A. were children.
   B. worked 12–16 hours a day.
   C. belonged to a union.
   D. lived in the suburbs.

Skill Practice

Directions: Read the passage. Then answer the questions that follow.

"Big" Business in the Industrial Revolution

John D. Rockefeller was important in the oil industry. Oil was not discovered in the United States until 1859. By 1863, Rockefeller decided that the oil business had great possibilities. By 1880, Standard Oil owned 90 percent of the oil refineries in the United States. It bought out most of its competitors. If the company owned 100 percent of the oil companies, it would have been a monopoly.

Rockefeller built his business through horizontal integration. First, he bought out other oil refining companies. To grow even more, Rockefeller and his partners set up a trust. Laws in some states prevented one company from owning stock, or shares, in another company. The goal of these laws was to prevent monopolies. The trust was meant to get around these laws. Stockholders exchanged their stock in an oil company for shares in the trust. The trust then managed the oil company and all the other companies in the trust. In all, 40 oil companies were part of the Standard Oil Trust. Rockefeller controlled the trust.

1. What is the best definition of horizontal integration?

   A. addition of businesses similar to one's own

   B. purchase of businesses in different industries

   C. illegal purchase of additional businesses

   D. management process for oil companies

2. Why did Rockefeller create a trust?

   A. to avoid a monopoly

   B. to help stockholders sell their oil company stocks

   C. to establish a monopoly

   D. to help his competitors create monopolies

3. Which term best describes Rockefeller?

   A. inventor

   B. scientist

   C. stockholder

   D. entrepreneur

4. The trust that John D. Rockefeller formed in gain control of the oil industry is an example of

   A. vertical integration.

   B. mass production.

   C. horizontal integration.

   D. a factor of production.

Writing Practice

Directions: Imagine you are a cottage industry worker in the early 1800s. Write a letter to a friend about the changes taking place in your village as a result of the factory system. Is your life better or worse? Why?

Directions: Choose the best answer to each question.

1. Which of the following statements describes the Roaring Twenties?

    A. Mass production made more goods affordable for middle-class families.

    B. The country suffered an economic recession, which increased poverty.

    C. Stock prices fell, and the Great Depression began.

    D. Few people were able to afford goods that made life easier.

2. What was one effect of President Hoover's public works projects?

    A. Fewer highways were built.

    B. Workers were paid higher salaries.

    C. New jobs were created.

    D. Business profits increased.

3. How did Roosevelt's actions align with John Keynes ideas about the economy?

    A. Roosevelt spent money on New Deal programs.

    B. Roosevelt entered World War II.

    C. Roosevelt closed banks after the stock market crash.

    D. Roosevelt proposed the American Recovery and Reinvestment Act.

4. Expansion of US economic interests in Hawaii is an example of _____.

    A. tariffs

    B. annexation

    C. foreign aid

    D. imperialism

5. Which statement best describes the effects of war?

    A. Wars create military-based business and help increase profits.

    B. Wars increase demand for goods, which grows business.

    C. Wars create unstable governments and scare investors.

    D. Wars improve the economies of the victorious nations.

6. When did the Scientific Revolution occur?

    A. from the late 1500s to the early 1600s

    B. from 1750 to 1900

    C. from the early 1900s to the late 1900s

    D. after 1990

Directions: Question 7 refers to the passage.

The Industrial Revolution and the Environment

The Industrial Revolution greatly changed how people affected the environment. In early farming economies, there was little need to use nonrenewable resources. Horses or oxen pulled plows, and water power moved the wheels that ground wheat. Women cooked over an open fire and sewed clothes by candlelight.

However, as nations began to industrialize, they needed more renewable and nonrenewable resources. Coal and petroleum became important sources of energy. The smoke from factories burning coal began to pollute the air in industrial cities. Wastes from factories and cities flowed into rivers and polluted them.

To reduce air pollution today, some nations are supporting efforts to develop other forms of energy. Among these alternative sources of power are solar, water, wind, and nuclear.

7. What is the main idea of the passage?

    A. The Industrial Revolution used renewable and nonrenewable resources.

    B. The environment has suffered from the effects of the Industrial Revolution.

    C. Nations today are developing ways to reduce air pollution.

    D. The Industrial Revolution changed the way women cook.

Directions: Questions 8 and 9 refer to the map.

European Industrial Centers, c. 1870

- ● Coal mining
- ▪ Iron ore deposits
- ◉ Major centers of industry

8. Based on the map, you would expect more factories to be located in _____.

   A. Russia

   B. France

   C. Ireland

   D. Sweden

9. According to the map, which country was a major source of iron?

   A. Italy

   B. Russia

   C. Great Britain

   D. Denmark

Check Your Understanding

Lesson	Item Number
Major Economic Events	1, 2
The Relationship between Politics and Economics	3, 4, 5
The Scientific and Industrial Revolutions	6, 7, 8, 9

WRITE ABOUT Reforms During the Industrial Revolution

When you write a persuasive essay, you try to convince your readers to agree with you about a particular issue. Unlike propaganda, which relies on emotional appeals, persuasion rests on rational arguments.

To begin, think about an issue about which you have strong feelings. Chances are excellent that someone during the Industrial Revolution also tried to address the same issue. Voting rights, civil rights, taxes, housing, child labor, prison reform, treatment for the mentally ill, immigration laws, fair wages, safe food, and decent public housing were all concerns of the late 1800s and early 1900s.

Read the excerpt on page 354 from *Children of the Poor*, published in 1892. Then write a persuasive essay about a reform during the Industrial Revolution. Put yourself in the place of a journalist arguing for a needed reform of that era.

BEFORE YOU WRITE Decide On an Arguable Point of View

What do you believe about your chosen issue from the Industrial Revolution? Are you for limits on immigration by country or ethnicity? Do you oppose child labor laws? To persuade others, you must be clear about where you stand. Your point of view becomes the topic sentence of the essay.

TIP   Use a Pro/Con Chart

You may find it helpful to write down your idea and then to make a two-column chart, listing pros and cons. For example, Jacob Riis clearly wanted better education and housing for the children of the poor. It might appear that no arguments could be made against those ideals. Yet struggling families, often immigrants from Europe, relied on the paid labor of their young children in factories and at home doing "piecework." For those parents, education often took second place to the need for food and shelter. Allowing children to attend school, when they could work at age 14—or sooner if they lied about their age—was not always a positive ideal for the family.

WHILE YOU WRITE Use Evidence

In persuasive writing, you use evidence to convince your readers. Each paragraph should make a single claim and then support it with evidence. The evidence may be data you have collected. It may also be anecdotal, or based on a personal story. Jacob Riis included both kinds of evidence in his writing.

Your final paragraph should restate your opinion and your strongest piece of evidence. Persuasive writing often ends with a call to action.

> **TIP** **Watch Out for Unclear Pronoun Reference**
>
> A pronoun refers back to another word, generally a noun known as its antecedent. (*Ante* means "before.") For example, in the sentence *Janelle loved her new outfit, Janelle* is the antecedent of the pronoun *her*. We as readers now know that the outfit belongs to Janelle.
>
> However, the writing may not always be so clear. Notice the following example.
> *Carlos told Wyatt that he would be ready soon.*
>
> We do not know if Carlos or Wyatt will be ready soon. The sentence needs to be revised so that the meaning is clear. Sometimes, this is most easily done with dialogue.
>
> Carlos said to Wyatt, "I will be ready soon."
> OR
> Carlos told Wyatt to be ready soon.
>
> As you write, make sure that your pronouns clearly refer to their antecedents.

AFTER YOU WRITE Rewrite from Another Point of View

To determine if your arguments are indeed persuasive, you may want to rewrite your piece from the opposing viewpoint. Will your reasoning hold up to an opinion different from your own? If you do not have time to rewrite completely, at least mentally argue with the points that you have made. Are any of them weak or in need of further factual support?

Chapter 8

Consumer Credit

A home is a big purchase, and most people cooperate with a financial institution to buy a home using credit. Lenders offer many forms of credit, from home loans to credit cards. Federal laws govern these forms of credit, to protect consumers from fraudulent lending practices. Financial institutions offer other products, including checking and savings accounts. A checking account allows the consumer to easily pay bills and purchase goods and services. A savings account allows the consumer to accumulate money for future needs.

In this chapter you will study these topics:

Lesson 8.1
Savings and Banking
Do you have both a checking account and a savings account with a financial institution? How do you use each type of account? Which account helps you to make purchases and manage bills? Which account helps you to accumulate money?

Lesson 8.2
Types of Credit
What kinds of credit are available to consumers? How are the types of credit different? Which type of credit is most useful for large or small purchases?

Lesson 8.3
Consumer Credit Laws
How does the federal government protect consumers who use credit? What are some of the consumer credit laws? Why are these laws important?

Goal Setting
How have you used bank accounts or credit in your everyday life? Have you financed a house or made other big purchases using credit?

What else would you like to know about consumer credit? What would you like to know about how consumer credit laws can protect you when you make a purchase?

LESSON 8.1   Savings and Banking

◼ LESSON OBJECTIVES

- Identify the types and uses of different financial institutions
- Describe how people use checking accounts
- Describe how people use savings accounts
- Explain the similarities and differences between checking and savings accounts

◼ CORE SKILLS

- Analyze Events and Details
- Get Meaning from Context

Key Terms

commercial bank
banks that originally served only businesses

credit union
a financial institution started by people with a common concern

deposit
to place money into a bank account

reserve
money banks retain for future use

Vocabulary

interest
a payment, or charge, for borrowed money

rationale
reason or explanation for something

Key Concept

Financial institutions provide consumers with services such as checking and savings accounts to help them manage their money.

When you were young, you might have kept your money in a piggy bank. Then when you got your first job, you might have cashed your paychecks and taken the money home as cash. Perhaps you paid for your meals, movies, and hobbies this way. What happens when your paychecks increase and you have more bills? You probably discovered that your money is safer in a bank or other financial institution. You might have discovered that you could make money on the interest in your savings or checking account. There are many advantages to using a bank to manage your money.

Banks

A bank is an institution that deals in money and provides a variety of financial services. Banks accept deposits and make loans. Banks earn a profit by charging more to borrow money than they pay to savers. They also charge fees for various services. Banks provide three basic services: keeping money safe, transferring funds, and loaning money.

Keeping Money Safe

A bank provides customers with a safe place to keep their money until they are ready to use it. Banks work on trust. When you make a **deposit**, or place money in a bank account, the bank promises to return that money. The bank even advertises that it will provide insurance to make sure it can honor that promise.

Transferring funds

Banks provide a way to transfer money from one person or firm to another. Carrying a large amount of cash or sending it through the mail is risky. Writing a check is an easier and safer way to make a payment. It is also possible to transfer funds by phone, by computer, or by authorizing the bank to automatically take a certain amount of money from an account to make a payment, such as for rent or delivery of your local newspaper.

Savings and Banking

Loaning Money

Another crucial service banks perform is loaning money to individuals and businesses. Where does that money come from? It comes from depositors. Since all of a bank's depositors are unlikely to want all of their money at the same time, banks hold back only a relatively small portion of cash for future withdrawals. That money is called a **reserve**—it is money set aside for future use. The rest is loaned to individuals and businesses.

 Think about Social Studies

Directions: Answer the following questions.

1. What can you conclude about the function of money?

   A. to signal power

   B. to carry out barters

   C. to show a person's importance

   D. to simplify the exchange of goods and services

2. Why do banks only hold a small reserve of cash for withdrawals?

   A. Because it is risky to hold all of the money in one location.

   B. Most money is transferred and not available for withdrawal.

   C. It is unlikely that other customers will all withdraw their money at the same time.

   D. The majority of banks deal with electronic transfers and have very little actual cash.

Types of Banks

There are several types of banking institutions. At one time, each played a distinctive role in the economy. Today, most of those distinctions are gone.

At first, **commercial banks** were banks that served only businesses. Today, most commercial banks offer accounts to everyone. Savings banks, savings and loan associations, cooperative banks, and credit unions are often classified as thrift institutions. Each originally concentrated on meeting the needs of people who were not covered by commercial banks. Savings banks provided accounts for workers who wanted to save some of their income. So did savings and loan associations and cooperative banks. These banks also helped workers buy homes.

People with a common concern started financial institutions known as **credit unions**. These people might work for the same company, belong to the same labor union, or live in the same community. At one time, a credit union's main function was to provide emergency loans for its members, many of whom were unable to get loans from other lenders. Those loans were often used to pay medical bills or for home repairs.

CORE PRACTICE

Analyze Events and Details

In order to understand the complex ideas and events you read about, it's helpful to make a web diagram like the one shown below. Write the main idea or event in the center circle, then write everything you know about it in the surrounding circles. You can even expand one of your smaller circles into its own web diagram if needed. Research the financial crisis of 2007 and 2008. Identify the events that are believed to have caused the crisis and fill out a web diagram with details about those events.

WORKPLACE SKILLS

Understand the Rationale Behind Workplace Policies

Banks have many workplace policies, such as protecting customer privacy, never using insider information for personal gain, and not engaging in money laundering. There is a **rationale**, a reason or explanation, behind every workplace policy, even if it is not readily apparent to the workers. Select one of the workplace policies listed here and do some research to find out why it is a policy. Write a paragraph explaining the rationale behind the policy.

Today, all of these types of banking institutions offer similar services. Commercial banks offer car and home loans; thrift institutions and credit unions make loans to factories, shops, and other businesses.

 Think about Social Studies

Directions: Determine whether each statement is true or false.

1. Commercial banks are only open to businesses.
2. A credit union is a type of commercial bank.
3. Savings and loan associations helped workers buy homes.
4. People who worked for the same company or belonged to the same union often started savings banks.

Personal Banking

When you take your money to a financial institution like a bank, you are entrusting your money to their care. They will provide you with a variety of services, some of which they will charge a fee.

Checking Accounts

One service banks offer customers is the use of a checking account. This is a type of account into which the holder deposits money so they can write checks against that money and use an automated teller machine (ATM) to get cash. A check is a written order to pay money called a bill of exchange.

When you write a check to another person, that person must endorse, or sign, the check and take it to his or her bank. Checks are payable on demand, which means the bank must pay it immediately. When this happens, the paper check is exchanged for cash. The cash can be in the form of currency or it can be an electronic transfer of funds from one institution to another.

How does money get into a checking account? Most people deposit their paychecks into their checking accounts. Money can also come from gifts, sales, dividend checks, and other sources. Once money is in a checking account, an account holder can use it to pay bills, such as the phone, cable, mortgage, and credit card bills. They can do this by writing out a paper check or by having the money transferred electronically. Sometimes people set up bill payments from their checking accounts so the money is withdrawn automatically. For instance, if the same car insurance bill is due the first of every month people could have their banks automatically send a payment to the insurance company at that time every month.

When you have a checking account, it is important to keep careful track of your account balance, which is the amount money of in your account. If you write a check for more money than is in your account, you may be charged a penalty fee from the bank for insufficient funds. You could also be charged a fee from the company you wrote the check to. If you do this too many times, the bank might close your account.

One way to understand the meaning of an unfamiliar word or phrase is to look at its context within surrounding text. What other words in the sentence offer clues to the unfamiliar word's meaning? Look closely at how the word is used. Then figure out its meaning by how it is used in a sentence or paragraph. Take a look at this sentence: "If you write a check for more money than is in your account, you may be charged a penalty fee from the bank for insufficient funds." Using the context of the sentence, determine the meaning of the word "insufficient."

Savings Accounts

Another service banks offer their customers is a savings account. In economics, savings refers to money set aside for future use. Until it is time to spend that money, savers can choose to invest it. That is, they can use their money—usually with the understanding that there is some risk involved. Those investments are essential to growth in a market economy.

Suppose you received a sum of money as a gift. If you decided to save it, you would have several choices. You could keep the money hidden in a drawer in your bedroom until you were ready to spend it. Or you could open a savings account—an account at a bank on which interest is paid and from which withdrawals can be made. **Interest** is a payment for borrowed money.

When you deposit your money in a bank, the bank makes a promise to return that money to you. It even buys insurance to make sure it can honor that promise. The bank also agrees to pay you interest on your deposit. Why does the bank pay you interest? One reason is to attract more depositors. Another reason is because the bank uses its deposits to make loans to other customers. Interest is your payment for letting them loan your money to someone else.

WRITE TO LEARN

What kind of financial institution do you use for your money? Do you have a checking account, a savings account, or both? Write a paragraph explaining the similarities and differences between these types of accounts. Use examples from your own experiences with these accounts as you compare and contrast them.

 Think about Social Studies

Directions: Choose the best answer to the following question.

1. What is one major difference between most savings and checking accounts?

   A. Checking accounts are not insured.

   B. Not all checking accounts pay interest.

   C. Money in savings accounts cannot be loaned.

   D. Automatic deposits are only available with checking accounts.

Vocabulary Review

Directions: Complete the sentences using the following key terms and vocabulary words.

deposit   commercial banks   credit union
rationale   reserve   interest

1. Banks keep some money in _____ so that they can pay savings account holders when they need their money.

2. In the past, _____ only served businesses, but now they serve everyone.

3. A payment for borrowed money is called _____.

4. One _____ for using a bank is to keep your money safe.

5. A bank provides customers with a safe place to _____ their money.

6. People who work for the same company often use a _____ for emergency loans such as home repairs.

Skill Review

Directions: Choose the best answer to each question.

1. What assumption are banks making about depositors when they give out loans?

   A. Most depositors will also want a loan at some point.

   B. Very few depositors will want to withdraw all their money at once.

   C. Most depositors will be transferring their money from one account to another.

   D. Few depositors will actually need insurance on their accounts.

2. Why do you think most financial institutions now offer the same services?

   A. to ensure that money is kept safe

   B. to offer higher interest rates

   C. to be competitive with one another

   D. to provide a variety of home loans

3. Which of the following is the best use for a savings account?

   A. to deposit your weekly paycheck

   B. to withdraw using your ATM card

   C. to transfer money from one account to another

   D. to set aside money for a car loan

4. Checking account holders should keep track of how much money is in their checking accounts

   A. to see how it will be invested.

   B. to see how much interest they have earned.

   C. to avoid a fee if they write a check without sufficient funds in their account.

   D. to ensure the bank is protecting their privacy.

Skill Practice

Directions: Read the passage. Then answer the questions that follow.

First Bank of the United States

In 1790, Secretary of the Treasury Alexander Hamilton turned his attention to the nation's finances. During the Revolutionary War, Congress had borrowed about $42 million from the American people. It gave the lenders loan certificates, or IOUs, that it promised someday to repay in hard cash. Hamilton asked Congress to exchange these IOUs for bonds, or certificates, that earned interest. He also proposed that Congress pay the $25 million in loans owed by the states. Finally, Hamilton asked Congress to create a Bank of the United States. He said that a bank was needed to collect taxes.

Several congressmen opposed Hamilton's financial plan, particularly James Madison. He thought the plan favored speculators, or men who hoped to profit from wartime loan certificates. Many of the original lenders had IOUs for as little as 25 cents on the dollar. Under Hamilton's plan, the people who bought them could exchange the certificates for bonds at face value.

After much debate, Hamilton won enough southern votes in Congress to get his plan approved. In 1791, Congress passed the bank bill.

1. Under Hamilton's plan, why might someone exchange an IOU for a bond rather than for hard cash?

   A. Bonds will be used to pay off state loans.

   B. There is no hard cash available to give people.

   C. The face value of IOUs is too high.

   D. Bonds will earn interest into the future.

2. According to the passage, what is Madison's *main* objection to Hamilton's banking plan?

   A. Hamilton's plan favored speculators.

   B. IOUs could be exchanged for bonds.

   C. People could cash IOUs at the face value of bonds.

   D. Bonds could be cashed in for IOUs.

3. According to the passage, why does Hamilton believe the United States needs a bank?

   A. to exchange IOUs for bonds

   B. to collect taxes

   C. to pay back the American people

   D. to earn interest on bonds

Writing Practice

Directions: Think about something you would like to save money for. Maybe it's a new car, a vacation, or money for college tuition. Write a paragraph about how you would do this, including how much money you'd save each week, your savings goal, how much interest you would earn, and how your bank can help you reach your savings goal.

LESSON OBJECTIVES

- Identify several basic types of consumer credit
- Compare the different types of consumer credit
- Describe situations in which each type of credit is useful

CORE SKILLS & PRACTICES

- Sequence Events
- Judge the Relevance of Information

Key Terms

credit
a way of taking ownership of something before you pay for it

credit score
a report of how well you pay your bills

default
become unable to continue paying back a loan

installment loan
a loan repaid with interest in equal periodic payments

secured loan
a loan in which a borrower pledges an asset or property that the lender can seize in case of default

Vocabulary

judge
to form an opinion about something after carefully thinking about it

Key Concept

Different types of credit have different purposes and different advantages and disadvantages.

A credit card is easy to use and accepted by most businesses. But is it the wisest way to pay? When you pay with a credit card, the credit card company is actually giving you a loan so you can make your purchase. You can get into trouble if you can't pay back this loan.

Credit

When you use **credit**, you are taking ownership of something before you pay for it. Credit allows you to obtain an item when you want it and then pay back the creditor over time. Credit makes it easy to purchase items that you need, or must have, as well as items that you want, or would like to have. Card terminals at checkout counters and the ability to use credit cards for online purchases make it simple to use, and in some cases abuse, credit.

Types of Credit

Credit cards are one type of credit. A credit card is an identification card that allows you to borrow money from a company, usually a bank, when you make a purchase. As soon as you approve the purchase, you have created debt, or an amount of money that you must eventually pay back. Credit cards are an example of revolving credit. This type of credit allows you to borrow money up to a certain amount. It also allows you to make only partial payments until the debt is paid off. Credit card companies may charge fees and interest on any monthly debt until it has been paid off.

Installment loans are another type of credit. When you receive an installment loan, you borrow a set amount and then repay the loan in equal amounts over a specific period of time. Banks provide installment loans to consumers for large purchases, such as cars or houses. An installment loan also charges interest each month, although the interest rate on an installment loan is typically much lower than the interest rate on a credit card.

A **secured loan** is another type of credit. When you make a secured loan, you pledge an asset or property that the lender can seize in case you **default** on the loan, or are not able to pay it back. A secured loan may give you a

Corbis Premium RF/Alamy

lower interest rate than a credit card, but it can also put your home, car, or other assets at risk in case you default, or stop paying back the loan. One type of secured loan is a home equity loan. This loan will lend you a certain percentage of your home's current value minus what is owed in mortgages. Interest on a home equity loan may be tax deductible.

Credit Score

Your **credit score** is a report of how well you pay your bills. Credit agencies use information from banks and credit card companies to determine your credit score. You can increase your credit score by using credit wisely and paying all bills on time. A high credit score can allow you to obtain loans at lower interest rates. Falling behind on loan or credit card payments can reduce your credit score. A low credit score can interfere with your ability to obtain loans or low-interest credit cards.

Legally, you are allowed to look up your credit report once each year for free from a reputable consumer credit reporting agency. A credit report helps you see how well you are paying your debts and also can tell you if someone has illegally used your identity to purchase items. For example, a credit report might reveal that your credit was used to buy a television in a different state. With this information, you can contact the authorities to catch the criminals responsible and return your identity.

Comparing Types of Credit

Each type of credit has advantages and disadvantages. A secured loan can provide you with a large sum of money that can then be used for big projects, such as home repairs, or big purchases, such as a car. A secured loan may also reduce the amount of taxes that you have to pay during the year, if the interest is tax deductible.

An installment loan can be useful for making a very large purchase, such as a house. Although the entire loan is large, each installment can be small enough to fit into an average budget. A credit card allows you to carry less cash and to make purchases online. However, you may end up paying a lot of money in interest if you do not pay the balance each month.

 Think about Social Studies

Directions: Fill in the blanks.

1. A credit card allows you to _____ money when you buy something.
2. Revolving credit lets you make _____ payments until you pay off your debt.
3. Banks provide _____ loans for large purchases, such as a car.
4. If you default on a _____ loan, a lender can seize your property.
5. A _____ is something you must have and a _____ is something you would like to have.

CORE PRACTICE

Sequence Events

What might happen to your personal finances if you defaulted on a secured loan? Write the sequence of events that could occur after you stopped paying the loan. This exercise can help you to understand how damaging a default can be to your life.

CORE SKILL

Judge the Relevance of Information

Judging something means to form an opinion after carefully thinking about something. What information in this lesson is most relevant to your life? How did you judge it to be relevant? Write a brief paragraph explaining why the information is relevant to you.

WRITE TO LEARN

List the reasons that you might need an installment loan.

Vocabulary Review

Directions: Complete the sentences using the following key terms and vocabulary words.

credit   relevant   installment loan
secured loan   default   credit score

1. A mortgage is a(n) _____ that is paid back in equal monthly payments.

2. Your _____ shows how well you have paid your bills.

3. If you are not able to pay back a(n) _____, you may lose an asset such as your car.

4. Information about loans will be _____ when you need to make a purchase on credit.

5. People often use _____ instead of cash to make purchases.

6. You may _____ on a loan if you cannot make payments on time.

Skill Review

Directions: Choose the best answer to each question.

1. You will not incur debt if you pay for a car with which of these?
   A. cash
   B. secured loan
   C. installment loan
   D. revolving credit loan

2. Which of these actions is most likely to lower a person's credit score?
   A. taking out an installment loan
   B. using credit cards for purchases
   C. paying interest on a secured loan
   D. making late payments on bills

3. A small business owner that runs a sign-making shop needs to purchase a building to expand her business. What type of credit is she likely to pursue?
   A. credit card loan
   B. secured loan
   C. installment loan
   D. revolving credit loan

4. How has technology made it easier to use credit?
   A. Anyone who has a computer can get a credit card.
   B. Credit cards can be used at checkout terminals and to make online purchases.
   C. Online purchases can be made using debit cards.
   D. Credit cards can be used to establish a credit line.

Skill Practice

Directions: Read the passage below. Then answer the questions that follow.

Credit cards are now required for more and more things, including making hotel reservations, renting a car, or making online purchases. However, people who have never had a credit card or who have a low credit score may not be able to qualify for a traditional credit card. Some banks have addressed this problem by offering secured credit cards. A secured credit card requires a cash deposit. This cash deposit is then available as a credit line that can be used by the card holder. For example, if a card holder gives the bank $250 as a cash deposit, this amount is then available as a credit line. The card holder can then use the secured card to make $250-worth of reservations or purchases. A secured credit card might have a variety of fees, including an application fee and an annual fee. If you decide to get a secured credit card, it makes sense to shop around in order to get the best deal.

1. Which of the following is a secured credit card most like?

   A. a revolving credit loan

   B. a secured loan

   C. an installment loan

   D. a traditional credit card

2. How is a secured credit card more like cash than like credit?

   A. You do not incur debt when you use the card.

   B. There are no fees associated with the use of the card.

   C. You can use the card wherever cash is accepted.

   D. Use of the card does not affect your credit score.

Writing Practice

List a goal that could be achieved by taking out an installment loan, such as funding a college education. Write a paragraph listing the ways an installment loan could help you to achieve this goal. In this paragraph, also list the pros and cons of having an installment loan. Be sure to include an introductory sentence and a conclusion in your paragraph.

LESSON 8.3 Consumer Credit Laws

LESSON OBJECTIVES

- Explain the importance of consumer credit laws
- Describe consumer credit laws

CORE SKILLS

- Analyze Point of View
- Identify Author's Bias

Key Terms

Consumer Financial Protection Bureau
federal agency created to protect consumers

Consumer Credit Protection Act
umbrella consumer protection law passed in 1969

Credit CARD Act
limits credit card fees and rate increases and requires lenders to be consistent in payment dates and times

Equal Credit Opportunity Act
prohibits discrimination in credit transactions on the basis of personal characteristics

Truth in Lending Act
federal law that requires lenders to use uniform methods for computing the cost of credit

Vocabulary

liability
legal responsibility

Key Concept

The federal government enforces laws that provide many safeguards for the consumer using credit.

Americans often use credit for purchases—from the smallest toys to the largest houses. With so many households relying on credit, it would be tempting for lenders to take advantage of consumers, making lots of money in the process. Because of this possibility, the federal government has passed a variety of laws to protect consumers.

Consumer Credit Protections

Since the 1960s, the federal government has passed a variety of laws that protect the rights of consumers as they obtain and use credit. These laws prevent discrimination and ensure that consumers have clear information about the terms of credit. They limit fees and interest rates that lenders can charge. To understand all of the credit protections you have as a consumer, it is useful to look at each of the most important credit protection laws that have been passed.

The Truth in Lending Act

In 1968, Congress passed the **Truth in Lending Act**. This law requires lenders to use uniform methods for computing the cost of credit. It also requires lenders to state the terms of credit to the consumer in a uniform way. This act helps consumers by allowing them to determine the real cost of borrowing money. The Truth in Lending Act also limits a consumer's **liability**, or legal responsibility, for purchases if a credit card is stolen and used by someone else.

The Consumer Credit Protection Act

The **Consumer Credit Protection Act** was passed in 1969. It is an umbrella consumer protection law that has had other acts added to it over time. The Consumer Credit Protection Act and the acts contained under it are modified by Congress periodically. The Consumer Credit Protection Act includes the Truth in Lending Act as well as the following acts.

The Fair Credit Reporting Act The Fair Credit Reporting Act, passed in 1970, allows consumers to have access to their credit report and to correct any errors in that report. A credit report is a record of a consumer's credit history. It shows how much credit the person has taken out and whether he or she makes payments on time. Lenders use this information to decide whether to extend credit to a person and, if so, how much. This act was amended in the last decade to protect consumers against identity theft, allow consumers to obtain a free credit report annually, and to give consumers the right to prevent companies connected to lenders to market to them. They do so by using an Opt Out option, which a government agency explains this way:

> Section 624 gives a consumer the right to restrict an entity, with which it does not have a pre-existing business relationship, from using certain information obtained from an affiliate to make solicitations to that consumer. . . .
>
> Under Section 624, an entity may not use information received from an affiliate to market its products or services to a consumer, unless the consumer is given notice and a reasonable opportunity and a reasonable and simple method to opt out of the making of such solicitations. The affiliate marketing opt-out applies to both transaction or experience information and "other" information, such as information from credit reports and credit applications.

The Equal Credit Opportunity Act The **Equal Credit Opportunity Act**, passed in 1974, prohibits discrimination by lenders on the basis of race, color, religion, national origin, sex, marital status, or age. In other words, lenders must judge credit applicants fairly and cannot use those characteristics in turning down an application for credit. It also prevents discrimination based on economic status. This feature of the law allows people who receive public assistance to qualify for credit. This act also prevents lenders from discriminating against you if you have filed a complaint under the Consumer Credit Protection Act.

The Fair Credit Billing Act The Fair Credit Billing Act, also passed in 1974, requires credit card companies to post payments to a consumer's account in a timely manner and correct any mistakes on a consumer's bills. This act also allows consumers to dispute incorrect charges on credit card bills.

⚑ Think about Social Studies

Directions: Fill in the blank with the name of the correct consumer credit law.

1. The _____ requires credit card companies to credit payments in a timely manner.

Recent Credit Protections

Acts passed in the 1980s and 2000s have added even more protections for consumers in the area of consumer credit. These laws give consumers more information about their credit card accounts so that they can make wiser decisions about using credit.

WRITE TO LEARN

Write a blog post with bullet points that explains how consumers benefit from the Truth in Lending Act.

CORE SKILL

Analyze Point of View

Analyzing the point of view of the writer can often help you to better understand the meaning of a piece of writing. Read the information about section 624 of the Fair Credit Reporting Act. From what point of view was this regulation written? What kind of information did the writer of this regulation wish to convey?

The Credit CARD Act pushes financial businesses to adopt more of a customer focus, as it requires these businesses to provide detailed information to aid customers in their financial decision-making. Examine the graphic on this page. The information in this graphic is now required on every monthly credit card statement. How does this information maintain a focus on the credit card customer? How can the customer use it to make better financial decisions? Write a paragraph that answers these questions.

The Fair Credit and Charge Card Disclosure Act

The Fair Credit and Charge Card Disclosure Act was passed in 1988. It requires any company that issues credit cards to provide information about the card's annual percentage rate (APR) and any annual fee associated with the card. The APR states the yearly cost of credit if a balance on the card is not paid in full. This cost is stated as a percentage so that consumers can easily compare credit terms from one lender to another. The act also requires the lender to tell consumers the number of days they have to pay their bill before interest is charged.

Credit CARD Act

The **Credit CARD Act**, passed in 2009, limits the charges that credit card companies can require. It puts limits on late fees, inactivity fees, and interest rate increases and prevents credit card companies from increasing the interest rate on existing balances. It also requires companies that issue cards to contact customers forty-five days before increasing the interest rate for any new transactions. Finally, the act requires credit card companies to provide information about how long it will take a consumer to pay off a balance. The chart below is an example of information the credit card companies must provide under this new law.

Credit Card Information

New balance	$3,000.00
Minimum payment due	$90.00
Payment due date	4/20/12

Late Payment Warning: If we do not receive your minimum payment by the date listed above, you may have to pay a $35 late fee and your APRs may be increased up to the Penalty APR of 28.99%.

Minimum Payment Warning: If you make only the minimum payment each period, you will pay more in interest and it will take you longer to pay off your balance. For example:

If you make no additional charges using this card and each month you pay...	You will pay off the balance shown on this statement in about...	And you will end up paying an estimated total of...
Only the minimum payment	11 years	$4,745
$103	3 years	$3,712 (Savings = $1,033)

🚩 **Think about Social Studies**

Directions: Use the statement above to answer the question.

1. How much would a consumer pay on a $3,000 debt if they only paid the minimum payment each month for 11 years?

   A. $90   C. $3712

   B. $103   D. $4745

The Consumer Financial Protection Bureau

The **Consumer Financial Protection Bureau (CFPB)** has authority over most federal consumer protection laws and looks out for the interests of consumers who are shopping for financial products and services.

Creation of the Consumer Financial Protection Bureau

Before creation of the Consumer Financial Protection Bureau, government agencies involved with financial regulations had mainly been concerned with bank safety or monetary policy. No one agency focused on enforcing consumer credit laws and protecting consumers. In 2007, a severe financial crisis hit the United States. Consumers experienced significant problems as a result, as explained at the CFPB website:

> In the 2000s, there were widespread failures in consumer protection and rapid growth in irresponsible lending practices. Many lenders took advantage of gaps in the consumer protection system by selling mortgages and other products that were overly complicated.
>
> This left many Americans with loans that they did not fully understand and could not afford. Although some borrowers knowingly took on too much debt, millions of Americans who behaved responsibly were also lured into unaffordable loans by misleading promises of low payments. . . .
>
> Even those who avoided the temptations of excessively risky credit were caught in its web. Those who never took out an unaffordable mortgage nonetheless saw the values of their homes plummet when neighbors lost homes in foreclosure. Those who used credit cards and home equity lines of credit judiciously saw across-the-board increases in interest rates on credit cards and contraction of outstanding lines of credit. . . . . The costs of irresponsible lending were borne by tens of millions of American families.

In 2010, Congress passed the Dodd-Frank Wall Street Reform and Consumer Protection Act. It established the Consumer Financial Protection Bureau. The CFPB has these functions:

- Write rules, supervise companies, and enforce federal consumer financial protection laws
- Restrict unfair, deceptive, or abusive acts or practices
- Take consumer complaints
- Promote financial education
- Research consumer behavior
- Monitor financial markets for new risks to consumers
- Enforce laws that outlaw discrimination and other unfair treatment in consumer finance

---

⚑ Think about Social Studies

Directions: Answer the following question on a separate sheet of paper.

1. Why might overly complicated language in financial documents hurt consumers?

Identify Author's Bias

An author may show bias by favoring certain people, ideas, or opinions over others. When you read informational paragraphs, it is helpful to look for any bias as you evaluate any arguments made by the author. Read the passages about how consumers were affected during the financial crisis that began in 2007. Do you detect any bias by the author? How would that bias affect the arguments the author is making about consumer involvement in the financial crisis?

Vocabulary Review

Directions: Complete the sentences using the following key terms and vocabulary words.

Truth in Lending Act
Equal Credit Opportunity Act
Consumer Financial Protection Bureau

Consumer Credit Protection Act
Credit CARD Act
liability

1. The _____ is a financial government agency that protects and educates consumers.

2. If someone's credit card is lost or stolen, the Consumer Credit Protection Act limits the person's _____ for charges on that credit card.

3. The _____ prevents lenders from discriminating based on gender in granting credit.

4. The _____ requires lenders to use uniform terms to disclose the terms of credit.

5. Lenders must provide information about how long it will take to pay off a credit card balance because of the _____.

6. To protect consumers, Congress passed the _____, which contains various consumer credit acts.

Skill Review

Directions: Choose the best answer to each question.

1. A consumer learns that her credit card has been stolen when a charge for expensive shoes shows up on her credit card statement. Which act gives her the right to dispute this charge?

   A. Fair Credit and Charge Card Disclosure Act

   B. Truth in Lending Act

   C. Credit CARD Act

   D. Fair Credit Reporting Act

2. The Consumer Credit Protection Act helps a consumer in which of these situations?

   A. The consumer has lost her credit card and needs a new one.

   B. The consumer has gotten divorced and needs a credit card.

   C. The consumer has made a late payment on a credit card.

   D. The consumer wants to file a complaint about a bank.

3. What is the relationship between the Consumer Financial Protection Bureau and the Credit CARD Act?

   A. The bureau enforces the regulations set up by the act.

   B. The bureau and the act only regulate credit card lenders.

   C. Both were enacted in response to irresponsible consumers.

   D. Both focus entirely on consumer financial policies.

Skill Practice

Directions: Read the passage. Then answer the questions that follow.

Controversy and the Consumer Financial Protection Bureau

The creation of the Consumer Financial Protection Bureau was not without controversy. Although a Consumer Union poll in 2011 showed that 74% of respondents supported the new agency, congressional Republicans and many financial and business groups opposed it. Those in opposition argued that the agency would expand government power, divert bank resources toward compliance with regulations, and make less credit available to consumers. In an article in the *Los Angeles Times*, the chief executive of one bank in Whittier, California, stated: "We're trying to be a resource for our community. We want to make credit and financial resources available. . . . At the end of the day, there's more hoops for us to go through." Some consumers also expressed concern about the new agency, wondering if it would have enough staff and resources to adequately address the extensive mortgage issues that resulted from the financial crisis. Elizabeth Warren, the Obama administration advisor who was put in charge of the bureau, warned that it needed time to have any positive effect. At the same time, she promised that the bureau would work hard toward "making the price clear, making the risk clear, and making it easier to compare products."

1. According to bureau officials, which of these is a goal of the Consumer Financial Protection Bureau?

   A. expand government regulatory power

   B. reduce the availability of credit

   C. allow comparisons of financial products

   D. eliminate consumer financial risk

2. Which statement reflects the view of the CFPB held by the chief executive of the California bank?

   A. It will create roadblocks that prevent consumers from obtaining loans.

   B. It will allow financial products to be more understandable to consumers.

   C. It will greatly increase the financial costs of regulatory compliance.

   D. It will cause political problems for politicians who voted for it.

Writing Practice

Directions: Write a paragraph that explores why the values of different politicians, consumers, or businesses would cause them to have different opinions about the Consumer Financial Protection Bureau.

Directions: Read the passage, and then answer the questions that follow.

In February, 2011, William C. Dudley, President and Chief Executive Officer of the Federal Reserve Bank of New York gave a speech discussing trends in household debt in the region served by the New York Fed. His remarks included this statement:

"Looking forward, we see some signs that the region is turning the corner on the credit cycle. After declining during the (financial) crisis, credit applications have begun to increase, suggesting that the demand for credit is rising. Although housing debt is still declining and delinquencies are still high, households in many parts of the region have sought and taken on some new debt in recent months."

1. What is one reason housing debt might decline during a financial crisis?
   A. More people want to sell homes than buy them.
   B. Home prices rise significantly during a crisis.
   C. People are less able to qualify for housing loans.
   D. Banks lend at lower interest rates during a crisis.

2. Which of these came into being partly in response to the financial crisis to which Dudley is referring?
   A. Consumer Financial Protection Bureau
   B. Truth in Lending Act
   C. Fair Credit Reporting Act
   D. Fair Credit Billing Act

3. What could be the result of widespread credit delinquencies in the region due to the financial crisis?
   A. Credit scores decline, and people are unable to obtain credit.
   B. The number of installment loans increases, as opposed to secured loans.
   C. Employment related to the financial system declines.
   D. Credit card applications and credit card usage increase.

Directions: Use the following chart to answer questions 4–6.

The Financial System

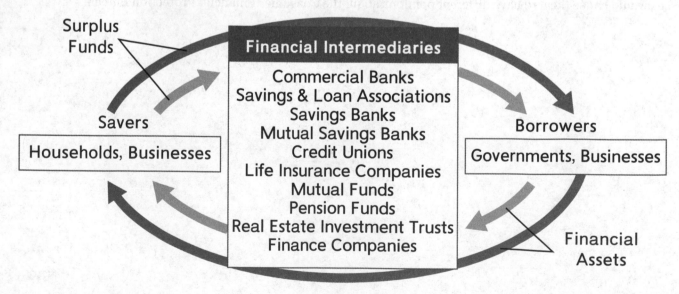

Surplus Funds

Financial Intermediaries

Commercial Banks
Savings & Loan Associations
Savings Banks
Mutual Savings Banks
Credit Unions
Life Insurance Companies
Mutual Funds
Pension Funds
Real Estate Investment Trusts
Finance Companies

Savers

Households, Businesses

Borrowers

Governments, Businesses

Financial Assets

4. Which financial intermediary in the chart started as an institution that provided emergency loans to its members?

A. commercial bank

B. credit union

C. savings bank

D. finance company

5. What does the chart make clear about the US financial system?

A. Financial institutions hold most of the money in the United States.

B. Governments borrow from banks but do not deposit funds.

C. Funds are constantly cycling through the economy of the United States.

D. There are more financial assets than surplus funds.

6. What is a critical service that intermediaries provide in the financial system?

A. They manage and safeguard money.

B. They prevent the transfer of funds.

C. They encourage saving instead of spending.

D. They reduce the need for borrowing money.

Directions: Read the following questions. Then choose the correct answer.

7. Which of these can allow you to borrow to make a purchase but also avoid paying interest?

A. installment loan

B. credit card

C. secured loan

D. paying by check

8. Which of these allows you to access your credit score annually for free?

A. Fair Credit Reporting Act

B. Credit CARD Act

C. Equal Credit Opportunity Act

D. Fair Credit Billing Act

Check Your Understanding

Lesson	Item Number
Savings and Banking	5, 6, 7
Types of Credit	1, 2, 4, 8
Consumer Credit Laws	3

WRITE ABOUT Consumer Credit

When you write with the purpose of evaluating data, you rely on information presented in graphics such as tables, charts, and graphs. Newspaper and magazine articles frequently present their facts in graphics. Evaluating data generally involves making inferences from the information presented. To make an inference, follow these steps:

- Identify the stated facts.
- Summarize the information.
- Apply any related information from your own knowledge or other sources.
- Use your own knowledge and the facts to reach a conclusion.

Read the essay on page 355, then analyze and evaluate data from the graph below.

General-Purpose Credit Card Holders by Age and Outstanding Balance

Age	Percentage having a credit card	Median balance (in dollars)
Under 35 years old	58.9	2,000
35 to 44 years old	68.1	3,400
45 to 54 years old	74.3	4,000
55 to 64 years old	78.9	3,500
65 to 74 years old	79.5	3,900
75 years old and over	66.0	900

BEFORE YOU WRITE Read the Graphic Carefully

The first—and most basic—step is to read the title to determine the topic. When dealing with financial matters, information can be very specific. For example, in the sample on this page, the chart deals only with general-purpose credit cards, not store credit cards.

Next, read the headings of rows and columns to find out what information the chart is presenting. If you are reading a line or bar graph, study it to determine whether the information represents an increase or a decrease. If you are examining a circle graph, pay attention to the size of each section, noting its percentage and portion of the entire graph. Study the facts and figures given, looking for patterns. Notice the relationships among facts and figures. You may wish to jot down some ideas before you begin to write. Doing so will help you organize your findings.

> **TIP** Use Correct Plural Forms
>
> Most regular nouns form their plural forms by adding s or es. However, some nouns are irregular. These nouns form their plurals in three major ways:
>
> - The plural and singular forms are the same.
> Examples: *deer, fish*
> - The noun has only a plural form.
> Examples: *clothes, eyeglasses, scissors*
> - The plural form requires a change in spelling.
> Examples: *woman/women, mouse/mice, tooth/teeth*

WHILE YOU WRITE Use Appropriate Terminology

At times, you will need to write about an issue that is unfamiliar and whose terminology you find confusing. Be sure to use reference materials—print or online—to try to gain understanding so you can clearly explain the issue to your reader. Your job as a writer is to make things clear to the reader, not to write in circles trying to avoid explaining difficult concepts. You must have a full understanding of the issue to be able to pass on to your reader in a clear manner the important elements of the issue. If all else fails, check a children's book on the subject. There are many excellent publishers of children's books that explain topics that may be hard for you to grasp. An effective writer is one who can plainly and succinctly outline facts and relationships to his or her reader.

TIP Watch Out for Faulty Reasoning

When analyzing data, it is important not to distort information to reach conclusions already held or desired. Hasty generalizations are based on lack of sufficient data or inconclusive evidence. Be sure that the results of any study include a large enough sample to be meaningful. Another danger is in seeing a cause when the evidence isn't there to support it. If one event occurs, it is not always the case that another, related event caused it. As you examine statistical data, be careful not to assume that unrelated events have a cause/effect relationship.

AFTER YOU WRITE Double-Check Your Work

Looking at information in charts or graphs can be tedious work, but misreading the data can lead to erroneous conclusions. Use a sheet of colored paper or a ruler to go over the table carefully. Be sure that you have transferred numbers and percentages correctly in your analysis. Go slowly.

Chapter 9

Societal Development

Have you ever visited a city like Rome? Ruins of an ancient
civilization sit next to modern buildings and roads. Although
these structures look quite different, ancient civilizations feature
some of the characteristics that modern civilizations still have.
For example, ancient cities were established by natural features,
such as rivers or mountains. The borders of modern cities, states,
or nations are often the same as natural boundaries. Ancient
cities also had population growth and economic development that
affected the natural world. Modern cities have overtaken many
natural areas, but modern planners have developed sustainable
practices to reduce the negative effects of human activity.

Societal Development

In this chapter you will study these topics:

Lesson 9.1
Development of Ancient Civilizations

What are the characteristics of a civilization? Did ancient civilizations have these characteristics? Where did ancient civilizations develop?

Lesson 9.2
Nationhood and Statehood

What are the boundaries and borders that separate cities or townships in your area? Do any of these borders follow natural features, such as rivers? How have people worked together to establish political borders? How have borders changed based on conflict?

Lesson 9.3
Human Activity and the Environment

How has population growth and economic development affected natural areas around where you live? How many people can your area support? Are there examples of sustainable development in your community?

Goal Setting

Do you live in a city, or have you ever visited one? What were the different features of the city, including its boundaries and its relationship with the natural world?

How do you think cities and civilizations developed? What kinds of features of ancient civilizations are still a part of modern civilizations?

LESSON 9.1 Development of Ancient Civilizations

LESSON OBJECTIVES

- Understand the development of ancient North Africa and the Indian Subcontinent
- Understand the development of the Early Chinese Civilization
- Understand the development of Ancient Greece and Rome

CORE SKILLS & PRACTICES

- Draw Evidence from Text
- Understand Cause and Effect

Key Terms

castes
categories that determined a person's occupation and social class

civilization
a society in an advanced state of cultural development

consuls
people who ran the Roman republic

dynasty
family of rulers

polis
Greek city-state that was a place and a governing body

Vocabulary

mandate
a command

Key Concept

Ancient civilizations shared the same six developments: cities, central government, religion, social and economic classes, art and architecture, and writing.

Most modern civilizations have a central government, an economy that provides goods and services, cities with buildings of all sizes, people of different social classes and religions, various forms of art, and an educational system. These characteristics of modern civilizations have their roots in many ancient civilizations, including those of North Africa, the Indian subcontinent, China, Greece, and Rome.

Ancient North Africa and the Indian Subcontinent

A **civilization** is a society in an advanced state of cultural development. In ancient North Africa, the Egyptian civilization grew up along the banks of the Nile River. In the Indian subcontinent, civilizations grew up along the Indus and Ganges Rivers.

Egyptian Civilization and Agriculture

Around 3100 B.C., a king named Menes united the peoples along the Nile River into the Kingdom of Egypt. He began the first **dynasty**, or family of rulers. Over time the Egyptian ruler became known as the pharaoh. Egyptians believed that the pharaoh represented the sun god Ra on Earth and was considered to be divine.

The civilization of ancient Egypt is sometimes called the "gift of the Nile." The Nile River valley is located in the Sahara Desert, where the climate is hot and dry. Without the waters of the Nile, the Egyptians could not have planted and harvested crops. Like the Tigris and Euphrates Rivers in modern-day Iraq, the Nile flooded each year. When the river flowed back within its banks, it left behind rich soil suitable for agriculture. The Egyptians learned to build dikes to control the flooding of the Nile. They also learned to build dams and irrigation ditches to bring the river water to their fields. Agricultural land was owned by pharaohs, nobles, and priests. A large class of peasant farmers worked this land and managed its irrigation.

Egyptian Religion and Culture

Like many ancient people, the Egyptians were polytheistic, believing in many gods. The sun gods and land gods became the chief deities of the Egyptians: Ra was the sun god; Osiris was the god of the Nile who brought the annual flood. The Egyptians thought life after death was similar to life on Earth. As a result, the pharaohs had themselves buried with all the things they would need in the afterlife. Pharaohs were also mummified, or preserved, for the afterlife and buried in tombs within large structures called pyramids. The Great Pyramid at Giza contains the tomb of King Khufu and was finished about 2540 B.C. The pyramids are one of the greatest achievements of the Egyptians. Other important achievements include the invention of papyrus (a paper-like material), a system of writing called hieroglyphics, and medical advances, such as surgery and the use of splints for broken bones.

Civilizations on the Indian Subcontinent

The earliest civilization on the Indian subcontinent began in the Indus River valley, around 2500 B.C. to 1500 B.C. Much of what we know is based on archaeological research from two cities, Harappa and Mohenjo-Daro. The two cities were laid out on a grid pattern. Houses had running water and indoor plumbing that drained into a citywide sewage system. A combined temple, palace, and fort stood over each city on a nearby hill. Both cities had villages and fields scattered around them and large warehouses where crops were stored.

The economies of Harappa and Mohenjo-Daro were based on farming. Like the Tigris, Euphrates, and Nile Rivers, the Indus flooded each year. Farmers used the rich soil left behind to grow crops such as wheat and barley. The farmers of the Indus Valley were the first to grow cotton and weave it into fine cloth. Cotton cloth became one of the trade goods of Indus merchants, along with grain, copper, and pearls. Harappa and Mohenjo-Daro had some form of central government, probably headed by a king or priest-king. The people of the Indus Valley were polytheistic and also worshiped animals. Although they had a written language, no one has been able to decipher it.

Aryan Invasion

Around 1500 B.C., nomadic Aryans from Central Asia invaded and conquered the Indus Valley. The Aryans spoke an Indo-European language known as Sanskrit. Like other ancient people, the Aryans were polytheistic. The Aryans developed a social system that divided the population into four major categories called **castes**. The castes determined a person's occupation and social class. Over time, Aryan culture and its caste system expanded across much of the Indian subcontinent.

⚑ Think about Social Studies

Directions: Fill in the blanks.

1. Because Egyptians believed in a(n) _____, pharaohs were buried with their worldly belongings.

2. The Aryans spoke a language known as _____.

3. The people of the _____ River valley were the first to produce cotton cloth.

4. The ancient _____ civilization formed in the Nile River valley.

WRITE TO LEARN

At a library or online, research the burial tombs of the early Egyptians. Write a paragraph describing the tombs. If researching online, remember to use reputable sources.

CORE SKILL

Draw Evidence from Text

The section "Civilizations on the Indian Subcontinent" gives detailed information about the earliest civilization on the Indian subcontinent, even though no written records exist. What statements in the text allow you to understand how historians know about this civilization? What kind of evidence implied by the text allows you to understand how the people in this civilization lived?

Early Chinese Civilizations

Like the early civilizations in Egypt and the Indian subcontinent, the first civilization in China began in a river valley. Chinese civilization was based on dynasties, and family was important to the structure of Chinese society.

Agriculture and Chinese Civilization

Like the Tigris, Euphrates, Nile, and Indus Rivers, the Huang He (HWAHNG HUH) River (Yellow River) was an agricultural resource. When the river flooded and then returned to its banks, it left rich soil behind. Like other people, the Chinese learned to build dikes and irrigation systems to control the river and water their fields. However, every few years, the floods of the Huang He overtook the dikes and caused widespread loss of life and damage to property. The Chinese began to call the Huang He the "river of sorrows."

The First Chinese Dynasties

China has been ruled by a succession of dynasties. The earliest Chinese dynasty was the Xia (SHYAH), which began around 2200 B.C. This was a prehistoric civilization, with no written record. Their economy was based on farming, although there is archaeological evidence that some people lived in cities. The Xia knew how to make bronze tools. Archaeologists have also found pottery and large tombs.

Legend indicates that Tang, the leader of the Shang (SHAHNG) people, overthrew the last Xia ruler. Tang established the Shang Dynasty around 1750 B.C. Like the Xia, the Shang were farmers, but many people lived in large, walled cities. Like the Xia, the Shang knew how to make bronze. The Shang also developed a writing system for the Chinese language and began what is called ancestor worship. Ancestors are members of a family who have lived and died. Like other early people, the Shang believed in life after death. They buried the dead with things that the person might need in the afterlife. The Shang also believed that the dead could either help the living or bring them bad luck. As a result, the living began to offer sacrifices to their ancestors. This form of religious worship continued for thousands of years.

Development of Ancient Civilizations

The Zhou Dynasty and the Mandate of Heaven

The Zhou (JOH) people rebelled against the Shang in 1045 B.C. The Zhou set up their own dynasty and ruled in central China. To explain why they overthrew the Shang, the Zhou developed the principle of the Mandate of Heaven. A **mandate** is a command. The Zhou said that the deities in heaven ordered the Zhou to replace the Shang ruler. The Zhou used this principle to justify, or support, their overthrow of the Shang.

According to the Mandate of Heaven, the king and all later emperors ruled by divine right. Their power came from the gods. In time, the Chinese expanded the theory. Rulers did not always act in the best interests of the people. Then the Mandate of Heaven gave the people the right to rebel against their ruler. The result was the development of the dynastic cycle. This is the rise, rule, and then fall of a dynasty over a number of years. Over time, the Mandate of Heaven became the basis for the way the Chinese changed their rulers.

The Family in China

The family was the basic unit of Chinese society and the most important. Each member of a family had a duty and responsibility to every other member. This duty was known as filial piety, and it governed the relationships among family members. Sons and daughters were to obey their parents. Parents were to obey their parents. All family members were to obey the oldest male of the family, who was considered to be the head of the extended family. An extended family contained all the related members of a family, including grandparents, parents, children, aunts, uncles, and cousins.

Early Writing in China

Written Chinese first developed during the Shang Dynasty. English is based on a 26-letter alphabet. To read English, a person has to learn those 26 letters and their 43 phonetic sounds. Chinese is based on characters, not letters. Each character stands for either a picture of something or an idea. There are thousands of characters in Chinese. An elementary school student knows at least 1,500 characters.

 Think about Social Studies

Directions: In a notebook, write a paragraph that discusses the relationship between the dynasty system of rule and the place of the family in ancient Chinese society.

Ancient Greece and Rome

Greece and Rome are located in the Mediterranean region. As in other areas, the ancient civilizations in the Mediterranean region developed in river valleys.

Greece and the Rise of City-States

The Greek Peninsula and nearby islands are mountainous, with river valleys and small, low coastal plains. At some time in the ancient past, groups of people settled in these valleys and plains. The mountains kept these groups separate from one another. Over time, people living in the groups developed independent, self-governing city-states.

Understand Cause and Effect

Sometimes, when you are shown an effect, you can determine a clear cause for that effect. Other times, the cause is not as clear. What was the likely cause for the Zhou development of the principle of the Mandate of Heaven? Explain your answer.

Critical Thinking and Problem Solving

The paragraph about Sparta states that it was a military polis with strict rules that cut itself off from the rest of the world and discouraged the study of literature, the arts, and philosophy. What do you think are the advantages and disadvantages of a society cutting itself off from the rest of the world? Use a graphic organizer to arrange your ideas to determine the connections between strict rules, isolation, and the discouragement of particular topics of study. Write about these connections in a short paragraph.

The Greek city-state was called a **polis**, which was both a place and a governing body. The English word *politics* comes from the Greek word *polis*. City-states were built around a hill. At the top of the hill was an area called the acropolis, where temples and public buildings were built. The rest of the city was built below the acropolis on flat land. One area of the city, called the agora, was kept as open space. Citizens assembled there for meetings and used it as a marketplace. Over time, the area surrounding the city came under the control of the city-state.

The earliest city-states were monarchies ruled by kings. In some city-states, wealthy aristocrats were able to overthrow the king and set up rule by oligarchy, which is a state that is ruled by a few people. The 500s B.C. marked the rise of tyrants. A tyrant was not always a cruel ruler, as the word means today. In ancient Greece, a tyrant was a government ruled by one man. Rule by tyrants was the first step toward democratic rule, as they were often caring and fair rulers. In some cities like Athens, tyrants made important reforms to help the poor. But overall, Greeks turned away from absolute rule and toward democracy.

Sparta and Athens

Over time, Sparta and Athens became the most important city-states in Greece. During the 700s B.C., Sparta became a military polis. Harsh laws governed all parts of Spartans' lives. Sparta's government was controlled by two kings, a ruling council, and a council of elders, with voting input from an assembly of citizens. The only job for a Spartan citizen was soldier. All other work such as farming was done by people captured in battle and enslaved. To protect its way of life, Sparta cut itself off from the rest of the world. The study of literature, the arts, and philosophy was not encouraged.

The earliest government of Athens was a monarchy. In the 700s B.C., an oligarchy of aristocrats replaced the king. Between 560 B.C. and 510 B.C., tyrants ruled Athens. By 512 B.C., Cleisthenes had the support of enough Athenians to gain control of the government and change its structure. Cleisthenes is regarded as the founder of Athenian democracy, in which male citizens could vote. By the 400s B.C., Athens was an important trading center. It grew much of its own food but also imported grain in large amounts. Some of its trade goods were wine and olive oil. Slave labor was used to manufacture these goods.

The Roman Republic

The Roman Republic began along the banks of the Tiber River in Italy. The river runs through the plain of Latium, which is about halfway down the west side of the Italian Peninsula. Sometime around 1500 to 1000 B.C., people began moving into the Italian Peninsula from the north. By 800 B.C., they had set up small villages on seven hills along the Tiber River. Around 650 B.C., Etruscans moved into Latium from the north. They seized control of much of central Italy and turned the seven villages into the city of Rome.

In 509 B.C., the Romans overthrew the Etruscan king and set up a republic. In a republic, citizens elect representatives to govern. This is different from the democracy that Athens developed, where citizens govern directly through voting. In Rome, wealthy landowners called patricians initially made most decisions regarding who would govern. Small landowners, farmers, craft workers, and merchants, known as plebeians, had little say.

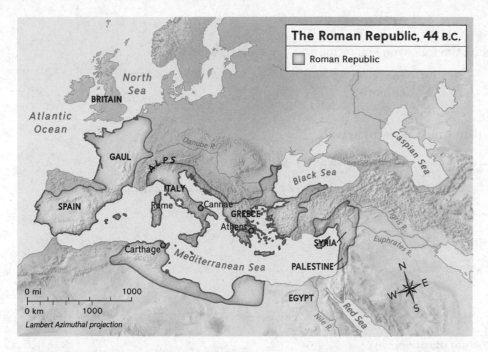

The Roman Republic, 44 B.C.

☐ Roman Republic

The government was headed by two **consuls**, or people who ran the Roman government. The consuls issued laws and orders and could veto each other's decisions. A senate made sure that the laws and orders of the consuls were carried out, and advised the consuls on issues. In time, the plebeians gained a larger voice in Roman government. By 409 B.C., plebeians had gained the right to hold public office. After 287 B.C., the Assembly of the People, which included all male citizens, could make laws that all Romans had to obey.

The Romans gradually extended their control beyond Rome. By 261 B.C., the entire Italian Peninsula was under Roman control. By 146 B.C., the Roman army had gone far beyond Italy, to control areas throughout the Mediterranean. Through the Roman Confederation, a series of alliances between Rome and other areas were forged. In return for loyalty, member city-states were allowed to rule themselves. They received trading rights with Rome and other benefits. In exchange, member city-states had to provide soldiers for the Roman army.

 Think about Social Studies

Directions: Study the map above. Choose the best answer to the following questions.

1. In 44 B.C., how far north did the Roman Empire extend?
   A. Carthage
   B. Italy
   C. Gaul
   D. Syria

2. Where was the city of Athens located?
   A. Carthage
   B. Greece
   C. Italy
   D. Palestine

Vocabulary Review

Directions: Complete the sentences using the following key terms and vocabulary words.

civilization   dynasty   castes
mandate   polis   consuls

1. A _____ is both a place and a governing body.

2. One characteristic of a _____ is an emphasis on cultural development.

3. In the Indian subcontinent, the Aryans introduced social classes called _____.

4. Many people lived in walled cities during the Shang _____.

5. A _____ is a command.

6. The _____ in Rome issued laws and orders.

Skill Review

Directions: Choose the best answer to each question.

1. Many ancient civilizations share which of these geographical features?
   A. high mountain ranges
   B. river valleys and flat plains
   C. shorelines on seas or oceans
   D. low-lying swamps or bogs

2. Religious beliefs in ancient Egypt appear to be most similar to religious beliefs in which of these other ancient civilizations?
   A. Indus River valley
   B. Roman republic
   C. Greek city-states
   D. Shang dynasty

3. Archaeological evidence suggests that people of the Indus River valley likely understood which of the following?
   A. Rivers eventually dry up in a desert area.
   B. Certain animals can be raised for food.
   C. Human wastes could lead to illness.
   D. Different groups of people should remain separate.

4. Member city-states in the Roman Confederation were
   A. part of Rome's expansion.
   B. exempt from military duty.
   C. allowed to rule other member states.
   D. not allowed to trade with Rome.

Skill Practice

Directions: Study the map and read the information below. Then answer the questions that follow.

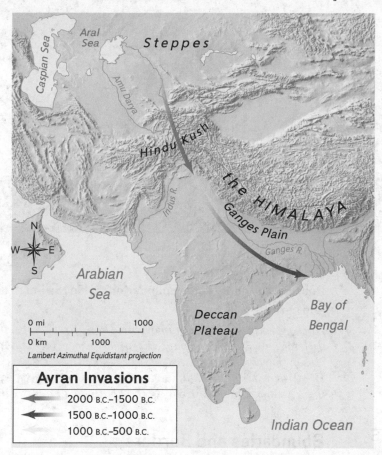

The Aryan invasions of the Indian subcontinent occurred over the span of 1500 years. During this time, Aryan cultural practices displaced the practices of other civilizations.

1. When did the Aryan culture most likely begin to impact the cities of Harappa and Mohenjo-Daro?

   A. Around 1000 years ago

   B. Around 2000 years ago

   C. Around 3000 years ago

   D. Around 4000 years ago

2. What geographical feature most likely influenced the direction taken by the third wave of Aryan invasions?

   A. the Ganges River

   B. the Himalaya mountain range

   C. the Bay of Bengal

   D. the Indus River

3. What area most likely had the largest settlements of people who farmed and traded?

   A. Deccan Plateau

   B. Ganges Plain

   C. coast of the Bay of Bengal

   D. Himalaya mountain range

4. What most likely prevented the Aryans from moving north from the Ganges Plain?

   A. the Himalaya

   B. the Caspian Sea

   C. the Bay of Bengal

   D. the steppes region

Writing Practice

Directions: Write a paragraph that compares any two of the ancient civilizations featured in this lesson.

LESSON 9.2   Nationhood and Statehood

LESSON OBJECTIVES

- Compare boundaries and borders
- Explain why borders often follow natural features
- Discuss how cooperation and conflict influence the division of Earth's surface

CORE SKILLS & PRACTICES

- Synthesize Ideas from Multiple Sources
- Analyze Author's Purpose

Key Terms

geometric boundaries

straight-line borders that follow imaginary lines on Earth

meridians

lines of longitude

parallels

lines of latitude that run parallel to each other

physical boundaries

natural features that separate two areas from each other

political boundaries

lines that separate countries and states

Vocabulary

coincide

occur together

Key Concept

Political and geographic boundaries divide the Earth into different regions and nations.

Have you ever studied a map of Europe? At first glance, the lines that differentiate European countries might seem arbitrary. But when you look closer, you can see some reasons for boundaries, such as mountains or rivers. However, some of the boundaries are not based on geographic features. How were Europe and other areas on Earth divided up into different nations?

Boundaries and Borders

Boundaries are lines that separate one area of Earth from another area. Borders are lines separating political regions, such as a state or country, from another. Borders create statehood and nationhood.

Physical Boundaries

When you look at a globe or map of Earth, you'll see many different geographic features. Mountain ranges, rivers, seas, deserts, and lakes all look different from each other on a map, and they represent distinct areas on Earth. Many of these features serve as physical boundaries on Earth. **Physical boundaries** are natural features that separate two areas from each other. A mountain range is a good example of a physical boundary. Mountains can be difficult to cross, so they can serve as a physical barrier to travel between one area and another.

Mountain ranges, rivers, oceans, deserts, and other geographic features that are physical boundaries can also be **political boundaries** or borders that separate countries and states. The western coastline of the Atlantic Ocean is both a physical boundary and a political boundary that separates the United States from countries in Europe and Africa. The Rio Grande River is also a physical and political boundary that separates the United States from Mexico. Physical boundaries that serve as political boundaries can occur between states within a country as well. The Mississippi River, for example, helps to define the borders, or political boundaries, between ten states within the United States.

Nationhood and Statehood

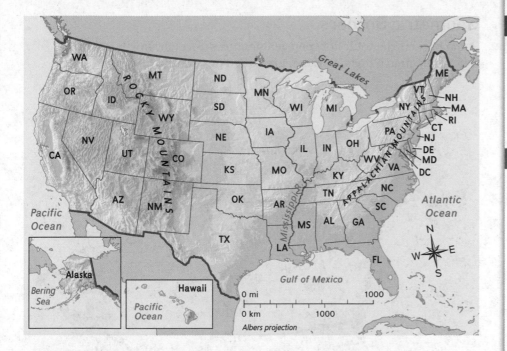

List some of the physical boundaries in the region where you live.

CORE PRACTICE

Synthesize Ideas from Multiple Sources

Examine the map of the United States on this page. Link the ideas from the text with the visual information on the map to describe the political boundaries, or borders, of six states that also coincide with physical features.

Physical Boundaries and Borders in the United States

This map shows all fifty of the United States. Many of the states have borders that **coincide**, or occur together, with physical boundaries. One of these states, Hawaii, has borders that coincide completely with coastline within the Pacific Ocean. A variety of north central and northeastern states have borders that coincide with the shoreline of the Great Lakes. Some states have borders that coincide with mountain ranges.

Relationships Retween Physical and Political Boundaries

Why would a physical boundary also become a political boundary? Physical features such as mountain ranges can be difficult to cross, so they might become a natural border between two groups of people. Mountains have difficult terrain and can also serve as a protective barrier that prevents aggression between groups on either side.

Wide rivers, large lakes, and seas or oceans can provide the same type of protection. Rivers can create a natural boundary that is also easy to see, which would help two groups of people to keep track of exactly where the border is located.

 Think about Social Studies

Directions: Use the map on this page to match the physical boundaries to political boundaries.

1. western border of Oregon   A. Appalachian Mountains
2. eastern border of Michigan   B. Bering Sea
3. eastern border of Tennessee   C. Mississippi River
4. western border of Illinois   D. Pacific Ocean
5. western border of Alaska   E. Gulf of Mexico
6. southern border of Louisiana   F. the Great Lakes

When you are taking a test, you may come across a long paragraph and a detailed image that are associated with a short question. The paragraph and image contain some information that will help you to answer the question, and some information that will not help. When you see something like this on a test, it helps to read the short question first, to determine exactly what it is asking. Then read the long paragraph and look at the image with the purpose of gathering only the details that will help you to answer the short question. Write these details down and ignore any other information in the paragraph or image. Use this test-taking skill to answer the questions in the Skill Practice section at the end of the lesson.

Geometric Borders

Some borders do not follow physical features. Straight-line borders that follow imaginary lines on Earth are called **geometric borders**.

Lines of Latitude and Longitude

Some borders follow imaginary lines of latitude and longitude. Latitude lines run east to west, but measure distance from north to south. Latitude lines are parallel to each other, so they are sometimes called **parallels**. The units of lines of latitude include degrees and locations in relation to the Equator. The Equator is at 0 degrees latitude. Any latitude in the Northern Hemisphere is greater than 0 degrees North. Any latitude in the Southern Hemisphere is greater than 0 degrees South.

Lines of longitude run north to south, but measure distance from east to west. Because they all converge at the poles, lines of longitude are not parallel to each other. Lines of longitude are also called **meridians**. They start at the Prime Meridian, which passes through Greenwich, England, and marks 0 degrees. There are 180 degrees of longitude west of the Prime Meridian, as well as 180 degrees of longitude east of the Prime Meridian.

Political Decisions and Geometric Borders

African countries have many geometric borders instead of borders based on physical boundaries. This is due to Africa's colonial history. During the late 19th century, many European nations controlled portions of Africa. Leaders of these nations were unfamiliar with many physical boundaries in their African colonies. During the Berlin Conference of 1884-1885, these leaders created straight-line border divisions for areas that had not been explored.

The Creation of Borders

Political boundaries are created by humans. Borders can be created when groups fight with each other. They can also be created when groups work together.

The First Borders

Beginning about 5000 B.C., the Nile River valley in northeast Africa provided the agricultural conditions for many permanent settlements to develop. The Middle East and the coastal regions of the Mediterranean Sea, as well as the Nile Delta, were the locations for the beginnings of many early civilizations, including Babylonian, Sumerian, Phoenician, Persian, and Greek. This close proximity allowed for trade and also created competition for land and resources. Competition for land and resources created the need for borders between civilizations.

Borders and Conflict

Borders can change during times of conflict. As armies claim territories, national borders can shift. At the end of conflict, new nations may form, or old nations may rise again. The Russian Revolution of 1917 gave rise to the formation of the Soviet Union in 1922. Nation states that had previously been independent were folded into this new nation. By the 1980s, the USSR, or Union of Soviet Socialist Republics, spanned two continents. Changes in the political climate finally led to a dissolution of the USSR in 1991 and the re-emergence of independent nations, some with new borders.

Borders and Cooperation

Borders can also change through cooperation, as countries work together to achieve the same end. European countries with colonies in Africa cooperated during the 1884 Berlin conference to create borders for African countries. This cooperation did not include leaders or citizens from Africa, however. The Jay Treaty of 1794 and the Treaty of 1818 established the border between Canada and the United States. Although the United States and Britain cooperated to produce this treaty, the border was established without input from Native American groups in the United States and Canada. West Virginia and Virginia used to be one state. When the Civil War started in 1861, West Virginia separated from Virginia because most West Virginians did not own enslaved people.

 Think about Social Studies

Directions: Answer the following question.

1. Which city has a higher latitude: Havana, Cuba or Oslo, Norway?

Analyze Author's Purpose

The topic sentence of a paragraph is often the first sentence in a paragraph. Authors use topic sentences to tell readers their purpose for writing the paragraph: whether they are arguing a point or just presenting information. Read the first sentence in the paragraph under the heading "Borders and Conflict." What is the author's purpose in the paragraph? Is the author presenting an argument or simply giving the reader information. Now read the rest of the paragraph. Do these sentences support the topic sentence? Are they presenting evidence and facts? In your own words, summarize what the author is saying about borders and conflict between nations.

Vocabulary Review

Directions: Complete the sentences using the following key terms and vocabulary words.

meridians   physical boundaries   political boundaries
coincide   geometric borders   parallels

1. Political boundaries along a river are also _____.

2. The imaginary lines that run from pole to pole on a map or a globe are known as _____.

3. _____ are also called borders.

4. Some borders can _____ with lines of latitude.

5. The imaginary lines on a map or globe that run from east to west and measure distance from the Equator to the Poles are called _____.

6. Borders that runs along parallels are _____.

Skill Review

Directions: Choose the best answer to each question.

1. Which of these is both a physical boundary and a political boundary?
   A. the border between the Yukon Territories and Alaska
   B. the 49th parallel
   C. the Rio Grande
   D. the border between New Mexico and Arizona

2. Why might a colonial power establish geometric borders in a territory that is far away from them?
   A. Without exploration, physical boundaries may be unknown.
   B. Geometric borders are easier to defend than other borders.
   C. Political boundaries may not be clear to the colonial power.
   D. Many territories do not have distinct physical boundaries.

3. Which of these is most true about political boundaries?
   A. Only acts of nature can change these boundaries.
   B. They are always distinct from geometric borders.
   C. They are established using imaginary lines on Earth.
   D. Conflicts can change these types of boundaries.

4. Lines of latitude measure distance on Earth
   A. in miles.
   B. in kilometers.
   C. in an east-to-west direction.
   D. in a north-to-south direction.

Skill Practice

Directions: Read the excerpt below. Then answer the questions that follow.

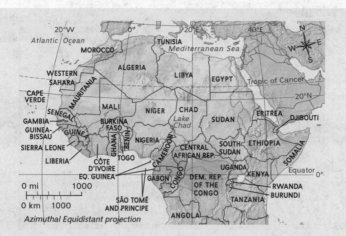

Chad-Libya International Boundary Study

In a United States State Department document, the Office of the Geographer outlines the history of the international boundary between Chad and Libya in Africa. According to the Geographer:

> The present-day territory of Libya came under Turkish suzerainty [control] as part of the Ottoman Empire in the latter half of the 16th century. In the decade following 1890, French military forces gradually extended their control to the lands south and east of Lake Chad. On June 14, 1898, France and the United Kingdom signed a convention delimiting their spheres of influence east of the Niger River. Supplementary to the 1898 convention, an Anglo-French declaration of March 21, 1899, indicated that the French zone was delimited to the northeast and east as follows:

> . . . by a line which shall start from the point of intersection of the Tropic of Cancer with the 16th degree of longitude east of Greenwich (13°40' east of Paris), shall run thence to the south-east until it meets the 24th degree of longitude east of Greenwich (21°40' east of Paris).

> Italy was interested in obtaining territory in North Africa at this time. In an exchange of notes with France on November 1, 1902, Italy concurred in the line specified by the 1899 Anglo-French declaration as the northern limit of French expansion.

1. Which of these best explains how the boundary between Chad and Libya was established?

A. Conflict between Africans in Chad and Libya led to the establishment of a border.

B. Colonial powers cooperated to establish territorial boundaries in North Africa.

C. Physical boundaries were used to create a political boundary between these countries.

D. Geometric borders were drawn after a period of conflict between colonial powers.

2. Which of these were used to establish the border between Libya and Chad?

A. the Niger River

B. Lake Chad

C. meridians

D. mountains

Writing Practice

Directions: In 100 years, would you expect all borders in North America to have remained the same? Write a paragraph explaining your answer.

LESSON 9.3 Human Activity and the Environment

LESSON OBJECTIVES

- Discuss the effects of population growth and economic development
- Explain carrying capacity and global warming
- Define sustainability and give examples of sustainable development

CORE SKILLS & PRACTICES

- Draw Evidence from Text
- Analyze Ideas

Key Terms

climate change
long term alteration of weather pattern

greenhouse effect
ability of Earth's atmosphere to trap heat from the sun

nonrenewable
not replaceable or replaceable only over millions of years

renewable
quickly replaceable

Vocabulary

deplete
to use up or reduce a resource

sustainability
living within limits when it comes to the use of Earth's resources

Key Concept

Economic development and a growing population are affecting the environment on Earth. Many people want to enact new policies to conserve Earth's natural resources.

Do you live in a large city, or have you ever visited one? Large cities are packed with people, living and working in tall buildings. The feeling of a city may be vibrant, but sometimes its environment seems stressed. Air quality may be lower in a city, due to excessive exhaust from cars and trucks. The amount of green space may be limited. Water quality in nearby lakes or rivers may be poor due to waste generated by the large population.

Population Growth and Economic Development

Earth's cities are becoming larger and larger as population growth and economic development progress. Earth's rural areas are changing too, as resources are mined, forests are cleared, and farmers and herders push onto new lands in an effort to produce more food. Around the world, human activity is putting strains on the environment.

A Developing World

Over the last 50 years, Earth's population has more than doubled, to reach over 7 billion people. All of these people need basic necessities, such as clean water, healthy food, and shelter from changing weather. As human population grows, more of Earth's resources are used up providing for these basic needs.

Earth's resources are also being used to support a higher standard of living around the world. Population growth and economic growth are occurring simultaneously in countries in South America, Asia, and Africa that had not had developing economies in the past. As economies improve, these growing populations build modern homes, purchase cars, and obtain a wider variety of goods. All of these products are made with natural resources and increase the need for energy resources.

Draw Evidence from Text

The text in this section suggests that human activity is straining Earth's resources. What evidence is given in the text to support this conclusion? Cite at least two pieces of evidence.

Natural Resources

Natural resources include wood, water, plants, animals, soil, minerals, natural gas, and fossil fuels such as coal and oil. Resources such as wood, plants, and animals are **renewable**, which means they can be replaced quickly after use. Resources such as soil, minerals, and fossil fuels are **nonrenewable**, which means they either cannot be replaced or it takes a very long time to replace them. Some nonrenewable resources, such as coal and oil, take millions of years to form.

Growing demand **depletes**, or reduces and possibly uses up, natural resources. As populations increase, they demand more agricultural products, forest products, food from oceans and other waterways, and clean water. Growing factories and cities demand energy and raw materials. All of this increasing demand places stress on Earth's forests, open lands, atmosphere, and waterways.

Carrying Capacity

In looking at how people live in their environment, economists and geographers use the term *carrying capacity*. Carrying capacity is the number of individuals in a population that an area can support with its resources. When we talk about the carrying capacity of all humankind, we are talking about the number of people that the entire planet can support with its resources. As populations grow and economic development increases, resources become depleted at a higher rate. As a result, the human population gets closer to Earth's carrying capacity.

⚑ Think about Social Studies

Directions: Fill in the blanks.

1. Coal is a _____ resource, because it cannot be easily replaced.
2. The growing demand for wood _____ forests around the world.
3. The _____ of the human population is the number of people that Earth's resources can support.
4. Corn is a _____ resource.
5. Basic human necessities include food, water, and _____.

WRITE TO LEARN

In a paragraph, describe what happens to the climate because of the greenhouse effect and state, based on what you have read, whether you think human actions are the cause of that phenomenon.

21ST CENTURY SKILL

Environmental Literacy

Use the Internet to learn more about climate change and its effects on human populations. Look for information from trusted sources, such as the National Oceanic and Atmospheric Administration (NOAA) and the Environmental Protection Agency (EPA). After you have researched this topic, prepare a small booklet that includes your findings.

Global Warming and Climate Change

Carbon dioxide is one of many gases that cause Earth's **greenhouse effect**, or its ability to prevent some heat from the sun that reaches Earth from traveling back into space. Without the greenhouse effect, Earth would be too cold for life. The greenhouse effect keeps Earth warm.

As human population grows, more people drive cars and use more energy. Much of this energy use involves the combustion of wood, coal, natural gas, or oil. Coal, natural, gas, and oil are all called fossil fuels because they were formed as a result of the decaying of the corpses of dead animals and plants millions of years ago that were then buried and transformed by pressure within the Earth. Burning wood or fossil fuels releases carbon dioxide, which is added to the atmosphere. This additional carbon dioxide traps even more heat than is normal and contributes to a rise in Earth's surface temperature, or global warming. Global warming leads to **climate change**, or a long-term alteration in weather patterns.

Climate change can cause changes in rainfall patterns, resulting in floods in some areas and drought in others. An alteration in rainfall can cause crops to fail, resulting in food shortages or even famine. Hurricanes and other storms can become stronger and more frequent with climate change. More powerful storms can destroy coastal areas and lead to loss of human life. Warmer temperatures can cause rising oceans and flooding of coastal areas, as polar ice caps melt. An overall increase in temperatures can allow diseases to become more widespread.

 Think about Social Studies

Directions: Choose the best answer to the following question.

1. Would population growth in one location affect the environment in other locations?

   A. No, because the affects are limited to one area.

   B. No, because population growth does not affect the environment.

   C. Yes, because population growth causes people to move to other areas.

   D. Yes, because population growth causes an increase in carbon dioxide in the atmosphere and global climate change.

Human Activity and the Environment

Sustainability

Population growth and economic development can cause a reduction in resources and an increase in the greenhouse effect and climate change. To combat these problems, individuals, communities, and businesses can implement sustainable development, which focuses on **sustainability**, or living within limits when it comes to the use of natural resources.

Sustainable development is economic development that uses natural resources to meet present needs without endangering supplies for the future. In other words, those who favor sustainable development believe people must make better use of resources. They believe that each generation must ensure that there will be an adequate supply of natural resources left for future generations.

Those who support sustainable development ask people to use fewer natural resources. For example, an advocate for sustainable development would not support more oil drilling. Instead, this person would try to influence automakers to produce—and consumers to buy—smaller, more fuel-efficient cars. Companies practicing sustainable development might obtain energy from renewable sources, such as solar and wind, instead of nonrenewable sources, such as coal or oil.

Individuals that practice sustainability often focus on reusing and recycling resources as well as reducing their use. Using washable containers instead of plastic bags to store food is one sustainable practice. So are turning out lights that are not being used and conserving water when showering, washing dishes, or brushing teeth. Recycling materials instead of throwing them in the trash saves materials that can be used again. Biking to work or walking instead of driving saves fossil fuels.

 Think about Social Studies

Directions: Choose the best answer to the following questions.

1. What is one way that practicing sustainability can help to prevent climate change?

   A. Using resources such as solar and wind instead of coal and oil can reduce the greenhouse effect.

   B. Drilling for more oil influences people to buy smaller, more fuel efficient cars.

   C. Using nonrenewable resources instead of renewable resources can slow climate change.

   D. People who believe in sustainable development believe we should not use any natural resources, which contribute to climate change.

CORE PRACTICE

Analyze Ideas

What are some of the ideas about sustainability practices in this section? Write down practices that you can try. Think of other ways that you can adopt a sustainable lifestyle and write down these ideas.

Vocabulary Review

Directions: Complete the sentences using the following key terms and vocabulary words.

climate change   depletes   greenhouse effect
nonrenewable   renewable   sustainability

1. An increase in severe weather events can result from _____.

2. One example of a _____ resource is oil.

3. A _____ resource can be replaced quickly.

4. A community that lives within the limits of its resources is practicing _____.

5. The _____ prevents some heat from leaving Earth's atmosphere.

6. When a population _____ a nonrenewable resource, less of that resource is available.

Skill Review

Directions: Choose the best answer to each question.

1. How has the human population changed in the past fifty years?
   A. It has decreased slightly.
   B. It has stayed about the same.
   C. It has more than doubled.
   D. It has more than tripled.

2. Which of these is a renewable resource?
   A. iron
   B. beef
   C. stone
   D. plastic

3. Someone who is practicing sustainability would most likely do which of the following?
   A. take a long shower every day
   B. leave a phone charger plugged in
   C. leave a porch light on at night
   D. only wash full loads of laundry

4. To address the issue of _____, a country could pass laws to lower the amount of fossil fuels that are burned.
   A. low water levels
   B. urban growth
   C. global warming
   D. population growth

Skill Practice

Directions: Study the graph and then answer the questions that follow.

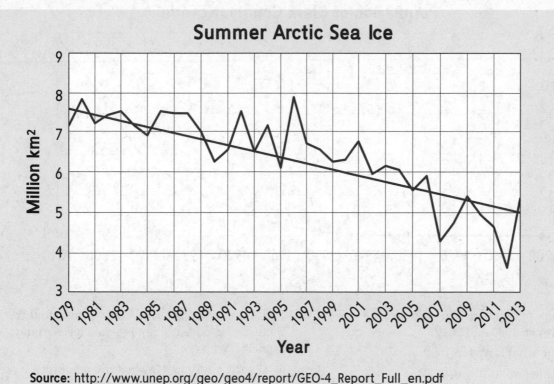

Summer Arctic Sea Ice

Source: http://www.unep.org/geo/geo4/report/GEO-4_Report_Full_en.pdf

1. The straight line on the chart shows the average amount of summer Arctic sea ice between 1979 and 2013. About how many years did it take for sea ice to decrease from an average of 7 million square kilometers to an average of 6 million square kilometers?

   A. about 5 years

   B. about 10 years

   C. about 15 years

   D. about 20 years

2. Based on what you have read in this lesson, which action could slow the decline in summer Arctic sea ice?

   A. a reduction in ship traffic in the Arctic

   B. an increase in the use of renewable energy

   C. an increase in human population

   D. an increase in the use of wood for fuel

3. What is the smallest amount of Arctic sea ice from 1979 to 2006?

   A. 8.0 million km²

   B. 7.2 million km²

   C. 6.8 million km²

   D. 5.5 million km²

Writing Practice

Directions: Write a paragraph that discusses how governments could encourage citizens and businesses to conserve resources and practice sustainability.

Directions: Use the graph to answer questions 1–3.

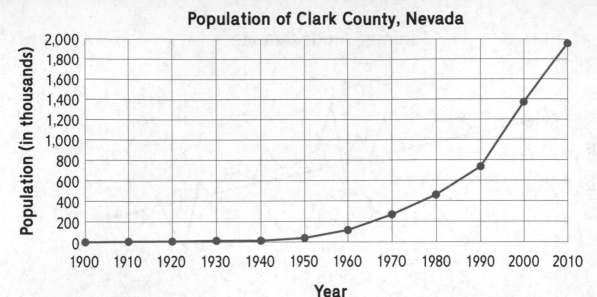

Population of Clark County, Nevada

1. How has the population of Clark County changed between 1960 and 2010?

   A. It is double what it was in 1960.

   B. It is five times what it was in 1960.

   C. It is ten times what it was in 1960.

   D. It is fifteen times what it was in 1960.

2. What kind of effect is the population growth shown in the chart likely to have on resources in the area?

   A. It is likely to strain supplies of drinking water.

   B. It is likely to decrease the use of renewable resources.

   C. It is likely to increase mining of resources in the area.

   D. It is likely to lead to more agriculture in the area.

3. The human population of Clark County and Las Vegas has apparently not reached its carrying capacity. Why not?

   A. Clark County has few natural resources.

   B. Human populations use less as they become larger.

   C. Resources are available to be imported to meet demand.

   D. The population plateaued in 1990.

Directions: Read the following questions. Then choose the correct answer.

4. How were the ancient Egyptian and ancient Chinese civilizations similar?

   A. Both practiced a system of divine right.

   B. Both had extended family systems.

   C. Both worked with metals to make tools.

   D. Both developed a type of caste system.

5. Which of these allowed the dissolution of the USSR and the establishment of independent nations with new borders?

   A. the end of World War II

   B. the Russian Revolution of 1917

   C. changes in the political climate

   D. wars between soviet countries

Directions: Use the following map to answer questions 6–8.

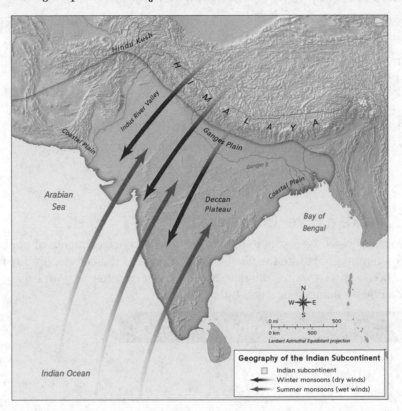

Geography of the Indian Subcontinent
- Indian subcontinent
- Winter monsoons (dry winds)
- Summer monsoons (wet winds)

6. What is the physical boundary separating the Indian subcontinent from countries to its east?

   A. Himalaya mountains

   B. Deccan plateau

   C. Arabian Sea

   D. Indus River

7. The ancient civilizations of Harappa and Mohenjo-Daro relied on which of the natural features shown on the map to grow crops such as wheat and barley?

   A. Indus river valley

   B. Deccan plateau

   C. Ganges plain

   D. Bay of Bengal

8. The pattern of monsoons shown in the diagram is most likely to be affected by which human activity in the next few decades?

   A. population growth

   B. mining of minerals

   C. sustainable agriculture

   D. fossil fuel combustion

Check Your Understanding

Lesson	Item Number
Development of Ancient Civilizations	4, 7
Nationhood and Statehood	5, 6
Human Activity and the Environmen	1, 2, 3, 8

WRITE ABOUT Human Activity and the Environment

A descriptive essay paints a word picture that relies on sensory terms. A good piece of description helps the reader imagine the scene or event.

Humans have been affecting the environment for centuries, for good and for ill. Whether it was the Mesopotamians irrigating their fields, the Romans building aqueducts, or the Chinese designing a wall to protect them from northern invasions, early peoples modified their surroundings. That tendency continues to this day. One example is the Green Belt Movement (GBM), begun in Kenya in 1977. After reading the essay on page 356, write your own descriptive essay on how human activity affects the environment.

BEFORE YOU WRITE Make a Five-Column Chart

Descriptive writing appeals to the senses. As a way to brainstorm the sensory elements of your descriptive essay, make a five-column chart like the one below. For each of the senses, jot down ideas and key words to use as you begin to write. You may not cover every sense in your essay, but your writing will be more vivid by using sensory details.

Seeing	Hearing	Smelling	Tasting	Touching

TIP   Use Spatial Order

Sometimes the descriptive essay is best arranged in spatial order. For example, when describing a landscape, the writer usually writes as if holding a camera, panning from one direction to another, not jumping around at random. Without definite spatial order, the reader becomes confused and the scene jumbled. The description moves from left to right or close up to far away. Space order might also be organized from head to toe, or top to bottom, or from outside to inside. All of these methods can be reversed.

WHILE YOU WRITE Consider Objective and Subjective Description

Descriptive writing can be objective and impartial, as news articles, laboratory findings, and police reports tend to be. The writer does not intrude on the scene or event being described.

Subjective writing allows for the writer's feelings, opinions, and ideas. If you describe a house as cozy, that is a subjective statement.

One style is not better or worse than another. The same event or landscape could be described using either method. However, it is better to decide which type you are going to use and to be consistent throughout your piece.

> **TIP   Watch Out for Overuse of Modifiers**
>
> A descriptive essay should not rely on strings of modifiers to paint a picture. Rather, the best adjective or adverb is chosen. For example, instead of saying the climate was hot and moist, you could say it was humid. Overloading a sentence with modifiers simply makes it cluttered and plants the suspicion that you have padded the writing to reach a particular word count. Instead of counting words, make each word count.

AFTER YOU WRITE Work with a Partner to Revise

Find a writing partner with whom to trade descriptive essays. Each of you should go through the other's draft, circling descriptive words. Try to make a rough sketch of the place being described, based only on what is written down, even if you know the scene. Make suggestions for how the essay could be more descriptive.

Chapter 10

Borders Between People and Nations

At the Olympic Games, athletes of many nations come together to compete in different sports. At a gathering like this, the diversity of cultures around the world becomes apparent. As the Olympic Games move from place to place, the diversity of the world's landforms and environment becomes apparent as well. Culture develops in response to a region's environment and resources. Human populations can also affect their environment as they grow and change.

Fabrizio Bensch - IOPP Pool/Getty Images Sport/Getty Images

In this chapter you will study these topics:

Lesson 10.1
Concepts of Region and Place

What is the structure of Earth, and how is it divided into regions? What natural resources and ecosystems are present in different regions? How do weather and climate affect regions?

Lesson 10.2
Natural and Cultural Diversity

What are the physical landforms that make different regions so diverse? What are the diverse cultures on Earth? How does physical geography affect the development of culture?

Lesson 10.3
Population Trends and Issues

What is the study of demography? How can the environment affect human population growth, migrations, and settlement patterns? What are current human population trends?

Goal Setting

What do you know about the environment where you live? What are the characteristics of people who live in your region?

Why do you think people settled in the region where you now live? What do you want to understand about the interactions between human populations and the environment by the time you finish this chapter?

LESSON OBJECTIVES

- Understand how natural resources are utilized
- Recognize the many ecosystems on Earth
- Consider weather and climate

CORE SKILLS & PRACTICES

- Use Graphs
- Use Maps

Key Terms

culture
the customs, beliefs, and practices of a society

ecosystem
a community of organisms and the natural resources with which it interacts

plain
a large area of flat land without trees

plateau
a large, flat area that is elevated above other areas of land

Vocabulary

carbon dioxide
a gas that is produced when organic materials burned

isthmus
a narrow strip of land surrounded by water on three sides

Key Concept

The planet Earth is made up of many interconnected physical systems, including land, water, plants, animals, and weather.

When you look at Earth from space, you see vast oceans, broken up by large landmasses. Across the land are mountains, hills, valleys, and open spaces. Some of these areas are lush and green, while others are brown. Still others are white from ice and snow. You might also be able to see cities and other areas influenced by human activities. Above the oceans and land are clouds in an atmosphere that shapes Earth's weather and climate.

Earth's Structure and Regions

A region is a portion of Earth that is distinctively different from other portions of Earth. One large region is Earth's crust, which is a thin layer of rock at Earth's surface. Landforms create smaller regions and include mountains, hills, valleys, and deserts. Flat places on Earth include plains and plateaus. A **plain** is a large area of flat land without trees. A **plateau** is a large, flat area of land that is higher than other areas that surround it. Landforms near water include peninsulas and isthmuses. An **isthmus** is a narrow strip of land with sea on either side, connecting two larger land areas. Oceans, rivers, seas, lakes, streams, and ponds are all examples of waterways on Earth's crust.

The crust is the layer where humans live, along with all other living organisms. Beneath the crust is Earth's thickest layer—the mantle. This layer is about 1,800 miles in depth and consists mostly of rock. The innermost layers of Earth are the outer and inner core. The outer core is liquid metal and the inner core is solid metal. Both core layers are extremely hot.

Seven continents rise above Earth's oceans. These are Earth's largest landmasses and they include North America, South America, Asia, Australia, Europe, Africa, and Antarctica. The continents are distributed, or spread out, across Earth's surface unevenly. Most of the landmass of these continents is in the Northern Hemisphere, with only 11% of Earth's landmass in the Southern Hemisphere.

NASA-JSC

Regions Defined by Resources

Earth has many natural resources on or in its crust. Soil, water, minerals, plants, and animals are all resources that can be used by humans. Air is another critical natural resource. Natural resources are distributed unevenly across Earth's surface. For example, certain areas have rich coal deposits, while others have rich iron deposits. In some areas, the soils are very fertile and suitable for agriculture. In other areas, soils are thin and dry. Some areas of Earth have huge forests while others have vast deserts. Areas with similar resources are often called regions.

Different countries can have different regions that are rich in a certain resource. The circle graph shows the countries with regions of rocks rich in uranium that mined the largest quantity of this element in 2010.

Worldwide Uranium Production, 2010

Source: http://www.iaea.org/OurWork/ST/NE/NEFW/Technical_Areas/NFC/images/uranium_cycle/Topten_RBwp.jpg

Cultural Regions

Just as regions can be defined by mineral or other physical resources, they can also be defined by the **culture**, or the customs, beliefs, and practices shared by the people who live there. Cultural regions often include people who speak the same language, wear a certain style of clothing, have a similar diet, share similar customs, and practice the same religion. Continents and countries can have several different cultural regions. For example, there are many cultural regions in the United States where people have different ways of living.

Think about Social Studies

Directions: Fill in the blanks.

1. _____ regions can be defined by the people who live there and their customs.

2. Continents are part of the outer layer of Earth, called the _____.

3. Regions can be defined by their natural _____, such as minerals.

4. Earth's inner core is composed of _____ metal.

5. Plains and plateaus are both _____ areas of land.

Pick a culture you are familiar with and explain how the land the people live on has affected aspects of their culture.

CORE PRACTICE

Use Graphs

Uranium is an element that naturally occurs in Earth's crust. It is commonly used to power nuclear power plants. The circle graph shows uranium output from mining for different countries in 2010. Which three countries appear to have the largest uranium deposits that are being mined? How does uranium output from mining in the United States compare to output in Canada? How does uranium output from mining in the Russian Federation compare to output in Australia?

Use Maps

The map on this page shows the different ecological regions, or biomes, on each of the continents. Use the map and its key to describe where different types of forests are found on Earth. Predict how climate would be different for each forest type.

Ecosystems

An **ecosystem** is a community of organisms in an area and the natural resources with which the community interacts. Ecosystems on land include grasslands, forests, deserts, tundra, and even cities and other areas where people live. Ecosystems in water are found in lakes, rivers, coasts, and oceans. Each type of ecosystem has a specific community of plants, animals, and other organisms associated with it. A forest ecosystem, for example, has trees, shrubs, smaller plants, and mosses. It can also have bird species, insects, wolves, deer, rodents, fungi, and bacteria. A grassland ecosystem has grasses and flowering plants and few trees or shrubs.

Ecosystems on land are influenced by climate. Desert ecosystems receive very little rain, while tropical rain forest ecosystems are very wet. Ecosystems in temperate areas, such as prairies and temperate forests, have seasonal temperature changes. Tundra and boreal forest ecosystems are very cold for most of the year, while ecosystems in tropical areas stay warm all year long.

Ecosystems in water are influenced by many physical factors. All are influenced by temperature and water depth. Ocean ecosystems are influenced by amount of light, salt concentrations, and wave action. Lake ecosystems are influenced by sunlight. Ecosystems in rivers and streams are influenced by moving water.

Earth can be divided into ecological regions that have similar organisms and physical characteristics. These regions contain many similar ecosystems. Ecological regions on land are called biomes. Biomes are defined by their plant and animal species as well as their climate. The map shows how biomes are distributed across the different continents.

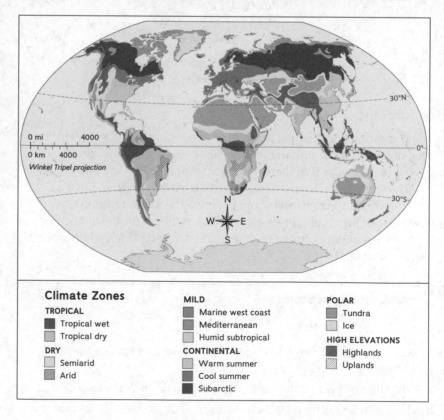

Climate Zones

TROPICAL	MILD	POLAR
Tropical wet	Marine west coast	Tundra
Tropical dry	Mediterranean	Ice
DRY	Humid subtropical	**HIGH ELEVATIONS**
Semiarid	**CONTINENTAL**	Highlands
Arid	Warm summer	Uplands
	Cool summer	
	Subarctic	

Weather and Climate

Weather changes daily, and includes conditions such as air temperature, wind speed and direction, cloud cover, and amount of precipitation. Climate is determined by the weather patterns that an area experiences over a long period of time. The weather in an area can be very hot one day and much cooler the next, but the climate of the area depends on the average conditions in that area.

Average temperature is an important factor in a region's climate. Average temperature can be affected by the distance the area is from the Equator. An area that is closer to the Equator tends to have a hot climate. An area that is closer to one of the poles tends to have a cold climate. Elevation can also affect average temperatures, with colder temperatures at higher elevations.

The amount of precipitation an area receives is another important factor in its climate. Precipitation includes rain, snow, sleet, and hail. Desert areas receive little precipitation. Many tropical areas receive large amounts of rainfall. Tundra areas receive large amounts of snowfall in winter.

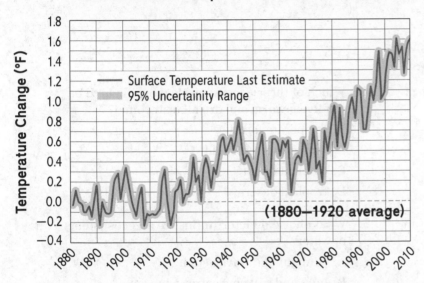

Global Surface Temperature Trends, 1880—2010

In recent decades, the burning of fossil fuels has caused an increase in carbon dioxide in the atmosphere. **Carbon dioxide** is a gas that is produced when people and animals breathe out or when fuels are burned and that is used by plants for energy. It prevents heat from the sun from escaping into space. An increase in carbon dioxide has raised Earth's average temperature. This increase in temperature is affecting climates worldwide.

🚩 Think about Social Studies

Directions: Choose the best answer to the following question.

1. How is weather different from climate?
    - **A.** Weather changes daily while climate is determined by weather conditions over an extended period of time.
    - **B.** Climate changes daily while weather is determined by weather conditions over an extended period of time.
    - **C.** Weather and climate both include cloud cover, but only climate includes amount of precipitation.
    - **D.** Weather impacts temperatures worldwide.

21ˢᵀ CENTURY SKILL

Apply Technology to a Task

Use the Internet to determine average monthly air temperatures and precipitation in your city or a city near your area. Graph these data to see any seasonal trends.

Vocabulary Review

Directions: Complete the sentences using the following key terms and vocabulary words.

culture	carbon dioxide	ecosystem
isthmus	plain	plateau

1. Although they are in the same continent, people in one area of Asia can have a different _____ than people in another area.

2. When fossil fuels burn they produce _____ that is used by plants for energy.

3. A flat area of treeless land that stretches across the landscape is called a(n) _____.

4. A large, flat area of land that is elevated above other areas of land that surround it is called a(n) _____.

5. A strip of land that connects two larger land areas is called a(n) _____.

6. Different plants and animals interact with the physical environment in a(n) _____.

Skill Review

Directions: Choose the best answer to each question.

1. A cultural region might be defined by which of the following?
   A. its weather and climate
   B. its mineral resources
   C. its plants and animals
   D. its language and customs

2. Which of these landforms is most similar to an isthmus?
   A. peninsula
   B. plateau
   C. mountain
   D. plain

3. Refer to the map on page 268. Which climate covers the most of the United States?
   A. highlands
   B. humid subtropical
   C. arid
   D. tundra

4. Which of these ecosystems is most likely to be relatively warm and dry all year round?
   A. temperate forest
   B. temperate grassland
   C. tropical forest
   D. tropical desert

5. What physical factors influence all ecosystems in water?
   A. sunlight and wave action
   B. light and salt concentrations
   C. temperature and water depth
   D. moving water and amount of light

6. Refer to the graph on page 269. Which statement best describes the activity during the period of time from 1950–1970?
   A. The temperature greatly increase.
   B. The temperature remained stable.
   C. The temperature greatly decreased.
   D. The temperature fluctuated greatly between highs and lows.

Skill Practice

Directions: Study the graph and then answer the questions that follow.

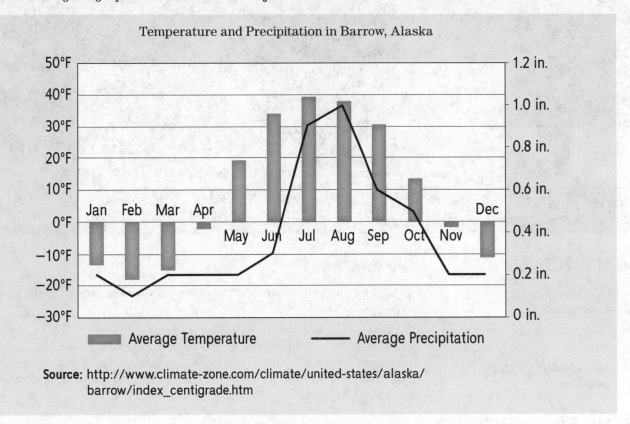

Temperature and Precipitation in Barrow, Alaska

■ Average Temperature   —— Average Precipitation

Source: http://www.climate-zone.com/climate/united-states/alaska/
barrow/index_centigrade.htm

1. For how many months is the average
temperature above 32°F in Barrow, Alaska?

A. 2 months

B. 3 months

C. 4 months

D. 5 months

2. Considering both average temperatures and
average precipitation in Barrow, how would you
describe ecosystems in this area?

A. They are cold and wet throughout the year.

B. They are dry in summer and wet in winter.

C. They are cold and dry throughout the year.

D. They are wet in summer and dry in winter.

3. The maximum average annual precipitation in
Barrow is

A. 1.2 inches.

B. 1.0 inches.

C. 0.5 inches.

D. 0.2 inches.

4. They average temperature in September in
Barrow, Alaska, is _____.

Writing Practice

Directions: Write a paragraph that describes how natural resources, culture, and ecosystems define the
region where you live.

LESSON 10.2 Natural and Cultural Diversity

LESSON OBJECTIVES

- Discuss the diversity of physical geography
- Discuss the diversity of human geography
- Explain how landforms affect human settlement

CORE SKILLS & PRACTICES

- Infer
- Evaluate Evidence

Key Terms

continent
major land mass

diversity
variety or differences

landform
natural feature of Earth's surface

multicultural
having many cultures

Vocabulary

density
concentration of people or things in a certain area

infer
conclude something from evidence and reasoning

Key Concept

Earth is rich in physical and cultural diversity, as seen by its landscapes and its people.

The world is a diverse place, with high mountains in some regions and flat plains in others. Anywhere you travel, you'll see landscapes that you may not have seen before. It's the same with people. Anywhere you go around the world, you'll find diverse people speaking different languages and solving daily problems in different ways than you might solve them.

Physical Diversity

What do you see when you travel around the region where you live? It's likely that you will see some physical **diversity**, or variety, in the landscape as you travel around. This diversity may be most obvious in the natural features of Earth's surface. A landscape of plains may be surrounded by hills or mountains that rise above the flatness. Rivers may flow through some landscapes, while others may be dotted with lakes. In the ocean, landforms rise from the sea to form islands and **continents**, which are the largest land masses on Earth.

Continents are one way that physical geographers categorize Earth's diverse land areas into regions. The seven continents include Africa, Antarctica, Asia, Australia, Europe, North America, and South America. Sometimes geographers also group the 30,000 islands in the Pacific Ocean into an eighth continent, Oceania. Geographers also divide the continuous global ocean into five main oceans: the Arctic, Atlantic, Indian, Pacific, and Southern.

Climate

Diverse climates also categorize Earth into regions. Climate in a region is determined by the region's latitude, or distance from the Equator. It is also determined by air currents, local landforms, and the region's location in relation to large bodies of water. For example, a coastal mountain range would have a climate characterized by large amounts of precipitation on the ocean-side of the mountains. However, the climate on the side away from the ocean, and in the shadow of the mountains, would be much drier, as precipitation is blocked from traveling over the mountains.

©Paul Springett/Alamy

Climates can vary from hot climates with large amounts of rain in tropical regions to cold climates with very little precipitation in arctic regions. Climates in temperate areas have seasonal changes in temperature and precipitation. There are at least 12 different climate types on Earth.

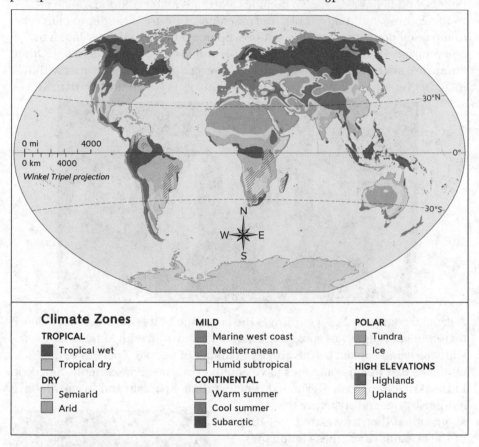

Climate Zones

TROPICAL
- Tropical wet
- Tropical dry

DRY
- Semiarid
- Arid

MILD
- Marine west coast
- Mediterranean
- Humid subtropical

CONTINENTAL
- Warm summer
- Cool summer
- Subarctic

POLAR
- Tundra
- Ice

HIGH ELEVATIONS
- Highlands
- Uplands

Climate affects the type of vegetation that can grow in an area, and the **density**, or concentration, of that vegetation. Tropical areas with a warm, wet climate year-round, such as tropical rain forests, have high diversity and density of vegetation. A high abundance of plants also leads to a high abundance and diversity of animals. Alternately, polar areas with a cold, dry climate year-round have low plant and animal diversity and density.

⚑ Think about Social Studies

Directions: Fill in the blanks.

1. _____ in an area can be influenced by the area's distance from the ocean.

2. A landscape with mountains, rivers, and valleys is high in physical _____.

3. According to the climate map, most of North Africa has a(n) _____ climate.

4. Oceania is considered by some geographers to be a _____, although it is composed of thousands of islands.

5. The climate map shows that the main climate type in areas around the equator is _____.

Infer

When you **infer** something, you come to a conclusion using evidence and reasoning. A desert is a region with a dry climate that can be very hot during the day. Use this information and other information in this section of the lesson to infer where deserts on Earth would be located.

Think of someone from a different culture than yours, and then write a paragraph about how they are similar and different from you.

Social and Cross-Cultural Skills

In the United States, there are often people who are originally from different cultures living in one community. If your community is multicultural, arrange to interview a person from a different culture about their experience in the United States. If your community is not multicultural, watch a film or read an article about another culture, and take notes about any cultural differences.

Cultural Diversity

Just as different physical features help to define places on Earth, so do different human cultures. Culture includes language, art, values, customs, beliefs, and behaviors. It also includes a group's material goods, such as food, clothing, buildings, tools, and machines. Culture is taught to children and passed down through generations. Some countries, such as Japan or Norway, have a distinctive culture that is similar all over the country. Other countries, such as the United States or Nigeria, have many cultures within different regions. A country with many cultures is called **multicultural**.

A crucial component of a culture is the language of its people. About 6,000 different languages are spoken throughout the world, with Mandarin Chinese being spoken by the greatest number of people. There is strong evidence that many languages have common origins. For example, Sanskrit, Latin, Armenian, Irish, German, French, Italian, Spanish, and Greek all have similar words and structure that suggest that they are related. Because of these similarities, these languages are all considered part of the Indo-European language family.

Language, food, art, customs, clothing, and other elements of culture all help to define a place. The various cultures along with the many natural features on Earth's surface combine to make Earth highly diverse.

Think about Social Studies

Directions: Choose the best answer to the following question.

1. Why do you think language is a crucial component of a culture?

   A. Because languages share common components.

   B. Language enables people to share ideas, sell goods and services, and establish laws.

   C. Languages help identify where a person is from.

   D. Because there are many languages spoken throughout the world.

Landforms and Human Settlement

Physical geography affects where people settle. Places with **landforms**, or natural features of the Earth's surface, that provide food, water, and shelter are most likely to be settled. People have chosen to live in river valleys for thousands of years, due to their abundant resources.

The valley between the Tigris and Euphrates Rivers in Iraq supported one of the earliest civilizations. These rivers provide drinking water, irrigation for crops, a good source of fish, and a way to travel. People have also settled along coastlines, especially where there are natural harbors or peninsulas. Coastal areas provide a reliable food source and may have a cooler climate than surrounding areas. Hilltops have also been common sites for settlement, as they provide a good view of surrounding areas, making them easy to defend from other groups of people.

Climate also has an impact on where people settle. Few people have settled near the poles, as these regions have extremely cold climates. Few have settled in the most extreme deserts on Earth, as they are dangerously hot and dry. Even lush rain forests can be difficult to settle, because their vegetation can be so thick. Population density is low in these areas. Population density is higher in areas with more moderate temperatures where people can grow or hunt food.

Wherever people live, their culture develops in response to the landforms, climate, and the environment around them. Local resources and community needs help to develop the culture's occupations. For example, seaside communities have many people with occupations related to the ocean, such as fishers and sailors.

Local materials and climate conditions dictate how structures are designed and built in the culture, and how clothes are made. For example, cultures in cold forest areas design and build sturdy structures out of wood and make warm clothing out of wool. Plants and animals that are available in the area are used to develop the culture's diet. For example, cultures in grasslands include grazing animals in their diets.

 Think about Social Studies

Directions: Study the map on page 273. Then choose the best answer to the following question.

1. What climate regions are located along the Equator?
   A. Warm Summer and Arid
   B. Tropical Wet and Tropical Dry
   C. Humid Subtropical and Highlands
   D. Tropical Wet and Arid

CORE PRACTICE

Evaluate Evidence

This section claims that landforms, climate, and the environment have an influence on how a culture develops. Write a paragraph that discusses whether or not the evidence used in the section supports these claims. Also discuss whether you have evidence from your culture that supports these claims.

Vocabulary Review

Directions: Complete the sentences using the following key terms and vocabulary words.

continents   density   diversity

infer   landforms   multicultural

1. South America and Asia are _____.

2. A festival that includes music from many different countries could be called _____.

3. Cities have a higher population _____ than rural areas.

4. You can use evidence to _____ the correct answer to a question.

5. Examples of _____ include mountains, valleys, and plains.

6. The continent of Africa has a _____ of cultures.

Skill Review

Directions: Choose the best answer to each question.

1. Where would you expect to find some of the hottest climates?

     A. near the Equator

     B. along a coastline

     C. near the poles

     D. away from water

2. Why would river valleys produce cultures that farmed food?

     A. The availability of water would attract wild animals.

     B. The river could be used to provide water to crops.

     C. Temperatures are usually more moderate near rivers.

     D. River valleys develop in areas with ample rainfall.

3. Where would you expect to find a culture that has hundreds of words in its language for the medicinal properties of many different trees and other plants?

     A. northern forest

     B. tropical forest

     C. arctic tundra

     D. tropical desert

4. Study the map on page 273. Which statement best describes the climates zones located along 30N and 30S.

     A. The climate zones are generally Tropical along 30N and Mild along 30S.

     B. The climate zones are generally Mild along 30N and Polar along 30S.

     C. The climate zones are similar and are generally Arid and Humid Subtropical with some Highlands.

     D. The climate zones along 30N are Continental while the climate zones along 30S are Tropical.

Skill Practice

Directions: Read the passage below. Then answer the questions that follow.

The BaMbuti are the real people of the forest. Whereas the other tribes are relatively recent arrivals, the BaMbuti have been in the forest for many thousands of years. It is their world, and in return for their affection and trust it supplies them with all their needs. They do not have to cut the forest down to build plantations, for they know how to hunt the game of the region and gather the wild fruits that grow in abundance there, though hidden to outsiders...They know the secret language that is denied all outsiders and without which life in the forest is an impossibility.

The BaMbuti roam the forest at will, in small isolated bands or hunting groups. They have no fear, because for them there is no danger. For them there is little hardship, so they have no need for belief in evil spirits. For them it is a good world.

—Excerpted from *The Forest People: A Study of the Pygmies of the Congo* by Colin M. Turnbull

1. Which of these is most likely part of BaMbuti culture?

A. growing of crops

B. building of cities

C. burning of wood

D. weaving of cloth

2. What evidence from the text supports the statement that the BaMbuti are the "real people of the forest"?

A. They do not believe in evil spirits.

B. They can find hidden food sources.

C. They hunt game in small groups.

D. They do not practice agriculture.

3. Which of the following had the most effect on BaMbuti culture?

A. food

B. climate

C. outside cultures

D. animals

4. Why do the BaMbuti not need to build plantations or farm?

A. There is plenty of food for sale outside of the forest.

B. The forest is so thick with trees that they are not able to clear an area large enough to farm.

C. The forest provides everything they need in game to hunt and fruit to gather.

D. They do not eat fruits or vegetables, only wild game that they hunt.

Writing Practice

Directions: Write a paragraph that describes how natural resources, culture, and ecosystems define the region where you live.

LESSON 10.3 Population Trends and Issues

LESSON OBJECTIVES

- Understand what is meant by the study of demography
- Recognize that population patterns tell a great deal about how humans interact with their environment
- Explain the trend toward urban growth in the United States

CORE SKILLS & PRACTICES

- Analyze Information
- Display Data

Key Terms

demography
the statistical study of the size, growth, movement, and distribution of people

migration
the movement of people from one place to another

mortality rate
death rate

population
all inhabitants of an area

Vocabulary

displaced
forced to move

outlying
surrounding

Key Concept

Humans interact with Earth by moving from place to place, building new communities, and expanding their populations.

The human population keeps growing and growing—and moving around the planet. How has population changed where you live in the last ten years or more? Have you seen people from different countries move into the area? Has the population of your area gotten bigger, gotten smaller, or stayed the same?

Demography

Governments gather demographic data to determine how many people live in and move in and out of an area. They also gather information about the people themselves.

Statistics

The statistical study of the size, growth, movement, and distribution of people is called **demography**. Governments gather demographic data periodically. Every ten years, the federal government of the United States conducts a census to count the **population**, or all the inhabitants, of every part of the country. It uses these statistics to see how the population is changing over time. State and local agencies collect demographic information on births, deaths, marriages, divorces, income, immigration, and occupations.

Governments use this demographic data to identify areas where population is growing or changing and more services may be needed. Businesses also often collect demographic data or use government data for marketing and planning for future growth. For example, a hospital might establish a new clinic in an area having high population growth.

Population Information

Demographic information includes birth certificates and death certificates. This information is collected to keep track of a population's fertility rate, or birth rate, and the **mortality rate**, or death rate. These measures can help demographers predict how populations will change in the future. For example, if mortality rates fall as fertility rates rise, the population may experience a large increase. However, if mortality rates rise as fertility rates fall, the population may experience a decline.

What factors affect mortality and fertility rate? Access to health care, clean water, nutritious food, and a safe living environment can all reduce mortality. Disease, famine, and war can increase mortality. Access to prenatal care can reduce mortality, as fewer infants and mothers die in childbirth. However, access to family planning can reduce fertility rates, as women use birth control to prevent pregnancies.

WORKPLACE SKILL

Use Data Effectively

The graph on this page shows population data from 1950 to the present, as well as estimated population data up to 2050. Does a line graph display this data in a useful and effective way? Does the data projection estimate make sense, in relation to the collected data? Why or why not?

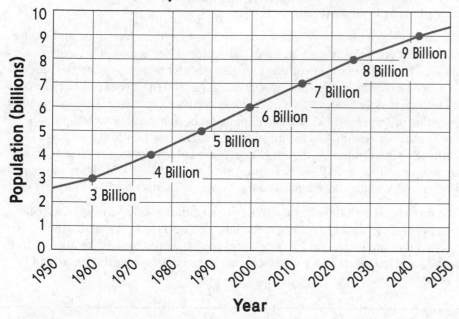

World Population Growth, 1950–2050

Source: U.S. Census Bureau, International Data Base, June 2011 Update.

Although population grows at different rates in different areas of the world, overall the human population has increased dramatically since 1900. The number of humans on Earth increased from 1.6 billion to over 7 billion from 1900 to 2013. The chart shows population growth between 1950 and 2013, with estimated population growth between 2013 and 2050.

Think about Social Studies

Directions: Fill in the blanks.

1. Disease can cause the _____ rate to increase in a population.

2. The world population _____ between 1960 and 2000.

3. The fertility rate in a population can _____ as a result of family planning.

4. When the mortality rate decreases and the fertility rate increases, a population will _____ quickly.

5. Every ten years, the U.S. government conducts a _____ to gather demographic information.

Migration and Population

People often move from one location to another when conditions where they live become too difficult. The problem may be a lack of resources or political or religious persecution. Sometimes large groups of people move, which can greatly affect the culture and economy of a region.

Migration is the movement of people from one place to another. The largest international migration occurred between the seventeenth century and World War II, when around 65 million people migrated from Europe to North and South America. Most of this migration involved individuals or families who were looking for economic opportunity or trying to gain religious and political freedom. Another large international migration took place in the late twentieth century, as almost 12 million people from Mexico and Asia moved to the United States.

Migration is not always voluntary but can be forced. In the 1600s and 1700s, millions of Africans were captured and taken to North and South America and sold into slavery. Migrations can also occur when people are **displaced**, or forced to move by conflict. World War II caused the displacement of over 30 million people by the Nazis government in Germany. The establishment of the state of Israel in 1948 and the expansion of that state onto other lands created about one million refugees. The apartheid policy of the white-controlled government in South Africa forced black South Africans to move to designated areas called homelands until the mid-1990s. Millions of people fled from Rwanda and Burundi to the Congo in the 1990s to escape civil war.

Migration can lead to cultural diffusion, as cultural traits are spread from one part of the world to another. Each region of the world has distinct groups that have brought their customs to the United States. As an immigrant nation, the United States has been enriched by the variety of these cultures.

 Think about Social Studies

Directions: Choose the best answer to the following question.

1. An example of a pull factor for migration is:

   A. a desire to escape war and persecution

   B. a higher paying job in a nearby city

   C. overcrowding

   D. reduction of rural farm workers

Urban Growth

During the last two centuries, there has been a trend toward the movement of people from rural, agricultural areas to urban areas, or cities. The period between 1800 and 1850 saw an increase in the population of cities in the United States, as workers moved from the countryside to live close to factories and mills.

During this time, living conditions in cities were terrible for workers. Families crowded into tiny apartments in five- and six-story apartment buildings called tenements. People got their water from hand-operated pumps. There was no organized fire or police protection. Cities also had no garbage collection or sewer systems, so waste piled up in streets and alleys and diseases spread quickly.

Laws have improved conditions in urban areas since the 1800s. However, since population density is still higher in cities than in the countryside, housing is often less spacious. Job opportunities are often better in cities and culture is more diverse, making cities attractive places to live. As a result, the trend toward urban population growth has continued in the United States, as shown by these maps. Metropolitan area refers to cities and surrounding suburbs, which are also considered urban areas.

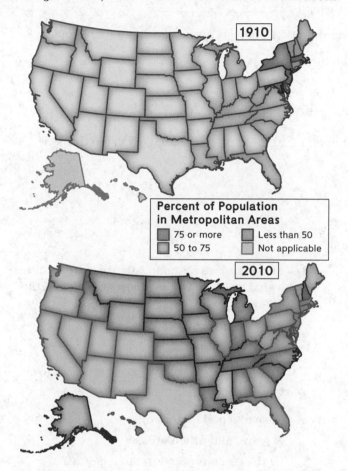

Percent of Population in Metropolitan Areas
- 75 or more
- 50 to 75
- Less than 50
- Not applicable

Although populations in cities are growing, there is also growth in **outlying** areas, or areas surrounding the city. Federal, state, and local investments in highways, bridges, roads, and public transportation have allowed more people to live in outlying areas and commute into the city for work. Modern transportation systems and trucking have also allowed businesses to move out of city centers into outlying areas, making the commute more likely to be between outlying communities. The movement of residential areas and businesses into outlying areas is called urban sprawl. Urban sprawl can alter the natural environment, as land is used for housing, shopping centers, businesses, roads, and other human activities.

Think about Social Studies

Directions: Choose the best answer to the following question.

1. Based on the map above, in 2010 the west coast of the United States had _____ population living in metropolitan areas.

A. 0%

B. less than 50%

C. 50–75%

D. 75% or more

In a paragraph, describe the living conditions of a tenement building in the Industrial Age.

CORE SKILL

Display Data

The data in the table show census figures from 1900 to 2010 for Cook County, Illinois, which includes the metropolitan area of Chicago. Calculate the mean, or average, of the data and find the median, or middle, value. Also find the range of the data. Range is the highest value and lowest value in a set of data. Then make a line graph of the data and describe what it shows about population growth in this urban area over the last century.

Census Date	Population
1900	1,838,735
1910	2,405,233
1920	3,053,017
1930	3,982,123
1940	4,063,342
1950	4,508,792
1960	5,129,725
1970	5,492,369
1980	5,253,655
1990	5,105,067
2000	5,376,741
2010	5,194,675

Vocabulary Review

Directions: Complete the sentences using the following key terms and vocabulary words.

demography   displaced   migration
mortality rate   outlying   population

1. All the people who live in Las Vegas make up the city's _____.

2. The study of _____ includes the statistical analysis of the distribution of people.

3. A(n) _____ population has been forced to move.

4. War can cause many deaths, leading to a high _____.

5. Suburbs are _____ areas because they are located just beyond a city.

6. Many people moved to the Americas during a mass _____ that occurred from the seventeenth century to World War II.

Skill Review

Directions: Choose the best answer to each question.

1. What caused the displacement of black South Africans during the twentieth century?

A. apartheid

B. civil war

C. famine

D. slavery

2. Which document would be most useful to someone studying demographic changes over time?

A. daily newspaper

B. current phone book

C. state highway map

D. county divorce records

3. What has contributed to the rise in population worldwide?

A. global migration

B. higher death rates

C. decreased birth rates

D. improvements in medicine.

4. As opposed to outlying suburban areas, cities would be likely to have more of which of the following?

A. residential homes

B. natural areas

C. ethnic restaurants

D. roads and highways

5. Push and pull factors refer to

A. rural and urban areas.

B. the reasons people go to a new area.

C. the increase and decrease in birthrate and death rate.

D. changing forms of government.

Skill Practice

Directions: Read the passage and then answer the questions that follow.

The region of Palestine was under British control between the two world wars. In the early twentieth century, groups of Jewish people had argued for the creation of an Israeli state. They wanted it located in the land known as Palestine, which they regarded as theirs since biblical times. Since being driven from the land by the Romans in A.D. 70, the Jewish people had been longing for a homeland. Sympathy for the Jewish people increased as people learned of the deaths of millions at the hands of Adolph Hitler during World War II. However, Palestine was primarily an Arab Muslim region, and old hatreds between the groups were strong. In 1948, the United Nations divided Palestine into Arab and Jewish portions despite the objections of Arab nations. As soon as Israel was declared a nation, these old enemies attacked. Israel defeated them in 1948 and again in 1967. In the 1967 fight, Israel took possession of parts of its neighbors land. Land disputes and hostilities have continued into the present.

1. Which group was displaced from Palestine in 1948?

   A. British

   B. Arab Muslims

   C. Jews

   D. Romans

2. What is one possible reason that the United Nations divided Palestine into Arab and Jewish portions?

   A. Palestine had a natural boundary at its center to serve as a border.

   B. A very large population of Jewish people already lived there.

   C. The history of the land included a Jewish population and culture.

   D. Jews and Palestinian Muslims had gotten along well together in the past.

3. Which two causes led to Palestine being divided into Arab and Jewish areas?

   A. the Jewish desire to have a homeland and British resistance to that idea

   B. worldwide sympathy for the Palestinians and old hatred between the two groups

   C. French control of Palestine and the deaths of millions of Jews during World War II

   D. worldwide sympathy for the Jews and the Jewish desire to rejoin their Palestinian neighbors in Palestine

4. The Jews were originally displaced from the Palestine area by

   A. Arab Muslims.

   B. the British.

   C. Romans.

   D. the United Nations.

Writing Practice

Directions: Write a paragraph that describes a migration that is currently occurring. Use the Internet to learn more about this migration before writing your paragraph. Describe the size of the movement, the groups and countries involved, and the reasons for it.

Directions: Choose the best answer to each question.

1. In which of these areas would human populations have been highest thousands of years ago?

   A. mountainous areas

   B. lush rain forests

   C. river valleys

   D. flat desert plains

2. River and lake ecosystems are influenced by many of the same physical factors. Which physical factor is more important in streams than in lakes?

   A. amount of sunlight

   B. flow of water

   C. amount of rainfall

   D. salt concentration

Directions: Read the passage below. Then answer the questions that follow.

One of the largest issues facing Mexico has been the status of its workers in the United States. As many as 3 million Mexicans work in the United States as undocumented immigrants. They do jobs that people born in the US don't want. These jobs offer low pay and, in some cases, are dangerous. Still, Mexican workers send about $9 billion each year back to family members in Mexico. The issue between the two countries is still not resolved. Many undocumented immigrants support amnesty, which is a general pardon for political offenses, including illegally entering a country.

3. According to the passage, which of these is a reason that millions of Mexicans immigrated to the United States?

   A. They support amnesty and are working toward that goal.

   B. They were happy to take on dangerous or low-paying jobs.

   C. They can find work and send money back to family members.

   D. They are criminals who want to be pardoned for their offenses.

4. What is the average amount that each undocumented Mexican worker exports back to Mexico annually, according to the passage?

   A. $300

   B. $900

   C. $3,000

   D. $9,000

Directions: Use this chart to answer question 5.

Phoenix, Arizona

Age	Population Estimate
Under 5 years	122,222
5-9 years	112,822
10-14 years	111,699
15-19 years	110,561
20-24 years	107,836
25-34 years	230,805
35-44 years	211,192
45-54 years	193,539
55-59 years	75,906
60-64 years	60,712
65-74 years	66,887
75-84 years	37,393
85 years and over	13,991

Source: http://factfinder2.census.gov/faces/tableservices/
jsf/pages/productview.xhtml?src=bkmk

5. Based on the information in the chart, which of these predictions is most likely to come true?

   A. The population of Phoenix will decrease in the next decade, due to mortality of its large aged population.

   B. The population of Phoenix will increase in the next decade, due to the number of people who are of reproductive age.

   C. The population of Phoenix will decrease in the next decade, due to a large number of young people who leave the city.

   D. The population of Phoenix will increase in the next decade, due to a large number of migrants entering the city.

Directions: Use the following map to answer questions 6–7.

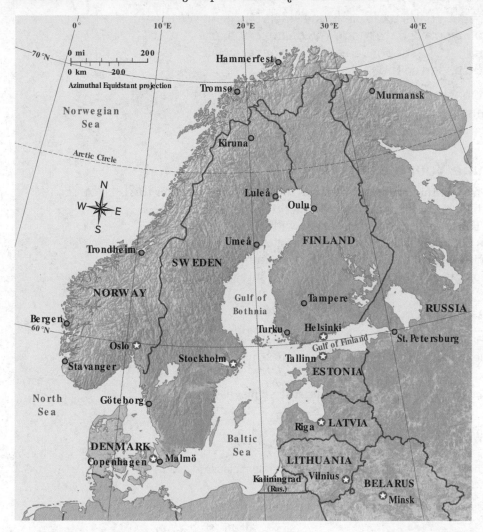

6. Which of these was most likely a staple in the Norwegian diet before the 20th century?

   A. ocean fish

   B. corn

   C. cattle

   D. fruit

7. Which of these Scandinavian cities is likely to have the coolest climate in summers?

   A. Copenhagen

   B. Helsinki

   C. Kiruna

   D. Oslo

Check Your Understanding

Lesson	Item Number
Concepts of Region and Place	2, 6
Natural and Cultural Diversity	1, 7
Population Trends and Issues	3, 4, 5

WRITE ABOUT Immigration and Population

When you write an argument essay, your goal is to present one side of an issue. Writing an argument essay is similar to arguing on a debate team. You do not try to present both sides but rather focus on facts that will support an opinion. Readers will determine whether your point is valid based on the facts you present.

Read the essay for chapter 10 in the back of your book. Then write an argument essay on an issue related to immigration and population.

BEFORE YOU WRITE Examine Your Biases

When writing an argument essay, it is important to keep an unbiased tone. This is not a letter to the editor, for example, or a social media post. It is a formal piece of writing that sets forth a position and supports it with reasons. Those reasons must be backed with facts or examples. Although you may have strong feelings about an issue, those emotions should not be part of your argument. You are striving for objectivity, regardless of your feelings. By knowing in advance what your weak spots are, you can be on guard against letting them creep into your writing.

TIP   Use Variety of Sentence Structures

When writing, it is easy to get stuck writing simple and/or compound sentences. Do not neglect the two longer sentence forms: complex and compound-complex. The longer structures will keep your writing from being monotonous.

A simple sentence has one independent clause and no dependent clauses. It may have phrases or compound subjects or verbs.

A compound sentence has two or more independent clauses, joined with a comma and conjunction or a semicolon.

A complex sentence is formed with an independent and at least one dependent clause joined together, often with a comma.

A compound-complex sentence has two or more independent clauses and at least one dependent clause.

WHILE YOU WRITE Use Parallel Structure

Any form of writing is made stronger when the ideas and sentences use parallel structure. The structure is balanced, pleasing to the eye and ear. In other words, if you begin using a prepositional phrase, as Roosevelt does in the second example below, stick with prepositional phrases. This is true for words, lists, phrases, and clauses. Look at these famous examples from political leaders to see how the force of their words increases with parallel structure.

"Ask not what your country can do for you—ask what you can do for your country."

John F. Kennedy

"With confidence in our armed forces, with the unbounding determination of our people, we will gain the inevitable triumph."

Franklin Delano Roosevelt

"We shall defend our island whatever the cost may be. We shall fight on the beaches, we shall fight on the landing grounds, we shall fight in the fields and in the streets, we shall fight in the hills. We shall never surrender."

Sir Winston Churchill

TIP Watch Out for Irregular Verb Forms

Most English verbs form their past tenses and past participles in regular ways. Generally, that means adding -d or -ed to the base: *work, worked, worked*. Occasionally, the final *y* becomes an *i* before adding -ed: *try, tried, tried*.

Some verbs have irregular forms and must simply be memorized. Sometimes, the verb changes its internal vowel: *begin, began, begun*. At other times, it changes radically: *bring, brought, brought*. At still other times, it does not change at all: *hurt, hurt, hurt*. Nonstandard or colloquial English may misuse these forms: *He brung a snack for lunch*. In formal writing and correct speaking, however, you will want to avoid such constructions.

AFTER YOU WRITE Attack Your Argument

In addition to checking your grammar, spelling, and punctuation, you will need to check your arguments for weak points. Imagine that you are on a debate team. Having argued one side of the issue, you are now to switch sides and argue the contrary. In that case, where would you then attack the rationales in your original arguments? Are they weak, in need of further sources to strengthen the argument? Is the thesis of the argument clear? Do the supporting facts, reasons, or examples hold up? Based on your attack, revise any weak spots.

This Posttest will help you evaluate whether you are ready to move up to the next level of test preparation. The Posttest consists of 60 multiple-choice questions that test your understanding of social studies concepts and your ability to read passages maps, tables, and charts.

When you have completed the Posttest, check your work with the answers and explanations on pages 301 and 302. Use the Check Your Understanding Chart on page 303 to determine the areas that you need to review.

Directions: Read the following question. Then select the correct answer.

1. Which of these terms best describes a person who opens their own art gallery?

    A. entrepreneur
    B. sales associate
    C. day laborer
    D. supplier

Directions: Read the following question. Then select the correct answer.

Credit Card Information

New balance	$3,000.00
Minimum payment due	$90.00
Payment due date	4/20/12

Late Payment Warning: If we do not receive your minimum payment by the date listed above, you may have to pay a $35 late fee and your APRs may be increased up to the Penalty APR of 28.99%.

Minimum Payment Warning: If you make only the minimum payment each period, you will pay more in interest and it will take you longer to pay off your balance. For example:

If you make no additional charges using this card and each month you pay...	You will pay off the balance shown on this statement in about...	And you will end up paying an estimated total of...
Only the minimum payment	11 years	$4,745
$103	3 years	$3,712 (Savings = $1,033)

2. Which piece of legislation forced credit card companies to add the information in the last three rows of this statement?

    A. Truth in Lending Act
    B. Equal Credit Opportunity Act
    C. Fair Credit Reporting Act
    D. Credit CARD Act

3. What percentage of the new balance is the minimum payment for this credit card?

    A. 3 percent
    B. 6 percent
    C. 9 percent
    D. 12 percent

Directions: Read the following questions. Then select the correct answer.

4. Sir Walter Raleigh established the
   - A. Continental Congress.
   - B. Plymouth colony.
   - C. Roanoke colony.
   - D. Mayflower Compact.

5. An "unconditional war on poverty" was declared by which president?
   - A. John F. Kennedy
   - B. Theodore Roosevelt
   - C. Woodrow Wilson
   - D. Lyndon B. Johnson

6. The ____ created an alliance of states.
   - A. Articles of Confederation
   - B. Virginia Plan
   - C. Anti-Federalists
   - D. Great Compromise

7. Many immigrants lived in crowded apartment complexes called
   - A. relocation centers.
   - B. skyscrapers.
   - C. tenements.
   - D. settlement houses.

Directions: Read the passage below from the Constitution. Then answer the questions that follow.

We the People of the United States, in Order to form a more perfect Union, establish Justice, insure domestic Tranquility, provide for the common defence, promote the general Welfare, and secure the Blessings of Liberty to ourselves and our Posterity, do ordain and establish the Constitution for the United States of America.

8. During which time period was this passage written?
   - A. 1600s
   - B. 1700s
   - C. 1800s
   - D. 1900s

9. What does the phrase "insure domestic Tranquility" mean?
   - A. American citizens will not have to pay taxes.
   - B. It means that traveling within the United States should be safe and free from criminals.
   - C. Americans will fight Britain until the colonies gain independence.
   - D. The Founders want the citizens of the new country to live at peace.

Directions: Use the map below to answer questions 10 and 11.

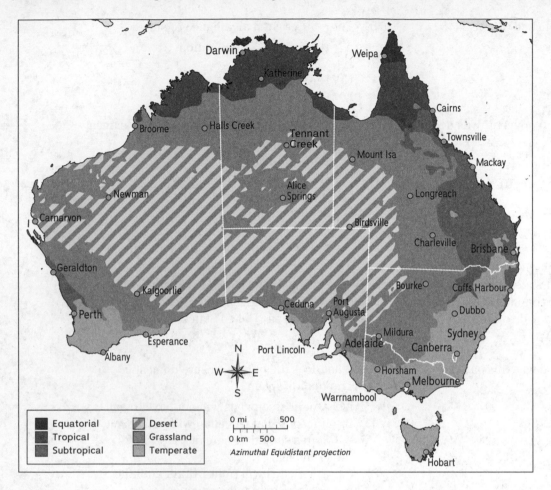

10. Which of these cities is likely to have the driest climate?

   A. Birdsville

   B. Bourke

   C. Brisbane

   D. Broome

11. Where might you expect to find trees that lose their leaves seasonally?

   A. Townsville

   B. Marree

   C. Mount Isa

   D. Adelaide

Directions: Read the following questions. Then select the correct answer.

12. After the Revolutionary War, why did many Americans fear a strong central government?

   A. They feared that taxes would be too high.

   B. They feared that the army would grow too powerful.

   C. They feared that a strong government would abuse its power.

   D. They didn't fear a strong central government.

13. Why was the Bill of Rights an important addition to the Constitution?

   A. It laid out in detail the rights that most Americans expected the government to respect.

   B. It made the Constitution long enough so the British king would pay attention.

   C. It separated the government into three branches so none of them would be too powerful.

   D. It set up the plan for the Senate and House of Representatives.

Directions: Read the passage below. Then answer the questions that follow.

One Japanese American named Fred Korematsu refused to leave California. He took his case all the way to the Supreme Court. In 1944, the Court ruled that the government had acted within its rights. According to the president's order, the War Department had the power to remove people from any area termed a military zone. That same day, in a different decision called *Ex parte Endo,* the Court ruled that loyal citizens could not be held against their will.

14. The court case described in the passage refers to
- A. the US military draft.
- B. US immigration law.
- C. US internment camps.
- D. US citizenship law.

15. What was the position of the Supreme Court regarding the resettlement of Japanese Americans like Fred Korematsu?
- A. The Court stated that California was not a military zone.
- B. The Court initially ruled that it was legal but later ruled differently.
- C. The Court attempted to block the resettlements from happening.
- D. The Court moved to take away citizenship from Japanese Americans.

16. Which Shawnee leader tried to unite Ohio Valley Native Americans against white settlers?
- A. Winnemac
- B. Baptiste
- C. Sacagawea
- D. Tecumseh

17. In 1836, American settlers in _____ declared their independence.
- A. Oregon
- B. Texas
- C. California
- D. Nevada

Directions: Read the following questions. Then select the correct answer.

18. Freedoms that are guaranteed by the United States Constitution are called
- A. due process.
- B. privileges.
- C. civil liberties.
- D. equal protections.

19. The poll tax was one method that was used to block African Americans' right to
- A. own property.
- B. vote.
- C. attend school.
- D. use public facilities.

Use the map below to answer questions 20 and 21.

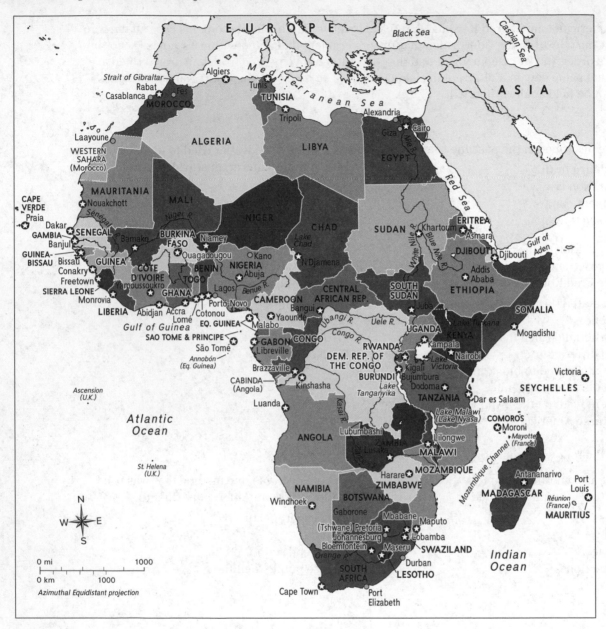

20. What physical boundary separates Africa from Europe?

A. Mediterranean Sea

B. Indian Ocean

C. Atlantic Ocean

D. Gulf of Guinea

21. Which of these two countries appear to have a border between them that is also a geometric boundary?

A. Algeria and Libya

B. Algeria and Mali

C. Eritrea and Sudan

D. Kenya and Ethiopia

Directions: Read the passage below. Then answer the questions that follow.

(1) In regard to these essential rectifications of wrong and assertions of right we feel ourselves to be intimate partners of all the governments and peoples associated together against the Imperialists. (2) We cannot be separated in interest or divided in purpose. (3) We stand together until the end. (4) For such arrangements and covenants we are willing to fight and to continue to fight until they are achieved; but only because we wish the right to prevail and desire a just and stable peace such as can be secured only by removing the chief provocations to war, which this program does remove. (5) We have no jealousy of German greatness, and there is nothing in this program that impairs it. (6) We grudge her no achievement or distinction of learning or of pacific enterprise such as have made her record very bright and very enviable. (7) We do not wish to injure her or to block in any way her legitimate influence or power. (8) We do not wish to fight her either with arms or with hostile arrangements of trade if she is willing to associate herself with us and the other peace-loving nations of the world in covenants of justice and law and fair dealing. (9) We wish her only to accept a place of equality among the peoples of the world, —the new world in which we now live, —instead of a place of mastery.

—*Woodrow Wilson, in an address to Congress, January 8, 1918*

22. What does Wilson say about Germany in this passage?

A. Germany's influence and power must be blocked.
B. Germany cannot be allowed a position of prominence in the world.
C. Germany should be allowed to remain an influential nation.
D. Germany should be occupied by democratic nations.

23. Why are the allied nations fighting against Germany?

A. to achieve peace by removing the causes that provoked war
B. to protect the right of nations to maintain empires
C. to reduce Germany's influence in the world
D. to establish permanent American influence in Europe

Directions: Read the following questions. Then select the correct answer.

24 Which of these describes a tax on bananas from Honduras that are imported to the United States?

A. budget
B. expenditure
C. subsidy
D. tariff

25. Most nations have a _____ political system.

A. one-party
B. two-party
C. multiparty
D. independent

26. What is the total number of electoral votes in the United States?

A. 100
B. 270
C. 438
D. 538

Directions: Use the map below to answer questions 27 and 28.

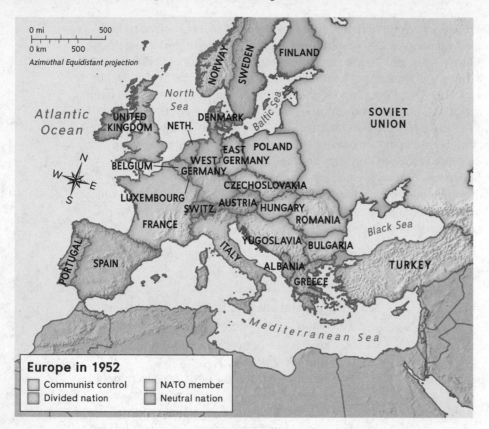

0 mi ———— 500
0 km ———— 500

Azimuthal Equidistant projection

Europe in 1952
- ☐ Communist control
- ☐ Divided nation
- ☐ NATO member
- ☐ Neutral nation

27. According to the map, which of these countries was a neutral nation in 1952, after the end of World War II?

   A. Austria
   B. Norway
   C. Spain
   D. Turkey

28. Which two countries were allied with one another in 1952, after the end of World War II?

   A. Austria and Hungary
   B. Belgium and Turkey
   C. Norway and Sweden
   D. Switzerland and France

Directions: Read the following questions. Then select the correct answer.

29. The trade routes that brought enslaved Africans to the colonies became known as the

   A. Underground Railroad.
   B. northwest passage.
   C. triangular trade.
   D. Trail of Tears.

30. President Lincoln issued the Emancipation Proclamation after the battle at

   A. Antietam.
   B. Gettysburg.
   C. Vicksburg.
   D. Shiloh.

Directions: Read the passage below. Then answer the questions that follow.

A great people has been moved to defend a great nation. Terrorist attacks can shake the foundations of our biggest buildings, but they cannot touch the foundation of America. These acts shatter steel, but they cannot dent the steel of American resolve. America was targeted for attack because we're the brightest beacon for freedom and opportunity in the world. And no one will keep that light from shining. Today, our nation saw evil—the very worst of human nature—and we responded with the best of America. With the daring of our rescue workers, with the caring for strangers and neighbors who came to give blood and help in any way they could.

—President George W. Bush, Address to the Nation

31. The excerpt comes from a speech made immediately after which of these events?

   A. United States invasion of Iraq
   B. initiation of the Gulf War
   C. bombing of USS *Cole* in Yemen
   D. attcks on the World Trade Center and Pentagon

32. According to Bush, the attacks mentioned have

   A. created fear in the United States.
   B. brought out the best in Americans.
   C. caused the spread of evil deeds.
   D. increased freedom and opportunity.

Directions: Read the following questions. Then select the correct answer.

33. A country at which of these latitudes is likely to have tropical rain forests?

   A. 2°N
   B. 22°S
   C. 47°N
   D. 55°S

34. A friend asks for advice about learning a new language. The friend would like to learn the language that would allow her to communicate with the most number of people in Asia. Which of these languages would you suggest?

   A. French
   B. Japanese
   C. Korean
   D. Mandarin Chinese

35. A capital investment at a company that manufactures yoga pants could include which of the following?

   A. sewing machines
   B. yoga mats
   C. employee benefits
   D. shake weights

Directions: Use the graph below to answer questions 36 and 37.

Price of a Market Basket of Goods 1913 to 2013

Directions: Read the following questions. Then select the correct answer.

36. What happened to the cost of a market basket of goods between 1973 and 1983?

   A. It stayed about the same.
   B. It fell by about half.
   C. It almost tripled.
   D. It more than doubled.

37. Inflation was lowest between which of these years?

   A. 1943 and 1953
   B. 1953 and 1963
   C. 1963 and 1973
   D. 1983 and 1993

Directions: Read the following questions. Then select the correct answer.

38. A government in which a small group of people rules with absolute power is a(n)

   A. democracy.
   B. dictatorship.
   C. oligarchy.
   D. constitutional monarchy.

39. _____ are financial institutions that serve people with a common concern, workplace, or community.

   A. Savings banks
   B. Community agencies
   C. Commercial banks
   D. Credit unions

40. Chinese and Japanese immigrants

   A. worked in construction in the western states.
   B. helped build industry in cities such as Chicago and Detroit.
   C. worked on farms on the east coast.
   D. settled mainly in the South.

41. People who believed in reform and the improvement of society were called

   A. isolationists.
   B. progressives.
   C. nativists.
   D. carpetbaggers.

Directions: Read the passage below. Then answer the questions that follow.

(1) Our greatest primary task is to put people to work. (2) This is no unsolvable problem if we face it wisely and courageously. (3) It can be accomplished in part by direct recruiting by the Government itself, treating the task as we would treat the emergency of a war, but at the same time, through this employment, accomplishing greatly needed projects to stimulate and reorganize the use of our natural resources . . . (4) The task can be helped by definite efforts to raise the values of agricultural products and with this the power to purchase the output of our cities. (5) It can be helped by preventing realistically the tragedy of the growing loss through foreclosure of our small homes and our farms. (6) It can be helped by insistence that the Federal, State, and local governments act forthwith on the demand that their cost be drastically reduced. (7) It can be helped by the unifying of relief activities which today are often scattered, uneconomical, and unequal. (8) It can be helped by national planning for and supervision of all forms of transportation and of communications and other utilities which have a definitely public character. (9) There are many ways in which it can be helped, but it can never be helped merely by talking about it. (10) We must act and act quickly.

—President Franklin D. Roosevelt, First Inaugural Address, 1933

42. This speech laid the groundwork for which of these?

A. Great Depression
B. Great Society
C. Roaring Twenties
D. New Deal

43. Which statement in the speech refers to ideas that were eventually used to start the Works Progress Administration?

A. statement 3
B. statement 4
C. statement 5
D. statement 6

Directions: Use the graphic below to answer questions 44 and 45.

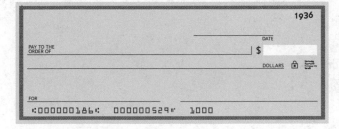

44. What is the account number on this check?

A. 1000
B. 1936
C. 000000529
D. 000000186

45. On which line would you sign this check?

A. bottom right line
B. top right line
C. bottom left line
D. line next to "Pay to the Order of"

Directions: Read the following questions. Then select the correct answer.

46. The power to establish courts to administer justice belongs to which branch(es) of government?

- A. federal
- B. state
- C. federal and state
- D. federal, state, and judicial

47. The presidential power to refuse approval of a law is called a(n)

- A. exclusion.
- B. override.
- C. regulation.
- D. veto.

Directions: Use the map below to answer questions 48 and 49.

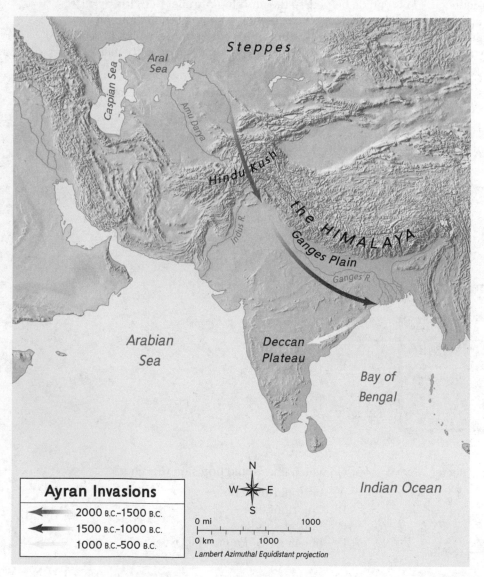

48. During which of these years were the Aryans moving from the steppes to the plateau?

- A. 2500 B.C.
- B. 1800 B.C.
- C. 1250 B.C.
- D. 800 B.C.

49. During the second period of Aryan invasion, which physical feature influenced movement?

- A. The Himalayan Mountains blocked the invasion.
- B. The Bay of Bengal forced the invasion to move to the southwest.
- C. The Arabian Sea forced the invasion to move to the southeast.
- D. The Ganges River influenced settlement.

Directions: Read the passage below. Then answer the questions that follow.

The Panama Canal

After the Spanish-American War, the United States had interests in the Caribbean and the Pacific. To get from one to the other, ships had to sail around the southern tip of South America. A canal across the isthmus of Panama would be the ideal solution.

In 1903, Panama was part of Colombia. When Panamanians rebelled, Roosevelt supported the rebels against Columbian troops. The new nation was grateful. It quickly agreed to lease to the United States a strip of land from the Pacific to the Caribbean. This 10-mile-wide strip became the Panama Canal Zone. In exchange for a 99-year lease, the United States agreed to pay $250,000 per year.

50. Before the Panama Canal was built, which government ruled Panama?

A. Colombia
B. France
C. Philippines
D. United States

51. The United States was interested in controlling the Panama Canal because it wanted to

A. trade with Panama.
B. start a war in Central America.
C. create efficient route for moving ships.
D. annex a Central American country.

Directions: Read the following questions. Then select the correct answer.

52. Military intervention in a conflict is an example of _____ policy.

A. foreign
B. domestic
C. economic
D. judicial

53. A trade group is an example of which type of interest group?

A. public
B. economic
C. civil rights
D. special

54. A(n) _____ is the amount of revenue that a country must borrow in order to meet its financial obligations.

A. bond
B. deficit
C. tax
D. surplus

55. The concept of "separate but equal" public facilities was used to justify

A. imperialism.
B. segregation.
C. nullification.
D. emancipation.

Directions: Read the following questions. Then select the correct answer.

56. Concentrating on the production of a few goods and services is called

   A. specialization.
   B. diversification.
   C. absolute advantage.
   D. efficiency.

57. What document was written by George Mason to guarantee individual rights and government by the people?

   A. Virginia Declaration of Rights
   B. Declaration of Independence
   C. Magna Carta
   D. Articles of Confederation

58. The increasing movement of people and businesses into outlying areas around cities is often called

   A. forced migration.
   B. urban sprawl.
   C. emigration.
   D. suburban expansion.

59. The period of prosperity and growth that preceded the Great Depression is known as the

   A. New Deal
   B. Great Society
   C. Roaring Twenties
   D. Progressive Era

60. _____ run from pole to pole on Earth.

   A. Lines of longitude
   B. Lines of latitude
   C. Geometric boundaries
   D. Physical boundaries

1. **A** An entrepreneur is someone who produces new products or provides new services.

2. **D** The Credit CARD Act established the rule that credit card companies had to provide detailed information about how much interest the consumer would pay if he or she only paid the minimum balance each month.

3. **A** The minimum payment of $90 is 3 percent of the new balance of $3,000.

4. **C** Raleigh led the colonization of Roanoke Island in the late 1500s.

5. **D** President Lyndon B. Johnson included a "war on poverty" in his Great Society programs meant to help needy Americans.

6. **D** The Articles of Confederation established the 13 colonies of the United States.

7. **C** Tenements were crowded apartment complexes that housed immigrants and other low-income workers and families.

8. **A** The United States was established with founding documents such as the Constitution in the late 1700s.

9. **A** Domestic tranquility means peace at home.

10. **A** Birdsville is in the desert, and the desert climate is usually the driest.

11. **D** A city in a temperate climate, such as Adelaide, is likely to have trees that lose their leaves before winter.

12. **C** Those living in the colonies had witnessed abuses of power and wanted to create a government that would prevent those abuses.

13. **A** The Bill of Rights provides statements that establish rights in detail.

14. **C** The passage refers to a case brought by a Japanese American who was being moved from his home and most likely to an internment camp.

15. **B** The court ruled one way in the Korematsu case and then ruled differently in the *Ex parte Endo* case.

16. **D** Tecumseh recruited tribes to fight with him against settlers during the War of 1812.

17. **B** Texas Independence Day was March 2, 1836.

18. **C** Civil liberties are freedoms that apply to all citizens.

19. **B** Voting occurs at polls.

20. **A** Europe is north of Africa and separated from that continent by the Mediterranean Sea.

21. **B** The straight-line boundary between Algeria and Mali appears to follow an imaginary line, not a physical boundary.

22. **C** Wilson states that Germany should "accept a place of equality among peoples of the world."

23. **A** The allied nations fought against Germany to remove the "chief provocations to war."

24. **D** Because bananas are foreign goods imported into the United States, the tax on these goods would be a tariff.

25. **C** During each election in most nations, candidates from a variety of parties run against each other.

26. **D** Electoral votes are assigned to the states based on population.

27. **C** The key shows that Spain was a neutral country during this period.

28. **B** Belgium and Turkey were part of the NATO alliance during this time period.

29. **C** Slave trade routes between Africa, North America, and Europe formed a triangle.

30. **A** The battle at Antietam provided a Union victory to allow Lincoln to issue the Emancipation Proclamation.

31. **D** Bush was President during this time period, and he refers to a terrorist attack on big buildings.

32. **B** Bush states that Americans responded with the "best of America."

33. **A** Tropical rain forests are found near the Equator, which is at 0° latitude.

34. **D** Mandarin Chinese is the language spoken by the greatest number of people in the world.

35. **A** A capital investment includes equipment such as machines that are used to produce other goods.

36. **D** The cost increased from $42 to $98, which is an increase of more than double but not triple the amount in 1973.

37. B The price of a basket of goods went up very little between 1953 and 1963.

38. C In an oligarchy, a small group has the ability to establish laws.

39. D Credit unions are financial institutions that serve members connected by a common workplace or other entity.

40. A Immigrants from Asia entered the western United States and worked on railroads and in other industries.

41. B Progressives have an agenda of reform and societal improvement through government.

42. D Many of the ideas in Roosevelt's inaugural speech were enacted in New Deal programs.

43. A The WPA was a government program that put people directly to work on projects.

44. C The second set of numbers along the bottom of the check indicates the account number.

45. A Your signature goes on the bottom right line of a check.

46. C The state and federal governments are able to try suspects in courts of law.

47. D The veto provides a check on the legislative branch by the executive branch of the federal government.

48. B The Aryan invasion from the steppes to the Deccan Plateau occurred between 2000–1500 b.c.

49. D The second Aryan invasion occurred along the Ganges River.

50. A Panama was part of Colombia before the canal was built.

51. C The United States needed a canal through Central America for moving warships and merchant ships.

52. A Military intervention in a conflict occurs outside of the United States, so it is part of foreign policy.

53. B Trade groups are groups that represent particular industries, such as the petroleum industry.

54. B A deficit is the amount of money that a country would need to borrow to meet all of its financial obligations.

55. B Supporters of segregation claimed that "separate but equal" schools and other facilities were a reasonable means of upholding the separation of people of different races.

56. A Specialization is the focus on producing only a few goods and services.

57. A George Mason was the author of the Virginia Declaration of Rights, which influenced the Declaration of Independence.

58. B The growing and often uncontrolled movement of residential areas and businesses into outlying areas is known as urban sprawl.

59. C The term "Roaring Twenties" refers to the decade of the 1920s and the prosperity in the United States prior to the stock market crash of 1929.

60. A Lines of longitude run from the North Pole to the South Pole, starting at the Prime Meridian.

Check Your Understanding

On the following chart, circle the item number of any question you answered incorrectly. In the Reference column, you will see the pages that address the content covered in the question.

Item #	Reference	Item #	Reference	Item #	Reference
1	pp. 146–151	21	pp. 248–253	41	pp. 86–91
2	pp. 228–233	22	pp. 98–105	42	pp. 122–127
3	pp. 228–233	23	pp. 98–105	43	pp. 194–199
4	pp. 66–71	24	pp. 176–181	44	pp. 218–223
5	pp. 122–127	25	pp. 48–53	45	pp. 218–223
6	pp. 66–71	26	pp. 48–53	46	pp. 28–33
7	pp. 86–91	27	pp. 114–121	47	pp. 28–33
8	pp. 16–21	28	pp. 114–121	48	pp. 240–247
9	pp. 16–21	29	pp. 78–85	49	pp. 240–247
10	pp. 266–271	30	pp. 78–85	50	pp. 200–205
11	pp. 266–271	31	pp. 128–133	51	pp. 200–205
12	pp. 22–27	32	pp. 128–133	52	pp. 54–59
13	pp. 22–27	33	pp. 272–277	53	pp. 54–59
14	pp. 106–113	34	pp. 272–277	54	pp. 176–181
15	pp. 106–113	35	pp. 152–157	55	pp. 40–47
16	pp. 72–77	36	pp. 140–163, 170–187	56	pp. 158–163
17	pp. 72–77	37	pp. 182–187	57	pp. 16–21
18	pp. 40–47	38	pp. 16–21	58	pp. 278–283
19	pp. 40–47	39	pp. 218–223	59	pp. 194–199
20	pp. 248–253	40	pp. 86–91, 278–283	60	pp. 248–253

Lesson 1.1

Think about Social Studies, page 17

1. representatives

2. monarchies

3. parliamentary

Vocabulary Review, page 20

1. analyze

2. autocracy

3. amendment

4. oligarchy

5. dictatorship

6. democracy

Skill Review, page 20

1. **D.** In representative democracies people vote for government officials to be their representative leaders. In constitutional monarchies, people vote for members of Parliament.

2. **B.** People in the United States elect leaders who represent them and speak for them in government.

3. **A.** The Declaration of Independence says, "Governments are instituted among Men, deriving their powers from the consent of the governed." The Virginia Declaration of Rights agrees: "all power is vested in, and consequently derived from, the people."

4. **A.** The people have the power to elect representatives, but they do not hold the power directly.

Skill Practice, page 21

1. **B.** The authors of the U.S. Bill of Rights were trying to prevent the government of the United States as a whole—not just the legislature—from taking actions like those taken by English monarchs that violated people's rights and freedoms.

2. **D.** The authors were probably concerned that, if they did not include Amendment 9, people might interpret the Bill of Rights as a list of all the rights people have—and thus the only rights people have.

Writing Practice, page 21

Answers will vary, but students should write a paragraph that describes their suggested amendment and explains why they would add this amendment to the Constitution.

Lesson 1.2

Think about Social Studies, page 23
1. **B**

Think about Social Studies, page 24
1. popular sovereignty

Think about Social Studies, page 25
1. **B**

Vocabulary Review, page 26
1. separation of powers

2. judicial branch

3. executive branch

4. federalism

5. legislative branch

6. relevant

Skill Review, page 26
1. **B.** Most states were satisfied with the Constitution and ratified it quickly.

2. **B.** 1788

3. **C.** those accused of crimes

4. **A.** Impartial means unbiased or without taking sides.

Skill Practice, page 27
1. **C.** This paragraph is about Sherman, who knew how to work with other delegates to solve problems.

2. **B.** The title of the passage provides a clue to the main idea.

3. **A.** Politicians must be able to work successfully with others, which includes the ability to compromise.

4. **D.** The convention may have been unsuccessful if not for the Great Compromise.

Writing Practice, page 27
The Articles of Confederation provided a weak central government, which could not tax Americans. After the war with England, the new American country was in debt, with no means to repay it. When courts began seizing farmers' property, a rebellion broke out, which the government did not have power to stop. The country's leaders realized the Articles of Confederation needed to change.

Lesson 1.3

Think about Social Studies, page 30

1. The president can veto, or overturn, acts of Congress.

Think about Social Studies, page 31

1. True

2. True

Think about Social Studies, page 31

1. executive

2. legislative

3. judicial

Vocabulary Review, page 32

1. bicameral

2. Senate

3. determines

4. veto

5. House of Representatives

6. referendum

Skill Review, page 32

1. **A.** The chart states the lieutenant governor presides over the senate. The senate is a part of the legislative branch.

2. **B.** The attorney general goes to court to represent the state in lawsuits.

Skill Practice, page 33

1. **B.** The judicial branch was granted the power of judicial review in several ways.

2. **A.** The Supreme Court gained this power through the Judiciary Act of 1789 and through the court case Marbury v. Madison.

3. **C.** The passage is explaining an official decision or declaration made by the court.

4. **D.** Judicial review strengthens the power of the Supreme Court by allowing it to review decisions made by Congress.

Writing Practice, page 33

Both state and federal governments have legislative, executive, and judicial branches of government. However, not all states have two houses in their legislatures, as the federal government does. The executive branch of the federal government is led by the president, whereas executive branches of state governments are led by governors. Governors do not have the same amount of power as the president. The federal judicial branch interprets laws at the national level, which can affect every state in the union. Although states have their own supreme courts, these courts can interpret only the laws that apply to their state.

Chapter Review

Review, page 34

1. **C.** In a direct democracy, all citizens meet and all citizens vote. This type of democracy does not work efficiently in large countries; therefore, those countries use another type of democracy, such as representative democracy.

2. **A.** The Declaration of Independence was written by members of the Second Continental Congress to declare independence from Britain and to explain the reasons why the colonies were rejecting British rule.

3. **D.** The compromised reached by delegates was that the lower house would follow the Virginia Plan and elect representatives based on population.

4. **B.** In a representative democracy, people elect representatives to speak for citizens in government business. The legislative branch includes those representatives.

5. **B.** Because Alaska and Rhode Island have almost the same number of representatives they must have similar sized populations.

6. **B.** The excerpt explains that amendments are sometimes necessary.

7. **C.** He believes Europe's laws and institutions have not progressed.

Write about Social Studies

Write about Social Studies, page 36

Answers will vary. Here are some ideas to consider:

- The essay should include information from all four paragraphs of President Reagan's speech.

- Possible relevant points include

  o The Soviet Union cannot provide goods and food for its people; only freedom brings prosperity.

  o Soviets may begin to understand the benefits of freedom. Some examples include allowing greater freedom to run businesses and releasing prisoners.

  o The question remains as to how genuine these reforms are. One sign could be given to confirm the intent of freedom.

  o Mr. Gorbachev, tear down this wall!

- The essay should avoid the use of passive voice.

- It should show evidence of careful editing for content and for correct grammar, mechanics, and word choice.

Lesson 2.1

Think about Social Studies, page 42

1. **A.** Due process includes the rights that are designed to protect the rights of someone under arrest. These include unreasonable search and seizure.

2. **D.** Freedom of assembly is more than just freedom of choice. It is the freedom to gather and meet.

Think about Social Studies, page 43

1. **B.** Segregation, or the separation of people based on race, was common in the south.

Think about Social Studies, page 45

1. **C.** Sandra Day O'Connor understands the importance of her position as the first female US Supreme Court Justice. However, she wants to stress that it is not gender but the strength of her legal arguments and knowledge that are important.

Vocabulary Review, page 46

1. civil liberties

2. suffrage

3. point of view

4. perseverance

5. segregation

6. civil rights

Skill Review, page 46

1. **A.** Women suffragists worked for the right to vote.

2. **C.** All other answer choices refer to the results of constitutional amendments or other pieces of legislation.

3. **C.** Martin Luther King, Jr. argued that segregation could never be just, under any conditions, because it makes people feel inferior and harms them in emotional ways.

4. **B.** Women wanted equal rights, including equal pay and the right to vote. They pressured the government by protesting and working to change the laws.

5. **B.** Women wanted the same rights as men and to be viewed as equal in the eyes of the law.

Skill Practice, page 47

1. **B.** The Court ruled that during wartime speech that is a "clear and present" danger to the nation is not protected by the First Amendment, but it did not outlaw all free speech.

2. **C.** Point of view is based on ideas and beliefs. Sentence 6 states Schenck's idea that he was protected by the First Amendment.

3. **A.** The Court believed that Schenck's speech would not pose a danger during peacetime; therefore they would rule to protect his freedom of speech during peacetime.

4. **B.** In the passage, espionage includes any actions that can harm the nation.

Writing Practice, page 47

Answers will vary but should contain some of the ideas in the following-. sample essay: Effective leaders are open-minded, motivated, and fair. Leaders must be open-minded and accept diverse people as followers and listen to a variety of ideas. Effective leaders are also motivated to create change. They also must motivate others, which can be accomplished more easily if they are motivated themselves. Effective leaders must also practice fairness. They must weigh the effects of decisions and make a choice that is fair to all.

Lesson 2.2

Think about Social Studies, page 49

1. **D.** A party platform describes the beliefs and position on important issues.

Think about Social Studies, page 50

1. **C.** Campaign reform laws were designed to stop abuses of campaign finance.

Think about Social Studies, page 51

1. Answers will vary, but may include: Political parties nominate candidates for public office; interest groups do not. Political parties work for solutions to a variety of issues. Interest groups generally focus on one or just a few issues.

Vocabulary Review, page 52

1. **E.** people who work to sway public officials toward a particular opinion

2. **C.** to combine things in order to make something new

3. **F.** a group of people with common concerns who join together to influence government policy on a particular issue

4. **B.** an organized group of people who share common values and goals

5. **A.** people who belong to no organized political party

6. **D.** something that represents something else

Skill Review, page 52

1. **C.** Both the donkey and the elephant are fishing out of the same pool, which is full of campaign issues. Yet they are fishing from different sides: the donkey from the left and the elephant from the right.

2. **A.** The Electoral College meets to vote for a president. The electors are chosen by citizens.

3. **C.** Because the two major parties have about equal numbers of members, major-party candidates need the votes of independents to win elections.

4. **B.** To become an informed voter, it would be helpful to read the political party's platform. Advertisements and talk shows are not always reliable sources of information. While a candidate's website would help you learn about a candidate, it would not help you learn about a political party.

Skill Practice, page 53

1. **C.** Answers will vary, but may include: Power shifts between the two major parties has occurred several times in America's history.

2. **B.** Answers will vary, but may include: The policies of the Republican president were not working, so voters elected a Democrat for president.

3. **D.** The passage details the economic problems related to political parties, such as the Republicans supported businesses, laborers, and high tariffs. During the Depression, the Democrats supported labor unions and Social Security.

4. **C.** In this case, dominant refers to the party that won the most elections.

Writing Practice, page 53

Answers will vary, but may include: Political action groups contribute millions of dollars to candidates. In return, political action groups expect candidates to return the "favor" by voting in such a way that would benefit those in the political action group. The candidate might abuse his or her office by ignoring the wishes of the general citizens and instead working solely for the action group.

Lesson 2.3

Think about Social Studies, page 55

1. The process is continuous because at the evaluation stage, which is the last step in the process, new policies are changed, or they are eliminated and the entire process starts over.

2. foreign

Think about Social Studies, page 57

1. E

2. P

3. E

4. S

5. S

Vocabulary Review, page 58

1. conclude

2. issues

3. domestic

4. accountable

5. public policies

6. bias

Skill Review, page 58

1. **C.** Public policies affect everyone in society. This water conservation law is a state policy that affects everyone in the state. The other options are personal decisions.

2. **D.** Minimum wage refers to economics, or financial, matters. Therefore, it is economic policy.

3. **A.** Lobbyists represent public interest groups.

4. **C.** The issue with texting and driving is that it can cause accidents, which affect people's health.

5. **A.** Reasoning includes facts. Opinions, bias, and judgment are not included in logical reasoning.

6. **D.** Special interest groups can help everyday citizens have their voices heard.

Skill Practice, page 59

1. **A.** Obama states that lobbyists have not funded his campaign and that they will not run the White House. He uses these statements to show Americans he will not be swayed by special interests.

2. **C.** Obama's statements about the influence of money as the "original sin" of politics and lobbyists setting the agenda in Washington show that he believes funding is necessary but can lead to unethical practice.

3. **A.** In the Senate floor speech, Obama admits to accepting money from wealthy people to fund his campaign, although he knows it's a dangerous practice. In his later presidential speech, he states that he has never taken money from lobbyists for his presidential campaign. These two statements seem to show a contradiction.

Writing Practice, page 59

Answer: Letters will vary, but may include: Lobbyists are a necessary part of US government today. Lobbyists represent various groups in society. Without lobbyists, most Americans would not be heard in Washington. Lobbyists have the funding and the inside knowledge of government to influence legislators. If lobbying were not allowed, ordinary citizens would not have the power to influence public policy.

Chapter Review

1. **C.** The Equal Pay Act made it illegal to pay men and women differently for the same job. Based on this graph, the Equal Pay Act has not been successful. One can conclude that women still face discrimination on the job.

2. **C.** The Establishment Claus was created so that government did not endorse any one religion, such as Great Britain did with the Church of England. Colonists wanted religion and the state to be separated.

3. **D.** In *Brown* v. *Board of Education*, the Supreme Court ruled segregation of school unconstitutional.

4. **B.** Interest groups can be very powerful, and their power is linked the amount of money they have. Campaign finance reforms are intended to limit the power and abuses of these groups.

5. **C.** The relationship between voters and elected officials creates a system in which people can influence public policy. Officials are accountable to their voters and thus will vote as their constituents want them to.

6. **D.** The steps of the policy-making process are 1) Problem identification, 2) Policy creation, 3) Policy adoption, 4) Policy evaluation.

7. Due process protects a person's right to life, liberty, and property.

8. **A.** All answer choices except for A can be proved. Therefore, A is an opinion.

9. **B.** Because current laws regulate only hard money, laws are needed to control the raising of soft money.

Write about Social Studies

Write about Social Studies, page 62

Answers will vary. Here are some ideas to consider.

- The essay should address a policy issue.
- Students' essays should use sentences of varying length.
- Essays should include time signal words as transitions to indicate sequence.
- Events should be in correct sequence order.
- It should show evidence of careful editing for content and for correct grammar, mechanics, and word choice. Homonym misuse in particular should be considered.

Lesson 3.1

Think about Social Studies, page 67

1. **B.** It was the first time colonists attempted to create a constitutional government, and it later became a model for the U.S. Constitution.

Think about Social Studies, page 68

1. Only war will determine whether the colonists remain under British rule or become their own country.

Think about Social Studies, page 69

1. false
2. true

Vocabulary Review, page 70

1. boycott
2. charter
3. colony
4. declaration
5. minutemen
6. unicameral

Skill Review, page 70

1. **A.** Charters were the laws of written code for colonies.
2. **C.** A group of colonists, angry over Townshend's tax plan, attacked a group of British troops.
3. **A.** The colonists threw tea into the harbor because they did not like the Tea Act, which Parliament had passed.
4. **B.** The Articles of Confederation created an alliance of states and set out a plan for government.

Skill Practice, page 71

1. **A.** The pamphlet convinced many colonists to urge the members of the Continental Congress to vote for independence.
2. **B.** The central idea is that the Declaration defends the human rights of all people. All people have the right to life, liberty, and the pursuit of happiness and to overthrow governments that abuse those rights. Because Jefferson included all people in the Declaration, it is a document for human rights, not simply the rights of the colonists.
3. **D.** Tyranny is a government in which a king or other ruler abuses the rights of citizens.
4. **B.** Oppressive means severe or harsh in this passage.

Writing Practice, page 71

Possible answer: Common Sense appealed to the sense of injustice that many colonists were feeling. Common Sense sold many copies, and it helped convince the delegates of the Continental Congress to vote for independence.

Lesson 3.2

Think about Social Studies, page 73

1. **B.** The Northwest Ordinance allowed for the spread of slavery by allowing settlers to create their own governments.

Think about Social Studies, page 74

1. B
2. A
3. D
4. C

Think about Social Studies, page 75

1. **D.** This was a time of unity and strong national sentiment.

Vocabulary Review, page 76

1. true
2. true
3. true
4. false
5. false
6. true

Skill Review, page 76

1. **C.** Washington, D.C., was burned in 1814. The British and the United States fought at New Orleans in 1815.

2. **A.** The Louisiana Purchase gave the settlers rights to the Mississippi River, which gave them a shipping route.

3. **D.** By calling himself Mr. President, he showed people that he was not in a higher position than they were.

4. **A.** Americans moved west to settle land. As they did, they took land from Native Americans. Westward expansion did not benefit Native Americans.

Skill Practice, page 77

1. **D.** The last sentence describes the number of Cherokee who died on the journey.

2. **A.** The passage describes the negative and cruel treatment of the Cherokee that the author witnessed. Seeing such treatment of Native Americans would likely cause the author to disapprove of Indian removal.

3. **C.** The word *tears* implies sadness, and the trail refers the journey to the west.

4. **D.** The passage is referring to the many people who were forced to walk.

Writing Practice, page 77

A hawk is a bird that hunts prey. Congressmen who were proponents of war were characterized as hawks because they supported war, which included attacking others.

Lesson 3.3

Think about Social Studies, page 80

1. **D.** Slavery was prohibited in The Oregon Territory by the Missouri Compromise.

2. **D.** The Missouri Compromise allowed slavery in the Arkansas Territory.

Think about Social Studies, page 82

1. factories

Think about Social Studies, page 83

1. **B.** It did not punish Southern states but allowed them back into the Union and back into Congress.

Vocabulary Review, page 84

1. surrender

2. persuasive language

3. slave codes

4. sectional

5. abolitionists

6. triangular trade

Skill Review, page 84

1. **A.** The North had more men of military age to send into battle. Farms and enslaved workers were advantages of the South.

2. **C.** With the cotton gin, cotton could be processed faster. Northern factories bought more cotton and produced more textiles.

3. **D.** President Lincoln believed that freed enslaved people would join the Union army of the North.

4. **B.** Abolitionists included men and women who believed in the Declaration of Independence, which states that all men are created equal. Abolitionists did not believe in enslaving others or that white men should determine the rights of others. Land ownership was not a major issue for abolitionists.

Skill Practice, page 85

1. **A.** Lincoln believes in a united nation. The last sentence states his main purpose of the address: to remain united and begin a "new birth" of freedom.

2. **C.** People should not forget why the men on both sides died, and they should work to avoid battling each other in the future.

Writing Practice, page 85

Speeches will vary but should include words that evoke feelings in the reader and facts that support the writer's point of view, such as equality of all men as it is given in the Declaration of Independence.

Lesson 3.4

Think about Social Studies, page 87

1. **B.** The idea reflected immigrants' belief that the United States offered economic opportunity and a better life.

Think about Social Studies, page 88

1. **B.** Most middle-class Americans lived in the suburbs at this time.

2. **C.** The number of people moving to the cities to work in the factories led to over-crowding and sanitation problems.

Think about Social Studies, page 89

1. **C.** Most immigrants were arriving from Northern and Southern Europe.

2 **C.** The total number includes those from both China and Japan.

Vocabulary Review, page 90

1. nativists

2. push factors

3. pull factors

4. settlement houses

5. tenements

6. social class

Skill Review, page 90

1. **D.** Japanese and Chinese immigrants settled mainly in the West.

2. **D.** New machinery replaced farm workers. These workers moved to cities in search of work.

3. **D.** Jane Addams was a reformer, so she had the most in common with progressives, who strove to make conditions better for people.

4. **A.** Religious freedom pulled Jewish immigrants to the United States. Religious persecution pushed them from their home country.

Skill Practice, page 91

1. **D.** Sentence 1 describes the entire passage. The other answer choices are details.

2. **C.** Sentence 5 is about the unsafe and unsanitary conditions in the meatpacking industry. The other sentences do not relate details about workplace safety.

3. **B.** Muckrackers exposed corruption in business and politics to help create fairness and equality for all people.

4. **A.** Poor children were most likely to have to work to help support their families. John Spargo worked to end child labor, which would affect poor families.

Writing Practice, page 91

Answers will vary but should include the idea that nativists wanted to ban immigrant groups from coming to the United States and helped create legislation to do so. Progressives, such as Jane Addams, wanted to reform society to make life better for immigrants as well as others.

Chapter Review

1. **C.** The colonists protested the Stamp Act by boycotting British goods. This pressure caused Parliament to repeal the act.

2. **B.** The pilgrims established a colony in North America in 1620. The other events listed occurred in the 1700s.

3. **D.** The blue stars depict victory of American colonists; the other battles were won by Britain.

4. **A.** The stars depict battle locations. Most of the stars are located in the New England area.

5. **C.** By signing the Treaty of Greenville, Native American tribes agreed to leave the Ohio Valley.

6. **B.** This is discrimination against a person because they are Jewish.

7. **B.** Answer choice B best describes the entire passage. The other answer choices relate only isolated facts from the passage.

8. **C.** One persuasive tool is emotional language. The imagery of the phrase "beardless boys . . . . mutilated in every imaginable way" evokes emotion in the reader.

Write about Social Studies

Write about Social Studies, page 94

Answers will vary. Here are some ideas to consider.

- The essay should focus on an aspect of the American Civil War, highlighting the cause-effect nature of the event.

- Students' essays should use compound sentences correctly.

- Essays should include cause-effect signal words, such as those listed in the student edition.

- Possessive nouns should be correctly written.

- The essay should show evidence of careful editing for content and for correct grammar, mechanics, and word choice. Excess use of strings of prepositional phrases should be avoided.

Lesson 4.1

Think about Social Studies, page 99

1. **D.** The desire for more natural resources and new markets for goods caused the increase in imperialism, which led to increased colonization.

Think about Social Studies, page 102

1. **D.** The Zimmermann Telegraph

Think about Social Studies, page 103

1. sovereignty

2. national self-determination

3. reparations

4. kaiser

Vocabulary Review, page 104

1. imperialism

2. alliance

3. diplomacy

4. revolution

5. League of Nations

6. nationalism

Skill Review, page 104

1. **D.** The first three answer choices occurred before the United States entered the war. Six months after entering the war, the Russian czar was overthrown and the new Russian government signed a treaty with Germany.

2. **A.** The Treaty of Versailles limited the size of the German army and navy, which reduced militarism in Germany.

3. **C.** The assassination was the spark that set off the war. All other answer choices are long-term causes of the war.

4. **A.** After men went to war, women and African Americans began to work in factories to produce goods needed during the war.

Skill Practice, page 105

1. **D.** Wilson saying the United States has no wish to "injure her" refers to his idea that Germany not be punished.

2. **A.** In the first sentence, Wilson states "intimate partners of all the governments," which refers to other world powers.

3. **B.** Wilson's plan did not punish Germany but it required Germany to exist peacefully with other countries and not try to conquer them.

4. **A.** Provocations refers to the things that are causing war.

Writing Practice, page 71

Answers will vary. Students should choose a clear side, either Germany/Austria or France/Britain. Students should cite logical evidence for their choice, such as stipulations in the Treaty of Versailles, including redrawn maps that cost Germany/Austria land, reparations, and limited military forces of Germany.

Lesson 4.2

Think about Social Studies, page 107

1. **B.** Treaty of Versailles

Think about Social Studies, page 110

1. 2
2. 1
3. 4
4. 3

Think about Social Studies, page 111

1. **C.** The War Department knew this would allow them to remove Japanese citizens from the area.

Vocabulary Review, page 112

1. propaganda
2. isolationism
3. fascism
4. totalitarian government
5. internment
6. depression

Skill Review, page 112

1. **A.** The depression in Germany angered Germans. Hitler took advantage of this thinking to take a position of power as a Nazi leader.

2. **C.** The United States refrained from entering the war until the attack on Pearl Harbor. The next day, the United States declared war on Japan.

3. **A.** Hitler felt Jews were undesirables. Hatred of Jewish people is called anti-Semitism. The other answer choices are not factual.

4. **B.** American military leaders believed an invasion of Japan would be prolonged and cost many Americans and Japanese people their lives.

Skill Practice, page 113

1. **D.** In the last line of the pamphlet, the Nazis refer to themselves ("our lines"). They reassure US soldiers that the Nazis will let them "safely" pass if the soldiers agree to stop fighting and go home.

2. **C.** The propaganda intends to put troubling ideas into soldiers' minds so that they will surrender and go home. The main idea is relayed in the sentence "Escape from this bloody business."

Writing Practice, page 113

Answers will vary but should include evidence related to the unfair treatment of Japanese-American citizens and the specific conditions these citizens lived under in the camps.

Lesson 4.3

Think about Social Studies, page 115

1. Great Britain

2. Soviet Union

3. Soviet Union

4. United States

Think about Social Studies, page 117

1. **B.** He used the policy of containment, which prevented the spread of communism throughout Europe, and Marshall Plan aid, which helped countries of Western Europe rebuild their economies.

2. **A.** They and their allies agreed to the Warsaw Pact, in which they pledged to defend each other in case of attack.

Think about Social Studies, page 119

1. **A.** Chicago and New York are in the orange area, which is the medium ballistic range.

Vocabulary Review, page 120

1. refugees

2. Truman Doctrine

3. NATO

4. Marshall Plan

5. containment

6. negotiated

Skill Review, page 120

1. **C.** The location of Miami would be the most logical entry

2. **A.** They hoped to prevent people from fleeing.

3. **C.** This type of action could easily lead to another world war.

4. **B.** Both sides were reluctant to agree to a compromise.

Skill Practice, page 121

1. **D.** When he states "neither will we shrink from that risk at any time it must be faced," the risk he is implying is worldwide nuclear war.

2. **B.** Hitler aggressively took over other nations, which led to World War II.

Writing Practice, page 121

Answers will vary but should include evidence related to the Cold War and the build-up of Soviet weapons in Cuba and thoughtful reasoning regarding the possible effects of Kennedy's tough stand or of allowing the missiles to stay.

Lesson 4.4

Think about Social Studies, page 123

1. False

Think about Social Studies, page 124

1. **B.** to quit or step down

Think about Social Studies, page 125

1. 4

2. 1

3. 2

4. 3

Vocabulary Review, page 126

1. Great Society

2. impeach

3. détente

4. scandal

5. media

6. poverty line

Skill Review, page 126

1. **C.** Americans disapproved of the war because they saw the media reports, and they realized the United States was not winning against the guerilla warfare of the Viet Cong.

2. **A.** The Voting Rights Act gave federal officials the power to register African Americans to vote. Therefore, African Americans did not have to take literacy tests to vote. This enabled more African Americans to vote.

3. **B.** Nixon realized that avoiding nuclear war was more important than being firm with communist nations.

4. **C.** Gorbachev's policy allowed satellite nations to govern themselves. As a result, the Soviet Union would not enforce communism in those nations.

Skill Practice, page 127

1. **C.** The sharp rise in inflation after the election of Jimmy Carter leads one to conclude that his policies were not good for the economy.

2. **A.** The first statement best relays all of the information in the text. Answer choices B, C, and D are details and do not relay the main idea of the entire text.

Writing Practice, page 127

Answers will vary but should include evidence related to Nixon's foreign policy, domestic policy, and economic policy as well as the Watergate scandal.

Lesson 4.5

Think about Social Studies, page 130

1. C.

Think about Social Studies, page 131

1. terrorists

2. NATO

3. Iraq

Vocabulary Review, page 132

1. militants

2. conduct

3. embassy

4. insurgents

5. foreign policy

6. terrorism

Skill Review, page 132

1. **C.** President Bush addressed the world in an appeal for help in the fight against terrorism.

2. **A.** Although Saddam Hussein refused to allow UN inspectors into Iraq, the UN would not declare war against Iraq.

3. **C.** After the attacks, the United States took the position of actively pursuing and capturing terrorists worldwide and taking action against governments that support terrorists.

4. **B.** The insurgency cost the United States more lives than the formal attack.

Skill Practice, page 133

1. **D.** All answer choices except D can be proven with facts. Answer choice D is an opinion.

2. **B.** The reference to the violence of the September 11th attacks and the imagery used in the phrasing will most likely affect listeners' emotions.

3. **A.** The fact that no armies descended upon the shores implies that this attack signaled a different kind of war.

4. **D.** Sentence 8 states that the homeland is more secure.

Writing Practice, page 133

Answers will vary but should include specific references to the Constitution and the Patriot Act. Essays may also include emotional appeals and other persuasive devices.

Chapter Review

Review, page 134

1. **A.** The assassination of the archduke, which occurred in 1914, was one of the factors that led to World War I.

2. **B.** Germany was required to pay reparations for the damage incurred during the war. The actions listed in the other answer choices were not part of the Treaty of Versailles.

3. **B.** The president is making the case for war against Japan. He used the speech to win the approval of Congress to go to war.

4. **C.** The GI Bill provided money for education, housing, and job counseling for returning soldiers.

5. **B.** President Roosevelt's purpose was to have Congress declare war on Japan.

6. **C.** The president is appealing to the American people.

7. **D.** NATO member-nations are depicted in green. Spain is purple and therefore not a NATO member.

8. **C.** The term *poverty* means "poor."

9. **B.** The Berlin Wall separated East and West Germany. The fall of the Berlin Wall led to a new, united Germany.

10. **B.** All terrorist groups use fear to accomplish their goals. Not all terrorists have the same goals. The other answer choices are goals of various terrorist groups.

Write about Social Studies

Write about Social Studies, page 136

Answers will vary. Here are some ideas to consider.

- The essay should focus on the propaganda art in the student edition.

- Students' essays should point out techniques such as the image of New York City in flames with Lady Liberty in the foreground and the extreme language of liberty perishing.

- Essays should include well-constructed paragraphs with main idea and supporting details.

- Essays should be free of sentence fragments.

- The essay should show evidence of careful editing for content and for correct grammar, mechanics, and word choice.

Lesson 5.1

Think about Social Studies, page 141

1. buyers, goods, services

2. buying, selling

Think about Social Studies, page 142

1. Competitive

Think about Social Studies, page 143

1. B., D., E.

Vocabulary Review, page 144

1. service

2. monopoly

3. outcome

4. competition

5. goods

6. markets

Skill Review, page 144

1. **C.** The government wants to ensure competition in the marketplace. Freedom of choice enhances competition.

2. **C.** Self-interest is when ordinary people decide for themselves what to buy and sell.

3. **A.** Competition forces sellers to use resources efficiently and respond to consumer needs. When a product is less unique it doesn't need to compete with similar products.

4. **C.** Monopolies can charge higher prices and deliver lower quality because consumers have fewer choices.

Skill Practice, page 145

1. **D.** Drug companies would not develop new drugs.

2. **B.** Professional authors, songwriters, artists, and photographers would eventually stop creating new works for publication.

3. **A.** This provides for your family after your death. It is a good idea because families often make sacrifices for the artist's career. It can be a bad idea because most works are not famous and can disappear completely instead of remaining a part of the.

4. **C.** limited or reserved

Writing Practice, page 71

Answers will vary but should contain some of the same ideas expressed in the following writing sample: The Internet has increased competition in our town. For example, people can now order office supplies online, so our two major office supply stores merged. They are consolidating into one location where they can offer better service and more personal attention. They also offer free same-day delivery. Delivery services are booming here. There is even one that will pick up a food order from any eatery in the city and bring it to your house for $6. I think there will be more services like this soon. We have already lost our camera shop. People buy high-tech equipment online. In general, businesses that sell small special-interest items that can be shipped may fade away. Businesses with both virtual and brick and mortar components may thrive. If each business looks for and exploits its competitive advantage, it will succeed.

Lesson 5.2

Think about Social Studies, page 147

1. Scarcity is characterized by people wanting something that has value and a limited supply, so not everyone can have as much as they want.

2. People can choose the things they need or want the most and skip things that are less important to them. People can make their own decisions, which lets them make the best use of resources.

3. Answers will vary, but may include: Water is not abundant all over the world, so humans who live in dry climates or locations affected by drought will find that water is a scarce resource.

Think about Social Studies, page 148

1. natural
2. labor
3. nonrenewable
4. renewable

Think about Social Studies, page 149

1. D

Vocabulary Review, page 150

1. entrepreneurship
2. opportunity cost
3. labor
4. natural resources
5. capital
6. scarce

Skill Review, page 150

1. **C.** The reason entrepreneurs are important to a market economy is innovation.

2. **D.** Capital is defined as tools, machinery, and buildings. Goods and services cannot be produced or created without these things.

3. **A.** Scarcity describes the idea that people have unlimited wants and needs but must deal with a limited number of resources. Thus, they must make choices between resources.

4. **D.** Ford's use of the assembly line increased production and lowered prices.

Skill Practice, page 151

1. **A.** It's faster and cheaper to hire and train workers than to build and equip a new factory.

2. **C.** The equipment will start to wear out and workers will not have room to do their jobs effectively.

3. **D.** Natural resources are the hardest to control. Weather, wars, and other factors can interrupt supply.

4. **A.** An entrepreneur could develop a new shoe assembly strategy or invent a new machine to perform tasks more efficiently.

Writing Practice, page 151

Answers will vary but should include some of the ideas from the following example: While hiring labor in other nations can have advantages for U.S. companies, it is not necessarily a good idea. A decade ago, wages in many countries were a fraction of what they were here. As economies in Asia and elsewhere have improved, pay for workers has risen. Labor unions are forming. As labor costs increase, shipping expenses become an issue for businesses. Advances in robotic technology have eliminated the need for many assembly jobs. Manufacturing tasks can now be performed domestically for the same price or less than in other countries. A growing "Made in the USA" consumer movement has added value to products built here. It's time for American companies to come home.

Lesson 5.3

Think about Social Studies, page 153

1. expenses

2. profit

3. risk

Think about Social Studies, page 154

1. production, opportunity cost, capital

Think about Social Studies, page 155

1. A

Vocabulary Review, page 156

1. strategy

2. market economy

3. depreciation

4. net income

5. productivity

6. incentive

Skill Review, page 156

1. **D.** Profits are the incentive to taking risks.

2. **C.** Capital resources, human resources, and natural resources alone cannot produce anything. But when they work together, they can.

3. **C.** By keeping expenses low, businesses can conserve some of their capital and not lose everything.

4. **B.** Technological innovations help create modern economies.

Skill Practice, page 157

1. **C.** The traditional economy is being phased out in favor of an economy that mixes traditional elements with a market economy. People were starting to have incentives to learn new skills, acquire tools and other capital, and to do work different from that of their family.

2. **D.** Some trade unions still offer apprenticeships, but they are not the same as those in the Middle Ages.

3. **B.** Blacksmiths and shoemakers are still around, but their trades are no longer central to the economy.

4. **C.** This means they had no other options but to farm the land.

Writing Practice, page 157

Market economies are based on self-interest. Another word for that could be greed. People talk about caring for others, but most want more for themselves. It's just human nature. Market economies take advantage of a basic human drive and use it in a special way. By helping others to get what they want and need, people can get more for themselves. An entrepreneur who risks much or all of his wealth to start a new business hopes to make a generous profit. He will only make that profit if his business serves the wants and needs of many other people. The results of his efforts will be more health, happiness, or comfort for thousands of others, perhaps for decades. There will also be more money for him. Yes, that is greed, but it is also a service.

Lesson 5.4

Think about Social Studies, page 157

1. **A.** Specialization enables a country to focus on the goods for which it is best suited to produce.

Think about Social Studies, page 159

1. specialization

2. trade-offs

3. does not need to

Think about Social Studies, page 159

1. **C.** Trade solves the problem of scarcity by helping countries acquire the goods they need.

Vocabulary Review, page 160

1. comparative advantage

2. efficient

3. specialization

4. absolute advantage

5. interdependence

6. opportunity cost

Skill Review, page 160

1. **B.** To read the graph, look for 6 bushes along the y-axis, then read across to the production possibilities curve and down to the x-axis to find the number of lawns mowed at that point on the curve, which is 8. Subtract that from the total number of lawns that can possibly be mowed (20) to arrive at the opportunity cost of trimming 6 bushes: 12 lawns mowed.

2. **D.** 14 lawns can be mowed.

Skill Practice, page 161

1. **D.** While Indian companies perform services related to insurance claims, loan applications, and medical x-rays, they specialize in information technology.

2. **B.** The exchange of information and services, which happens when U.S. companies hire an Indian company, is an example of interdependence.

3. **B.** While statements A, C, and D may be true, they do not provide a reason for U.S. companies to export their services to India. Because the transfer of information over the Internet is cheap, and Indian companies specialize in information technology, we can infer that U.S. companies export their services to India because it is less expensive there.

Writing Practice, page 161

Students should include detailed steps describing a task. The steps should be in chronological order, and basic steps should not be left out. Jargon and technical terms should be defined. The steps should have correct grammar and punctuation and be written with clear, precise prose.

Chapter Review

Review, page 164

1. **A.** Specialization allows more efficient production of products

2. **A.** These two producers are interdependent because they rely on each other for goods and services.

3. **C.** When multiple companies compete to sell a product, the price of the product generally goes down.

4. **C.** In a market economy, individuals and businesses can own property, which gives them an incentive to produce goods and services.

5. **D.** Barter does not work as well in a market economy where people perform specialized tasks.

6. **A.** Land, capital, labor, and entrepreneurs participate in factor markets.

7. **B.** Investment in labor and capital can increase productivity, which increases the production of goods and services.

8. **B.** Entrepreneurs invent and sell new products and services to make money.

Write about Social Studies

Write about Social Studies, page 166

Answers will vary. Here are some ideas to consider.

- The essay should focus on processes needed in a business.

- Students' essays should use compound sentences correctly.

- Essays should include correct subject-verb agreement.

- Possessive nouns should be correctly written.

- The essay should show evidence of careful editing for content and for correct grammar, mechanics, and word choice. Excess use of strings of prepositional phrases should be avoided.

Lesson 6.1

Think about Social Studies, page 169

1. D

Think about Social Studies, page 170

1. buyer

2. seller

3. buyer

4. seller

Think about Social Studies, page 171

1. C

Vocabulary Review, page 172

1. market equilibrium

2. median

3. trend

4. demand curved

5. supply curve

6. law of demand

Skill Review, page 172

1. **D.** At $5, 8 CDs would be sold. The lower the price, the more CDs sold, so if priced less than $5, more than 8 CDs would be sold.

2. **B.** $12.50 is between $10 and $15 on the graph. The corresponding point on the x-axis is 4.

3. **C.** The median is the middle number after the numbers are sorted in ascending order: 0, 0, 1, 3, 5, 8. The median is the mean of the two numbers in the set: $1 + 3 \div 2 = 2$.

4. **B.** The mean number is 3.5.

Skill Practice, page 175

1. **A.** The war left many people without shoes. Machinery was able to produce more shoes in less time than before the war to meet the demand.

2. **C.** The first paragraph states "the existing shoe factories had during the war only been able to supply the northern states," implying that those in Southern states were "shoeless."

3. **B.** The price would decrease because supply increased.

4. **C.** Bind means to fasten or secure something.

Writing Practice, page 173

Answers will vary but should contain the following ideas: The law of demand relates to buyers. It states that the higher the price of a product or service, the less of it people are willing to buy. The lower the price, the more people will buy. The law of demand reflects a negative relationship on the demand curve. The law of supply relates to suppliers. It states that the higher the price of a product or service, the more of it suppliers will offer for sale. As the price falls, so will the quantity supplied. The law of supply shows a positive relationship on the supply curve.

Lesson 6.2

Think about Social Studies, page 177

1. Answers will vary but may include: National Defense: This expenditure could make my family safer by preventing terrorist activity; Human Resources: My dad was a veteran and uses health services for veterans; Physical Resources: This expenditure funds transportation infrastructure so my family can be safe while driving on roads and over bridges.

Think about Social Studies, page 179

1. C.

Vocabulary Review, page 180

1. tariff

2. fiscal policy

3. expenditures

4. subsidy

5. contrast

6. monetary policies

Skill Review, page 180

1. B. A corn subsidy is a payment to a corn producer, so it is a government expenditure.

2. D. When an economy is increasing, money is increasing, so the Fed removes money. When the money supply is high, the Fed may raise interest rates to prevent inflation.

3. C. Because the Fed can increase or decrease interest rates, this would affect the interest rate of a homeowner's loan.

4. A. Income taxes account for almost half of the revenue

Skill Practice, page 181

1. A. Bernanke says that the central bank provides liquidity during periods of panic or incipient panic.

2. D. By having cash easily available, the Fed can loan money and help businesses who need immediate financial assistance.

3. B. One way the Fed regulates interest rates is through inflation. It can achieve credibility by providing financial stability.

4. D. When something is resilient it is able to withstand hardship, or able to recover from something difficult.

Writing Practice, page 181

Answers will vary but may include how revenue would be raised and how expenditures would be changed.

Lesson 6.3

Think about Social Studies, page 183
1. B.
2. C.

Think about Social Studies, page 184
1. inflation
2. decrease (fall)
3. deflation
4. less

Think about Social Studies, page 185
1. C
2. D

Vocabulary Review, page 186
1. unemployment rate
2. deflation
3. inflation
4. integrate
5. gross domestic product
6. cyclical

Skill Review, page 186
1. C. Only final goods and services made in the United States and consumed in the year they were made are included in the GDP.
2. D. The unemployment rate only counts those who are unemployed and trying to find work.
3. A. As inflation increases, the purchasing power of the dollar decreases, which means households have less money to spend.
4. A. As deflation occurs, the purchasing power of the dollar increases.

Skill Practice, page 187
1. C. An increase in unemployment during a recession—when output is down because consumer spending is down—indicates that lack of demand is causing employers to cut back on their workforce.
2. D. The chart shows that unemployment in 2012 was at a much higher level than in previous periods, indicating that there could be a structural problem as well as cyclical unemployment related to recession.

Writing Practice, page 187
The essay should include a topic sentence, a summary sentence, and sentences comparing and contrasting economic conditions during periods of high and low unemployment. Students should recognize that low unemployment is connected to rising demand, which pushes produces to produce, and results in growing prosperity for workers—who have incomes from their jobs—and rising profits. High unemployment is linked to shrinking demand, lowered output, and a general decline in prosperity.

Chapter Review

Review, page 188

1. **C.** Job training programs are necessary when the demand for a particular skill decreases and workers must learn new skills.

2. **B.** The proposed tax credits are meant to change the behavior of companies so that they hire more workers and spend money on equipment.

3. **D.** Funding for highway and transit projects is the only one of these that requires funds directly from the government.

4. **C.** The amount sold is lower when tablet price is higher.

5. **D.** The point where the supply and demand curves cross represents market equilibrium.

6. **B.** The graph shows an increase in demand, which allows more sales at higher prices.

7. **D.** This is the point where market equilibrium is reached during the final demand.

8. **B.** Because the demand from initial to final increases, so does the price.

Write about Social Studies

Write about Social Studies, page 190

Answers will vary. Here are some ideas to consider.

- The essay should show evidence of either a block or alternative comparison or contrast method of development.

- Students' essays should include transitions indicating comparison and contrast, such as those given in the student edition.

- Essays should be free of dangling or misplaced modifiers.

- Essays should include a strong conclusion restating the main idea and incorporating main points.

The essay should show evidence of careful editing for content and for correct grammar, mechanics, and word choice.

Lesson 7.1

Think about Social Studies, page 195

1. C

2. D

3. B

4. A

Think about Social Studies, page 196

1. C. People took out loans to buy stocks. When stock prices fell, people who bought on margin could not pay back those loans. This situation caused more people to sell and the prices of stock to in turn keep dropping. On a day that massive selloffs occurred, the stock market crashed.

Think about Social Studies, page 197

1. FDIC

2. AAA

3. WPA

Vocabulary Review, page 198

1. business cycle

2. recession

3. standard of living

4. expansion

5. Great Depression

6. stimulus

Skill Review, page 198

1. A. People could not repay loans to the banks, leaving the banks without money.

2. C. The assembly line came first. The other events came in 1929 or later, when the assembly line had already been in use.

3. C. Roosevelt believed that federal involvement in the economy might lead to socialism.

4. B. The Tennessee Valley Authority (TVA) was a complex project that built many dams to control flooding and generate electricity. The other answer choices refer to other programs, none of which were to provide electricity to a rural area.

Skill Practice, page 199

1. C. Obama states "only the government can break the cycles that are crippling our economy." This shows he believes the federal government has a role in economic activities.

2. D. A trough is a low point in economic growth. The president is describing a recession, which is a trough.

3. B. President Obama believes that the federal government should act to create jobs and improve the economy, much as Roosevelt did.

Writing Practice, page 199

Answers will vary but all should include evidence from the chapter to support the opinion.

Lesson 7.2

Think about Social Studies, page 201

1. D. Laissez-faire means to leave alone, or let it be.

Think about Social Studies, page 202

1. 1

2. 4

3. 3

4. 2

Think about Social Studies, page 203

1. A. The Open Door policy was intended to help the United States trade with China. If opened the door for any nation to be able to do so.

Vocabulary Review, page 204

1. Open Door Policy

2. humanitarian

3. foreign aid

4. annexation

5. industrialized nations

6. laissez-faire

Skill Review, page 204

1. D. The United States wanted to protect its interests in China. By ensuring all countries had equal access to China, the United States protected itself.

2. B. The United States needed to expand its economy and sell products to people of other countries and territories. Imperialism provided the United States with new markets for its products.

3. B. Nations provide foreign aid to war-torn countries for a variety of reasons, including humanitarian reasons as well as to gain allies, establish military bases, and provide opportunity for foreign investment.

4. C. President Roosevelt used Keynes ideas in the New Deal plan to create government programs to put people to work, regulate business, and protect workers. This economic stimulus would end the Great Depression.

Skill Practice, page 205

1. A. The United States sent warships to threaten Colombia, who then allowed the Panamanian rebels to declare independence. In repayment, Panama allowed the United States to control the canal.

2. B. A French company had already started building the canal, which likely means that France had military or economic interests in the area.

3. C. By sending ships to threaten Colombia, President Roosevelt showed his intention of obtaining control of the canal.

4. A. This statement supports the assumption that the United States was more powerful than Colombia's army and was forced to give in to their wishes.

Writing Practice, page 205

Answers will vary, but points made in the argument should be directly tied to the Declaration of Independence. For example, those arguing for imperialism might tie the argument of pursuit of happiness to the desire for economic expansion through imperialism.

Lesson 7.3

Think about Social Studies, page 207

1. **B** Earth orbits the sun. The sun does not orbit anything. The stars do not orbit Earth, and the moon does not orbit the sun.

Think about Social Studies, page 208

1. **B** Cottage industry workers had to work in factories for factory owners after inventions were put to use in factories.

Think about Social Studies, page 209

1. cities

2. suburbs

3. labor unions

Vocabulary Review, page 210

1. cottage industry

2. scientific method

3. urbanization

4. Scientific Revolution

5. innovation

6. Industrial Revolution

Skill Review, page 210

1. **D.** Cities did not have services, such as waste disposal. The large increase in city populations created more waste and unsanitary living conditions.

2. **B.** The Industrial Revolution changed the way people worked, lived, communicated, and enjoyed culture. The changes were profound. The industrial Revolution did not cause violent revolts or result in leaders begin overthrown. The revolution was the result of scientific advances and did not stop future advances.

3. **A.** Several factors gave rise to the Industrial Revolution in Great Britain, including investment money, workers, markets, and natural resources.

4. **B.** The steam engine powered machines that factories needed. Steam engines allowed for the growth of factories, which increased the population of cities.

5. **B.** Horrible working conditions led to the creation of labor unions.

6. **B.** All of the descriptions could apply to an industrial worker at the time, but not the majority of them. Most, however, did work 12-16 hours a day.

Skill Practice, page 211

1. **A.** The passage describes Rockefeller buying other oil companies and building a trust to avoid monopoly laws. Therefore, horizontal integration is best defined as owning other businesses similar to one's own.

2. **C.** Trusts were not illegal. In establishing the trust and controlling it, Rockefeller was able to have a monopoly.

3. **D.** Entrepreneurs establish new business and assume the risk for it. Rockefeller established oil companies and then purchased more, assuming the risk for those companies. He may have owned stock in his companies, but his main role was as an entrepreneur.

4. **C.** Rockefeller was able to gain control of the oil industry through a process known as horizontal integration.

Writing Practice, page 211

Answers will vary but should include facts about the rise of the factory system, the working life of a factory worker, and the decline of the cottage industry.

Chapter Review

Review, page 212

1. **A.** In the 1920s, more people wanted goods that would make their lives easier. Mass production technology made it possible for businesses to meet the demand for these goods.

2. **C.** President Hoover's public works projects created new jobs and provided relief for the unemployed. Among the projects were highways, dams, and public buildings like libraries.

3. **A.** John Keynes believed that the government should manage its economy by creating demand. It could create demand by spending money.

4. **D.** Imperialism is the governing of weaker countries or colonies by more powerful nations.

5. **C.** Wars create unstable governments, which scares away investment. Without investment, countries cannot develop their economies.

6. **A.** The Scientific Revolution preceded the Industrial Revolution.

7. **B.** The main idea can often be found in the title of the passage. Answer choice B best restates the title.

8. **B.** According to the map, major centers of industry are depicted with a red dot.

9. **C.** Iron ore deposits are noted with triangles. Of the answer choices, Great Britain has the most iron deposits.

Write about Social Studies

Write about Social Studies, page 214

Answers will vary. Here are some ideas to consider.

- The essay should focus on a reform of the Industrial Revolution. Possible topics include but are not limited to voting rights, civil rights, taxes, housing, child labor, prison reform, treatment for the mentally ill, immigration laws, fair wages, safe food, and decent public housing

- Essay should include clearly state the point of view.

- Students' essays should include factual evidence to support the main idea.

- Essays should be free of unclear pronoun references.

The essay should show evidence of careful editing for content and for correct grammar, mechanics, and word choice.

Lesson 8.1

Think about Social Studies, page 219

1. D.

2. C.

Think about Social Studies, page 220

1. false

2. false

3. true

4. false

Think about Social Studies, page 221

1. B.

Vocabulary Review, page 222

1. reserve

2. commercial banks

3. interest

4. rationale

5. deposit

6. credit union

Skill Review, page 222

1. B. Banks assume that most depositors will leave most of their money in the bank so the banks can use this money for loans.

2. C. If one financial institution offers a wide range of services, it's hard for the others to compete unless they too offer the same services.

3. D. Banks set up savings accounts for customers to keep their money in the bank and earn interest so they can save up for future uses.

4. C. If the account holder does not track the money that is deposited in and withdrawn from their checking account, they could write a check they do not have the funds to cover.

Skill Practice, page 223

1. D. Bonds will earn interest and continue to make more money. Hard cash is a onetime payout.

2. A. While it's true that IOUs could be exchanged for bonds and that people could exchange them for the face value of bonds, they are just part of the main reason for Madison's object. The main objection is that Hamilton's plan favors speculators.

3. B.

Writing Practice, page 223

Answers will vary, but may include details such as weekly amount to save, the end dollar amount, how long it will take to reach their goal, how the bank will increase their actual savings by paying interest.

Lesson 8.2

Think about Social Studies, page 225

1. borrow

2. partial

3. installment

4. secured

5. need, want

Vocabulary Review, page 226

1. installment loan

2. credit score

3. secured loan

4. relevant

5. credit

6. default

Skill Review, page 226

1. **A.** All other items in this list besides cash cause you to borrow money and take on debt.

2. **D.** Credit score may drop if you make late payments. Using credit can actually increase your credit score.

3. **C.** Installment loans are useful for purchases of large assets, such as property.

4. **B.** People can use credit cards to make purchases electronically.

Skill Practice, page 227

1. **B.** A person must pledge an asset to get either a secured credit card or a secured loan.

2. **A.** Since you provide the cash for a secured credit card ahead of time, you do not incur debt when you use the card.

Writing Practice, page 227

Answers will vary, but the student should list a goal and then write a paragraph explaining how the goal could be reached with an installment loan and how the installment loan could help or harm their financial life.

Lesson 8.3

Think about Social Studies, page 229

1. The Fair Credit Billing Act

Think about Social Studies, page 230

1. **D.** $1,745 in interest ($4,475 total payment over 11 years - $3,000 borrowed)

Think about Social Studies, page 231

1. Consumers might not be able to understand all the terms in financial documents with overly complicated language, so they might make poor financial decisions.

Vocabulary Review, page 232

1. Consumer Financial Protection Bureau
2. liability
3. Equal Credit Opportunity Act
4. Truth in Lending Act
5. Credit CARD Act
6. Consumer Credit Protection Act

Skill Review, page 232

1. **B.** The Truth in Lending Act allows consumers to dispute fraudulent charges on their credit card bills.

2. **B.** Under the Equal Credit Opportunity Act of the Consumer Credit Protection Act, a lender cannot discriminate against a consumer based on marital status.

3. **A.** The Consumer Financial Protection Bureau enforces federal laws regarding consumer finances, including the Credit CARD Act.

Skill Practice, page 233

1. **C.** According to Elizabeth Warren, who launched the agency, the CFPB would make financial product comparison easier.

2. **A.** The chief executive of the bank states that he wants to make credit and financial resources available, but there will be "more hoops to go through" which could restrict the availability of credit.

Writing Practice, page 233

Answers will vary, but students should use information from the passage to discuss how the different values and perspectives of consumers, politicians, and bankers might cause them to have different opinions about the value of the CFPB. Students should include an opening and summary sentence in their paragraph.

Chapter Review

Review, page 234

1. **C.** During a financial crisis, banks may tighten standards for granting loans and make credit less available.

2. **A.** The Consumer Financial Protection Bureau was established in the wake of irresponsible lending practices that led up to the financial crisis of the late 2000s.

3. **A.** Delinquencies would negatively affect credit scores and the ability to obtain more credit.

4. **B.** Credit unions started as institutions that would provide emergency loans to members in the same company or labor union.

5. **C.** The chart shows that funds cycle, with financial institutions as intermediaries.

6. **A.** Financial institutions keep money safe but they also manage its use within the financial system.

7. **B.** If you pay off the balance each month, you can avoid paying interest on credit card purchases.

8. **A.** The Fair Credit Reporting Act allow consumers to obtain a free credit report annually.

Write about Social Studies

Write about Social Studies, page 236
Answers will vary. Here are some ideas to consider.

- The essay should focus on the data presented on p. 236 of the student edition.

- Students' essays may include the following points: credit card use increases with each age group until age 75 or older; balances rise with each age group until 55–64, dip, rise, and dip again; median balances are comparable in ages 35–44 and ages 55–64, as well as in ages 45–54 and 65–74.

- Essays should show evidence of careful reading of the chart and include appropriate terminology.

- Analysis should avoid faulty reasoning and attribution of causality where none is shown.

- Essays should use plural forms correctly.

The essay should show evidence of careful editing for content and for correct grammar, mechanics, and word choice.

Lesson 9.1

Think about Social Studies, page 241

1. afterlife

2. Sanskrit

3. Indus

4. pyramids

Think about Social Studies, page 243

1. Answers will vary, but may include how the importance of the family unit and the structure of obedience within the family in ancient Chinese society can be seen on a larger scale in the importance of each dynastic unit and its rule by divine right.

Think about Social Studies, page 245

1. C.

2. B.

Vocabulary Review, page 246

1. polis

2. civilization

3. castes

4. dynasty

5. mandate

6. consuls

Skill Review, page 246

1. B. All of the civilizations mentioned in the lesson developed in river valleys and their surrounding plains.

2. D. Ancient Egyptian and Shang dynasty civilizations believed in an afterlife and buried their dead with items that had been used in life

3. C. Buildings in the two ancient cities located in the Indus River Valley had indoor plumbing and a city-wide sewer system, which would indicate that the people in this civilization understood that containing waste could improve health.

4. A. By 146 BC, Rome had expanded its control throughout the Mediterranean and formed alliances with other areas known as member city-states.

Skill Practice, page 247

1. D. The Aryans invaded the area of the Indus River Valley between 2000–1500 B.C., which was between about 4000 and 3500 years ago.

2. C. The Bay of Bengal forced the third Aryan invasion to change direction and move along the coastline and down to the Deccan Plateau.

3. B. The Ganges Plain was level and near the Ganges River so it provided ideal conditions for farming and trading.

4. A. The Himalaya would have prevented a huge obstacle to Aryans attempting to move north.

Writing Practice, page 247

The student should compare the intellectual, cultural, and material developments of two ancient civilizations. The paragraph should open with a topic sentence and close with a summary sentence.

Lesson 9.2

Think about Social Studies, page 249

1. D
2. F
3. A
4. C
5. B
6. E

Think about Social Studies, page 249

1. Oslo, Norway is farther away from the equator, so it would be at a higher latitude. 3. Meridians, because meridians run from pole to pole.

Vocabulary Review, page 252

1. physical boundaries
2. meridians
3. political boundaries
4. coincide
5. parallels
6. geometric borders

Skill Review, page 252

1. **C.** Of these choices, only the river can be a physical boundary
2. **A.** A colonial power that is far away may not know the physical boundaries in a territory, so borders may be established with straight lines on a map.
3. **D.** War and other conflicts often change political boundaries or borders.
4. **D.** Lines of latitude do not measure distance in miles or kilometers. Latitude lines run east-to-west, but measure distance in a north-to-south direction.

Skill Practice, page 253

1. **B.** France, Britain, and Italy established boundaries related to Libya, Chad, and other North African countries through treaties.
2. **C.** Lines of longitude (meridians) were used to establish the border between Libya and Chad

Writing Practice, page 253

Answers will vary but should be supported by evidence based on information in the lesson.

Lesson 9.3

Think about Social Studies, page 255

1. nonrenewable
2. depletes
3. carrying capacity
4. renewable
5. shelter

Think about Social Studies, page 256

1. **D.** Population growth can lead to climate change which affect the world.

Think about Social Studies, page 257

1. **A.** A business might practice sustainable development to save money and to make a positive contribution to the community

Vocabulary Review, page 258

1. climate change
2. nonrenewable
3. renewable
4. sustainability
5. greenhouse effect
6. depletes

Skill Review, page 258

1. **C.** The human population has more than doubled in the last 50 years, to reach over 7 billion people.
2. **B.** More beef can be produced quickly by raising cattle when this resource is temporarily depleted
3. **D.** Waiting to do only full loads of laundry saves detergent, water, and energy.
4. **C.** One of the causes of global warming is the burning of fossil fuels such as coal, oil, and natural gas.

Skill Practice, page 259

1. **C.** Summer Arctic sea ice decreased from 7 to 6 million square kilometers between around 1986 and 2000, which is closer to 15 years than to the other figures provided as answer options.
2. **B.** An increase in the use of renewable energy sources could reduce the use of fossil fuels, thereby reducing the emission of carbon dioxide, which causes global warming, which leads to a decrease in Arctic sea ice.
3. **D.** Arctic sea ice dropped to 5.5 million km^2 in 2005.

Writing Practice, page 259

The student might include ideas for laws and regulations that would either reward or punish particular behaviors related to resource use.

Chapter Review

Review, page 260

1. **D.** The population increased from just over 100,000 to nearly 2,000,000 between 1960 and 2010.

2. **A.** A large population boom in a desert area would put a strain on water supplies.

3. **C.** If resources are not available within the country they can be imported to meet demand.

4. **A.** The Mandate of Heaven allowed Chinese emperors to rule by divine right. Egyptian pharaohs were also considered to be divine.

5. **C.** The U.S.S.R. dissolved in 1991 due to political changes, not war.

6. **A.** The Himalaya Mountains separate the Indian sub continent from countries located to the east.

7. **A.** Harappa and Mohenjo-Daro were cities in the Indus River Valley that relied on flooding to grow crops.

8. **D.** Combustion of fossil fuels adds carbon dioxide to the atmosphere. This contributes to climate change, which could affect the pattern of monsoons.

Write about Social Studies

Write about Social Studies, page 262

Answers will vary. Here are some ideas to consider.

- The essay should be descriptive and consistent.

- Essays should use plural forms correctly.

The essay should show evidence of careful editing for content and for correct grammar, mechanics, and word choice.

Lesson 10.1

Think about Social Studies, page 267

1. cultural
2. crust
3. resources
4. solid
5. flat

Think about Social Studies, page 269

1. **A.** Weather describes temperature, precipitation, and other conditions each day, whereas climate describes long-term weather patterns.

Vocabulary Review, page 270

1. culture
2. carbon dioxide
3. plain
4. plateau
5. isthmus
6. ecosystem

Skill Review, page 270

1. **D.** A cultural region is defined by the customs of its people.

2. **A.** Part of both a peninsula and an isthmus has contact with the sea.

3. **B.** Temperate mixed forest climate covers the majority of the United States.

4. **D.** A desert in the tropics would be warm with little rainfall.

5. **C.** All ecosystems in water are influenced by the physical factors of temperature and water depth.

6. **B.** There was little change in the temperature during this time.

Skill Practice, page 271

1. **B.** Average temperature is above 32°F in the summer months of June, July, and August.

2. **C.** Barrow, Alaska stays cold throughout the year with little annual precipitation.

3. **B.** The maximum amount of annual rainfall received is 1.0 inch.

Writing Practice, page 271

Students should describe the types of resources, people, plants, and animals in their community.

Lesson 10.2

Think about Social Studies, page 273

1. climate
2. diversity
3. arid
4. continent
5. tropical wet

Think about Social Studies, page 274

1. B.

Think about Social Studies, page 275

1. B.

Vocabulary Review, page 276

1. continents
2. multicultural
3. density
4. infer
5. landforms
6. diversity

Skill Review, page 276

1. A. Some of the hottest climates are in tropical areas near the Equator.

2. B. Civilizations that developed in river valleys developed methods of irrigation to water crops.

3. B. A forest in the tropics has a high diversity of trees and other plants, which would most likely lead to more words being added about these organisms to the language.

4. C. The climate zones along these locations are generally similar.

Skill Practice, page 277

1. C. As a forest people, the BaMbuti likely burn wood to provide warmth and cook food.

2. B. The text states that the BaMbuti know the secret language of the forest, and that they can find food that is hidden to outsiders.

3. A. The climate of the forest had the most effect because it dictated how the BaMbuti hunted and lived within the forest.

4. C. They do not have a need for plantations of farms because they have learned how to acquire everything they need through hunting and gathering.

Writing Practice, page 277

Answers will vary, but students should describe the types of resources, people, plants, and animals in their community.

Lesson 10.3

Think about Social Studies, page 279

1. mortality
2. doubled
3. decrease (or decline)
4. increase (or grow)
5. census

Think about Social Studies, page 280

1. B.

Think about Social Studies, page 281

1. D.

Vocabulary Review, page 282

1. population
2. demography
3. displaced
4. mortality rate
5. outlying
6. migration

Skill Review, page 282

1. **A.** The South African system of apartheid forced black South Africans to move to designated "homelands."

2. **D.** Divorce records would give the demographer a sense of how the frequency of divorce has changed over time.

3. **D.** The population has increased worldwide because improvements in medicine and access to medical care are helping people live longer.

4. **C.** The more diverse population found in cities would promote the establishment of many different ethnic restaurants.

5. **B.** Push and pull factors refer to the reasons people leave or go to an area. These terms do not describe birthrate, death rate, forms of government, or types of landscape.

Skill Practice, page 283

1. **B.** When the state of Israel was founded in 1948, Arab Muslims that lived in the area of the new state were displaced.

2. **C.** Jews were driven from the land in 70 A.D., so they were part of the history of that land.

3. **D.** The Jews wanted to live in Palestine since they were driven away in A.D. 70 by the Romans. That, and the worlds' sympathy for them after World War II, led to the UN dividing Palestine into two areas.

4. **C.** The Romans originally displaced the Jews from the Palestine area.

Writing Practice, page 283

Students should describe a mass movement of people from one country to another that is occurring at this time. They should explain what group is moving, what places they are moving from and to, how many people are moving, and why they are moving

Chapter Review

1. **C.** Many early civilizations formed around river valleys, to take advantage of the water supply for crops and drinking water.

2. **B.** Flowing water affects organisms in a stream.

3. **C.** Undocumented immigrants will do work that others will not to be able to make money for their families, including those back in Mexico.

4. **C.** 9 billion ÷ 3 million = $3,000.

5. **B.** The demographic group with the largest population in Phoenix is the 25–34 year old group.

6. **B.** Due to the large numbers of people who are at or near reproductive age in Phoenix, it is likely that the population will increase in the next decade.

7. **A.** Norwegians most likely took advantage of their vast coastline to harvest fish.

8. **C.** Kiruna is farthest north and away from the coast.

Write about Social Studies

Answers will vary. Here are some ideas to consider.

- The essay should use parallel structure.

- Essays should use plural forms correctly.

The essay should show evidence of careful editing for content and for correct grammar, mechanics, and word choice.

Remarks on East-West Relations at the Brandenburg Gate

In the 1950s, Khrushchev [then the leader of the Soviet Union] predicted: "We will bury you." But in the West today, we see a free world that has achieved a level of prosperity and well-being unprecedented in all human history. In the Communist world, we see failure, technological backwardness, declining standards of health, even want of the most basic kind— too little food. Even today, the Soviet Union still cannot feed itself. After these four decades, then, there stands before the entire world one great and inescapable conclusion: Freedom leads to prosperity. Freedom replaces the ancient hatreds among the nations with comity and peace. Freedom is the victor.

And now the Soviets themselves may, in a limited way, be coming to understand the importance of freedom. We hear much from Moscow about a new policy of reform and openness. Some political prisoners have been released. Certain foreign news broadcasts are no longer being jammed. Some economic enterprises have been permitted to operate with greater freedom from state control.

Are these the beginnings of profound changes in the Soviet state? Or are they token gestures, intended to raise false hopes in the West, or to strengthen the Soviet system without changing it? We welcome change and openness; for we believe that freedom and security go together, that the advance of human liberty can only strengthen the cause of world peace. There is one sign the Soviets can make that would be unmistakable, that would advance dramatically the cause of freedom and peace.

General Secretary Gorbachev, if you seek peace, if you seek prosperity for the Soviet Union and Eastern Europe, if you seek liberalization: Come here to this gate! Mr. Gorbachev, open this gate! Mr. Gorbachev, tear down this wall!

—President Ronald Reagan - June 12, 1987

Post-note: Two years later, in November 1989, East Germans issued a decree for the wall to be opened, allowing people to travel freely into West Berlin. In some cases, families that had been separated for decades were finally reunited. The wall was torn down altogether by the end of 1990 upon the collapse of Communism in Eastern Europe and in Soviet Russia itself, marking the end of the Cold War era.

Nineteenth Amendment to the U.S. Constitution: Women's Right to Vote (1920)

The Nineteenth Amendment guarantees all American women the right to vote. Achieving this milestone required a lengthy and difficult struggle; victory took decades of agitation and protest. Beginning in the mid-19th century, several generations of woman suffrage supporters lectured, wrote, marched, lobbied, and practiced civil disobedience to achieve what many Americans considered a radical change of the Constitution. Few early supporters lived to see the final victory in 1920.

Beginning in the 1800s, women organized, petitioned, and picketed to win the right to vote, but it took them decades to accomplish their purpose. Between 1878, when the amendment was first introduced in Congress, and August 18, 1920, when it was ratified, champions of voting rights for women worked tirelessly, but strategies for achieving their goal varied. Some pursued a strategy of passing suffrage acts in each state—nine western states adopted woman suffrage legislation by 1912. Others challenged male-only voting laws in the courts. Militant suffragists used tactics such as parades, silent vigils, and hunger strikes. Often supporters met fierce resistance. Opponents heckled, jailed, and sometimes physically abused them.

By 1916, almost all of the major suffrage organizations were united behind the goal of a constitutional amendment. When New York adopted woman suffrage in 1917 and President Wilson changed his position to support an amendment in 1918, the political balance began to shift.

On May 21, 1919, the House of Representatives passed the amendment, and 2 weeks later, the Senate followed. When Tennessee became the 36th state to ratify the amendment on August 18, 1920, the amendment passed its final hurdle of obtaining the agreement of three-fourths of the states. Secretary of State Bainbridge Colby certified the ratification on August 26, 1920, changing the face of the American electorate forever.

The Road to Revolution

Three-hundred years ago, Great Britain and France were often at war in Europe. This antagonism extended to the New World. The British continued to expand their colonies in North America. As a result, the French grew worried about their own holdings, especially in Canada. The French and Indian War, fought in North America from 1754 to 1763, was an extension of the combat in Europe known as the Seven Years' War.

Britain had won the war and gained territory in North America from France. To protect the new lands as well as the colonists already settled there, more soldiers were sent. Because of the expense of the war, Britain was out of cash, so British lawmakers decided that the colonists should pay for their own defense. They were required to feed, house, and pay salaries of British soldiers.

A series of new taxes levied on the colonies by Parliament led to the cry of "No taxation without representation!". To avoid paying taxes of the Townshend Act of 1767, colonists began smuggling goods. Consequently, Britain closed Boston Harbor and seized ships. Angry Bostonians rioted in protest, causing even more British troops to be sent. By the end of 1769, the city of about 15,000 people also had 4,000 British soldiers. The stage was set for what became known as the Boston Massacre, the first bloodshed of the American Revolution. Five of the rioting Boston citizens were killed in the fighting. For that reason, the British soldiers accused of firing the shots were arrested. The remaining soldiers left the city.

Gaining Support for World War I

Most people in the United States had little interest in the Great War that began in Europe in 1914. William G. McAdoo was Secretary of the Treasury from 1913 to 1918. The following is an excerpt from a speech he gave in 1918 explaining the decision to enter the war. Underlined words indicate the emotional language McAdoo used to stir up patriotic feelings.

"American Rights"

The Kaiser insolently commanded our vessels and our citizens not to sail the high seas within his own of about 500 miles surrounding Great Britain, France, Belgium, and Italy. He said: 'if you do, I will sink your ships without notice, kill your citizens, and destroy your commerce.' He did this in defiance of all international law and in violation of Germany's treaty obligation with this government. No self-respecting nation could permit any alien despot to order it to surrender rights that are vital to the national integrity and security. If we had not courage enough to defend our rights on that ground, then our material interests were so involved, that it was absolutely essential to America's continued life and prosperity that the Kaiser's order should be defied. A zone five hundred miles in extent, surrounding Great Britain, Belgium, France and Italy, meant this: that if we kept our commerce out of these waters, our intercourse with those countries would cease, and a market for more than one half of all that this country exports each year would have been lost. If we had submitted to that order, and that had been destroyed, what would have happened? Disaster upon the farms of America, disaster to the manufactories of America, disaster to the mining interests of America, disaster to the labor interests of America. To every productive activity of the American people there would have come irreparable injury. Never could we submit to that.

Every man and woman who stays at home, and for whose liberties, property, and sacred institutions our boys will shed their blood, must be moved by a spirit of sacrifice equal to that which animates our gallant troops. We must be willing to give up something of personal convenience, something of personal comfort, something of our treasure—all, if necessary, and our lives in the bargain, to support our noble sons who go out to die for us. We fight for our sacred rights and for our noblest ideas. America has never lost a war for freedom, and with God's help we shall not fail now. Let us organize our strength, marshal our resources, vindicate our rights, reestablish a just peace, and keep the torch of liberty burning throughout the world.

Henry Ford's Assembly Line

Henry Ford began assembly line production in 1913, three years after he opened an automobile-making factory in Highland Park, Michigan. His brilliant idea was to bring the work to the men, rather than having the men go to the work. Every worker had only one task on moving conveyor belts at waist height. The assembly had three floors, with different parts of the car being made on each floor.

First, tires were made on the top floor. They then arrived downstairs by means of chutes. In another part of the factory, engines and gasoline tanks were made. When they were completed, they were delivered to a lower level, where the chassis was built. The middle floor was the place where the auto bodies were assembled. One worker would attach the left door, for example, while another attached the right door. After the bodies were completed, a pulley dropped each one onto the chassis waiting below. The assembly line cut production time of a single Model T Ford from 12 hours 8 minutes to 1 hour 33 minutes. The rate continued to drop until, by 1925, a car rolled out of the factory every 10 seconds! As a result, the price of the vehicle dropped from $850 to $295 within 16 years.

Henry Ford believed that by lowering the cost of the car, sales would increase. He was right, and other manufacturers soon adopted the practice of mass manufacturing. The age of mass consumerism had begun.

Competition Versus Monopoly

In a market economy, businesses must compete with one another. Certain parts of the economy have many businesses, so there is a great deal of competition. For example, the fast food industry has many restaurants, so competition is fierce.

One the other hand, some areas of the economy include only a few businesses. The aluminum industry, for instance, has just a few very large corporations. A market with few sellers of a product is called an oligopoly. There is usually very little price competition among the sellers. Instead, they compete by advertising and offering special customer services.

In contrast, a monopoly exists when there is only one seller of a product. Actually, a pure monopoly has never existed. Instead, the word has come to mean a situation in which one seller controls most of the market. In 1994, for example, Microsoft agreed to end monopolistic practices after the European Commission as well as the United States brought charges against the computer giant. Microsoft had been using its licensing agreements and nondisclosure agreements to choke competition.

Government in the Economy

The United States has a market economy. However, it does not operate solely according to market forces. Both federal and state governments manage the economy in various ways.

Demand management, or fiscal policy, is one way that the government influences the economy. Demand management refers to how the government budget and taxes are used to influence demand in the economy. Before the Great Depression in the 1930s, the government did little to control the level of demand. Since then, to avoid another catastrophe of that size, the government has tried to create more demand for goods and services.

One method of using demand management is by increasing government spending when the private sector spending slows and unemployment rises. By increasing government spending, more money flows into the economy. For example, the government might extend unemployment benefits to place more money in the hands of those without jobs. When these consumers spend that money, demand is created, benefiting the economy. In 2008, this is precisely what happened. Congress enacted up to thirteen more weeks of unemployment benefits for the entire country.

Conversely, when the economy picks up again, the government reduces unemployment benefits or other spending to slow inflation. The program to extend unemployment was revised at several points, and in 2012, Congress declared that the program would end on January 1, 2014. By that time, the economy had improved.

Reforms During the Industrial Revolutions

The following excerpt is taken from an exposé by Danish immigrant Jacob Riis. This work, *Children of the Poor*, published in 1892, was only one of several books Riis penned. He was a newspaper reporter and photographer, providing shocking visual and verbal documentation of what he saw. He is considered the father of modern photojournalism.

It was only last winter I had occasion to visit repeatedly a double tenement at the lower end of Ludlow Street, which the police census showed to contain 297 tenants, 45 of whom were under five years of age, not counting 3 peddlers who slept in the moldy cellar, where the water was ankle deep on the mud floor. The feeblest ray of daylight never found its way down there, the hatches having been carefully covered with rags and matting; but freshets [the rise of water due to heavy rains or melted snow] often did. Sometimes the water rose to the height of a foot, and never quite soaked away in the driest season. It was an awful place, and by the light of my candle the three, with their unkempt beards and hair and sallow faces, looked more like hideous ghosts than living men. Yet they had slept there among and upon decaying fruit and wreckage of all sorts from the tenement for over three years, according to their own and the housekeeper's statements. There had been four. One was then in the hospital, but not because of any ill effect the cellar had had upon him. He had been run over in the street and was making the most of his vacation, charging it up to the owner of the wagon, whom he was getting ready to sue for breaking his leg. Up-stairs, especially in the rear tenement, I found the scene from the cellar repeated with variations. In one room a family of seven, including the oldest daughter, a young woman of eighteen, and her brother, a year older than she, slept in a common bed made on the floor of the kitchen, and manifested scarcely any concern at our appearance. A complaint to the Board of Health resulted in an overhauling that showed the tenement to be unusually bad even for that bad spot; but when we came to look up its record, from the standpoint of the vital statistics, we discovered that not only had there not been a single death in the house during the whole year, but on the third floor lived a woman over a hundred years old, who had been there a long time. I was never more surprised in my life, and while we laughed at it, I confess it came nearer to upsetting my faith in the value of statistics than anything I had seen till then. And yet I had met with similar experiences, if not quite so striking, often enough to convince me that poverty and want beget their own power to resist the evil influences of their worst surroundings.

Credit Card Debt

Credit card use in the United States continues to be popular. As the chart below indicates, a majority of people rely on their general-purpose credit cards from companies such as Discover, MasterCard, and Visa. Several inferences can be drawn from the information in the chart below.

The percentage of general-purpose credit card holders has declined somewhat since the high of 2001. However, troubling data in the last three columns paints a picture of people relying too heavily on their credit cards. In the three-year period from 2001 to 2004, median new charges grew by $100 per month. At $300 a month for the median of new charges, an average person adds $3,600 a year in credit debt.

This amount might not be troublesome in itself, except that families are not paying off their balances promptly. The percentage of those carrying balances has risen to nearly 60 percent. Furthermore, that balance has continued to climb, jumping from $2,000 to $3,000 in twelve years.

The effect of this use of credit cards without paying off balances is a drop in disposable income for the cardholder. Many general-purpose credit cards charge fees of more than 20 percent on the unpaid balance, which may explain the growing median balance. An item bought on sale is no longer a bargain if it cannot be paid for within a month. Clearly, instruction in the responsible use of credit is called for, beginning in high school, when many companies begin to target potential new users.

Use of General-Purpose Credit Cards by Families, 1995–2010

Year	Percentage of credit card holders	Median number of cards	Median new charges on last month's bill	Percentage having a balance	Median balance
1995	66.4	2	$200	56.0	$2,000
2001	72.7	2	$200	53.6	$2,100
2004	71.5	2	$300	56.2	$2,300
2007	70.2	2	$300	58.3	$3,000
2010	68.0	*	*	55.1	$3,300

* Data not available

[Source: Board of Governors of the Federal Reserve System (at least, the info 1995-2007 is)]

The Green Belt Movement

Dr. Wangari Maathi missed the trees of her native Kenya. The ground was baked hard from the sun; there was no smell of rain yet. Her eyes ached to see green again. Birds and small animals had moved away, their habitat cut down.

She could her the women talking as they walked to find enough wood for the day's fuel needs or for building fences to keep the animals safe. As more trees were cut down, their walks grew longer. Soil eroded without tree roots to hold it in place. Without shade from the trees, both people and animals felt hotter.

Women in much of Africa were responsible for everything that had to do with food. They grew edible plants and cooked the meals over open fires. Women also had a low status. Often they could not go to school; if there was money to send a child to school, a boy child went. As a result, women had little self-esteem.

Dr. Maathi wanted to change the perceptions of women and to preserve the environment. Why could those two goals not be merged? Women knew how to plant—they could be trained and paid to plant trees. Earning money would give them more independence, and planting trees would improve the Earth.

As the movement spread, sometimes a large-scale project was planned. More than a thousand seedlings were planted in rows, forming a "green belt," which gave the movement its name. These green belts were planted near watersheds. As Dr. Maathi said, "If you destroy the forest then the river will stop flowing, the rains will become irregular, the crops will fail and you will die of hunger and starvation."

Local dignitaries came as guests of honor, dressed in their finery. Women carried signs: "Start with little, but start now," said one. Another proclaimed, "Green Belt Movement: the Answer to the Fuel Wood Crisis."

Beginning in 1977, women began to plant trees in Kenya, and the movement soon spread. Thus far, more than 51 million trees have been planted. They now sway, green and lovely, over the rivers of Africa.

Chinese Immigration to the United States

A case study of the immigration of Chinese nationals to the United States demonstrates that U.S. policy toward various ethnic groups has not always been just or fair. Prior to 1882, people from all countries were welcomed. The lines from Emma Lazarus' poem etched on the base of the Statue of Liberty were meant to convey this feeling. "Give me your tired, your poor, / Your huddled masses yearning to breathe free, / The wretched refuse of your teeming shore. / Send these, the homeless, tempest-tossed, to me: / I lift my lamp beside the golden door!"

Following the California gold rush of 1849, however, many on the West Coast resented the Chinese immigrants who were arriving in great numbers. In addition to mining, Chinese laborers helped build the Transcontinental Railroad during the 1860s. They also opened small businesses, such as laundries, in the Chinatowns of San Francisco and other cities. They made up one-fourth of the California labor force by 1870.

West Coast settlers, many of them descended from European immigrants, felt threatened. They believed that the Chinese were the cause of low wages and unemployment. They also were racially prejudiced against Asians. In 1882, President Chester A. Arthur signed into law the Chinese Exclusion Act. The act was made permanent in 1902. Although it was repealed in 1943, only 105 Chinese immigrants were allowed annually, and the act remained at least partially in force until 1965.

Immigration laws that are rooted in racial prejudice are by their nature unfair. The idea that some races are in any way better than others has been shown to have no scientific basis. Blaming the business cycle's fluctuations on one group of people does not make logical sense. When people from other nations come to take jobs that citizens do not want to do, they do not cause unemployment. The Chinese Exclusion Act was unfair and prejudicial to a group of people merely trying to better their lives in America, as European immigrants had done from the seventeenth century onward.

Directions: Use this rubric to guide your writing and to evaluate your finished work on a 1 to 4 scale. A score of 4 indicates a mastery of the element; a score of 1 indicates a need for extensive revision.

4	3	2	1
Development of Ideas/Organizational Structure			
Main Idea There is one fully developed main idea.	**Main Idea** There is one mostly developed main idea.	**Main Idea** There is a partially developed main idea.	**Main Idea** There is no main idea.
Details Accurate and directly relevant details support the main idea.	**Details** Accurate and mostly relevant details support the main idea.	**Details** Some of the details are accurate and relevant to the main idea.	**Details** There are no details relevant to the main idea.
Structure The writing has an introduction, a body, and a conclusion. The introduction states the main idea. The body presents information that is clearly relevant to the main idea. The conclusion restates or summarizes the main idea. Paragraph and text structures are clear and appropriate to the topic and purpose.	**Structure** The writing has an introduction, a body, and a conclusion. The introduction states the main idea. The body presents information that is mostly relevant to the main idea. The conclusion restates or summarizes the main idea. Paragraph and text structures are mostly clear and relevant to the topic and purpose.	**Structure** The writing has an introduction and a body. The introduction states the main idea. The body presents some information relevant to the main idea. There is no conclusion. An attempt is made to use paragraph and text structures that support the topic and purpose.	**Structure** The writing does not introduce a main idea. The purpose of the content in the body is unclear. There is no conclusion. Paragraph and text structures are not clear or appropriate to the topic and purpose.
Author's Purpose, Analysis of Arguments, and/or Use of Evidence			
Purpose The purpose for writing is clear. The writer has full knowledge of the topic and provides thorough supporting evidence. The writer uses appropriate techniques to connect to the audience.	**Purpose** The purpose for writing is somewhat clear. The writer has some knowledge of the topic and provides some supporting evidence. The writer makes some effort to connect to the audience.	**Purpose** The purpose for writing is unclear. The writer has little knowledge of the topic and provides some supporting evidence. The writer makes some effort to connect to the audience.	**Purpose** The purpose for writing is unclear. The writer has no knowledge of the topic and provides no supporting evidence. There is no attempt to connect to the audience.
Arguments/Evidence The writer develops a logical argument that includes a clearly stated claim related to the prompt and cites sufficient evidence from texts and other sources that is specific and relevant. If appropriate, the writer analyzes and evaluates the logic and validity of arguments in source texts.	**Arguments/Evidence** The writer's argument is generally logical; the claim is clear and relevant to the prompt; evidence is provided from texts and other sources but is not specific, sufficient, or relevant. If appropriate, the writer attempts to analyze and evaluate the logic and validity of arguments in source texts.	**Arguments/Evidence** The writer's argument contains logical flaws; the claim is stated, but does not relate directly to the prompt; some relevant evidence is provided. If appropriate, the writer mentions arguments in source texts, but the analysis/evaluation of them is incomplete, superficial, or incorrect.	**Arguments/Evidence** The writer does not develop an argument, or the argument is not logical; no claim is stated, or the stated claim is irrelevant to the prompt; little or no relevant evidence is provided. If appropriate, the writer may mention arguments in source texts, but fails to analyze or evaluate them.

4	3	2	1
English Conventions and Clarity			
Clarity The writer makes varied word choices that help readers visualize the content. Words and phrases are vivid, powerful, and engaging. Sentences are varied in style and length and read naturally. Relationships between ideas, sentences, and paragraphs are clear and frequently reinforced by signal words and phrases.	**Clarity** The writer makes some varied word choices that help readers visualize the content. The language is frequently engaging. Sentences exhibit some variety in style and length and are generally fluent. Relationships between ideas, sentences, and paragraphs are usually clear and sometimes reinforced by signal words and phrases.	**Clarity** The writer makes limited word choices that minimally help readers visualize the content. Few words and phrases engage readers. Sentences have little variety in style or length and at times read awkwardly. Relationships between ideas, sentences, and paragraphs are sometimes clear and occasionally reinforced by signal words and phrases.	**Clarity** The writer makes repetitive word choices, often incorrectly. Words and phrases do not engage readers. Sentences show little or no variety in style or length; the text does not flow naturally. Relationships between ideas, sentences, and paragraphs are unclear and are not reinforced by signal words and phrases.
Conventions All sentences are well constructed. There are no errors in spelling, grammar, or mechanics.	**Conventions** Most sentences are well constructed. There are almost no errors in spelling, grammar, or mechanics. Any errors do not affect comprehension.	**Conventions** Some sentences are well constructed. There are several errors in spelling, grammar, and mechanics. It is sometimes hard to understand what the writer means to say.	**Conventions** Sentences are poorly constructed. There are many errors in spelling, grammar, and mechanics. It is often hard to understand what the writer means to say.

Name _____ **Date** _____ **Class** _____

Name _____ Date _____ Class _____

1.

2.

3.

4.

Name _____ **Date** _____ **Class** _____

Name_____ **Date**_____ **Class**_____

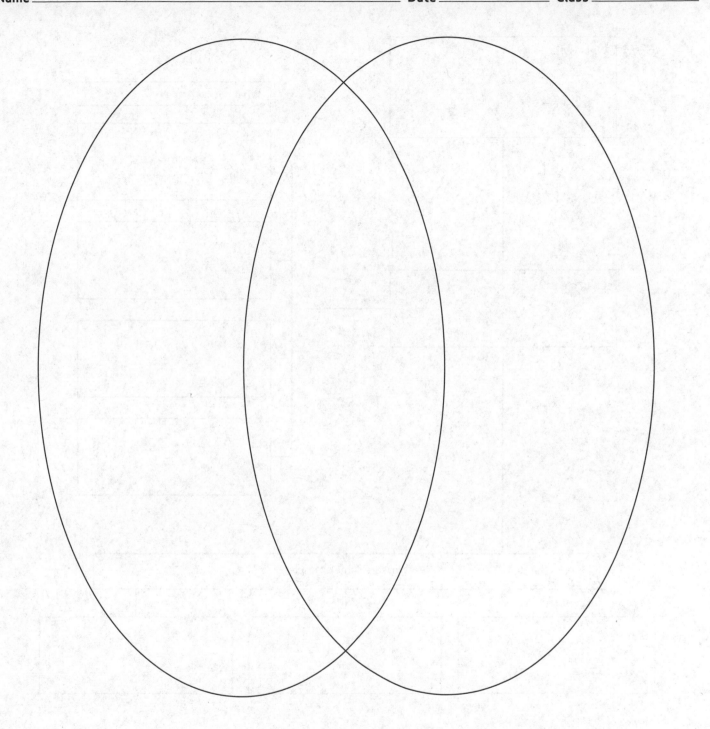

Name_____ **Date**_____ **Class**_____

What is it?

What is it like?

Characteristics:

What are some examples?

Name _____ **Date** _____ **Class** _____

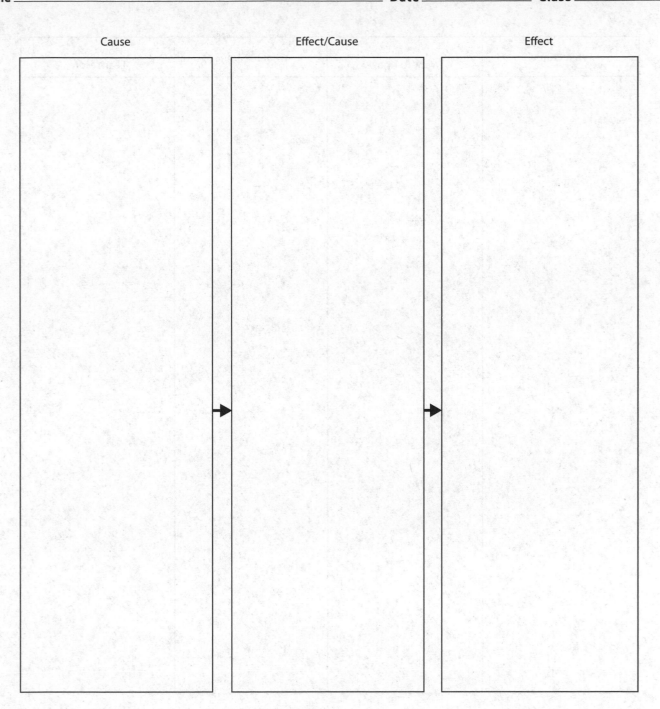

Cause

Effect/Cause

Effect

Name _____ **Date** _____ **Class** _____

What I Know	What I Want to Know	What I Learned	How Can I Learn More

GLOSSARY

A

abolitionists people who wanted to end slavery

absolute advantage the ability to produce a product or service using fewer resources than other producers require

accountable to be responsible

alliance a group of countries joined together in a common cause

amendment changes or additions to a constitution

analyze to break information into parts

annexation taking control of another country or territory

autocracy a government in which a single person holds all power

B

bias belief that certain ideas or people are better than others

bicameral two houses

boycott to refuse to buy

business cycle the repeated pattern of growth and decline of an economy

C

capital equipment used to process natural resources into goods or to deliver services

carbon dioxide a gas that is produced when organic materials are burned

castes categories that determined a person's occupation and social class

charter a written code of rules or laws

civil liberties freedoms guaranteed by the U.S. Constitution

civil rights rights everyone has to equal protection under the law

civilization a society in an advanced state of cultural development

climate change long term alteration of weather pattern

coincide to occur together

colony a geographic area in a new land that remains loyal to the parent nation

commercial bank banks that originally served only businesses

communism totalitarian system of government in which the state plans and controls the economy, and all goods are shared by the people

comparative advantage the ability to produce goods or services at a low opportunity cost compared to other producers

competition a process of offering price, quality or other advantages to two or more suppliers to try to gain the business of a buyer

conclude to decide

conduct to perform

consuls people who ran the Roman republic

Consumer Credit Protection Act umbrella consumer protection law passed in 1969 that includes the Equal Credit Opportunity Act, the Fair Credit Billing Act, the Fair Credit Reporting Act, and the Truth in Lending Act

Consumer Financial Protection Bureau federal agency created in 2010 to protect consumers by carrying out federal consumer financial laws

containment US policy to block further Communist expansion

continent major land mass

contrast to show differences

cottage industry system in which workers manufacture products at home

credit a way of taking ownership of something before you pay for it

Credit CARD Act federal law passed in 2009 that places limits on credit card fees and rate increases and requires lenders to be consistent in payment dates and times

credit score a report of how well you pay your bills

credit union a financial institution started by people with a common concern

culture the customs, beliefs, and practices of a society in any given place or time

cyclical reoccurring in the same order

D

declaration a formal statement

default to become unable to continue paying back a loan

deflation a drop in the general level of prices over time

demand curve a graph that illustrates the quantity of a good demanded at different prices

democracy a type of government in which the power to rule comes from the people

demography the statistical study of the size, growth, movement, and distribution of people

density concentration of people or things in a certain area

deplete to use up or reduce a resource

deposit to place money into a bank account

depreciation a decrease in value

depression a period of low economic activity and high unemployment

détente a relaxing of tensions

determine to identify

dictatorship a government in which one person has absolute authority over citizens' lives

displaced to be forced to move

diversity variety or differences

domestic relating to one's own country

dynasty family of rulers

E

ecosystem a community of organisms in an area and the natural resources with which it interacts

efficient to be capable of producing desired results with little waste

embassy a building that houses an ambassador and other representatives

entrepreneurship human creativity that produces new products or services

Equal Credit Opportunity Act federal law passed in 1974 that prohibits discrimination in credit transactions on the basis of certain personal characteristics

executive branch the branch of government that is headed by the president and carries out the nation's laws

expansion period when the a country's GDP grows

expenditures money that is paid out by a government

F

fascism a dictatorship in which the state is more important than individuals

federalism shared power between the states and the national government

fiscal policy taxing and spending policies of a government

foreign aid money, goods, and services that the government of one nation gives to help the government of another nation

foreign policy the principles used to guide interaction with other nations

G

geometric borders straight-line borders that follow imaginary lines on Earth

goods products made to be sold

Great Depression a severe decline in the US economy during the 1930s

Great Society a set of policies in which the American government helped those in need

greenhouse effect ability of Earth's atmosphere to trap heat from the sun

gross domestic product (GDP) the dollar value of all final goods and services produced in a nation during a single year

H

House of Representatives federal body that protects the rights of large states

humanitarian concerned with improving the lives of others

I

impeach to charge a public official with misconduct with the intent to potentially remove from office

imperialism governing of weaker nations or colonies by more powerful nations

incentive encouragement to try new ideas or invest new products

independents people who belong to no organized political party

Industrial Revolution the time when machines replaced hand tools in the manufacturing of goods

industrialized nations countries with developed economies, advanced infrastructures, and high standards of living

inference to reach a conclusion or opinion based on facts or evidence presented

inflation a rise in the general level of prices over time

Innovation the process of introducing something that is new

installment loan a loan repaid with interest in equal periodic payments

insurgents rebels

integrate to combine to make a whole

interdependence two or more producers' reliance on one another

interest a payment, or charge, for borrowed money

interest group a group of people with common concerns who join together to influence government policy

internment the confining or segregating of people during war

isolationism a policy of avoiding involvement in international affairs

issues concerns

isthmus a narrow strip of land surrounded with land on three sides

J

judicial branch the branch of government made up by the court system

judge to form an opinion about something after carefully thinking about it

L

labor efforts of people who process natural resources or produce services

laissez-faire "let it be" approach to governing business

land grant gift of land

landform natural feature of Earth's surface

law of demand as the price of a good rises, the demand falls; as the price falls, the demand rises

League of Nations an organization designed to help nations settle disputes peacefully

legislative branch the branch of government that makes the laws

liability to have legal responsibility

limited government the principle that a ruler is not all-powerful

lobbyists people who work to sway the opinion of public officials

Louisiana Purchase US purchase of land between the Mississippi River and the Rocky Mountains

M

mandate a command

Manifest Destiny belief that the United States should extend boundary to the Pacific Ocean

market a relationship that makes buying and selling easier

market economy an economy where people are free to decide what, how, and for whom to produce goods and services

market equilibrium the point at which demand is equal to supply

Marshall Plan US plan to provide economic aid to help Europe rebuild after World War II

media methods of communication used to reach the public

median middle number when numbers are sorted least to greatest

meridians lines of longitude

migration the movement of people from one place to another

militants people who use violence to achieve their goals

militarism a policy of aggressive military preparedness

minutemen soldiers in the colonial militia who were ready to fight at a minute's notice

monetary policies strategies for controlling the size of the money supply and the price of credit

monopoly the control or domination of an industry by a single supplier

mortality rate death rate

multicultural to have many cultures

N

nationalism a feeling of pride in and loyalty to one's nation

nativists native-born people who wish to limit immigration

NATO organization designed to stop Soviet expansion in Europe

natural resources anything found in nature that can be used to produce goods and services

negotiate to discuss something formally in order to make an agreement

net income the amount left over after total expenses are subtracted from income

nonrenewable not replaceable or replaceable only over millions of years

O

occupy to take possession or control of

oligarchy a type of government in which only a few people rule

Open Door Policy a policy proposed by the United States that gave all nations equal trading rights in China

opportunity cost the alternative that one gives up when making choices

outcome result or consequence

outlying surrounding

P

parallels lines of latitude that run parallel to each other

persevere to continue doing something under difficult circumstances or strong opposition

persuasive language – language used to influence a reader's opinion

physical boundaries natural features that separate two areas from each other

plain a large area of flat land without trees

plateau a large, flat area of land that is elevated above other areas of land that surround it

point of view how a person feels about, or what a person thinks about, something

polis Greek city-state that was a place and a governing body

political boundaries lines that separate countries and states

political party an organized group of people who share common values and goals

population all inhabitants of an area

poverty line the minimum that the government believes a family of four needs to live adequately

productivity the amount of goods and services a worker can produce in a certain amount of time

propaganda false or exaggerated statements

public policy actions that affect everybody

pull factors reasons that bring people to the United States

push factors reasons that force people to leave their native countries

R

rationale reason or explanation for something

recession a decline in a country's GDP for at least two quarters

referendum allows citizens to overturn legislation that was passed by legislature or by voters

refugee a person who flees a country because of war or danger

relevant information that is connected to information you already know

renewable to be quickly replaceable

reserve money banks hold back for future use

revolution the overthrow of a government or ruler and replacement with another government

S

scandal an event that is legally or morally wrong

scarce to be rare or in short supply

scientific method the process used by scientists for testing theories using careful observation

Scientific Revolution the time period when numerous scientific theories were developed

sectional local

secured loan a loan in which a borrower pledges an asset or property that the lender can seize in case of default

segregation separation of races

Senate federal body that protects the rights of small states

separation of powers division of central government

sequence the order in which something happens

service useful work that does not create an actual product but meets someone's need and is sold in the market

settlement houses privately run neighborhood centers that provide services for the poor

slave codes laws that enslaved African Americans and their children

social class levels of society that are based on economic success

specialization to concentrate on the production of a few goods and services

standard of living the necessities or comforts essential to life or aspired to by an individual

stimulus government policies to provide relief for workers and create business reforms

strategy carefully devised plan

subsidy government payment to an individual or business to encourage or protect a particular economic activity

suffrage the right to vote

supply and demand forces that influence the exchange of goods and services in a market economy

supply curve a graph that illustrates the quantity of a good that is supplied at different prices

surrender to stop fighting

sustainability living within limits when it comes to the use of Earth's resources

symbol a person or object that represents something else

synthesize to combine things in order to make something new

tariff tax on an import

tenements large buildings of apartments where the poorest people live

territory an area of land that is controlled by a government

terrorism political strategy that uses violence against people or property to achieve a goal

totalitarian government a government that controls all aspects of a nation

triangular trade triangle shaped trade route

Truman Doctrine US policy of aiding countries threatened by communism

Truth in Lending Act federal law passed in 1968 that requires lenders to use uniform methods for computing the cost of credit and stating the terms of credit

unemployment rate the percentage of people in the labor force who actively looked for a job during a particular month but could not find one

unicameral a legislature with one chamber

urbanization significant increase in the number and size of cities

veto power of the president to refuse a law

INDEX

Laws:
consumer credit, 228–231
federal, 31
state, 31
unconstitutional (*See* US Supreme Court)
Leadership, perseverance in, 45
League of Nations, 98, 102, 103, 106, 115
Lee, Robert E., 81, 82
Legislative branch (state), 31
Legislative branch (US), 23, 29 (*See also* Congress)
definition of, 22
and division of powers, 30
state representation in, 23
Lenin, Vladimir, 102
Lewis, Meriwether, 73
Liability, 228
Liliuokalani, queen of Hawaii, 202
Limited government, 18
as basic principle for US, 23
definition of, 16
Lincoln, Abraham, 17, 80–82
Literacy tests, for voting, 43
Lithuania, 103
Loans:
from banks, 219
types of, 224, 225
Lobbying, 51
Lobbyists, 51
definition of, 48
public policy affected by, 57
Local governments, public policy made by, 54
Lodge, Henry Cabot, 103
Longitude lines, 250
Louisiana, secession of, 80–81
Louisiana Purchase, 72, 73
Lusitania, 100
Lynching, 45

M

Macroeconomics:
and GDP, 182
and government policy, 176–179
inflation and deflation, 184
unemployment, 185
Madison, James, 19, 25
Magna Carta, 19
Maine, 79
Make inferences (core practice), 147, 202
Make predictions (core skill), 99
Mandate (term), 240
Mandate of Heaven, 243
Manifest Destiny, 72, 75
Mantle (Earth), 266
Market(s), 140–141
competitive, 141–142
definition of, 140
failure of, 179
foreign, 202
microeconomic influences of, 170–171
new, 201

Market economy(-ies), 141
definition of, 152
incentive in, 155
market failures in, 179
risks and profits in, 152–153
supply and demand in, 170–171
traditional economies vs., 155
Market equilibrium, 170, 173
Marshall Plan, 114, 116
Maryland, 81
Mason, George, 18
Massachusetts:
Pilgrims in, 66
Puritans in, 67
Shays's Rebellion, 22–23
Mayflower Compact, 66
McClellan, George B., 81
McKinley, William, 202
Media, 122
Media literacy, 123
Median, 170, 172
Medicare deductions, 176
Menes, 240
Meridians, 248, 250
Mexican American War, 75
Mexico:
immigration from, 87, 89, 280
and Zimmermann Telegram, 101
Microeconomics, 170–173
Middle class, 87, 209
Migration, 278, 280
Militants, 128
Militarism, 98, 99
Military powers, 29
Minor parties, 48, 49
Minutemen, 66, 68
Mississippi, 80–81
Mississippi River, 81, 248
Missouri:
admission of, 79
Civil War, 81
Missouri Compromise (1821), 79
Mohenjo-Daro, 241
Monarchies, 16
constitutional, 16
early city-states as, 244
Monetary policies:
definition of, 176
of US government, 177, 179
Money:
and banking, 218–219
loaning, 219
Money supply, 179
Monopoly(-ies), 140, 143, 179
Morocco, 108
Mortality rate, 278, 279
Multicultural (term), 272
Multicultural countries, 274
Multiparty system, 49
Mussolini, Benito, 16, 106, 107

INDEX

Supply:
:   definition of, 171
:   and market equilibrium, 173
Supply and demand, 170
Supply curve, 170, 172
Supply schedule, 172
Supreme Court, US (*See* US Supreme Court)
Surface temperatures, 269
Surrender, 78
Sustainability, 254, 257
Sweden:
:   as monarchy, 16
:   World War II, 108
Switzerland, 108
Symbol, 48, 50
Synthesize (term), 48
Synthesize ideas from multiple sources (core practice), 142, 249

T

Taliban, 129–131
Tang, 242
Tanzania, 128
Tariff(s), 176, 178, 202
Taxation:
:   to affect voting rights, 43
:   of businesses, 178
:   congressional power for, 29
:   early rebellions against, 22–23
:   by England, 67–68
:   fiscal policies directing, 177–178
:   by states, 31
Technological advances:
:   assembly lines, 154, 195
:   cotton gin, 80
:   in Industrial Revolution, 80, 98–99, 207–209
:   in Scientific Revolution, 206–207
Technology literacy:
:   compare types of communication, 143
:   Internet research, 119
Technology skills:
:   apply technology to a task, 75, 103, 269
:   and unemployment, 185
Tecumseh, 73, 74
Tenements, 86, 87, 209
Tennessee, 81
Tennessee Valley Authority (TVA), 197
Tenth Amendment, 24, 30
Territory(-ies), 72
Terrorism:
:   definition of, 128
:   global War on Terror, 130–131
:   in United States, 128–130
Terrorist organizations, 128
Test-taking skills:
:   eliminate unnecessary information, 250
:   gather information, 51
:   understand the question, 196
:   use prior knowledge, 89

Texas, 80–81
Textile industry, 80, 208
Theocracy, 129
Third parties, 48
Thirteenth Amendment, 42, 81, 82
Thrift institutions, 219, 220
Tiber River, 244
Tigris-Euphrates valley, 275
Tippecanoe, Battle of, 74
Title IX, 45
Totalitarian government(s):
:   communism as, 114
:   definition of, 106
:   following World War I, 106, 107
Townshend, Charles, 67
Townshend Act, 67, 68
Trade:
:   slave codes, 78
:   triangular, 78
Trade-offs, 147
Traditional economies, 155
Trail of Tears, 75
Transportation, 80
Treaty of 1818, 251
Treaty of Ghent, 74, 107
Treaty of Greenville (1795), 73
Treaty of Paris (1783), 68, 72
Treaty of Versailles (1919), 102, 103
Triangular trade, 78
Trough (in business cycle), 194
Truman, Harry S., 110, 116
Truman Doctrine, 114, 116
Truth, Sojourner, 80
Truth in Lending Act, 228
Tundra, 268, 269
Turkey:
:   aftermath of World War I, 102
:   aftermath of World War II, 114, 116
TVA (Tennessee Valley Authority), 197
Twenty-Fourth Amendment, 43
Two-party system, 48–49
Tyrants, 244

U

UN (*See* United Nations)
Understand author's bias (core practice), 107
Understand cause and effect (core practice), 243
Understand the main idea (core skill), 110
Unemployment:
:   causes and effects of, 185
:   during Great Depression, 196
Unemployment rate, 182, 185
Unicameral (term), 66
Unicameral legislature:
:   under Articles of Confederation, 69
:   in Nebraska, 31